W9-ABP-612

LEXINGTON

LEXINGTON

THE EXTRAORDINARY LIFE AND TURBULENT TIMES OF
AMERICA'S LEGENDARY RACEHORSE

Kim Wickens

BALLANTINE BOOKS

NEW YORK

Published in the United States by Ballantine Books, an imprint of Random House, a division of Penguin Random House LLC, New York.

BALLANTINE is a registered trademark and the colophon is a trademark of Penguin Random House LLC.

Photo credits are located on page 385.

LIBRARY OF CONGRESS CATALOGING-IN-PUBLICATION DATA
Names: Wickens, Kim, author.
Title: Lexington: the extraordinary life and turbulent times of America's legendary racehorse / Kim Wickens.
Description: First edition. | New York: Ballantine Books, [2023] | Includes bibliographical references and index.
Identifiers: LCCN 2022060488 (print) | LCCN 2022060489 (ebook) | ISBN 9780593496701 (hardcover) | ISBN 9780593496718 (ebook)
Subjects: LCSH: Lexington (Race horse), 1850–1875. | Race horses—United States—Biography. | Horse racing—United States—History—19th century.
Classification: LCC SF355.L4 W53 2023 (print) | LCC SF355.L4 (ebook) | DDC 798.40092/9 [B]—dc23/eng/20221220
LC record available at https://lccn.loc.gov/2022060488
LC ebook record available at https://lccn.loc.gov/2022060489

Printed in the United States of America on acid-free paper

randomhousebooks.com

2 4 6 8 9 7 5 3 1

First Edition

Title-page art courtesy of the National Museum of Racing and Hall of Fame

Book design by Caroline Cunningham

To Mike and Connor

All over the sunny South went the word "Lexington." Far up into the North, even into parts where the race-horse was not known, traveled the word "Lexington." There came a day when any little child of America could have told you the story of Lexington. And the time is not yet past when that name is synonymous with everything that is greatest in a horse. Lexington belonged not alone to the turfmen. He was the heritage of the nation. He was Lexington in the minds of the people, and after him there were merely other horses.

—CHARLES E. TREVATHAN, "The Last Race of
Lexington," *The American Thoroughbred*

When the memory of the race takes in . . . the crowds in the hotels, the noted men and women from all over the South who had come for the match, the whirl of carriages, and cabs, and vehicles of all kinds along the shell road, a kind of race track itself, the grandstand, exclusive as a private ball-room, glittering with ladies in toilets from the ateliers of the great modistes . . . and the men, from all over the South glittering too . . . the track—that superb track of old Metairie—the jockeys petted and spoiled like ballet-girls—and the horses! A volume would not hold it all before we even get to Lexington and Lecomte, and after that, a library would be needed to contain it. . . . That was what horse-racing meant then.

—GRACE KING, *New Orleans: The Place and the People*

CONTENTS

PART II

PART III

LEXINGTON

BOTTOM

GRIT. THAT'S WHAT nineteenth-century Thoroughbred racing was about. Back then, the sport in America wasn't so much about a horse's speed—although speed was important—as it was about stamina. A racehorse was no good unless it could run a distance of four miles or greater. The term used to describe a gifted racehorse was "bottom." Bottom was what carried a horse beyond the brink, past the exceptional, and into the extraordinary. It was the embodiment of an undefined quality buried somewhere in a horse's soul. Bottom was a measure: how much courage, stamina, heart, and strength a horse had before it hit that realm where it could go no further. To say that a horse had "bottom" meant, essentially, that it had no bottom. It had staying power.

Stamina and courage played into every aspect of nineteenth-century competition. When prizefighter James Ambrose, better known as Yankee Sullivan, faced John Morrissey on October 12, 1853, the boxers dueled bare-knuckled for thirty-seven rounds. That's when Morrissey swayed, "waiting," noted the New York sporting paper the *Spirit of the Times,* "for his seconds to lift him up." As Morrissey stumbled out of the ring, Sullivan bounced on his feet, jabbing his fists in the air, yelling at Morrissey to come back and finish.

America, severed less than a century from Great Britain, was a young country. Americans expected much of themselves and much more from their horses. Besides politics and religion, nothing brought more intense feelings to them than racing and the race-horse.

Horse racing came about in order to test and improve equine quality. Through breeding, the Thoroughbred horse evolved to meet the high demands of racing—tests of courage, strength, and stamina. The better the horse was able to meet the tests, the better it was equipped to serve man's realistic needs in everyday life. And in battle.

A racehorse in nineteenth-century America needed bottom and plenty of it. Today races consist of single-digit furlongs—each fur-long being about 660 feet. America's longest modern-day race, the Belmont Stakes, is one and a half miles, or twelve furlongs. In the nineteenth century, horses ran heats consisting of one, two, three, or four miles each. Per nineteenth-century racing regulations, a horse had to win at least two heats to earn the purse. It was there-fore unknowable at the race's outset how many heats a horse would actually end up running. In a race with four-mile heats—the top tier of American nineteenth-century racing—horses would run a minimum of eight miles, and that was only if one horse won the first two heats. If, however, different horses won heats one and two, a tie-breaking third heat would send them off for another four miles—a total of twelve miles run in a single race. This sce-nario could play out into additional heats until eventually, the same horse had won two heats. Four-mile heats, therefore, required an animal of supreme strength and bottom to withstand the pounding of bone and the pulling and stretching of sinew and muscle for eight, twelve, sixteen, or even twenty miles around an oval track at extreme rates of speed. Races of this distance were not uncommon. In that era, racehorses were trained differently: not to sprint but to endure.

Cooling periods separated the heats to allow some modicum of recovery. Depending on each racecourse's regulations, and the duration of the heats involved, cooling periods could last anywhere from fifteen minutes for a one-mile heat race up to forty-five minutes for a four-mile heat. During these compacted minutes, a small fleet of horse grooms armed with arsenals of buckets, rags, scraping brushes, and whiskey swarmed upon each horse as if it were their only task in life. Dousing rags with the liquor, grooms washed away the grime of four miles before massaging the numbing liquid over the horse's aching body. After pulling and tucking wool blankets around their charge in a moisture-wicking papoose, they walked it in circles to loosen its muscles. All the while, grooms fought back the deluge of betting men and turf writers who had gathered around the heaving horse to hurl their weighted questions: How's he faring? Is he lame? Can he go again?

Betting tables were, after all, still open for the next heat's speculations.

Heats were tough on the jockeys too. Steering a twelve-hundred-pound animal at a full run for eight or twelve miles required not only strength but tremendous stamina. Jockeys, then as now, weighed less than average men, typically about ninety pounds. A minimally weighted man riding on an empty stomach during the heat of the day *and* regulating a powerful animal running at the top of its speed often failed to meet the challenge. Some riders fainted during the race. Others lost the strength to steer their mounts. Exhausted jockeys occasionally rode horses off course or collided with their competitors.

These cooling periods were, therefore, equally important for the equines' counterparts. Back at the cooling circle, grooms pulled limp rag-doll jockeys out of their saddles and propped them in straight-backed chairs to regain their breath. Dragging over the water buckets and whiskey that had first been used for the horses, grooms worked to massage the life back into jockeys' spent arms and legs. If massage and liquor couldn't revive a man over the next forty-five minutes, he was replaced—usually over hard-fought pleas and false assurances that he could go another four. Generally, it took at least two jockeys to ride a single horse in a four-mile heat race. Unusual was the man who could endure multiple heats. Those jockeys were rare, and they earned top dollar.

During the 1850s, horse racing was America's supreme spectator sport, attracting everyone from high-ranking political figures to anyone who could afford the one-dollar entry fee. Racecourses were *the* gathering place: a place to be seen, and a place to take a betting chance in an atmosphere dense with opinions. Horse racing was so popular in the mid-nineteenth century that anyone desirous of seeing a race would be hard-pressed *not* to find a racecourse somewhere in the then-existing thirty states. Fifty-nine tracks operated to a profit in the Southern states. New Orleans alone offered enough fanfare and patrons to support four racecourses. The North funneled horse-race patrons into twenty-one courses in New York, New Jersey, and Pennsylvania. Four of those tracks were located on Long Island. Seldom in today's vastly arrayed sporting spectrum can a city support more than one racecourse.

In the nineteenth century, when a race involved a phenomenal horse—a horse that had shown exceptional bottom in past performances—hosting cities were often overwhelmed by the multitudes who thronged there for a glimpse of the spectacle. A race that featured a star horse induced mania to the extreme. By post time, a hosting city, whether New Orleans or New York, ceased functioning, having lost nearly every soul to the racecourse. News of the results was so eagerly awaited that newspaper reporters carted in carrier pigeons to their trackside tables in the hope of expediting bulletins prepared between heats to the printing press. This hurried endeavor was in no way unappreciated. On race day, those people who were unable to attend gathered on the sidewalks outside newspaper editors' offices, waiting to hear the outcome at first opportunity.

Horses in those days were celebrities in their own right. Their feats of courage were discussed in parlors, stores, and businesses, and at the family dinner table. And it was a celebrity that was well earned, since, even by that era's unrelenting standards, a horse that could run a demanding four-mile heat race was a rarity. Even harder: to find a horse that not only had bottom but could capture the heart of a nation. It was in this era of pioneering tests of strength that a colt named Lexington rose to fame. It took two equally pioneering men to guide Lexington into becoming what one nineteenth-century writer described as "a name synonymous with everything that is greatest in a horse."

PART I

CHAPTER 1

___

REBIRTH

RICHARD TEN BROECK had always been exceptional, though not entirely in the best ways. His path was curved. Always had been. As if, by forging twists and turns into the straightaway, he could create a more complex and grander route than one that was quiet and mundane.

He was easy to spot if you knew to look for the steady stream of smoke rising from his cigar. Otherwise, his appearance was so unremarkable you might well miss him. Instead of neckties popping with color like those worn by most men of the era, Ten Broeck chose the black and understated d'Orsay cravat, always immaculately tied, worn around a stiff upright collar. Aside from his eyes, which were deep blue and impenetrably faraway, the rest of his face was unexceptional, hidden as it was behind a light brown beard that was trimmed to even-sided perfection. Slim, medium in stature, he might have been mistaken for an oversize jockey. He enjoyed the misimpression and in fact occasionally rode his own horses in races. Even then, the cigar never left his mouth.

But beneath the deadpan exterior was a master of wits who could bluff a royal flush while holding nothing but a high card, a risk-taker so self-assured that others thought he *must* know something they didn't. He usually did. Always five steps ahead, Ten Broeck had already played out every conceivable scenario in his head before he made his next move. And so, when Richard Ten Broeck said he was going to accomplish something, no matter how fantastical it seemed, few among his broad group of acquaintances ever questioned him.

However unassuming his appearance may have been, the Ten Broeck name stood out among the mightiest, having established itself in a patriarchal lineage of military and politics. In 1663, Dirck Wesselse Ten Broeck emigrated from Holland to New Amsterdam. He became rich exporting animal pelts, and helped found the city of Albany, New York, and its Reformed Dutch Church. Since then, just about every Ten Broeck male had either served in the U.S. Army or at the helm of New York's government. Young Richard Ten Broeck's was a golden path, paved for him by the dedication and hard-earned respectability of generations of forefathers. All he had to do was follow it.

Born in 1812, by age seventeen, Richard—"Dick" to most people—had soared through the prestigious Albany Academy while simultaneously accumulating an unending list of disciplinary infractions and enduring more cracks from his headmaster's cane than a promising boy ought. To enhance Richard's chances for life success, his father secured him a paid position running messages as a page in the New York House of Assembly. It was a spoiled life, unearned and therefore taken for granted—flippantly burning through opportunities as if there were always another and better one around the corner. In Richard's case, there usually was. In 1829, rebellions aside, his academic accomplishments and family name awarded him a coveted cadetship to West Point. But in less than a year, he faced resignation or expulsion after challenging his superintendent, Colonel Sylvanus Thayer, to settle their differences in a duel. Richard had only been doing what it had been ingrained in him to do—uphold honor at all costs. Instead of polishing his derringer, walking ten paces, and firing at the cadet, Colonel Thayer urged the military brass in Washington to expel the upstart.

Back in Albany, Richard's father scurried around the city, elbowing his way into important offices to have a discreet word about his son. His political pull worked, and in January 1830, young Ten Broeck wrote a letter to the secretary of war, John Eaton, tendering his resignation as a cadet "with the consent of my parents," accompanied by a scribbled note of approval from his father "in accordance with the requests of my son."

Although the family's honor remained intact, the West Point debacle sent Ten Broeck out on his own, undoubtedly with a stern order from his father to figure life out for himself. No longer was Richard the golden son. No longer was he one of the "favored children of the nation—the future men of America," as the cadets had been dubbed in 1825 by the then secretary of war, James Barbour.

Tossing aside his wool uniform and packing what was left of his two Academy-issued candles, eighteen-year-old Ten Broeck set out on a faraway path unbridled by regulations and discipline. A new world full of promises and adventure awaited him. He boarded a train headed southwest toward the Mississippi River.

The Mississippi and all it had to offer made sense to wanderers. Snaking through twelve hundred miles of jutted bluffs and banks of mustard-colored soil, the river teemed with a society unto itself. Steamboats cut through dark rapids, transporting a menagerie of people over the river's magical and mysterious wonderland. On board, vagabonds, wealthy Southern sugar planters, Northern bankers, bishops, and gamblers sat elbow to elbow as deckhands tossed tobacco over to Old Al, the river god of folklore, to appease his pipe and create a foggy ambiance, or spun stories about the river's voodoo spells and ghosts moaning over some bygone wrong. Inside the common rooms, it was not unusual to find a deck of playing cards sitting pepper-and-salt beside a Bible, while out on the balcony, ladies corseted in fragile Parisian silks and wearing hats sprouting fountains of feathers gossiped with men swathed in buckskin leather with bowie knives strapped to their belts. All coexisted handsomely—if only for a short while—as they steamed north or south. For everyone, the river was a gateway to new worlds, and the artery through which Southern life pulsed.

The sound of Southern life had attracted the young rebel. Not the bustle and mechanical motion of the big Northern cities, but rather, a society whose many great pleasures involved languid afternoons on porches flanked by dogwoods and French hydrangeas. All the while bantering and drinking an unfathomable number of juleps to celebrate the setting sun, only to then gamble with a hazy brain until the sun rose. Card playing wasn't confined to the South's richly green landmass. The recreation extended beyond the muddied banks and to the river. So much so that nineteenth-century author Emerson Bennett declared that "any man living on the lower Mississippi, who was not in favor of playing all sorts of games for all manner of sums, would have been at once pronounced no gentleman or a minister of the Gospel." Unlike in the North, where moral conservatives eschewed card playing—considering it a destroyer of all incentive to industry and therefore taxing gambling with a stinging effect—the river brimmed with steamboats whose captains happily obliged the incessant running of card tables. Northerners with a penchant for cards naturally went south.

In the roughly eight to ten days it took to travel the Mississippi from St. Louis to New Orleans, there were scarcely fifteen minutes when cards weren't played. One steamboat captain recalled that at any hour, there were "four to six gambling tables stretched out in the main cabin in full blast for money." Sometimes the captain himself was the most skilled gambler on board. Everyone—from passengers of all classes to the cabin steward and the cook—played, and it was not unusual for $1,000 to change hands in a single game. With cards, fortunes could be made or lost. Marriages wrecked.

Professional gamblers, termed "cardsharps," generally appeared to be gentlemen, polite to a fault. They wore fine clothes, carried gold watches, and looked the way a Southern cotton planter should. They bet their lives daily to make a profit and coolly affected living by the maxim "I don't give a damn." Cardsharps were shrewd, and having perfected the art themselves, could easily spot a man's bluff. Cheating was scorned, and those who did cheat faced the end of a six-shooter and a permanent baptism in the Mississippi. One swindler unlocked the door to his cabin room only to find his opponent's wife on the inside, aiming her pistol in his face and demanding her husband's money. Another crooked gambler was seized, flogged, tarred and feathered, then placed in a canoe and pushed into the dark currents of the river with *only one* bottle of whiskey.

Ten Broeck plunged into this funhouse world of twisted images and false angles. He had no money or accomplishments, but he was smart and began matching wits against a spectrum of men. Over the Mississippi's churning waters he began to hone an awareness of man's desires and fears and to understand that failure was largely dependent on how he chose to view it. He found a new life, fusing himself into the Mississippi's rich amalgam of personalities.

The young man from Albany spent the next decade gambling at the river's card tables, gallivanting from Southern city to Southern city, never putting down roots, or much less staying in one place too long. The river was his home, and on it he emerged a formidable opponent—and not just at the card table. "I back my opinions. Each event in life is a wager," he later wrote, "whether I gain or lose."

The Mississippi eventually relinquished Ten Broeck, depositing him in St. Louis. He still had no legitimate profession or social standing. All he had was the hard currency he won gambling. And his resilience.

It didn't take long for the wandering cardplayer to find the race-track. But gambling on horses was a whole lot different from playing poker at the buckaroo river tables. Betting on a horse wasn't just about winning money. Nor was it about feigning one's way through a bluff. Horse-race betting was very much a spectator event. *Everyone* went to the racecourse, including important men with big titles and lots of money—Commodore Cornelius Vanderbilt, the railroad magnate; John Cox Stevens, the yachtsman and steamboat-manufacturing heir; and President Andrew Jackson—men who had the clout and the means to make things happen. Many of them owned racehorses, and some owned the racecourse itself. In the South there was a lot riding, so to speak, on the way a man bet a horse.

In the nineteenth century, there was no private betting at a window and receiving a paper ticket shrouded in secrecy. Instead, bets were made publicly, so the whole world knew how much a man wagered and with whom. At the racecourse, betting tables lined up row after row in a roped-off area near the grandstand. The betting ring was an odd place, with odd men called Knowing Ones, who had a lingo all their own. These men spent their days watching horses exercise around the track. If they hadn't seen enough there, they headed to the bars or dining parlors to buy a round of drinks for grooms, jockeys, or anyone who might be willing to share reliable information. On race day, the Knowing Ones stood near the betting tables, yelling out whatever bets and odds they proposed along with the terms. *"Who will give me one hundred dollars on Bay Maria to take both heats?"* *"Fifty dollars?"* And then a somewhat plaintive *"Will any gentleman back anything?"* and so on, until someone took the wager by calling out, *"Done!"*

Not only were men betting; they were watching. And they weren't just watching to see how much a man bet, or whether he was drawn to bays over chestnuts. They watched to see if a betting man had the judgment to pick a winner. If he did, and won consistently, he probably carried that skill into all walks of life. Business in particular. Conversely, a man who bet on a losing horse—or worse, a horse that had to be withdrawn from a race because it was too fatigued to go on—was reckless, a fool. He should have known what he didn't know. Wagering on horses, and doing it right, became a way to get a foot in the door of a desirable business enterprise, or an introduction to a group of men who moved and shaped society, or a betrothal to a rich man's daughter.

Getting a foothold was precisely what a young man who'd been forced out of society years before desperately needed. But a way back in wasn't the only thing Ten Broeck desired. Horses had been in his blood since childhood. Even his orange-and-black family crest featured rearing white horses. Back before the anti-gambling craze seized the North, horse racing had flourished there. On childhood summer days, Ten Broeck's father had taken him to the track near Albany, where the boy had elbowed his way to the rail along the homestretch.

One memorable day, when he was eleven, young Richard sat in a carriage beside his father on the crowded roadway to the Union Course in what is now Queens, on Long Island. The attraction that afternoon was the first in a sensational series of horse races, monikered the "North versus South." Originating in 1823, the race aimed to highlight the growing split in a nation fresh off the 1820 Missouri Compromise. It pitted the best horse from the South and the best horse from the North against each other. By post time on May 27, 1823, sixty thousand people had crammed into the Union Course—nearly half of New York City's population of 123,000. Upward of $200,000 ($4.5 million today) was wagered.

Racing for the North was the sportsman John Cox Stevens's firecracker stallion American Eclipse. For the South, turfman Colonel William R. Johnson settled on a relatively unknown Sir Henry, chosen undoubtedly not just for speed but for his ability to withstand the arduous miles of rickety rail travel from Virginia to Long Island. The North versus South race was Ten Broeck's introduction to grand-scale mania: tens of thousands of people shouting, backing their horses with cash and passion. Sitting next to his father in the stands, the boy fixated on the power and drive of Eclipse and Henry. Their hooves beat a percussion that rumbled through him, accompanied by deafening cheers and piercing shrieks from all around. The horses battled for twelve miles before the Northern horse won by a nose. Ten Broeck was hooked. Eighteen years later, he became immersed.

Ten Broeck rode into horse racing on the coattails of the same flamboyant, wild-haired promoter who had showcased Sir Henry in that 1823 North versus South race. Colonel William R. Johnson was better known as "the Napoleon of the Turf," or "Old Nap" by those who really knew him. The sobriquets had nothing to do with his height and everything to do with his giant reputation. In 1807, at age twenty-five, Johnson raced sixty-three horses and won sixty-one races. Napoleon Bonaparte was then the undefeated dictator of Europe, and American turfmen saw a comparison. Ever since, Johnson wore the title like a badge of the *Légion d'honneur.*

Aside from fancy French nicknames, Johnson also answered to the title of Colonel, which in that era was a Southern honorific applied to any gentleman whose persona was grand enough to carry it off, and Johnson's was. Dressed in frilled shirts and midnight-hued velvet frock coats, he sported a shock of white hair that never agreed to be tamed by a comb. His whole en-

"Old Nap" portrait by Thomas Sully. William R. Johnson, the gregarious Southerner, took racehorse promotion to another level. His North versus South races showcasing famous horses drew multitudes and generated large revenues for hosting cities and racecourse jockey clubs.

semble was punctuated by coal-black eyes that, according to his jockey, Charles Stewart, "snapped fire at you."

That spirit was what drove Johnson. His dear friend John Davis described Old Nap as suave, amusing, and "ready to resent an insult." A believer in respecting every man's rights, Johnson stood, according to Davis, in an adored realm, highest of the high. Johnson was also one of the South's most venerated hosts. He made sure the front doors at Oakland, his Virginia plantation, swung open to visitors from every corner of life. The place had notoriously reformed many a teetotaler from his erring ways of abstinence.

Born in North Carolina, Johnson had walked the halls of that state's legislature as an elected official until 1816, when he migrated to Virginia, married the daughter of a plantation owner, and assumed Oakland's operations. Politics drew Johnson again, and he served another twenty years in the Virginia General Assembly.

Taking advantage of Oakland's location near Richmond, an area heavily involved in breeding Thoroughbreds, he began acquiring and breeding them himself. Above the main entrance to Oakland he hung a sign that read, "There is nothing so good for the inside of a man as the outside of a horse." Rumor had it he could walk by a horse and tell how far it could run—just by eyeing it. Johnson's opinion alone could make or destroy a racehorse and its breeder. Stallion advertisements often quoted him saying that the featured horse was "by far" the best racehorse he had ever seen . . . or ever would. And the ploy worked. Johnson's promotions of racehorses and horse races created a roster of successes. The North versus South races were, after all, his idea.

The gregarious Southerner was the ideal man to give Ten Broeck his start.

By 1841, Ten Broeck was twenty-nine years old and filled with a sense of his future. His supreme confidence, plus the respect and money gained from his winnings at the card tables and on horses, paved his way to Johnson. Though the when and where of the partnership's beginnings are unknown, at some point the two men sat down for a round of their favored mint juleps to discuss the current state of horse racing and Johnson's illustrious career. At age fifty-nine, he managed racecourses all over the South and was involved in some manner with just about every racehorse worth mentioning. Although diametrical opposites in demeanor and appearance, they found their commonality in horses. Ten Broeck summed it up this way: "Owing to my fondness of racing, and his good opinion of me, Colonel William R. Johnson determined to take me into partnership in his many racing ventures"—though in what way, or to what extent, he never stated. Nevertheless, before long, Ten Broeck was standing next to Old Nap on the racecourse, being doused in horse-race lingo and whatever sage proverbs Johnson chose to share. He soaked up the knowledge and soon earned enough of a favorable impression that Old Nap started relinquishing the management of a few of his horses to the would-be turf-man.

Late that year, Ten Broeck gambled on himself and bought his first racehorse. He quickly bought another and started racing them to trophy-winning success. Horsemen soon took notice. Ten Broeck's aptitude for sizing up horses began opening doors to clubs where important men drank Sazerac and talked about local affairs—including horse racing, that sport that consumed their world above all others.

It was in that 1840s decade of tutelage when one horse in Old Nap's stable profoundly shaped Ten Broeck's view of racing and the animals it showcased. He was a super-horse, really. The epitome of bottom. A common chestnut with a white blaze that earned him the endearment "Old Whitenose," Boston didn't look like a standout, yet he was anything but common. Even his name had a story. Boston was christened not for the city but for the whist game in which he was anted up as eight hundred dollars' worth of collateral by John Wickham, the Richmond, Virginia, lawyer who defended Aaron Burr on a charge of treason.

The winner of the card game was a man named Nathaniel Rives, who wasted no time in turning the colt over to Old Nap for training under the skilled hand of the Englishman Arthur Taylor and his assistant, John Belcher. In a span of ten years at Old Nap's training stables, Boston competed in forty-five races, most of which were four-mile heats, for a total of 265 career miles. He lowered his colors only five times. Twice he received forfeit to win after every other contending horse was withdrawn before the race even started.* Other owners simply felt their horses stood no chance against him. Their beliefs weren't unjustified. Many speculated that Boston could go in harness, pulling a buggy, and still beat his competition. The horse packed grandstands with not only senators and congressmen but all colors and realms of society. Even Canadians and the English had heard his name. *Bell's Life in London,* the English weekly sporting magazine, occasionally gossiped about the wagers Londoners had made on Old Whitenose. Wherever Boston raced, cities seemingly stopped functioning, having lost their populace to the racecourse. The *Spirit of the Times,* a New York–based sporting periodical, wrote in 1838, "Boston now stands alone in his glory." No horse could touch him.

Boston remained as the pinnacle of racing until May 1842, when, at the age of nine, he faced one of the most formidable opponents of his career. His rival was a sensational mare owned by William Gibbons, a quiet man from New Jersey who, oddly, de-

---

* Per nineteenth-century racing regulations, if a horse was the sole entry in a race, it was required to walk once around the racecourse to show nothing was amiss—that it could race if required—in order to claim the purse. In the case of Boston, he received forfeit twice, meaning that other owners paid to withdraw their horses prior to the race, believing they could not win against him. On one of those occasions, out of respect for Boston, who was by then a proven racehorse, track officials broke from the regulation requiring that he walk the course once. Without objection from the owners who had withdrawn, Boston was awarded the purse without ever leaving his stall.

tested almost everything involved with racing horses except the horses themselves. Shunning all forms of gambling, he raced only horses he had bred, and he never placed a bet. Not even on his own entries. In 1837, Gibbons had sent his mare Bonnets o' Blue to the imported English Thoroughbred, Trustee. The result was the star-faced chestnut filly he named Fashion. By the age of four she had won six of her seven starts, against not just other mares but also stallions and geldings alike; horse races were never separated by gender back then. Fashion kept winning with such ease and courage that Northern turfmen were hailing her as one of the greatest racehorses of the generation. Some even spoke her name and the word "immortal" in the same breath. In 1842, she was half Boston's age.

Boston by Edward Troye, based on an 1833 portrait by Henri De Lattre. Nicknamed "Old Whitenose," Boston was the epitome of "bottom."

By 1839, Boston had been sold to a boisterous high-dollar gambler named James Long, who kept the horse in training with Old Nap. For the undreamed-of price of $12,000 ($363,000 today), Long had bought the one horse who, more than any other, could pave the man's way into the national spotlight. And to guarantee he got noticed, Long challenged Gibbons by wagering $20,000 ($682,000 today) that Boston would beat Fashion in a four-mile heat race on her home turf, Long Island's Union Course. In December 1841, after two months of public demand to see the horses matched, the anti-gambling Gibbons wrote the *Spirit* publicly, accepting the challenge. Given the competitors' geographical origins, it made sense to stage the race as the next installment in Old Nap's North versus South race series.

On May 10, 1842, an estimated seventy thousand people thronged the Union Course to watch the race, completely disregarding rules of order. Fans who were legitimately inside the gates found they had no view at all, while those outside were nonetheless determined to get in. Thousands began tearing down sections of fences, breaking down doors, and storming the course. For a while, officials questioned whether they should call off the race. Finally, someone tracked down local prizefighter Yankee Sullivan in the crowd, paid him two hundred dollars, and sent him off to tame the trespassing masses. For those less than compliant, Sullivan swung with his right—the same right that was known to send other prizefighters stumbling to the floor.

Nearing post time, thousands of people lined both sides of the field. Two judges climbed into the stands, each holding a chronometer—a watch that measures time in quarter-second increments—that had been made in Europe expressly for the legendary match between Sir Henry and American Eclipse.

As space cleared for the horses to enter, Fashion walked gracefully to the post. When Boston set foot on the track, the crowd erupted. Tossing his head wildly, the stallion yanked his two grooms in every direction. Per regulations that required horses to carry weight according to their age—not ability—Boston, age nine, carried 126 pounds to Fashion's five-year-old weight of 111. For a race of this caliber, Long had reached deep into his pocketbook to retain one of the best jockeys in the nation, Gilbert Patrick—

known simply as Gilpatrick. The jockey pulled himself up on Boston and gathered up the reins. Joe Laird, the lightweight son of Fashion's trainer, Samuel Laird, was given a leg up onto the mare. Receiving their orders, both jockeys brought their horses to the post and waited for the drum's single tap—a sound that to every nineteenth-century racehorse meant, "GO!"

Boston charged for the lead as if the race were a mere sprint. Drawing the inside track, he led the first half mile. With Fashion nowhere in contention, he passed the judges' stand, completing the first mile. As Boston continued, Fashion threatened to take the lead. Boston pushed and again passed the judges' stand, claiming the second mile. He then completed the third mile at a blistering speed, running the three miles in the fast time of 5:37 ½.

On the turn of the fourth mile, Laird raised his whip over Fashion's head, shaking it for her to see, then sank his spurs deeply, sending Fashion forward at a tremendous pace. In six strides, she took the lead. Refusing her an inch, Boston caught and held parallel to her along the backstretch.

As the horses rounded the final turn, Gilpatrick urged Boston. But the horse's drive was too powerful for even the experienced and renowned jockey to hold steady. Gilpatrick pulled too tight to the inside, ramming Boston into the rail and crashing him against a post. A nail sank deeply into Boston's hip, ripping through eight inches of muscle. From the stands the crowd saw the stallion jar off course, falter, and appear to stop. Three lengths ahead, clouds of dust trailed Fashion.

With a torn hip and the home turn in sight, Boston dug into the track, closing on the mare to within a few feet. The crowd, eager to see the drama firsthand, pushed onto the track, so that only a narrow path existed for the horses to run. With screaming fans only an arm's length away, the horses squeezed through the crevice. Boston increased his speed. Someone in the crowd shouted, "Rouse up your mare! Boston's on you!" Laird raised his whip and drove it down. Fashion regained focus and ran first to the wire, almost a length ahead of Boston.

With tens of thousands of race patrons shouting—a sound, noted the *Spirit,* equaled only by the "explosion of a steamboat boiler"—many did not hear the judges announce the official time. Fashion had run the four miles in 7:32 ½, breaking the American record for horse racing's four-mile speed. Boston crossed the wire less than a second behind.

At the cooling circle, Arthur Taylor tossed his lucky sorrel-colored derby off his head. Even Old Nap's unfaltering smile had been replaced by something far more determined. Ten Broeck stood nearby watching as grooms worked the life back into Boston's aching body. The horse snapped his massive jaws at them and struck out with his hooves, warning them against rubbing their towels too abrasively on his sensitive skin or torn hip. Outside the Union Course's gates, William Gibbons sat tucked away behind closed curtains in his carriage—too nervous to watch his mare race Boston; too nervous, even, to see Fashion's physical state between heats. Someone knocked on his carriage door and delivered him the news that Fashion had beaten the American speed record. Still, Gibbons didn't budge.

At the bugle's sound, Gilpatrick wedged Boston through a human barricade covering the track and steadied the horse at the post for the second heat.

Fashion broke to the front, leading Boston down the backstretch by three lengths. The stallion challenged and passed, giving rise to a tremendous thunder from the grandstand. Laird dug his spurs into Fashion, sending her a neck's length into the lead. As Fashion passed, Boston snapped at her twice, reprimanding, biting the mare severely on the second attempt. She continued on, completing the second mile three lengths ahead.

Gilpatrick eased off Boston, but as the half-mile post neared, he drove the horse to a desperate effort. Sensing a futile expulsion of energy, Laird pulled Fashion back, allowing her to rest. Boston pushed on, claiming the third mile. The pace was electric. "Nothing short of limbs of steel could stand up under such a press," wrote the *Spirit*.

On the first turn of the final mile, Fashion rushed for the lead. Catching Boston opposite the quarter-mile post, she passed him with ease. Fashion won the heat, clinching the match win, with Boston trailing by sixty yards. Gilpatrick pulled Boston up and walked him over the finish line.

Though he'd been beaten, many held Boston in higher regard for his incredible effort and his courage in defeat. Competing with an open wound and burdened with fifteen pounds more than the mare, he'd nevertheless run that first heat faster than any American horse besides Fashion ever had. Many turfmen viewing the race felt Boston had more speed than Fashion, and that, had he not crashed into the post, he would have defeated the mare. Boston was worth more after the race than before.

The following day at the Union Course, after the enormous crowds had dissipated, leaving behind only a few devoted turfmen, Ten Broeck ran one of his own horses to a spectacular victory. But the win felt surprisingly hollow. There was a difference, he realized, between what he saw that day and what he'd seen the day prior. Boston wasn't just a horse to rack up purses, providing prestige to his owner. The horse mattered to the people. His life's hardships and setbacks resonated with them, and they were moved by his unfailing *bottom*. Horses like Boston came around only once in a lifetime. Ten Broeck knew as much.

CHAPTER 2

WARFIELD'S PROPHECY

IN KENTUCKY, LEXINGTONIANS awoke on Sunday, March 17, 1850, to squeeze into their best garments and fineries, then head to church. Although it was St. Patrick's Day, celebratory parades had been postponed until Monday worldwide, out of respect for religious observance.

At The Meadows, a sprawling 123-acre swath of bluegrass on the outskirts of the city, Dr. Elisha Warfield shunned his shined shoes and skipped church entirely. Since twilight of the preceding day, he had sat by candlelight, fidgeting away the minutes in a state of high expectation. Sometime during the night, his temperamental mare, Alice Carneal, had started pacing her stall, restless and sweating. By early morning, she had lowered herself to the ground and, lying on her side, begun birthing a foal. The colt emerged as he should, forelegs first, his nose tucked between. The sack covering his face was pushed back, allowing his first breaths to fill his lungs. The world was shadows to him: blurry, dark, and cold. He would soon gain his sight—the refined perception of objects and what they meant. Alice Carneal stood and began to lick him clean, reassuring him with her touch and presence.

Birth was nothing new to Warfield. At seventy-one, with tousled white hair and a face etched by time, he had long been Lexington's most venerated obstetrician and surgeon. By this point in his career, he had delivered the better portion of the city's human population of 7,920, including Mary Todd, the future Mrs. Abraham Lincoln. Warfield also taught obstetrics and surgery to an endless roster of medical students at the nearby Transylvania University while serving as the department's chair and a university trustee. When he wasn't occupied with biped birth, Warfield was standing outside the stall of one of his numerous broodmares, ready to assist in her foaling.

Having bred horses for fifty years, he was often called "the father of the Kentucky turf." Warfield gained his vast knowledge from his personal library, which housed endless volumes of turf registries from England and America—monthly periodicals with handed-down stories of horse-racing lore stamped onto their rag-paper pages. Pedigree books and England's Weatherby's *General Stud Book* also lined his shelves. Conspicuously absent was any equivalent stud book from America. One didn't yet exist. Therefore, Warfield became the recognized expert on the centuries-long evolution of the Thoroughbred. For a simple barter of candles, gunpowder, hemp, whiskey, or brown sugar, he could tell anyone the historical lineage of the most noted stallions in the world, or settle a dispute about a horse's genealogy.

But it was his own stables that benefited the most from his knowledge. Warfield was a master of determining the best stallions to cross with his mares. His most beloved mare, Alice Carneal, had delivered five previous foals before this morning's new arrival, all of them sired by stallions with crowning pedigrees and headline-grabbing victories. Planning for his prize mare's sixth foal, Warfield had paid a fifty-dollar stud fee and sent Alice Carneal to be bred to the racehorse Boston.

The celebrated stallion had retired from his grueling race schedule six years before and begun his stud career in Virginia. Three

years later, in February 1847, arrangements were made to send
Boston to Kentucky. Reportedly, he was *walked* 435 miles, over
weather-beaten and unpaved roads, from Virginia to Versailles.*
There Boston entered the wood-planked stables of George Edward "Uncle Ned" Blackburn, the same stable where John Cox
Stevens had sent his American Eclipse to stand as a sire. Uncle
Ned's was beyond a doubt the place to be for a stallion whose
owner intended to produce a generation of racehorses. Central
Kentucky had long been prized for its limestone-enriched soil that
strengthened the bones and muscles of the animals that grazed
there. By 1794, the Thoroughbred, originally imported from England into Virginia in 1730, had made its way into the Bluegrass
State. Over time, Kentucky took the reins from Virginia and began
in earnest establishing the Thoroughbred's American bloodline.

As Boston walked the long journey from Virginia to Kentucky,
the *Spirit* trumpeted his sire services in an advertisement worthy of
the champion racehorse:

> Boston's prodigious power, size, and substance, make him
> an admirable cross . . . and we hope to hear that he is liber-
> ally patronized. On the score of family, game, and turn of
> speed, not less for training on during a career unparalleled
> for its brilliant achievements and its no less wonderful con-
> tinuance, he commends himself to the breeders of the coun-
> try. His colts are remarkably promising and if *'like begets*

---

* It is mind-boggling to consider that Boston was walked the entire distance. At his
apex as a racehorse, he was worth an estimated $15,000 (about $546,000 today). His
financial potential as a sire would also have been considerable. The dangers posed to
his health, as well as the possibility of being harmed or stolen by roadside thieves,
would have made the journey extremely risky. Nonetheless, history records that
Boston was indeed walked the distance. When the stallion was sold to James Long,
he unfortunately fell into the hands of a man who cared little for the animal's wel-
fare. Long was ruthless with the horse, running Boston in many questionable races,
even against his race promoter Colonel Johnson's objections. The stallion's health
never having been foremost of Long's concerns, it is possible that the man refused to
pay the expense of having Boston shipped to Kentucky by rail or river.

like,' the admirers of [American] stock may confidently
look forward to a succession of cracks who, like him, will be
too fleet for the fast and too stout for the strong.

Warfield didn't need glowing words to convince him of Boston's
potential. The horse belonged to an ancestral line that began with
the Byerley Turk, an English battle horse who had long been regarded for his stamina and courage. In 1690, he had triumphantly
carried Captain Robert Byerley through the sword-slashing Battle
of the Boyne in Ireland. Both survived and returned to England,
where the stallion began siring a generation of racehorses. Boston's
dam was a full sister to Tuckahoe, a noted stallion from Maryland
who ran in the North in the early nineteenth century. In pedigree books, breeders scribbled down her name simply as "Sister to
Tuckahoe," as if that was all that needed to be said. It wasn't until
after Boston had achieved fame that Tuckahoe was finally referred
to as the brother to Boston's dam.

Alice Carneal, named in honor, or maybe in jest, of one of Warfield's daughters-in-law, was a bay Thoroughbred mare who went
back in ancestral lineage to the Cullen Arabian of England, one of
the many blood strains that comingled early on to create the Thoroughbred horse. Out of the mare Rowena, Alice Carneal was sired
by the mighty Sarpedon, an English stallion who had either won,
placed, or showed in eighteen of his twenty-two starts in races all
over the United Kingdom—races that focused on speed over bottom. Alice Carneal had a good pedigree for racing.

Boston's cover of Alice Carneal took, and eleven months later,
on March 17, she foaled his son. As Warfield eyed the colt that
chilly St. Patrick's Day morning, he noted how strikingly similar
the foal was to the Darley Arabian, another of England's three primary Thoroughbred sires. In one of his many books, Warfield had
seen the eighteenth-century paintings by John Wootton and John
Nost Sartorius, and how splendidly they depicted the Arabian high-
stepping along the English countryside on slender, spindle-shaped

legs—riderless, supreme, and ethereal—as if human touch would mar him. Most pronounced in both depictions was the white blaze that stretched from the Arabian's crown to cover his nose. Like the Darley Arabian, Warfield's colt bore a white strip, made prominent by his contrasting dark velvety color. A bay. But Warfield noticed a small difference: The Arabian had three white socks; this colt had four.

The doctor watched as the colt struggled to rise, teetering on his wobbly limbs, so unreliable in offering their support. With effort the colt splayed his legs and found his balance, succeeding in the first of his life's trials. He raised his head and looked around at the parameters of his stall, peering at the shadows, examining Warfield and the stable grooms staring back at him. He was such a new creature, so fragile and vulnerable, but surely he would grow into something as magnificent as the Arabian in Wootton's painting. Warfield liked the little foal immediately. He named him Darley.

Over the next two years, Darley indeed grew into a form as splendid as Boston's. Standing fifteen hands, three inches, a good height for that era, Darley was born with the build of a runner. His bones were slender, except his backbone, which was unusually large due to his wide chest: a genetic formation inherited from Boston. Where other horses outweighed Darley by two hundred pounds, he made up for that heft in muscular build. His large nostrils, wide jawbone—so wide that one man compared him to a squirrel with a cheek full of acorns—and deep chest combined to give him an exceptional ability to breathe. Like Alice Carneal's, Darley's shoulders were slanted, wide, and strong, enabling the colt a greater reach with his forelegs and a longer stride. The enormous size of his rib cage made his front legs appear shorter than they were. His pasterns connecting his hooves to his fetlocks were long, slightly upright, and firm, springing each of his steps and giving him excellent flexibility. The hocks of his hind legs were angled more than on most horses, affording him an increased ability to withstand strain from concussive, high-impact running. Darley's entire hind leg conformation combined to provide him great mobility and an incredible forward reach—a dynamite punch of propulsion.

But it was his eyes that best conveyed the soul beneath his build. The engine to the machine. One man described Darley's expression only as "resolute." At the time, the horse had been doing nothing more than walking off a railcar.

Despite owning a powerhouse of a horse, Warfield's horse-racing hands were tied. By the time Darley was born, the doctor's health had started to decline, and out of concern, his wife, Maria, ruled him off the turf and forbade him from having anything further to do with racehorses . . . or else! Toeing the line on the house rules, Warfield sat back, fidgeting under his newly imposed constraints, and did his best to suppress his ardor for everything equine.

But if anyone cared to ask, they'd get a wistful earful of grand memories about the early days when Warfield became a member of the first Lexington Jockey Club, which had been formed in 1797. For a one-guinea (one pound, one shilling, or about $1.50) entry fee per horse, Warfield ran his colts in three-mile heat races for a chance to win almost double that. They ran carrying his registered silks: sky-blue cap and white jacket. When the Lexington Jockey Club folded in 1823, Warfield took his horses to his good friend Senator Henry Clay's Ashland estate in Lexington and ran them there on Clay's makeshift racecourse. For a while, Clay's friends were content to let their horses run ovals into Ashland's manicured lawns, but eventually the turfmen of Lexington yearned for something more structured, for something that gave legitimacy to what they were doing. Racing horses wasn't just about a Sunday gathering and a chance to drink juleps in the shade. Finally, on July 23, 1826, Warfield and about sixty other men met at the Phoenix Hotel in Lexington and organized the Kentucky Association to promote the breeding and racing of the Thoroughbred horse in their state. They bought sixty-five acres of land outside Lexington, built a one-mile oval racetrack, and formed the Kentucky Association Race Course—no doubt with much gratitude from Henry Clay's groundskeeper.

The following year Warfield paid $3,690 to buy the 123 grassed acres adjacent to the Association Race Course. He sold his downtown home, packed up Maria and their children, and moved to what became The Meadows, complete with a nine-thousand-square-foot colossus of a house that sprouted four chimney stacks. The house had been configured so that the attic's crescent-shaped window overlooked the racetrack, giving an unobstructed view of racecourse happenings. Warfield soon built his stables, paddocked off fields, and set out with purpose to breed racehorses. By 1850, his love of horse racing was operating at full throttle. Life was perfect until Maria's sentence of doom.

Further prompted by his wife, Warfield started selling some of his horses, ostensibly to ease his burdens. He kept Darley. The horse was then two, an age when other horses run their first races. But Warfield could do nothing with the horse without igniting Maria's ire. Instead, Darley ran circles in the grassed paddock next to Warfield's house, untrained and unraced. Over time, The Meadows became barren of any racing stock except for Alice Carneal, Darley, and just a handful of other young horses. Warfield had pointed Darley out to potential buyers, telling them that the Darley Arabian's mirror-image colt would make a good racehorse.

Dr. Elisha Warfield, "Father of the Kentucky Turf," by L. Rawley Jacobs.

He went further on one occasion, telling a New York newspaper editor, "I am an old man. I cannot live long, but you will live to see the day when the best racehorses in America trace to Warfield's Darley."

The editor wasn't in the market for a professed would-be champion, but there was one man who liked everything he saw in Warfield's bay colt. Harry Lewis, affectionately known as Old Harry to everyone who had anything to do with racing, was a freed Black man who had lived his life tending to horses. He was the trainer to see if you needed to turn a promising horse into a full-fledged racer. Deeply serious about his work, Lewis usually wore an impatient expression. It wasn't that he didn't enjoy the company of others, it was just that he had more pressing thoughts. Two steps ahead of everyone, he walked with purpose. You had to step up to keep up. And you had better not disrespect him by showing up in his presence in some ragtag ensemble. Lewis had gone through much in his life and had worked hard to be where he was. He not only wanted to be a part, he wanted to look it, and he was surely known to several haberdasheries around Lexington. They performed a remarkable job outfitting his tall frame with extra-long green velvet coats and sharp gray trousers. But it was the black silk top hat that announced he had arrived.

Thanks to Lewis's skilled training, Kentucky figured heavily in the national competition to produce winning horses. At some point, Kentucky turfman Captain Willa Viley bought Lewis from the Robert Burbridge family for fifteen hundred dollars. Although the date is unclear, by possibly 1853, Viley reportedly gave Lewis his freedom and then retained him at five hundred dollars per annum to train his racehorses—the equivalent of $16,680 today. It wasn't much money, but Old Harry was free.

Lewis had crossed a forbidden barrier. Pre–Civil War horse racing was built on the tireless work of untold thousands of enslaved jockeys and trainers. Black horsemen had the knowledge of horse care learned from work with plantation field horses. Enslaved men

Richard Singleton by Edward Troye, circa 1834. Harry Lewis, the trainer of Richard Singleton, is pictured saddling the horse for a race. Also pictured are "Charles," Singleton's groom; and "Lew," his jockey. Lewis was much younger here than when he assumed the training of Darley some nineteen years later.

and boys were the ones in the barns, riding the horses, feeding, medicating, and training. They were highly sought by racehorse owners, and, even though enslaved, they were paid. Sometimes handsomely. Old Nap Johnson's enslaved jockey Charles Stewart traveled all over the North and South, not only to ride Johnson's horses but also, eventually, to train and run an entire string of the colonel's racehorses. "I went all alone," Stewart said of his early jockey days, "and when I was up on the stage at Petersburg in my new suit o' store clothes, with ten dollars in my pocket and more to come, I was 'high come up,' I tell you." As early as 1823, Stewart commanded up to three hundred dollars to ride a horse in a race. "I had plenty of money and nobody to say nothing to me," Stewart recalled.

National newspapers also occasionally lifted Black jockeys, enslaved or freed, out of the stranglehold of inequality and anonymity by crediting them with the same level of skill and courage as their white counterparts. Skilled jockeys, Black and white, were coveted, and, according to nineteenth-century author Grace King, "petted and spoiled like ballet girls." Black jockeys and trainers usually enjoyed a rare freedom, privilege, and authority that were otherwise unheard of in the lives of enslaved people. They had the ability to travel at will and alone. Historian Dale Somers wrote that "riding Thoroughbreds served one of the functions that professional sports have traditionally served—it provided an egress from poverty and humiliation for members of afflicted minority groups." But despite the freedom, fame, and financial upswing, the lot of an enslaved horseman was just as uncertain and fearfully precarious as that of his brothers in the fields. At any time, he could be sold back into a life where he had no value.

In 1853, freedman Harry Lewis rode out to The Meadows to take a look at the young bay horse who had inspired Warfield's prophesies of eternal bloodlines. At the front door of the pilastered mansion, the doctor greeted Lewis with a hopeful handshake. Old Harry had trained Kentucky's champion Thoroughbreds Grey Eagle and Richard Singleton. If Lewis would just take a look at Darley, he too would see that glimmer of greatness that Warfield intuitively believed was at the core of this colt. Warfield pointed to the paddock next to his house, and to Darley romping around and playfully kicking out. The spirited horse was already supremely powerful. Eager. Far too much animal to be unworked and relegated to a paddock. He could soon become unmanageable, even for breeding. But where Warfield saw in Darley thousands of future racehorses, Lewis saw a compact build, a deep chest, and muscular legs. He asked to lease Darley's racing rights—the right to train and race the horse while Warfield remained the owner. Warfield readily agreed, and Lewis took the reins.

In Lewis's hands, Darley was started under saddle. Sadly, details of his early training have not surfaced in history, but if he was anything like his sire, Boston, the process was pure hell. Books of the era expounded training techniques to deal with horses of all temperaments. For a wild and unbroken colt, one manual advised,

enter alone, with a long whip in your right hand held pointing behind you. When you enter the stable, stand still, and let the horse look at you a minute. As soon as he is settled in one place, approach him slowly, with the right hand hanging by your side, and the whip trailing on the ground, the left bent, and the elbow projecting.

But such precision was a near impossibility with horses like Boston. Training manuals were most likely tossed aside.

To break Boston, one of Old Nap Johnson's trainers, John Belcher, had surrendered his best stable hand, a young man named John Alston, to the wild stallion. When Alston first approached the horse, Boston flared his nostrils and pawed the ground like a bull ready to charge. Still, Alston managed to slip on a bridle and girth on a saddle. But the horse swung his hind end and violently jerked his head back, wrenching the reins out of Alston's hands. Alston grabbed the reins again, tightened his grip, and lowered Boston's head, pulling the horse's nose back toward the animal's shoulder. Holding the horse in submission, Alston climbed aboard.

The weight on his back was a decidedly unpleasant sensation to the horse. Boston lunged forward and bucked, kicking out twice before his rear hooves hit the ground. Skilled and fearless, Alston managed to stay aboard through the fire-and-brimstone fight. Boston jumped back, whirled around, and sidestepped in a frenzied staccato, as if dancing to some unknown rhythm playing only for him. Eyeing a fence, Boston ran to it, leaned in, and dragged his side against the planks, but Alston didn't budge. The stallion turned in a tight circle and quieted, as if pondering a chess move. Then, from a dead stop, he sprang into a gallop toward a crop of trees with branches that swayed low to the ground. Boston rushed under them, but Alston flattened himself against the horse's neck and dug in his spurs. Boston jumped sideways, then plunged low and kicked up toward the sun. Alston landed in the dirt. From that point forward the use of spurs on Boston was *highly* discouraged.

Whatever amount of respect Boston afforded the young stable hand from that day forward was evidently enough for him to ride the horse in future races. But during those early years, if anyone other than Alston tried to board, Boston played his ultimate coup de main by dropping to the ground and rolling the rider from his back. After a couple of lackluster race performances, Boston finally matured into the phenomenal racehorse he was.

Not only did Darley come to Lewis carrying the baggage of his sire's obstinacy, he came weighted with the reputation of his dam's irascible temper and anxiety. "Her nerves were as delicately tuned as those of a girl reared inside convent walls," one turfman said. Although fast and headstrong, Alice Carneal could never last through a training session without panic; sweat poured down her sides and dripped from her belly as if she had come in out of a wrath of rain. For whatever reason, she was so terrified of any work that the decision was made not to race her at all until she had matured to the age of five. But age did nothing to calm her. Finally, a now-or-never decision was made, and Warfield entered Alice Carneal in her first race.

At the sight of the track the five-year-old trembled convulsively, broke into a lather, and became so unmanageable at the post that track officials deemed her a hazard to herself and others. Warfield entered her in another race, hoping that she would mature—not from age but from experience. But the mare remained wildly ungovernable. At age seven, she competed in a two-mile heat race at the Association Race Course next door to The Meadows. She failed to show any effort and ran unplaced, or "distanced," meaning that by the time the leading horse crossed the wire for the win, Alice Carneal had not passed the distance pole that was located one hundred yards from the finish. Despite her potential, Alice

Carneal won only one of her seven races. But Warfield still believed in her. He retired his mare from the turf and started making plans for her broodmare career.

When Lewis took on Darley, the horse was a spirited, unbroken three-year-old. But the trainer had handled more than his share of highly tuned horses. He survived the breaking of Darley and rechanneled the horse's energy into daily workouts on the Association track. When Darley reached the age of three, Lewis aimed him toward his first race—his maiden. The Association Stakes was a one-mile heat race (a potential of two miles, three miles if a tie-breaking heat was required), a relatively easy race for well-conditioned horses of that era. Some of Kentucky's best colts would be entered, trying to win their maiden in order to advance to more challenging and lucrative races.

Back at The Meadows, Maria had gone looking for her husband. He wasn't anywhere in the nearly empty stables. Nor was he in the parlor or even in his book-filled library. Finally, she resolved to search him out in the one place she feared he might be. Leaning into the stairway banister, she started the unpleasant climb up three flights of stairs. As suspected, Maria found the doctor in the attic sitting at the crescent-shaped window. In one hand he held his field glasses—pressed firmly against his eyes, squinting out toward the Association racetrack where Old Harry had Darley stretched into a full run. In Warfield's other hand he held his chronometer. Each time Darley reached a certain point on the track, Warfield clicked the button and checked the time. He must have known then that Alice Carneal's sixth colt was singular.

CHAPTER 3

THE METAIRIE

A YEAR AFTER BOSTON lost to Fashion, Richard Ten Broeck found paradise. It came in the form of a city that a visiting cleric had once declared was a depot on the way to hell. Bishop Henry Benjamin Whipple listed twenty reasons to condemn New Orleans, most of which had to do with the fact that gambling and just about any form of entertainment—masked balls, sword fights, Italian fantoccini—occurred somewhere in the city every day of the week, the Sabbath included.

By the late 1830s, New Orleans had garnered a reputation as a mecca of the spectacular. Everyone went there to experience what the city boldly held up as the scepter of indulgence. On any given week, the Port of New Orleans received as many as two hundred steamboats, steamships, brigs, and schooners. Many flew brightly colored foreign-national flags, turning the port into a miniature international enclave. Money and goods—cotton, barrels of whiskey, Parisian silks, Chantilly laces, feather compositions, and other bric-a-brac—funneled into New Orleans. The city swirled with every decadence, and because of these riches, it grew into an economic power to be envied.

Open to all comers, the city particularly catered to those in pursuit of a lavish lifestyle, the kind author Grace King called "fine living and generous spending of lordly pleasure, and of haughty indifference to the cost." Risk, and the chance to earn a self-made fortune, brought turfmen from Virginia, New York, Kentucky, and Tennessee down to the Deep South to speculate in what was quickly becoming the hotbed of horse racing. So much so that by 1838, New Orleans had enough money and horse-racing interest to support two separate jockey clubs and three separate racecourses.

The Eclipse Course, operated by the New Orleans Jockey Club, looked about as opulent as an opera house. Thanks to a promotional sales wizard named Yelverton N. Oliver, who aimed to style the racecourse after the city, the Eclipse boasted a Baroque-inspired parlor with pink chaise lounges, carpeted floors, and gilt-framed mirrors almost as large as the walls themselves. Not to be outdone, the city's Louisiana Jockey Club opened its own Louisiana Course that was figureheaded by a wealthy French Creole named Bernard Xavier Philippe de Marigny de Mandeville. Bernard claimed he could trace his lineage to an ancestor upon whom Louis XIV had bestowed a title, and therefore lived as if he were indeed the descendant of royalty. More tangible was the seven-million-dollar estate Bernard had inherited when he was all of fifteen years of age. Well accustomed to an unbridled existence, when he wasn't lounging around at the Louisiana Course, he was swallowed up in a pool of velvet inside his gold-encrusted coach drawn by two magnificent fairy-tale-looking horses, no doubt en route to one of his many sword duels. An expert swordsman, Bernard gallivanted around New Orleans, challenging and successfully defending as many as fifteen duels, all in the name of afflicted love and gentlemanly honor.

But for all the Baroque parlors and colorful figureheads, it was the third racecourse that would become a mainstay in New Orleans. The Metairie came about in 1838, when the New Orleans Jockey Club leased two tracts of land from the New Orleans Canal

& Banking Company for purposes of building a racecourse. The region known as Metairie, a term for a farm run under a twelfth-century French sharecropping system, had once been owned by early European settlers and freed Blacks. The tracts abutted Shell Road, a five-mile stretch of crushed oyster shells that ended at the Port of New Orleans. After leasing the land, the New Orleans Jockey Club built a mile-long oval track, walled by an uprising of live oaks tangled in Spanish moss, and set up a wood-planked grandstand along the homestretch.

Metairie's track was something beyond supreme. Built on the upper Metairie ridge, one of the highest plateaus in New Orleans, the land offered excellent drainage for its fifty-eight annual inches of rainfall. And, when properly maintained, the soil compacted, preventing a horse from sinking too deep. The result was a spring-board dirt surface—a responsive track that bounced energy back into the ligaments of the horse, allowing it an easier run. There wasn't a track of its quality anywhere else in America.

It was only a matter of time before the Metairie, and all of New Orleans, reeled in Ten Broeck. By the mid-1840s, he had begun racing his own horses under the colors of his family crest: orange cap and jersey, black belt. He had also managed Old Nap's horses at tracks all over the South and even in the North. But in May 1837, a financial panic sent many New York City businesses into bankruptcy, collapsing banks and upending people's lives and liveli-hoods. In one month alone, New York City saw mercantile failures amounting to over $100 million—worth nearly $3 billion today. In 1839, another financial panic struck, decimating what was left of New Yorkers' fortunes.

Over the ensuing years, Northern horse racing was almost com-pletely wiped out. Long Island's famed Union Course, where Bos-ton raced Fashion, held one race meeting a year, lasting just three days. Pittsburgh held only one meeting too, lasting four days—this in open contravention of Pennsylvania laws prohibiting horse racing and gambling under the most stringent of penalties including confiscation of all racehorses. With the foreclosure of Northern tracks and the anti-gambling laws lashing out severe blows to racehorse owners, Ten Broeck routed his and Old Nap's horses down South.

Among the planters and merchants, Ten Broeck thrived. He was likable. Deft. A chameleon who adapted himself to any culture and minded his own business. His calm, accommodating nature eventually helped land him the coveted position of managing the Bascombe Race Course in Mobile, Alabama.

Managers were often hired by jockey clubs to run the race meets and were put in charge of every detail from the creation of stakes races and the setting of purse sizes to collecting admission fees, supervising the layout and appearance of the venue, crowd control, and even catering. If the manager also understood and appreciated horse racing, all the better. Honesty was everything. So was loyalty. Finding the right man was key to a successful track. With its track in the correct hands, a jockey club could earn a profit, and so too the man who ran it.

But the job was more than just a busy one. A successful track depended on the right publicity and promotion. Since a manager's profit depended on attracting as many people as possible to the racecourse, he had to create the types of events people would pay to see. Matches like Old Nap's North versus South series fed enormous amounts of money into racecourses and their corresponding jockey clubs. But promoting racing meets that drew not only turfmen but also people who had never been to a horse race was an especially creative art. Not everyone who managed racecourses could do it. Some courses—like the Bingaman, the Metairie's sister course—resorted to gimmicks such as, in one instance, a match between a bear named Andrew Jackson and Columbus the bull.

Three thousand people attended to see Columbus gore Andrew Jackson back into his cage. Although a financial success for the Bingaman Race Course, the event was widely criticized as barbaric.

The construction of the courses posed a different problem. Wooden grandstands splintered and warped, and when thousands of people loaded onto them, they became sagging hazards to humanity. In 1845, Ten Broeck stood in the middle of an overcrowded, dilapidated grandstand in Camden, New Jersey, bracing himself as an excited crowd rattled and shook the structure beyond its engineered capacity. "Crash went the stand and I with it," he recalled. "Fortunately, I fell beside a hogshead of beer, and the rafters being on top of the hogsheads, furnished me a good berth."

Not all racecourse hazards were viewed so good-naturedly. In 1847, the New Orleans Jockey Club was sued for $1,000 in damages when stands at the track allegedly buckled, causing one man to break his leg. The problem, the Jockey Club contended, wasn't the grandstand. Instead, the litigious man had left his seat in the stands to join several other men in ascending the weakly constructed rooftops of the refreshment booths—obviously a viewing area to which no sane racecourse manager would have ever sold tickets! The lawsuit's outcome was not reported, but it was inevitable that racecourse management contributed to, as well as suffered from, the advancement of modern-day tort law.

Still, for those willing to contend with these downfalls, racecourse management brought not only monetary reward but also a chance to receive national recognition. Ten Broeck was a genuine fit for the position. He impressed most people as reticent and philosophic—in other words, savvy and intuitive. Racehorse trainer William Day said he had "extremely gifted abilities," and an "unusual acumen and unwonted foresight." Ten Broeck's typist called him "the strangest genius I ever met."

By 1849, thanks to his successful management of the Bascombe Race Course, as well as his audacious but shrewd betting on horses, Ten Broeck's bank account was flourishing, and his name was becoming intermeshed with the sport itself. But managing race-courses wasn't all he aspired to. He wanted to own a track. To be the one man with whom no one interfered. The man fully able to orchestrate the kinds of races Old Nap had created so many years before, with Sir Henry and later Boston. Everyday stakes races were one thing. National headlining and fan-swooning races, the kind that attracted tens of thousands of people, were another. Ten Broeck needed a racecourse he could take over.

Oddly, the timing couldn't have been better. New Orleans's gold luster had dulled. The city could no longer support the horse-racing bubble that had been created in the 1830s. The dismal effects of the financial panic of 1837 had spread throughout the country. Although New Orleans had initially survived it, the depression that followed barreled through the city, knocking down many people who had previously stood unassailable. The riches that had enabled its citizens to build and sustain three racecourses were slowly pulling away from horse racing. Other matters became more pressing: families had to be supported, mercantile and planting businesses kept afloat. By the 1840s, Bernard Xavier de Marginy, who was now on the verge of losing a sizeable portion of his fortune, turned away from his membership in the Louisiana Jockey Club, taking many of his established Creole brethren with him. They too were feeling the shock of financial depression and had little to invest in the sport. Yelverton Oliver had also lost money and saw a dreary outlook ahead. In 1840, he left the Crescent City for Louisville to establish the Oakland Course. His Eclipse Course closed in 1849, barely able to sustain its two race meetings a year—one in the spring and one in the fall. Only the Metairie, having outperformed her sister courses and therefore having a more permanent base of supporting members, survived. But it was a remnant of its former glory.

Despite this bleak scene, Ten Broeck turned his interest away from the Bascombe Course and directed his full focus on buying the struggling Metairie. Since the Metairie's inception in 1838, the

New Orleans Jockey Club had been shoveling cash to the Canal &
Banking Company to pay rent so they could operate their racing
meets on those two land parcels out by the bayou. But still, the
bank could sell the land out from under the Jockey Club any day,
sending it scrambling to find another venue. Impermanence inspired little financial investment from club members. No one
wanted to sink their dollars into a structure that might be torn
down and sold off. So, as the years turned into a decade, the Metairie's once beautiful façade began to wear. It was outdated, in
need of a facelift—and more—if the course was to capably host the
city of New Orleans, and eventually, the nation.

After forming the Metairie Association, a joint-stock company
in which he held the majority of shares, Ten Broeck knocked on
the door of the Canal & Banking Company and, in April 1851,
paid $9,000 toward a $27,000 purchase price to buy the Metairie
outright. Then, as the racecourse's new proprietor, he rebuilt the
facility.

He started by enlarging the grandstand to run the entire length
of the 2,122-foot homestretch, creating seating to cram in as many
people as possible. More patrons meant more tickets sold. While
the grandstand was being overhauled, work crews were busy saw-
ing wood and hammering nails to improve the stables to hold the
kind of horse talent Ten Broeck hoped to attract—star contenders
like Boston, who could entice multitudes into a racecourse. He
then focused on the lackluster parlors of the Metairie. Borrowing a
page from Yelverton Oliver's creation of the Baroque-style Eclipse
Course, Ten Broeck revamped the Metairie's salons to supremacy.
Gone were the haphazard-looking edifices that only offered rain-
warped, wood-planked seating, replaced by wedding-cake mold-
ings, cushioned chairs, and silk curtains that pooled in rippled
patterns on the floor.

Ten Broeck focused next on the patrons. In that era, horse racing was regarded as a "gentleman's sport." Yet it was clear that the
heartbeat of competition pumped just as fervently in women. Ten

Broeck shunned the notion of "men only" and broke down the barriers of what was considered appropriate or fashionable for the women of New Orleans by giving them a presence and a voice. The Metairie not only welcomed them to debate their well-reasoned horse-racing predictions but provided a women-only parlor that rivaled the stuffy old mahogany smoking rooms of the sporting clubs that were exclusive to men. Female patrons could now talk about horses while they sat under cascading tiers of crystal chandeliers amid frescoes of Shakespearean characters. They drank bottomless glasses of champagne and indulged in meals created by chefs Ten Broeck had hired to outshine the city's fanciest restaurants on the waterfront, just a mile down the road.

First Futurity by L. Maurer, 1889. This racecourse at Sheepshead Bay, New York, was active forty years after Ten Broeck's Metairie. Yet the grandstand and judges' stand depicted here still hearken back to the grandeur and elaborate construction of racecourses like the Metairie at the time when Lexington raced. Noteworthy is that the Black and white jockeys shown here still rode in a position that aided stamina, having not yet adopted the crouched position over the horse's back, the English jockey position favored for speed.

After the Metairie had been dressed up to host the likes of kings and queens, Ten Broeck focused on satisfying the turfmen. Luxurious indulgence aside, the Metairie was a true racecourse. Unlike its sister establishments, such as the Bingaman—notorious host to the bear-and-bull fight—the Metairie catered only to horse racing. Ten Broeck tripled the number of stakes races, backing them with heavy purses. He also insisted that horses run carrying colors, or silks, designated by their owners—a practice that wasn't always followed at other courses. He set up regulations to decrease the potential for fraud, since jockeys were sometimes paid to lose, either by their opposition or by someone placing a high-dollar bet. Deliberately losing could be accomplished by carrying extra weight secreted in the saddle, causing the horse to slow its speed. Jockeys would now be weighed with saddle in hand, not only before the race but between heats and afterward. Turfmen could be assured that if they went to the trouble and headache of shipping their horses to run in New Orleans, the race would be fair and the results honest.

Next, to turn the Metairie into a first-class horse-racing venue, Ten Broeck needed community backing, which meant Creole support. Against a backdrop of French and Spanish architecture as elaborate and complicated as New Orleans itself was a mixed people saturated in European customs. Americans were viewed as latecomers. Or worse, as foreigners. By the 1830s, New Orleans's European Creole families had already established a practice of attending animal sports. They crowded at street corners to watch roosters fighting, or in larger arenas to see matadors twirl their colorful capes at ground-pawing bulls. Yet horse racing, an English sport adopted by the Americans, was an unfamiliar pastime. It took some convincing to draw people whose mindsets were in many ways still stuck in Old Paris. Early attempts by American turfmen had already piqued the interest of the established Creole population. But Ten Broeck wanted the Creole society not only to interact with the sport as fans or merely to serve as fancy figureheads like Bernard the swordsman. He wanted Creoles also to have a say at the board of directors' table. In February 1852, with Ten Broeck at the helm, the Metairie Jockey Club hosted its annual members' gala at the St. Charles Hotel—an evening packed with "great hilarity and good feeling," reported the *Spirit*. Gathered around a "table furnished with everything in the most luxurious style," the Metairie's members elected Colonel Paul Octave Hébert as its second vice president.

Since masquerade balls were a much-loved New Orleans tradition, the Metairie hosted several grand galas to celebrate horse racing and increase membership. Ten Broeck also engaged the Metairie in the community. In years past, the Metairie's ticket gates had funneled any profit back into the club itself. Now, on various occasions, half the proceeds of every ticket purchased to enter the track was donated to local orphanages and other needy projects, meaning that a day at the races could double as an entertaining charitable outpour. Owing to Ten Broeck, more people started patronizing the high-banked Metairie Race Course.

By 1853, horse racing was once again booming in New Orleans. "The Metairie Course," the *Spirit* reported, "is now in every respect superior in accommodations to any other course in the country." The city flourished from the thousands of visitors who disembarked from carriages and steamboats, eager to see firsthand what all this talk was about.

At the same time that Ten Broeck was enjoying the fruits of his success, America was weathering Congress's attempts to unify the country. The Fugitive Slave Act of 1850 had turned the free states into slave-hunting grounds. Now, with unbounded authority, Southern slave owners could search the North for escaped persons. Any Northerner who had knowledge of the whereabouts of a fugitive was required by law to report that information. Passage of the law meant no one was safe. The Underground Railroad continued to function, funneling enslaved people clandestinely through the North and to freedom in Canada, and by 1852, Harriet Beecher Stowe had written her original short-story version of *Uncle Tom's Cabin* for the abolitionist paper *The National Era*. The fissure that would divide a nation was well established.

Hoping to exploit what was left of American camaraderie in 1853, the North-hailed Ten Broeck, racing impresario of the South, envisioned a race different from the North versus South series. Talk of a multistate race had been rolled out the previous season when turfmen from various parts of the country met at one of New Orleans's sporting clubs to debate the merits of each region's horses—along with the sire lines that were thought to be most influential. There, among the esteemed horsemen, Ten Broeck conceived a grand contest he would promote at the Metairie. The race would not pit divisive territories against one another but combine an aggregate of states to compete for the title of "best horse." He gave the race a decorative title, the Great State Post Stake, and encouraged any of the then-existing thirty-one states to enter. All a state had to do was select its very best horse and post a whopping $5,000 entry fee. Ten Broeck aimed for the Great State to be the most sensational horse race the nation had ever seen. He dreamed of people from all over the country jam-packing into New Orleans, filling its hotels and restaurants, and piling through the ticket-charging gates of the Metairie. To make a decent show of it, he figured he needed no less than four or five contending states.

He'd crammed the national papers with advertisements to promote the event and had even lured—possibly paid—some newspaper editors to craft their own promotions. "The most brilliant sporting event of the age," trumpeted New Orleans's *Daily Picayune*. "In proof of this we might instance the Olympic Games of Greece, the Gladiators of Rome, the Chariot races, the Tournaments, the Bull Fights, and, more than all, the deeds of bravery, skill, and strength exhibited in thousands of instances amid the pomp and circumstances of bloody wars." Louisiana, naturally, was in. Alabama too. Rumors circulated that Mississippi and North Carolina were also on the verge of entering and had already started combing the tracks for their best candidates. But Kentucky, home to great turfmen and horses, was uncommitted, if not outright aloof. Ten Broeck bought a ticket for the next steamboat headed up the Mississippi. His big race needed Kentucky. And he needed a Kentucky horse to run in it. He didn't plan on coming home until he found him.

CHAPTER 4

OUTMANEUVERED

THE CLOUDS HAD turned the sky into a bruised palette. During the last forty-eight hours they had dropped a sea of water. On May 22, 1853, the rain still hadn't stopped. On the outskirts of Lexington, Kentucky, over at the Association Race Course, the deluge had churned the track into knee-deep mud. Darley and eleven other contenders sloshed to the post and lined up to await the tap of the drum. The race was in heats of one mile each, a minimum of two heats, three to break a tie. Darley's first race.

Ten Broeck waded through the Association's grounds, leaving a wake of whispers about why the auspicious turfman was *here*. He was likely shown a seat in the grandstand sheltered from the showers but opted to stand near the track so he could survey the field of young horses trudging to the post. He tugged his hat down tighter to filter off the rain, then asked his hosts about this horse named Darley. They shook their heads and waved away the question. Darley was the least-bet colt in the field.

Darley was under his jockey's tight rein, prancing sideways, arching his neck high, and wild-eyeing his competition, all of whom exuded the angst of unseasoned horses. What happened next is anyone's guess. It could've been as simple as someone in the grandstands waving a hat, or possibly an earsplitting crack of thunder from the heavens. What ignited the fuse attached to the spool of frantic energy spinning within Darley is unknown, but before the drum ever tapped, he dug into the slop and bolted away from the start. Two other horses lost all sense and cut loose too. Darley's jockey pulled, then pulled harder, but the horse took hold of the bit, found a higher gear, and ran faster. As rain assailed the track, Darley circled the mile-length oval, once . . . twice . . . then another three-quarters before his jockey's tugs and pulls snapped reason into the horse's brain. Darley slowed only to a trot, blew through his nostrils, and shook his head side to side from frustration. The two other horses slowed behind him as their jockeys wrangled to bring them back to manageable rein. One horse was breathing so hard he was withdrawn from the race.

Lining up at the start again, the horses champed their bits as their bodies tensed from anxiety, making them feel to their jockeys like twelve-hundred-pound explosives under a saddle. When the drum tapped, Darley took off down the homestretch and into the lead. Staying out in front of eleven of Kentucky's most promising young horses, he sailed across the wire to win the first heat. Only four horses crossed the line behind him. The remaining six were too worn-out even to finish the mile. After a fifteen-minute cooling period, Darley came to the post. Only three other horses had recovered well enough to contest the second heat. At the drum's tap, Darley took the lead and won, breaking his maiden. Considering the distance he'd covered in the false start, he had run nearly five miles on a track of deep sludge: the type of ground that pulled horses down, exhausting them. Darley was barely spent.

After the race, Ten Broeck said nothing. He just looked at his hosts incredulously. They shrugged—*Who would have known?*—and told him Darley was owned by Dr. Elisha Warfield. Ten Broeck set out to find him.

Old Harry Lewis shook Dr. Warfield's hand, then made his way over to the edge of the track to wait for the doctor's horse. Darley walked in, head high, unfazed that he had run harder than most racehorses ever would. Lewis took the reins and started his inspection of the mud-slathered horse to ensure he had come out of the race without injury.

Although Lewis was a freed Black man, and although he had leased the rights to race Darley, he still wasn't allowed to use his name to enter the horse in the Association Stakes. The horse had been registered instead as "Warfield's Darley." Even though Lewis had posted half of the $100 subscription fee, Darley ran his maiden carrying Warfield's blue-and-white silks. The grand prize that day was a shining silver plate valued at $100 and a $1,700 cash purse. The winnings totaled over three times Lewis's $500 annual salary from turfman Willa Viley. Having paid half the entry fee, Lewis stood to gain half the winnings. Warfield had agreed to collect the purse and distribute it equally between them, the silver plate going to whomever had the mantel space to show it off. Warfield had four fireplaces.

After the race, Lewis shook a few more hands and accepted congratulations for a job well done. But the men quickly moved on to Warfield, whose circle of admirers was expanding tenfold. There was one man, however, who may have lingered a little longer next to Lewis and Darley. Ten Broeck most likely put several questions to the trainer—blunt ones that ventured into areas of little interest to the casual onlooker. Was the horse ever amiss? Did he train well? Was the performance this horse just delivered typical or a fluke? Was he really only three years old? Because this horse's stamina seemed like that of a seasoned animal. Would it be all right if Ten Broeck just took a quick look at the horse's teeth to verify his age? Was the horse beyond a doubt sired by Boston?

Lewis would have obliged the turfman and answered the questions honestly, knowing full well that a horse of Darley's caliber called for greater things beyond race meets with horses that could barely keep up. Ten Broeck glanced over at the large circle around

Warfield, then turned back to the horse and studied him from head to tail. He nodded to Lewis and walked away.

A few feet from Darley, Warfield was most likely also dodging a slew of questions. An array of men shouted, What are your plans for Darley? Is he for sale? How much? I'll give you $1,000 right now. Did Old Harry train him? How did that go for Harry? Warfield pushed his way through the clamorous circle and headed toward the racecourse gates with a quickened pace to get back to Maria and The Meadows, where he could escape all the noise and the bold requests to buy his horse. As his mind turned the matter over, he realized he had to assess his own position about Darley.

It might have been the same day that a man named Louis E. Smith knocked on his door. A few weeks before, Smith had assembled a team of Alabama turfmen who pooled $5,000 to enter the Great State. Smith submitted the nomination for Alabama and registered an unnamed contender. Toward the end of May 1853, he boarded a steamboat headed to Kentucky, certain he'd find Alabama's horse nestled there somewhere, contentedly grazing on a hillside in Lexington or nearby Versailles. How could he have known that as he sat on that boat, Ten Broeck was aboard another steamboat also forging its way to Kentucky? And that the Metairie's new owner was also searching for a horse? But not one to run under Alabama's crimson-crossed flag.

Once inside Warfield's house, Smith told him that he wanted to buy Darley. The *Spirit of the Times* was calling the Great State "a race without a parallel in the annals of the American Turf!" Representing Alabama would place Warfield's horse center stage nationally. And wasn't that what he wanted? Wasn't that the dream of most horse breeders? To have an animal good enough to stand among the best? An animal born from a man's idea of what blood crossings would bring about the fastest of the fast? Smith told Warfield to name his price. Warfield responded by showing Smith the exit, leaving the Alabaman staring at a closed door and wondering where his talk had gone wrong.

Not long after Smith's departure, Warfield answered another knock. It was Ten Broeck, who would have explained that he owned the Metairie Race Course and was promoting the Great State. But Warfield interrupted, telling Ten Broeck the horse wasn't for sale and sending him away as well.

Smith and Ten Broeck weren't the only ones interested in Darley.* They were just the first ones to approach Warfield. Both men had greatly underestimated the doctor's attachment to his horse and what it might take to sever it. They had also misunderstood their own potential roles in relation to the horse and how to characterize the advantages of their ownership. Over the next couple of days, while other groups of turfmen were forming syndicates, pooling their resources, or simply pondering their chances of owning Darley, Old Harry was making other plans.

Although Warfield had yet to sell Darley, his trainer knew that the doctor's days with the stallion were numbered. Darley had come out of the Association Stakes race fine—uninjured and unfatigued. The Citizens' Stakes for three-year-old horses, a two-mile heat race, promised a second silver trophy along with a cash purse of thirteen hundred dollars. The problem was that Warfield still hadn't paid Lewis his portion of the winnings from the last race—not a large amount to Warfield, but almost two years' salary to Lewis. Warfield certainly wasn't short on character, nor was his pocketbook shy on funds. But the offers for Darley weighed on his mind such that everything else was put off. Rather than approach Warfield about the Citizens' Stakes, Lewis went to see the doctor's son and asked if he could borrow the one hundred dollars to post the next entry. Lewis assured him: Darley is a winning type of horse; he will not let us down.

With the money now in hand from Warfield's son, Lewis entered Darley in the Citizens' Stakes under Warfield's name and the

---

* Historical sources diverge on this detail. Some sources only relate the stories of Smith's and Ten Broeck's attempts to buy Darley. Another source notes that there were several interested parties, but fails to identify who they were.

blue-and-white silks. Although the doctor may have known of Old Harry's desire to run Darley again, his horse was entered without Warfield's involvement, and possibly, without Warfield's knowledge.

Ten Broeck wasn't the kind of man who took no for a final answer. The Great State promised not only the best horse from each contending state but also a corresponding party of turfmen. Ten Broeck was in Lexington to find a horse to represent Kentucky. But he was also there to put together Kentucky's team.

Captain Willa Viley, the man who gave Old Harry his freedom, was one of the original Kentucky turfmen and had a reputation for scrupulous honesty. The same words could easily have described Dr. Warfield. And like Warfield, Captain Viley was a founding member of the Association Race Course and a champion of game and sport. The two men had spent many a day watching their horses outpace the herd over the limestone-flecked sands of Kentucky's tracks. Captain Viley had heard stories of Darley's phenomenal abilities from Old Harry and Warfield. So, when Ten Broeck approached him about forming a Kentucky syndicate for the Great State, and said that he aimed to buy Darley to run for them, the captain was fully on board and willing to go the distance. "I'll go half with you on the horse," Viley promised. They shook hands, then worked together to assemble their group.

Over at luxurious Ward Hall, a magnificent Greek Revival mansion that rivaled Dr. Warfield's, Captain Viley and Ten Broeck visited with Junius Ward, Viley's brother-in-law. Ward was also a member of the Kentucky Association and had bred and raced horses, whom he was fond of naming after people he knew or admired—Catherine, Emily Johnson, Dick Johnson, Plato. Convincing Ward to join them wasn't difficult. The money they would offer to buy Darley had already been covered. So, all he had to do was show up in New Orleans, stay at the city's palatial hotels, and wave to the multitudes at the Metairie as he stood beside Kentucky's horse. Ward readily agreed.

To cap the team off, the three men traveled out to Bosque Bonita Farm in Midway, on the outskirts of Lexington. There, they met with General Abe Buford, a hero of the Mexican-American War, who, by the 1850s, had turned his heroism and honor to the turf, becoming one of Lexington's preeminent horsemen and a burgeoning Thoroughbred breeder. After hearing the plan, which Ten Broeck excelled in delivering, Buford enlisted. Together, the Kentuckians and Ten Broeck became the Kentucky contingency for the Great State. Thus assembled, they agreed to focus their efforts on Warfield.

By then, Warfield had heard that Old Harry had entered Darley in the Citizens' Stakes. As he had done before, Warfield approached his trainer and told him he would post half the entry fee to receive half the purse. But the doctor *still* had not settled the winnings from the last race. Old Harry looked point-blank at Warfield and told him, "I don't know nothing about no halves!" Darley would still run for Warfield in the Citizens', but if he won, it would be in the doctor's honor only.

On May 27, the day of the Citizens' Stakes, Old Harry put on his green velvet long coat, his laced shirt, his pleated trousers, and his silken top hat, and walked briskly to The Meadows. Nearing the stallion's paddock, he gathered up the halter hanging by the gate and whistled for the horse. Darley galloped across the field. Lewis slipped on the halter and walked the horse up the washboard-ridged road to the Association Course. There, Lewis girthed a saddle around Darley and gave his rider a leg up. As seven jockeys lined their horses to face the start, a drum tapped.

There is almost no record remaining of that day's Citizens' Stakes. No one knew what lay in Darley's future. He was just another horse entered in another nondescript race on just another racecourse. Even his first race had been better recorded by the newspapers, and only because of the bizarre start that ended with such a miraculous finish. The *Spirit of the Times*'s editor, William T. Porter, received a good portion of his race reports from correspondents. He published what he received regarding the Citizens' race, which wasn't much at all.

While the newspapers had no apparent interest in the race, the turfmen who gathered at the Association Course that day were paying considerable attention, being curious whether Darley was just a one-shot wonder. He lost the first heat, finishing second—proving some of their predictions and sending potential buyers into a cooled aloofness. Ten Broeck may also have doubted his determination to reapproach Warfield, or may have seen an advantage allowing him to negotiate less aggressively. At any rate, whether Ten Broeck and his Kentucky contingency approached Warfield after the first or second heat is unknown. What *is* known is that Ten Broeck told the doctor that he wanted Darley to run in the Great State—not for Alabama or some other state but for Kentucky. These three men—Viley, Ward, and Buford—were Kentucky's team. Captain Viley took a look at Warfield, his lifelong friend, and told him that he was going half in to buy the horse with Ten Broeck. They offered Warfield $2,500 and another $2,500 if Darley won the Great State.

"Take him," Warfield said. "I know he will win it."

Darley won the Citizens' Stakes after taking the second and third heats. The Kentucky team shook hands and agreed to meet at the Metairie in a year. Ten Broeck patted Captain Viley on the back, and the two men walked to the winner's circle. Assuming that as Darley's new owners they had just won the purse, they asked Warfield about collecting the winnings. "Talk to Harry Lewis," Warfield told them. They did. But Lewis stood his ground, refusing to hand the purse over, since Warfield had paid none of the post entry and was, therefore, entitled to none of the winnings. Harry Lewis kept the money. Captain Viley got the silver pitcher, which he displayed on his mantel. And Ten Broeck got Darley.

When Louis Smith learned that he had been outmaneuvered by Ten Broeck, and that Darley would run not for Alabama but for Kentucky, he seethed with an anger that embedded itself deep within him. A month before, he had raced his mare Sallie Waters against a Ten Broeck horse. Sallie Waters had won on a controversial false start, and the matter had divided the two men. Knowing that the mare was a sore point with Ten Broeck, Smith caught up with him before he left Kentucky. Smith proposed a match: He'd run Sallie Waters against Darley in a race of three-mile heats, a minimum of six miles, over the Metairie that upcoming December. Ten Broeck accepted. But before his new colt would run in any future races, Ten Broeck had to resolve a matter that had bothered him since he first met Darley. His name.

The day following the Citizens' Stakes, Ten Broeck wrote a letter to the *Spirit* in New York. He informed the paper, and the nation, that Kentucky was entering the Great State, and that he had bought a powerful horse to be its contender. He wrote, "I have purchased Dr. Warfield's Boston colt for which I claim the name of *Lexington*."

CHAPTER 5

GETTING THERE

TEN BROECK ESCORTED his new horse to the city's train depot on Water Street. Twenty-two years earlier, Kentucky governor Thomas Metcalfe had stood there cheerfully waving to an enthusiastic crowd before swinging a sledgehammer to drive an iron spike into a rail, memorializing the first mile of track that would soon connect Lexington to Louisville. Lexington the horse may have been destined for the Metairie, but first he had to ship to his next home at the Pharsalia Race Course in Natchez, Mississippi, where he would recuperate and train to run four-mile heats. Getting there wouldn't be easy, even in that new day of progressive transportation.

On the Lexington & Frankfort Railroad, the horse rode ninety-four miles to Louisville, bracing against the jolts that came every fifteen feet where an iron rail joined unevenly into a new one, negotiating the sway of the train as it fishtailed around corners and bends. At Louisville, grooms walked Lexington to the wharf along the Ohio River where a steamboat waited. A gang of dockhands secured a canvas sling under his belly and tethered it to a breastplate so he wouldn't slip out. A cargo hook was attached to the sling, and then a dockhand signaled a man operating a derrick. The crane's winch started turning, taking up the slack of wire running along the boom, hoisting Lexington off the ground. He struggled, kicking out as the ground below him receded. The crane angled him high up over the dock before lowering him on the boat's deck. When he touched the solid platform, he pivoted and kicked out again, trying to rid himself of his entrapments. Deck hands carefully approached the horse and unhitched him before backing him into a six-by-six-foot stall. He would stand there for the next ten days of travel.

In the era when Ten Broeck shipped Lexington, travel catastrophes were an almost everyday occurrence. In a six-month period in 1851, *The New York Times* reported thirty-three wrecks on the railroad, on the rivers, and at sea, many of which resulted in fatalities. All of them were due to negligence. Trains collided head-on and buckled up, throwing passengers and precious cargo across the countryside. Brake switches failed to be pulled, boilers ran too hot, ships bottomed out in "iffy" waters, and captains and engineers either got sick, evacuated their posts, or just weren't paying attention. No mode of travel was immune from disaster.

Traveling on the Mississippi was always a concern. Cypress trees growing along the river's banks were prone to breakage, and when they did, their twisted branches toppled down and floated half-hidden below the water's plane, making them hard to see. A boat's encounter with such a tree could rip its hull open. If the boat sank, getting to shore meant swimming the one-to-four-mile width of the Mississippi, depending on where you happened to be. Many people and animals, subjected to such a misfortune, mixed into the river's current and undertow and were dragged down. Lives lost were numerous, lending the river an air of threat and mystery, a ghost hum echoed by the whisper of the swaying branches along the banks.

On board the boat, Lexington stood in the smallest of accommodations. The system of horse travel was designed to prioritize quantity over safety. Sometimes decks on ships were haphazardly converted to stables by throwing up a tarp roof and then tying horses in parallel rows, so tightly they touched like herrings in a box. At times they were shoved in *any* space available, even the bridge decks and coal bunkers. Ten Broeck most likely never transported any of his horses in such conditions. He once advised a friend to ship a horse in a horse box—a six-by-six stall with siding all around—which offered the animal more security. But even then, issues arose. In a heavy gale, stall fittings had to withstand the strain of one and a half tons of horse weight flinging around in every direction.

The sturdiness of the stalls was just one concern. Fatigue was sometimes a greater problem. Because of his stall's small confines, Lexington would have been forced to stand the entire trip. Every hour of travel added to the continual pressure on his joints, ligaments, and feet. Wave-induced pitching and rolling wasn't limited to cross-Atlantic travel. The Mississippi unleashed plenty of its own turbulence. Negotiating rough waters, Lexington would have resisted the rolling motion by throwing his body's weight in the opposite direction of the boat's motion. Maintaining balance wasn't always easy. Horses could slip and fall to their knees, where they struggled—many times violently—to regain their footing. Even if they were able to keep steady, horses' hindquarters aren't designed for continual balancing support. The bulk of a horse's natural balance is in its front. A horse's hindquarters have enough movement to allow it to spread-eagle for support, but it cannot maintain that balance for a prolonged period without enduring potential damage. In plain terms, balancing over the waters or any travel had the potential to induce lameness.

To help alleviate pressure on his limbs and joints, Lexington, like many horses, may have had a canvas sling stretched under his belly with the canvas ends attached to the stall's siding, in hopes he would ease his body into the sling's support. But not all horses took to the idea of canvas wrapped around them. Slings added pressure on respiratory and digestive organs. And, like the problem with bad stall fittings, when traveling through vehement waters, slings swung the animals against the sides of their stalls, bruising them or breaking their bones. At a minimum, slings had to be removed during rough weather to allow a horse to use its feet for balance. Unhitching a nervous horse from a sling during tumultuous waters was something reserved for experts or the brave. Many times, there weren't any experts around. Horse care was often relegated to the crew on board. Sometimes the sling stayed on.

Unloading a horse occurred the same way you loaded one, usually with the sling. A few steamboats had gangways, or planks, that allowed horses to walk on and off—most often blindfolded. Even this easy thoroughfare was far from horse-proof. When Lexington's sire, Boston, en route to a race, was walked aboard a steamboat, he quickly backed himself overboard, whereupon it probably took several ropes, pullies, and a few prayers to reclaim him. To everyone's relief they got Boston back aboard, and he later won the race. But for horses, the boat's gentle swaying motion foretold balancing challenges that sent their brains into an overdrive of uncertainty. No amount of coaxing, blindfolding, or coddling could ease their distress. The sling only intensified that fear; yet, for whatever reason, it became the preferred method for loading and unloading.

Even if the horse made it safely to the destination, recovering from travel was a lengthy process. Following a two- or three-week voyage, a horse could take weeks, even months, to recuperate. This meant the horse did nothing other than walk, sleep, and eat. Trotting and the other gaits were slowly added. Working a horse too fast and too soon could result in permanent lameness or death. To avoid these losses after traveling a lengthy journey, horses had to undergo a time-consuming, almost ritualistic conditioning process. Trips had to be planned and enough time given for the horse to recover before any pressures of work could be imposed. Travel was a tricky and precarious endeavor. That horse travel occurred as often as it did and with some success was, frankly, miraculous.

Departing from Louisville, Lexington stood hinged by fittings inside a cramped stall as the boat headed south. Thrown to the mercy of the temperamental Ohio and Mississippi rivers, he would stand hour after hour as one day rolled into the next, for up to ten days. If Ten Broeck was a spiritual man, he likely offered up a few prayers to the heavens to quell the legion of complications so fraught on the water.

CHAPTER 6

LOST LIGHT

T HE SUN SANK halfway beneath the water's edge. Above, black metal stacks exhaled smoke while lanterns in the pilothouse peered out, fusing a yellow haze with the river air. The water was exceptionally quiet, and the boat's slow movements rocked calmness into the hour. On the boat's fo'c'sle, Lexington leaned into his stall. The boat moved on, feeling her way over the water. By morning, she would dock at Natchez.

At the Pharsalia Course, Ten Broeck turned Lexington over to John Benjamin "J. B." Pryor, a man who had already amassed a reputation as being capable of training four miles into a horse and bringing him around between heats. Hailing from Virginia, J. B. was born to an ambitious family. His younger brother, Luke, had been elected to the United States Senate for the state of Alabama. J. B. was more introverted, not so outspoken, but his skills with horses nonetheless brought him national recognition.

Pryor had worked for a Mississippi cotton planter named Adam Bingaman, a Harvard-educated lawyer who had the gift of gab and a penchant for politics. Bingaman, whose name would be immortalized with New Orleans's Bingaman Race Course, was one of the

South's most preeminent turfmen. Besides the racecourse that bore his name, he established the Pharsalia Race Course in Natchez, and he roped in Pryor not only to manage the course but to train his horses. By common law, Pryor married Bingaman's biracial daughter, Frances Ann, Bingaman himself having had a lengthy relationship with a freed Black woman. Because he was a white man, Pryor's marriage to Frances Ann would certainly have been illegal, especially in Mississippi, which may explain why he kept to himself. But Pryor and Frances Ann's relationship stood true, producing five children, several of whom also went on to become racehorse trainers.

Pryor not only excelled in his duties for Bingaman but gained considerable clout in New Orleans among the hard-to-impress Creoles. They considered him a man of integrity. *Sans peur et sans reproche.* And it would take a fearless man to temper Lexington, who by all accounts had a resolute will.

The match race against Sallie Waters was a little over six months away, and Ten Broeck had no plans to race his horse before then. Time was on Lexington's side, affording him a lengthy recovery from his Kentucky journey, and a decent stretch of months to gain the muscle and stamina he would need to run against the Southern mare.

Under Pryor's watchful eye, Lexington's days took on a gentle rhythm. Every morning before sunrise, stable hands wrapped flannel blankets around his midquarters and girthed a saddle over them. Clothing was so paramount to the racehorse training process that the *American Turf Register*—one of the earliest publications to chronicle horse care—listed a racehorse groom's *essential* tools to include "plenty of horse clothes of all descriptions." The linen garments consisted primarily of three separate pieces: a hood, a breast cover, and a body cloth that covered the horse's torso. Wrapped head to tail in the blankets, horses resembled ghost creatures, like children costumed in white bedsheets with cutout eyeholes. Underneath the ghost sheet, woolen flannel hugged the horses, even in the summer, to wick them dry of all moisture.

Putting on the clothes was an art form in itself. Grooms tied, buckled, swaddled, compressed, smoothed, and tucked the wraps to conform snugly to the horses. Even though horses frequently gnashed at the garbs, violently attempting to free themselves, nineteenth-century trainers believed blanketed exercise—the sine qua non of training—necessary for removing obstructions in blood vessels and promoting circulation.

Horse clothes consumed the horse, head to tail, and, per custom and practice, were used in riding exercises to remove obstructions in blood vessels and promote better circulation. These clothes are similar to the three-piece ensemble worn by Lexington and other racehorses of his era.

Fully swathed, Lexington was ridden at a walk for an hour each morning, sweat drenching his sides, encouraged forward by his rider's soft low hum and gentle talk. At sundown, they repeated the same routine, the horse walking for another hour under heavy blankets. Pryor's nineteenth-century training methods required weeks of doing nothing other than walking. This snail's approach to training was touted as tried and true. Requiring a horse to go too fast too soon, it was believed, could injure it, ruining the conditioning already achieved. Instead, the gaits—trotting, cantering, and the running—were added incrementally.

One day, after many weeks, Lexington's rider pressed his heels in, signaling that now was the time to go faster. The horse broke into a canter. When the reins tugged slightly, he slowed to a trot. "Easy now," the young man said. They continued their training this way, trotting at a good clip, until Lexington had gained more strength. Only then was he asked for a faster gait. Regulated by his rider's weight and pull, the horse settled into a rocking canter. After two weeks of walking, trotting, and cantering, the horse heard his rider cluck his tongue and felt the man's heels press firmly against him. Lexington reached his hind legs far under his belly and leaped into a giant stride, coming into a gallop that filled his lungs, expanding them, giving him his wind. Awakened, the horse opened up into a tremendous run.

For a while, things went as they should with Lexington's slow, methodical training. Over the next five months, the horse was developing his form and strengthening. In fact, word started trickling down the Mississippi and into the ears of New Orleans's newspapermen: Ten Broeck's new Kentucky horse was powerful. Unstoppable. But the dark hours of one October night would not only test the depths of Lexington's will; they would change his life forever.

Lexington had spent the morning cantering around the Pharsalia. Afterward, he was turned out to graze for a few hours on Natchez's silt loam pastures. After his evening walk, grooms brought the horse back to his barn and fed him his nighttime grain. The stablemen left the barn for the evening, undoubtedly eager for their own meal and a few hard-earned hours of leisure. In their haste, someone forgot to latch the bars that secured Lexington inside his stall. Now, free to roam with no humans to foil his plans, Lexington nudged the door open and escaped. The next morning, when the men returned, they found a keg barrel lying on its side in the barn aisle. Its contents—about sixty-two quarts of golden corn kernels—were now mostly gone. They found Lexington standing in his stall looking content, the stall door wide open.

Feeding racehorses was a task that required precision. In that era, they were fed five times a day. Up to eleven or twelve quarts of grain, comprised of seven to ten quarts of oats and two quarts *only* of cracked corn or hominy, were given in varying portions throughout the day. A typical feed schedule looked as follows:

Daybreak:	1 qt.
After morning exercise:	3 qt.
11:00 A.M.:	3 qt.
Before evening exercise:	1 qt.
At night:	3 qt.

The smallest grain proportions were fed before exercising so that the horse would not work on a full stomach. Besides all the quarts of grain, a racehorse ate up to nine pounds of hay daily.

Just as Pryor's stable hands were beginning to put two and two together, the trainer arrived with Captain William J. Minor, at the time one of America's most prolific writers on horse racing, a turf-man in his own right, and a member of the Metairie Jockey Club. Minor's aggressive and sharp-tongued opinions about turf matters consumed perhaps more columns of national sporting publications than those of the papers' own editors. He was always ready with his quill to tell everyone "how it was, how it is, and how it will be" on just about every subject pertaining to horses, horse racing, horse breeding, jockeys, racecourses, horse speeds. Or anything else. Minor had heard the rumors about Kentucky's horse and had expressed a strong desire to see Lexington in action. Since Ten Broeck and Minor sometimes collaborated as a racing team, the thought may have been for Pryor to demonstrate Lexington's abilities to Minor. Pryor ordered Lexington saddled.

Pryor's grooms would surely have known the dangers of running a horse who had gorged on food. Grain overload, particularly from a grain as rich as corn, can impact a horse's hindgut, releasing toxins from the gut into the bloodstream, causing a condition known as endotoxemia. Galloping a horse after it has overeaten can amplify the release and circulation of toxins into the body. The problem was, with Minor standing beside Pryor, no stable hand was prepared to admit the stall-door-and-corn-eating fiasco. To Lexington's great misfortune, the men said nothing. They girthed a saddle around the stallion. As a rider was hoisted up, Pryor told the man to run Lexington two miles over the Pharsalia's sand to show Minor exactly what this horse could do.

Lexington ran sluggishly. Concerned, Pryor stopped the horse's work and ordered him returned to the barn. After ushering Minor away with assurances that Lexington was, indeed, an extremely impressive horse, the trainer returned to his barn, firing off a fusillade of questions at his stable hands. Much to his exasperation, the truth slowly emerged.

Throughout the day, Lexington developed a high temperature, closed both eyes, and refused all feed. Pryor bled the horse, but nothing changed. He swapped out blankets, wrapping Lexington in heavier flannel to try to sweat out the illness. The fever held fast. Over the next couple of days, other experienced horsemen likely offered thoughts on tonics and mixtures of mash and magical, hard-to-find herbs, but nothing helped. Within the week, Pryor had tried every recourse, but no amount of veterinary skill nor handed-down grooms' remedies could cure the horse. Rumors circulated around Pryor's barn that Lexington wouldn't be running in the Great State. He might not even survive. Pryor notified Ten Broeck, who, as was his wont, said absolutely nothing.

Over the next short weeks, Pryor turned Lexington out on Natchez's pastures. The horse recovered from his fever and started putting on much-needed weight. But the corn bingeing had done irreparable damage.

Lexington's eyes began to cloud. His right eye was worse.

The overeating and subsequent workout could certainly have triggered endotoxemia, causing an infection in his eyes. In turn, his eyes could have become compromised, rendering them susceptible to a condition now known as equine recurrent uveitis (ERU), commonly known in the nineteenth century as "moon blindness." ERU is an incurable and painful episodic inflammatory ocular condition that can lead to cataracts and loss of vision. An estimated 60 percent of horses who suffer from ERU are unable to return to their former riding routines. In the nineteenth century, cataracts were considered incurable, except by operation, which was not always recommended due to the often poor outcome. In short, moon-blind horses were usually retired.

"I have no doubt that working the horse full brought it about," Pryor later explained.

Lexington was going blind.

Horses see differently than humans. Humans see three-dimensional images in a 190-degree field of view, with what's known as binocular vision, because both eyes share a common focal point. By contrast, horses see in two-dimensional monocular vision. Because the eyes are placed laterally on the head, they do not have a common focal field. Horses do, however, have about a 65-degree range of binocular vision in the front, with only about a 3-degree blind-spot range in the rear. Because of their bilateral eye placement, they can see almost the entire length of their bodies. Monocular vision also allows horses to see two different objects at the same time. While the right eye may register a crouching bobcat, the left eye can spot a bird circling in an entirely different location. For a prey animal like the horse, this ability to see two sides at once is a considerable advantage, allowing it to discern multiple threats. For a rider, the horse's ability to see *everything* can be hell. If the horse identifies something startling in its field of vision, it can become distracted or get spooked, reacting to something that the rider might not even have noticed. What's more, some studies suggest that what a horse sees with one eye doesn't translate to the other.

Consequently, a horse that spooks at a flapping flag on the right may very well spook again when passing the same flag on its left, because technically, it's never seen it before.

While the human eye lens focuses by changing its shape with the use of ciliary muscles, giving us good depth perception, a horse's ability to perceive depth is compromised because its ciliary muscles are underdeveloped. Some studies suggest horses focus by adjusting their heads to project the clearest picture possible to the retina at the back of the eyes. Horses are estimated to have only six-tenths of the visual acuity of humans. The reason may simply be that detail isn't as important to horses as is their ability to detect motion or to grasp a larger view of their surroundings. But since equine eyes are the largest of all the land mammals', their oversize retinas see objects as larger than they actually are. The crouching bobcat may be dozens of yards away, but to the horse, the animal appears to be a close-up, menacing monster. An immediate threat.

When a prey animal such as a horse loses its vision, its instinctual survival skills are diminished. Its once bold stride is reduced to faltering steps. Its self-reliance is shattered, and the horse becomes dependent on people and companion animals to see for it and guide it. Dangers are amplified, leaving the animal less confident, more fearful, and prone to freezing in its tracks. A completely blind horse that spooks doesn't always bolt in a straight course but sometimes turns in tight, panic-driven circles, too afraid to run because it can't see, yet too afraid to stay put.

The sudden shock of losing vision in one eye can leave a horse bewildered until it learns to adapt. Given time, most horses that lose partial vision can overcome the setback. However, some horses never return to their full level of performance before blindness set in.

For partially blind *racehorses,* the animal's dependency on its one usable eye is another challenge. If dirt is kicked into that eye, as often happens if one horse is running behind another, it momentarily loses all ability to see and to discern the distance of advancing horses. It hears and feels the thunder of hooves without any ability to gauge its placement in the stampede.

Some blind horses fold under the unbearable pressure of losing their self-reliance. They experience depression. Others learn and adapt. How a horse adjusts to blindness has everything to do with the animal's personality rather than the disability itself. It begins to rely more on its auditory abilities and sense of smell. It learns to *feel* its way around. A horse's muzzle—its chin and nose—have numerous nerve endings in the follicles of its long whiskers. It's not unusual for a blind horse to run its face up and down the sides of walls, along the fenced perimeter, and against objects to form a map of its environment and to get a sense of its boundaries. It reads its surroundings with its whiskers much as a blind person uses fingers to read Braille. On their blind side, one-eyed horses rely more on their senses of sound and touch.

If the horse is brave and resilient, it can learn to function in partial or total darkness, taking several weeks, months, a year, or longer to adjust. Mostly, it's up to the horse how well it will cope.

In the weeks following the bingeing incident, Lexington's right eye remained clouded. The left had improved. Still, Ten Broeck and Pryor must have seen something promising in the horse's demeanor. They considered racing him again.

The Sallie Waters match against Lexington was set to occur on December 2, 1853, at the Metairie. Despite Lexington's illness and impaired vision, Ten Broeck made no effort to scratch the horse from competition. To what degree criticism can be cast on his decision is debatable. The science known then did not discourage people from working horses suffering from such conditions. And if Lexington was going to run the Great State—under the national spotlight—Ten Broeck and Pryor had to know if his courage and ability could overcome his compromised vision and propel him to the winner's circle.

Ten days before the match against Sallie Waters, and a mere four weeks after the grain accident, Lexington's grooms walked him out of his pasture in Natchez, slung him onto a steamboat, and shipped him down the Mississippi to New Orleans. There, Sallie Waters was already tearing up the track at the Metairie. Less than a year had passed since she had broken the Metairie's two-mile speed record. And only in November, she had again won a race of two-mile heats on her home track at Mobile. Sallie Waters was gaining a reputation as one hard-to-beat racehorse. In a little over a week, Lexington would face her in a match of three-mile heats, his first attempt at that distance.

When Ten Broeck's horse arrived at New Orleans's port, dock-hands took him from his box stall, attached the sling, and signaled for the derrick to lower him to the dock. Once he touched the ground, Lexington spun and kicked out to rid himself of the dreaded sling as dockhands danced a frantic two-step to avoid his flying hooves. Pryor stood back at a respectably safe distance. After the horse calmed, Pryor walked him five miles up Shell Road to a stall at the Metairie.

Owing to the short duration of travel—twenty-eight hours— from Natchez to New Orleans, Lexington was most likely able to be worked within a day of his arrival. He first stepped foot on the Metairie in the cool breeze of a November morning. Horses galloped the course, expelling breath that lingered in the morning's haze. After the track cleared, Pryor gave his Black jockey— unnamed in the history books—a leg up onto Lexington. The horse had only one week to ready himself to face the mare.

On Friday, December 2, 1853, the Metairie's grandstand was nearly bare. Gray clouds still hung over the course from the rain-

storm the night before. The track was heavy slop. Puddles in some
areas, and porridge-like sludge in others, made it difficult to run
through. The damp cold and muddied streets pushed most people
back inside to the warmth of their homes. Most anyone who might
have been interested in watching Sallie Waters race this unknown
Kentucky colt had brushed off the idea. With the Metairie turned
into a mud sty, the race would most likely be slow, uneventful.
Among the few people present at the racecourse were Louis Smith,
Ten Broeck, and Pryor. A few enthusiasts huddled in the grandstand alongside a handful of newspapermen, including Francis T.
Porter, editor of the *Picayune*'s sporting column—not to be con-
fused with his brother, William T. Porter, editor of New York's
Spirit of the Times.

Sallie Waters trudged through the muck in front of the stands
and headed toward the cooling circle. Grooms flung off her linen
blankets, revealing a bay coat that shined richly against the dull sky.
Now and again her muscles twitched in anticipation as grooms
girthed on a saddle and gave her jockey a lift up. He trotted the
mare along the track, then pressed her into a gallop to loosen her
up before the race. Off in the distance, Pryor walked alongside
Lexington as they made their way toward the stands. The people of
New Orleans hadn't yet seen this horse. They'd only heard rumors
or read descriptions about him in the *Spirit,* what few there had
been. Before their eyes he displayed himself impressively, pro-
nouncing each of his steps with a spring in an emphatic declaration
of his presence. Yet despite his vaunting parade, the crowd jeered
him. The sight of his four white socks sent many of them into
head-shaking sneers. White socks were considered a bad omen,
signaling weak feet. The men glanced over at Ten Broeck, supposedly a seasoned horseman, and wondered what he had been thinking. Most people wouldn't part with five dollars for such an animal.
As Lexington neared, one man yelled out, "Take him away!"

Porter and a few others decided to disregard the superstition
until they'd had a chance to visit the cooling circle and eye the

horse as he was saddled. Out from under his blankets, he showed in good condition. "A racehorse, *sure,*" said one observer. Porter also liked what he saw—the upright pasterns, the barrel chest. But the horse's eyes were glassy and discolored, noted Porter. He stared into them for any hint of the soul within, but they remained expressionless and distant. If there was anything that would betray the horse during the race, Porter believed it wouldn't be the animal's white feet; it would be his eyes. The editor made his way over to the betting tables and decided to take a chance on the Kentucky horse. He was one of the few who did.

Despite Porter's confidence in Lexington, Pryor and Ten Broeck were feeling unsure. The illness that had severely impacted his right eye and inflamed his left made his vision shadowy. Although the horse had shown abundant courage in his week of workouts—pressing through, regardless of his lost vision—he was far from his true racing form.

About the time Porter was placing his bet, Sallie Waters was walking back from her warm-up, slathered in mud. Her gallop through the heavy track hadn't fazed her, which stirred Ten Broeck to make a tough decision. He approached Smith and offered to draw the match so that each party could walk away without a win or a defeat. Smith refused.

At half past noon the drum tapped, and the two horses set off. Lexington dug into the mud and took the lead. Sallie Waters pressed forward and caught up, running parallel to the horse on his near-blind right side. Neck and neck, they completed the first mile. Lexington couldn't see Sallie Waters, but he could feel the vibrations of her run, and he could hear the heavy breaths propelling her every stride. Despite her proximity, he didn't swerve. Instead, he increased his speed and pulled ahead, leaving the mare trailing by two lengths, finishing the second mile in the lead. Sallie Waters's jockey desperately spurred her throughout the entirety of the third mile. But she offered no challenge, handing over the first three-mile heat to Lexington.

Over the thirty-five-minute cooling period, the mare struggled to recover. Grooms massaged her legs, offered her water, and walked her to loosen her muscles. But she couldn't rally. She hung her head low and dragged along during her walk. To the handful of turfmen present that day, the race had been over since the first mile. Inexplicably, and possibly still driven by vengeance over losing the purchase of Lexington to Ten Broeck, Smith ordered Sallie Waters saddled to contest the second three-mile heat. When bettors saw her at the post, they shook their heads and descended upon the wagering tables, throwing odds heavily in favor of Lexington.

At the drum's tap Lexington stretched into the first mile in an effortless glide. "The poetry of motion," wrote Porter. Sallie Waters struggled. When Lexington reached the distance pole 130 yards from the finish of the heat, the mare trailed him by two miles. She ran four miles to Lexington's six before she gave up.

Sallie Waters never recovered from that race. It was her last. According to one nineteenth-century source, her run against Lexington taxed her beyond her reserves, and the once promising mare and shining star of Alabama died. However, the *Spirit* reported that barely more than a month after the race, Sallie Waters died of lockjaw, the cause of which was not stated.

After the race, Porter wrote for the *Picayune,* "The horse that outruns Lexington in a sticky, heavy track, like that of yesterday, must be a sort of steam engine in disguise." But it wasn't just the horse's raw power. Lexington's makeup went beyond his immense muscular strength, upright pasterns, and barrel chest. Ability and stamina comprise half of a horse's bottom. The other half is made of courage.

The Great State contenders had not yet been officially named. Although rumors circulated about what horses *might* be entered, the four competing states—Alabama, Mississippi, Louisiana, and

Kentucky—seemed perfectly content to sit back and absorb the spectacle of aspirant owners showcasing the laurels of their horses. There were easily one hundred horses in the participating states that were presently training to run four-mile heats. All of them had shiny résumés, and each was fresh from claiming some victory somewhere in the South. They had been readied to endure. Strengthened to run faster. All belonged to owners or syndicates who hoped their prodigy would be chosen to represent their home state. By the end of February 1854, the hopefuls would converge at the Metairie to continue their training, in full view of everyone who had the power to decide their fates.

After the triumph at the Metairie, Ten Broeck shipped Lexington back to the Pharsalia in Natchez, where Pryor, with renewed conviction, put him in full training, with the goal of running him for Kentucky. Regardless of Lexington's failing vision, he would be expected to race as if he had no physical disadvantage. Pryor trained him accordingly, holding him to the same standard, and more, as any other horse.* Although Lexington had shown tremendous strength in the Sallie Waters match, he needed to be able to run a race of four-mile heats—a contest that could potentially require him to run top speeds for *twelve miles*. His stamina had to be superior.

Although horses then rarely trained by running a full four miles, Pryor believed that the only way to push Lexington into that powerful realm was to train him in trials of that distance. To strengthen him even more, Pryor released a fresh horse to challenge him at each mile of the trials. Consistently, Lexington outran every horse he trained against. Pryor then heaved an extra twenty-four pounds of lead into packs strapped behind the horse's saddle—weight de-

---

* The historical record makes no mention of how Pryor may have adapted his training methods to accommodate Lexington's loss of vision. From all accounts, it appears he did not. It is also unclear if Lexington's left-eye vision improved after the Sallie Waters match. While his right eye remained near-blind, if not completely blind, historical reports reveal that the degree of vision in his left eye often fluctuated.

signed to make Lexington work harder. The horse answered by finding a higher gear, outrunning his competition again and again. Over the months, Pryor continued to strengthen and test the horse to discern if he would ever reach his limit. Each time, Lexington delivered a decisive victory, registering no signs of fatigue or strain.

In early March, Pryor gave Lexington another trial run of four miles. As he had always done, the trainer brought four other horses out of his stable—one for each mile. Jim Barton was one of the fastest horses in Pryor's barn. Little Flea was another, and quite possibly faster than Jim Barton. Two other unnamed horses also stood ready.

At the start of the trial, Lexington and Jim Barton broke together. Around the mile they soared, Lexington outpacing Barton the entire way. As Lexington bounded into the second mile, Pryor withdrew Barton and entered one of the unnamed horses. Lexington ran the mile far ahead. As he crossed the wire to lead into the third mile, Pryor released the other unnamed and energized contender. The horse struggled to corral Lexington's tremendous pace. Engulfing yards of ground with every stride, Lexington entered the fourth mile as Pryor released Little Flea. Flea ran into the fourth mile with the same speed he would later use to break a speed record over a three-mile heat. He ran foot for foot beside Lexington. Whether he ran on the stallion's blind side is unknown. Flea tore away, passing Lexington before crossing over into his path, cutting him off. Whether Lexington saw Flea is unknown. But the son of Boston bore down upon Flea, colliding with him and sending him off the track. As Flea stumbled into a ditch, Lexington continued his tremendous drive to the finish. Completely unvexed.

By March 18, 1854, the nation knew the names of the Great State's horse contenders. Running for Mississippi was the undefeated horse Lecomte, who had set the nation's record for the fastest mile at 1:45 ¾ seconds and was then regarded by the *Spirit* as "the most promising and finest colt in America." Arrow, running for Louisiana, had won five of seven starts, all at three-mile heats. And Alabama's Highlander, the most experienced of all the contenders, had two seasons of wins and had never suffered defeat. As for bluegrass pride, Kentucky would rest its hope on the half-blind Lexington. Ten Broeck's confidence in his horse was surging at an all-time high.

CHAPTER 7

KENTUCKY'S HORSE

NEW ORLEANS WAS a candy-colored concoction, illuminated by a current emanating from its ever-pulsing pleasure principle. The whole of the city's energy intensified every year during Mardi Gras—a grand and monumental festival that outshone all the smaller celebrations that made up every other day of the year. New Orleans was the perfect city to host a contest. It was a city of risk, a sporting haven, and a mecca for horse racing.

In the month preceding the Great State, New Orleans was in the throes of Lent. The Roman Catholic practice—deeply embedded in New Orleans's culture—requires its followers to abstain from overindulgence and other "evils" for forty days. But that did nothing to temper interest in the upcoming race. "The most brilliant sporting event of the age," trumpeted the *Picayune*. "The day that this race is run will be a great day for New Orleans, for there will, without doubt, be a larger and more brilliant assemblage of persons than ever before assembled in this part of the country on any occasion." Indeed, as one Alabama man predicted, "The world and his wife will be looking at the race of races!"

Thousands of visitors would throng to the city. New Orleans was ready.

In 1854, there were over two thousand no-frills sports betting establishments in the city. These chairless, lusterless, and grimy taverns, called "coffee houses," served everything from whiskey to home-brewed grog. No one in New Orleans had to search for a drink. One cleric estimated that if all taverns were lined up and spaced thirty feet apart, they would extend over thirteen miles. Coffee houses not only served a man his choice of whiskey but took his bet at whatever odds were on offer for the sport of his choice—or any other in a vast array of amusements and wonders. People bet on endless oddities—footraces, a race between a man on foot and a wagon team of horses, whether a horse could trot a distance of one hundred miles without rest, or whether a man could walk 168 miles carrying ten pounds of weight on his back and, as the *Spirit* reported, an umbrella in his hand. *Anything* qualified for betting speculation.

Betting on everything from fantastical stunts to racehorses had become so prevalent in New Orleans that there was hardly anything left for the Sunday churchgoing congregations to pitch in. One Catholic priest decried from the pulpit, "No more pennies must be put in the box. We spend hours every week counting and stacking pennies, and it is a shocking waste of time. If you are so destitute that you can't afford at least a nickel to your church, come to the vestry, after mass, and we will look at your needs and give you the relief the church always extends to the poor."

Most horse-racing bets were cast in one of the city's two major hotels. In the American Quarter, separated from the French Quarter by Canal Street, stood the St. Charles, an enormous Federal-style structure that featured an expansive wall of Corinthian columns and a rotunda that evoked the U.S. Capitol. One traveler compared the hubbub that filled the lobby to the noise and confusion of the New York Stock Exchange. James Buckingham, a visiting Englishman, wrote that the St. Charles—with its polished marble floors, granite steps, grand mahogany staircases, and Italian-sculpted statues—was the "largest and handsomest hotel in the world. At least I remember nothing equal to it in any country that I have visited." To each his own. Frederick Law Olmsted, visiting from the North, wrote, "And at the second block, I was landed before the great Grecian portico of the stupendous, tasteless, ill-contrived, and inconvenient St. Charles Hotel." To spare its patrons the wincingly strong, throat-burning drinks sold at the wood-planked coffee houses, the St. Charles offered a swank drinking chamber draped in damask and velvet and walls crowded with paintings of Venus, Bacchus, and Vulcan hurling his flaming thunderbolts. People clustered around marble-topped tables and drank imported Madeira or Kentucky bourbon from sunup to sundown. After leaving the chamber doused with more than sufficient courage, guests ambled out to the rotunda to place their bold bets.

The French Quarter showcased its own hotel: the St. Louis. Also enormous, with its own vaulted dome, the St. Louis covered an entire city block bounded by St. Louis, Toulouse, Chartres, and Royal streets. Its barrooms catered to politicians, newspapermen, turfmen, and anyone able to spend the dime for a drink to learn the progress of the latest turf contenders. The overflow trickled back up to the St. Charles vicinity, and to the Boston Club, where members only could sit in their deep mahogany chairs and read sporting pages from foreign countries. Those who were not members funneled into the Orleans Club, a drinking and gambling establishment known for its raucous, up-all-hours excitement. With gaslit chandeliers, dense carpets, and red brocaded chairs, it boasted a membership including not only newspapermen but the organizers of the 1838 Mardi Gras Association—the ones who ensured that celebratory parades would forever be a New Orleans tradition. The club especially catered to racetrack devotees who gathered on

any given night to discuss the merits of different horses and all the ·
hoopla that Ten Broeck's Great State was churning up.

The Great State rivalry competition rode on the haunches of
four fast horses. "The race for everybody, and everybody for the
race!" proclaimed the *Picayune*. "Everybody who was anybody, or
wanted to be deemed anybody" was going. Thousands of people
from the contending states—Louisiana, Kentucky, Alabama, and
Mississippi—funneled proudly onto chartered vessels destined for
the Port of New Orleans. A mail boat from Mobile brought over
a large contingent of Alabamans, while another group from Fayette County, Kentucky, leased three stately and spacious steamers
to depart from Louisville. In Louisiana, several sugar planters chartered a New Orleans packet steamer only to brave a wind-and-rain
storm that ripped off the chimneys and delayed the boat by two
days. Passengers arrived just in time to join the procession to the
racetrack.

The attraction wasn't limited to Southern states. Northerners
too had an interest, even though they had no contenders; the financial panic of 1837 that had decimated Northern horse racing
may have been one of the reasons. Since then, the North had been
climbing out of the hole, and New York had successfully petitioned its legislature for a charter to open a new course. But for the
time being, Northern states turned their eyes toward New Orleans
and enjoyed their horse racing from afar. The *Spirit of the Times*
noted, "The principal topic of discussion in the Union is the Great
State Post Stakes . . . and the merits of the various horses. Opinions
differ widely in these matters, and lead to excitement, warm talk,
and high betting on the various points presented. It appears to be
the general opinion that many more persons will be collected in
New Orleans, to witness this Great State contest for supremacy
in blood horses, than has ever been gathered together by any event

in the Southern country." In one week, an estimated $500,000 changed hands nationally over the race—$15.5 million in today's dollars—with $100,000—some $3 million today—wagered in New Orleans and another $100,000 wagered in New York.

Former president Millard Fillmore traveled for two weeks from New York over back-jolting train rails and jostling Mississippi currents to view the race firsthand. Arriving six days ahead of time, he paraded down Canal Street, followed by an entourage of Louisiana political figures, public school teachers, clergy, and, as the *Picayune* noted, "distinguished strangers." Business owners on both sides of the street had draped American flags from balconies in his honor. At city hall, President Fillmore delivered a speech from a wrought-iron-laced balcony before being escorted to the plush presidential suite that the St. Charles had meticulously arranged for him.

The St. Charles leased out every one of its four hundred rooms, even moving cots into attic rooms normally reserved for cleaning staff. Down the street, dollar upon dollar piled into the cash registers of every store and restaurant. Memoirist Eliza Ripley recalled that Olympe Boisse, a milliner on Chartres Street, greeted every racecourse-destined customer at the front door, "Ah, Madame, I brought from Paris the very bonnet for you! No one has seen it; it is yours!" Woodlief's, also on Chartres, offered ladies' gloves, one button only and *never* white—best in lavender, lemon, pink, or bottle green. And the Herriman and Chessé tailor shop on Royal Street could barely keep its inventory of gowns in palm-leaf patterns or indigos and strawberry red in stock; for men, blue coats underscored by yellow-and-green-flowered vests were in high demand.

"The men," wrote Grace King, "show themselves more enslaved to fashion than the women, going about in the heavy clothing of Europe, heads sunk in high collars, arms and hands lost in long sleeves, chins buried in triple cravats, legs encased in high boots, with great flaps."

During the week of the race, Richard Ten Broeck worked to

ensure that the Metairie was ready. The Metairie Jockey Club had committed upward of $50,000 ($1.8 million) in course improvements, and another $50,000 for the stakes' purses. In the kitchens, chefs unpacked crates of champagne and assembled their demanding lists of rare ingredients to concoct their delicacies, while maître d's pressed their white jackets and polished silver platters. The bustle extended out to the track. Horses carted wagons overflowing with grasses and grains to the training stables, as well as bushels of tanbark to soak up the stench of excrement permeating the air near the stalls. On March 30, 1854, L. H. Filie, New Orleans's city surveyor, examined the stands, finding them strongly supported and in good order. The *Picayune* promptly relayed that fact, to the satisfaction of the race-going public. All week, the fever of the upcoming race pumped through the Metairie, with all its bustle and commotion and joyous spirit of what was to come. The vibe was no less felt throughout the city.

By April 1, the day of the Great State, some twenty thousand people—all with the goal of witnessing what the *Picayune* labeled "the most celebrated event in the annals of turf history"—had taken up temporary residence in the city. All of them purchased their grandstand tickets, which on this day were double the normal price. Those in the members' section basked in the knowledge they would dine on a *déjeuner à la fourchette* of eggs and thinly sliced meats and indulge in bottomless glasses of champagne. People filled the parlors and halls of every hotel and establishment with laughter and talk. Of the Kentucky women at the St. Charles, Ripley wrote, "How they talked, in the soft, Southern accent, so peculiarly their own! How they laughed! How they moved about, seemingly knowing everybody they met. How they bet!"

Despite the previous days of rain and wind, the day of the Great State was beautiful and warm. The mayor of New Orleans declared it a half-holiday. That morning, all the avenues leading out of the city were clogged with every means of transportation imaginable. Wooden carts and drays, loaded with people and hauled by

mules, wheeled slowly alongside grand carriages of polished mahogany with red velvet seats and gold-colored spokes. Gloved passengers opened picnic baskets filled with Southern-style arrays of
baked ham, chicken, brandy, beer, and, of course, cigars. Sporty,
bright-yellow curricles—two-seaters—zipped between larger carriages, leaving trails of dust and squeezing out riders on horseback.
A nine-passenger stagecoach owned by the St. Charles rolled
through, carrying far more than the allotted number, spiking the
air with a party-fevered pitch. The whole of the morning was an
exodus of sorts. A divestment from the city of nearly a fifth of its
population, all of whom were trying to make it out to the Metairie, the promised land.

There was one problem. The same rain-and-wind storm that
had ripped the chimneys off the New Orleans packet steamer had
turned the Metairie's track into a mud pit. Worse, as the winds
swept across the track, the dirt had stiffened into a clingy, glue-like
consistency. Mud, eight inches in depth, congealed atop the track.
The *Picayune* called it "tenacious," as if the mud had a mind of its
own. And though Lexington was a mudder, bettors doubted he
could prevail in his first attempt at four-mile heats. In the *Spirit,*
one man predicted, "I do not think [Lexington] has enough foot
for these flyers."

His questionable speed wasn't the only issue the gambling crowd
considered before parting with their hard-earned cash. Thanks to
the *Picayune*'s write-up about the Sallie Waters match, the reading
public was now aware that Ten Broeck's horse had questionable
vision. Those who had visited the horse tucked away in his Metairie stall had seen the opaqueness, the untracking gaze hauntingly
absent of life—as if part of his soul had vanished. The only glimmer of Lexington's spirit may have been the abrupt turn of his
head toward a noise, his incessant pawing at the ground, or his nose
nudging their shoulders, as if to say, "What do you see?" Whatever
physical power the stallion might have, his failing vision could
upend any chance of his winning. But his stellar victory over the

highly acclaimed Sallie Waters, when he had run nearly blind, gave bettors some assurance. Many of them took the risk. In the odds, Lexington trailed second to Alabama's Highlander.

By two o'clock, the Metairie's grandstand overflowed its capacity with white, Creole, and Black faces,* everyone sitting elbow to elbow: an astonishing scene in an America only seven years away from civil war. President Fillmore labored up into the judges' stand, waved to the grandstand behind him, and sat down in his reserved seat—one of the best in the house for unobstructed racetrack viewing. Those without tickets climbed oak trees or sat on fences, hedges, carriage tops, or any other high point on that bayou that promised a view of the race.

At a quarter after two, the four horses, draped in silk blankets, walked onto the track, prompting a shattering chorus of cheers. Lexington, wildly excited, pranced alongside his groom, who held him tightly. Never before had he appeared in front of so many people. The rowdy excitement in the stands had also taken hold of the infield crowd, causing shrieks and whistles to circle the horse, as if he were swirling inside a cyclone of pandemonium. He jerked his head now this way, now that, to discern what his right eye could not see.

---

* Scholars differ as to whether New Orleans society in that era was inclusive of freed Blacks. In *End of an Era: New Orleans, 1850–1860,* Robert Reinders writes of the favorable economic position of freed Blacks of that time. "They owned an estimated $15,000,000 worth of real estate; a few free men of color owned entire city blocks." They "served as jewelers, brokers, tailors, and money lenders." Although freed Blacks were respected by the white community, Reinders maintains that, in general, the two races did not comingle publicly. Conversely, Dale Somers in *The Rise of Sports in New Orleans, 1850–1900* writes,

> Negroes in New Orleans had long been interested in the turf as jockeys, as spectators, and even as owners of race horses. Before 1871, the city's racecourses had admitted black fans to any part of the track except the members' and ladies' stands, which were also closed to most white spectators. Racial harmony evidently prevailed at the track, if not in society at large.

John Dizikes, in *Sportsmen & Gamesmen,* writes that "blacks mingled freely with everyone else in the [racecourse] crowds." It is noteworthy that the era predated the late nineteenth century's enactment of the Jim Crow laws forcing racial segregation.

The four jockeys, saddles in hand, stepped up to the weighing scales—in those days, a seat separated from weights by a fulcrum. Nearby, J. B. Pryor wiped Lexington's nostrils and mouth with a wet sponge, then slipped on the bridle. Motioning for the jockey's saddle, he dipped a sponge in water and moistened the saddle girth so it would adhere to Lexington's sides and belly and not shift position during his run. With the saddle tightened in place, he turned to his jockey.

Henry Meichon, a young French Creole, was an eager up-and-comer. He'd ridden in a few races but was still considered a neophyte. The finely tuned skills of regulating a horse's energy, judging its speed, and knowing when to ask were matters in which he was not yet adept. Compounding his inexperience, he was riding a partially blind animal who was much harder to steer and not nearly as reliable as one who could fully see. But the Kentucky team had given Meichon the chance of a lifetime in the most publicized race of the decade. Under the national gaze, the young man was about to go head-to-head with some of the nation's most seasoned and best jockeys. He pulled himself up into Lexington's small saddle and took up the reins.

A few feet away, grooms lifted a saddle onto Alabama's Highlander under the watchful eye of his jockey, the famed Gilpatrick. As the principal rider for President Andrew Jackson and Old Nap, he was well accustomed to big-bannered races. He knew every dip in the Metairie's track and had more than likely walked the course before the race to discover that along the homestretch, the middle ground was harder and much faster than the eight-inch depth of sloshing and speed-slowing mud at the inner rail. Farther down the saddling paddock, Abe Hawkins, a solemn and steely-eyed enslaved Black jockey who, it was said, had a sixth sense when it came to horses, had been retained to ride for Louisiana. Whatever the nature of his skill was—magic or sheer know-how—he would be called upon to use it for Arrow. The horse was underweight, far too fragile to contend a four-mile heat race over a physically burdening track. A jockey identified only as John, most likely Black, was given a leg up on Mississippi's Lecomte.

At three o'clock, the drum tapped. Arrow dug into the mire with a force that betrayed his frailty.* Hawkins kicked him on, each stride propelling slop back into the face and eyes of Lexington, who had closed in behind. Farther back down the homestretch, Lecomte ran third. Trailing was the bettors' and Knowing Ones' favorite, Alabama's Highlander. Taking advantage of the hard middle ground in front of the stands, Gilpatrick guided Highlander there, and his horse duly increased his speed. Entering the second mile, Meichon brushed his spurs against Lexington. The horse burst into a tremendous charge, careening into the first turn and closing the gap on Arrow. By the time he rounded the turn, Lexington had taken the lead.

The stallion's speed now dictated the pace, and John, up on Lecomte, sensed it. Sinking his spurs between Lecomte's ribs, he urged the chestnut past Arrow and within a whisper of Lexington. Chopping the mud with each stride, Lexington maintained a steady speed, keeping his lead through the second and third miles. As the horses entered the fourth mile, the thick, clingy terrain had become especially difficult for Arrow. Over the last three miles, he had given Hawkins everything the jockey had asked, but now the horse labored unevenly, the gap between him and the rest of the field becoming unsurmountable. In the lead, Lexington continued digging into the mud with a ferocity that denied its existence. As the horses turned for home, Lecomte stretched deeper into his run. But Lexington increased his speed, winning the first heat under a strong pull—never reaching full stride. Three lengths behind, Lecomte finished second. Winded, Highlander merely sauntered to the finish. Arrow walked in, no longer in contention.

★ The *Picayune* places the initial order of the horses in the first heat differently, with Lexington leading the heat. Correspondent "Kentuck," who frequently reported for the *Spirit of the Times,* submitted his firsthand observation of the race to *The Kentucky Statesman* on April 11, 1854, placing the order as written here.

High-pitched whistling and cheering erupted inside the Metairie. For the hundreds of people outside the track who had been unable to gain entrance, news couldn't travel fast enough. Back inside the Metairie, Lexington sent fans scrambling to the betting tables.

During the forty-five-minute cooling period, grooms led Lexington away from the crowds gathering around him. They removed his bridle and cleaned out his mouth with a sponge drenched in water. With another sponge they wiped the grime of four miles from his eyes and face. Other grooms scraped the stallion's body to whisk away the sweat and mud that caked his sides and belly. Taking two sets of blankets, grooms pulled and tucked them around Lexington in a swaddle to prevent him from cooling too quickly. With equal parts water and wine, his mouth was rinsed again, allowing him to swallow small amounts of the concoction.

Over the next five minutes, grooms walked the horse to keep his muscles and limbs from locking up. They stripped the blankets from him and doused him with whiskey, massaging it into his limbs, shoulders, and hindquarters to deaden any pain. Lexington sipped more of the wine and water mixture while grooms wrapped him again in blankets. Then he was walked again. The process occurred in five-minute repetitions of walking and massaging until Lexington's coat dried and his breathing lowered to a normal rhythm. The heavy blankets were untucked, removed, and replaced with a light linen cloth. Once the horse had cooled, Pryor lifted his feet and examined his iron-plated shoes to ensure they remained firmly nailed in place. Grooms gave Lexington more water and wine, from which he was allowed no more than two swallows so his belly wouldn't become too full. They walked the horse draped in linen until the bugle announced the end of the forty-five-minute reprieve. At that point, Pryor saddled and bridled Lexington for the next heat.

At the drum's tap, Lexington, Highlander, and Lecomte darted ahead in a mad scramble. Lexington's placement in those initial strides was never reported. To what extent mud had been kicked in his face, blinding him further and affecting his own regulation and balance, is unknown. But as he ran down the homestretch, Lexington's feet got tangled in the mud. He stumbled and almost fell to the ground. Lecomte eased into the lead.* As Meichon and Lexington struggled to regain their footing, Gilpatrick rushed Highlander ahead on the hard ground. Behind, Lexington shook off his stilted stride and settled into a piston-pumping rhythm, a full-out onslaught to catch the field. Atop Highlander, Gilpatrick looked behind and saw the quickly approaching bay. He pushed his heels in, driving Alabama's horse faster. Rounding the first turn, Gilpatrick cut Highlander abruptly into the path of Lexington. Meichon pulled the reins hard, throwing the horse off his tremendous pace, then swerved him to the outside of Highlander to avoid a collision. Lecomte ran ahead, unimpacted by the battle behind him, the tenacious mud causing him little distress. Gilpatrick's antics at the turn ultimately failed. In that brief span of seconds, he had momentarily set Lexington back, causing him more work after he had already struggled so badly in the stumble. But the stallion had been challenged, and his resolve intensified.

Out of the turn, Lexington passed Highlander as Gilpatrick struggled to urge his horse into that mystical realm where bottom is tested. Over the next two miles, the position held: Lecomte, followed by Lexington, then Highlander. Every time the horses entered the homestretch, Gilpatrick took the hard ground's advantage, making several attempts to drive his horse past Lexington, who ran ahead in mud up to his shins. Each time, Kentucky's horse increased his run, but only enough to keep a slight lead over Highlander. By now, Lecomte's great speed had given him a hundred-yard advantage, and he continued on into the fourth mile unstressed and unchallenged. As Lexington and Highlander rounded the first

* The *Picayune* places the horse order in the second heat differently, with Lexington leading again. Kentuck describes Lexington's stumble at the beginning of the second heat, which caused the horse to fall behind.

turn of that final mile, Meichon brushed his spurs against Lexington's sides, pushing him faster. The horse sprang forward, eating away the yards of mud that separated him from Lecomte. His giant leaps through the mud indiscernible, he ran as if he floated on air. It was only his mud-splattered face and body that told the tale of his struggle. By the time Lecomte rounded into the final turn, Lexington had completely closed the hundred-yard gap. The multitudes in the grandstand stood on their feet, shouting louder and louder with each of Lexington's strides. He rounded the final turn in tandem with Lecomte.

At this point, the crowd all but lost its senses. "The uproar became quite deafening," according to Ripley, who described a woman from Kentucky jumping up, standing on her bench, and ordering her escort to "hold me while I holler!"

Down the homestretch Lexington ran, passing Lecomte and charging forward in vast outreaching strides. He beat Lecomte by four lengths, claiming the title of champion of the Great State.

Lexington walked off the track showing scant effect from his run. Grooms took the reins from Meichon and led the horse and his jockey to the weighing scales. The exertion of corralling the stallion's extreme drive over the last four miles had been too much for the young man. He swayed in the saddle, then doubled over in a blackout. Before Meichon fell from the horse, grooms pulled him off Lexington and propped him in the weighing scale seat, placing the saddle in his lap.

In spite of the speed-slowing mud, Lexington had run the first heat in eight minutes and eight and three-quarter seconds. Even with his stumble and Gilpatrick's antics around the mile turn, Lexington managed to improve his time in the second heat by four and a quarter seconds. Old turfmen who thought they'd seen everything were shocked by his numbers. Word rippled through the grandstand that the horse was more powerful than any of his record-breaking predecessors. For most of the race, Meichon had ridden Lexington under a tight pull to preserve the horse's energy.

Lexington could have run the race faster. It appeared that the stallion had not even come close to reaching his bottom.

Richard Ten Broeck said nothing after the race. He just gathered his horse, possibly congratulated his Kentucky team, and, as he
had done on other occasions following a dramatic win, returned to
the stables with Pryor. The *Picayune* labeled his silence "gracious."
Ten Broeck had every right to quietly bask in the national glow
about to descend on Lexington. Already, the electric fingers of the
Metairie's telegraph operator were dispatching dots and dashes to
Astor House in New York, where the Northern turfmen who no
longer owned horses were nevertheless sitting in the parlor anx-
iously awaiting the news.

The text was simple: KENTUCKY VICTORIOUS!

CHAPTER 8

LECOMTE

E VERY NOTABLE NEWSPAPER in the nation splashed "Kentucky Victorious!" across its pages. It was either that or the more elaborate "Old Kentucky Victorious—Lexington the Winner," as the *Boston Herald* proclaimed. The *New-York Daily Times* printed the win on page one, right below the election results for the Thirty-third United States Congress: "The great race was won by *Lexington* in two straight heats." The *Louisville Daily Courier* did similarly: "Kentucky Triumphant!" followed by the announcement of Kentucky's newest congressman. That year's congressional election issues weren't just the usual fare of mudslinging and impossible promise-making but something far more crucial. Congress was in heated debate over the Kansas–Nebraska Act, which, one month later, would repeal the Missouri Compromise of 1820 and create what came to be known as Bleeding Kansas. The whole affair would send small-town Illinois attorney Abraham Lincoln into word-swaying rhetoric against Illinois's Democratic senator, Stephen Douglas. But for now, alongside the congressional election results, news of the Great State's victor was paramount.

The Spirit of the Times.

in good	SAME DAY—Jockey Club Purse $400, for all ages, 3 yr. olds carrying 86lbs.—4, 1t0—5, 110—6, 118—7 and upwards, 124—allowing 3lbs. to mares and geldings. Two mile heats.	On startin with Lexi
meagre. ts, and opinion as such but lit-	S. M. Read's br. f. *Maid of Orleans*, by Bethune, out of Alice Carneal by Imp. Sarpedon, 4 yrs. .... 2 1 A. L. Bingaman's ch. g. *Wade Hampton*, by Boston, out of Margaret Woods by Imp. Priam, 5 yrs. .... 1 dist. Time, 4:09¼—4:38.	comto ma mile in ad mile. At only brusl distance, i

FOURTH DAY.

THE GREAT STATE POST STAKE.

KENTUCKY VICTORIOUS!

| So far opinion uld ran lashing steady. speci- speed rmerly favorite hands, . The by bet-ed him Blonde up to by four dy pull mance Blonde | Rarely has a lovelier Spring day opened on more brilliant hopes and expectation than that which yesterday dawned upon the thousands who, to a greater or less degree, were rushing forward to the great event of the day, with the most pleasurable expectations. The race! The great struggle of States for superiority in that contest which had for months enlisted so much feeling, so much State pride, so much individual competition, had been the ruling idea, in all circles, and scarcely any other topic had been discussed or thought of. Myriads of strangers, as the eventful day approached, had thronged our city, and almost nothing else was talked of but the probable or possible result of this great sporting affair. Opinions of every kind and shade were freely expressed. Each one of the gallant States that had so chivalrously come into the arrangement, had its host of representatives on the ground, and each indulged in earnest and eloquent eulogies upon his favorite. Banters were offered, bets were made, speculations were indulged in, predictions were ventured, hopes and fears were expressed, and the town had a topic that lasted up to the very moment when the tap of the drum gave signal for the start. Even the ladies caught the infectious excitement, and made up their pretty | ing throug On the tress, and as Arrow went to w striving ha quarter Le side by sic and cheer a torrent, but the sp stand abou cheers of t mile being Our rea merits of severity of would app the circum chances, i the contes persons in |

National and local headlines like this one from April 15, 1854, in the *Spirit of the Times* trumpeted the glorious win of Lexington in the Great State.

The citizens of Lexington took a further step by commissioning silversmiths Garner & Winchester to fire up the kiln and melt silver coin to form a commemorative bowl. The inscription read: *1854—Presented by the Citizens of Lexington, Kentucky, to Dr. Elisha Warfield as a Token of their Esteem for the Immortal Horse Lexington.*

Immortal! As if the horse, mere flesh and blood, were a

The Lexington Bowl presented to Dr. Elisha Warfield in 1854 by the citizens of Lexington, Kentucky, in honor of the Great State victor.

supreme and infallible being. The sentiment was shared. The *Nashville Union and American* wrote of Lexington's impeccable effort as "light and graceful . . . A bottom and constancy which could be depended on."

General Thomas Jefferson "T. J." Wells, the owner of Lecomte, was not pleased. In fact, he was bitter as vinegar. Lexington's win and the national press's reaction sent Wells into a frenzy of green envy. It didn't help that his mind had grown more unstable of late, his thoughts persistently drifting to odd insecurities, certain that others were conspiring against him. Although a mainstay and heavy supporter of the Louisiana turf since the 1830s, he wasn't universally liked. Many considered him far too aloof, venomously accusatory, and just plain cold. Turf historian John Hervey said of Wells that he "lacked *savoir faire* and was never easy to get on with."

Isolating himself at his Wellswood plantation, a vast landscape hugged by an endless row of live oaks along the Bayou Boeuf riverbanks in the parish of Red River, Louisiana, Wells spent his days watching his horses circle his one-mile oval racetrack. In 1849, just as Dr. Warfield was writing out a fifty-dollar note to Uncle Ned Blackburn so he could breed Alice Carneal to Boston, Wells wrote out his own fifty-dollar note and shipped his gifted race mare, Reel, to Uncle Ned's so that she too could visit Boston. The result was Lecomte.

Wells trained his colt at Wellswood, in close proximity to his namesake—Wells's friend and fellow turfman Ambroise Lecomte, whose idea it was to send Reel to Boston in the first place. Gladly lending his name to the product of that union, Lecomte, along with Wells, watched the gangly chestnut grow and train into a magnificent racehorse. Lecomte started racing in April 1853, just one month before Lexington's maiden at the Association Course. Throughout the year, while Lexington was ailing and going blind at the Pharsalia, Lecomte was racing in a competition-packed schedule, beating some of the South's most renowned horses— Conrad the Corsair, Zero, Argent, Joe Blackburn, and many others—running some of those races with a rest interval of only seven days. He even set a mile record of 1:45 ½ at the Metairie. After he had run the entire year unbeaten, Lexington had handed him his first defeat in the Great State.

That was what got Wells so furious. He believed that if the Metairie hadn't been a mud bog, Lecomte would have won. All the accolades and applause, all the glorified tributes and poetic grandeur would have come pouring down on Lecomte *and* himself. Confiding in his trainer, known only as Hark, Wells unleashed his anger. Unlike Lexington's dam, Alice Carneal, Lecomte's dam had won a few races and was deemed the superior mare. Of all things! That Lecomte should lose to a lesser, half-blind horse! Wells declared he wouldn't rest until his horse defeated Lexington.

Hark told Wells frankly that it wouldn't be any horse that brought down Lexington, but rather, a man. The *only* way to beat Lexington was to put Abe up on Lecomte.

Abe Hawkins was the highly acclaimed Black jockey who had ridden Arrow in the Great State. Before that race, he had moved from Mississippi to Louisiana, and into the hands of a heavy-pocketed turf magnate named Duncan F. Kenner. For the sum of $2,350, Kenner had "bought" one of the nation's best jockeys. Monikered "the Dark Sage of Louisiana," Hawkins was an ace when it came to horses. He, better than anyone, knew how to ride a horse steady to preserve its energy, and when to let it run full out. Hawkins also had the feel of an onrushing locomotive. His career was rising, and fast. Although enslaved, he operated in prestigious circles, in some ways sharing equal status with the top white jockey, Gilpatrick. Hawkins "enjoyed a professional life beyond the dreams of most whites," wrote historian Edward Hotaling. Accolades elevated Hawkins's reputation until he became, Hotaling wrote, "the second-best known Abe in the country, the other [later] residing in the White House." Abe Hawkins's skills made him so sought-after that he was, according to journalist Bob Roesler, "perhaps the first Black professional athlete to gain national prominence."

General Wells arranged through Duncan Kenner to hire Hawkins to ride Lecomte and aimed for the Jockey Club Purse, a four-mile heat race set to run a mere seven days after the Great State.

While Hawkins was prepping Lecomte in daily morning workouts, New Orleans was buzzing about Lexington. In the marble-and-mahogany rooms at the Boston Club, members waved away thick clouds of cigar smoke in order to see one another. They discussed their opinions about the Great State champion in alternating hushed and elevated tones. Was he a one-shot miracle? Was Lecomte the better horse?

Talk of Lexington and Lecomte wasn't isolated to the Boston Club. People discussed them underneath the rotunda at the St. Charles, in the lounge of the Orleans Club among writers from the *Picayune* and *The New Orleans Daily Crescent,* and over gumbo filé at Victor's. Perhaps the voodoo priestess Marie Laveau sold predictions about which horse was superior, having heard enough gossip during her daytime trade of coiffing hair to make the most educated guess in the city. Some speculators believed that if Lexington was raced over a dry, perfectly conditioned track, he would fail. The talk wasn't just about the two horses. The factor of Time was also hotly debated.

Time had been a silent contender in horse races since 1722, when the English racehorse Flying Childers, a son of the Darley Arabian, ran four miles, one furlong, and 138 yards over Newmarket's round course in 7:30. Then in 1755, the English horse Matchem, grandson of the Godolphin Arabian, ran four miles at Newmarket's Beacon Course in 7:20. It would take another sixty-eight years before an American horse could even come close to Matchem. In May 1823, Sir Henry raced four miles in 7:37 ½ during his famed race against American Eclipse. An American record, but still not as fast as Flying Childers or Matchem. Then, in May 1842, Fashion raced a four-mile heat in 7:32 ½ against Boston. Still slower than the English horses but catching up. After the Great State race, Time—capitalized in that era in recognition that

Time was a contender in all races—had still not been beaten. Although a horse could naturally become a champion by running a superlative race, if it also happened to lower Time in that race, that horse was assured of being catapulted into the stratosphere of immortality.

With all the buzz around Lexington and Lecomte, the itch for a rematch got the better of Ten Broeck. Lecomte was already entered in the Jockey Club Purse, now just a few days away, but Captain Willa Viley, as Lexington's half owner, had a say in this and wanted nothing to do with a rematch. In fact, what Viley did next broke from that era's well-founded theories on horse training.

After a race, a horse generally went through hours of around-the-clock observation to ensure it did not come down with a fever, wasn't lame, or did not become so. "Sometimes inflammation comes on rapidly and if it doesn't destroy him, can make him useless as a racer as it generally terminates his feet . . . several horses after a hard day can become blind," wrote the *American Turf Register and Sporting Magazine*.

Post-race observation and management included a crammed itinerary of chores and check-ins that were supposed to occur every twenty minutes over a twenty-four-to-forty-eight-hour span. During those initial hours, grooms painstakingly provided pails filled with small amounts of water to prevent the horse from drinking too much too soon. They brushed the horse briskly several times throughout the night and day to increase circulation, and soaked its hooves in buckets of hot water; the idea then was to draw out any infection that might set in. They also wrapped its legs in flannel to bring down swelling and fed it oats mixed with tonics of sulfur to help heal ligaments and tendons.

If a horse developed a fever, the protocol recommended that two quarts of blood be let from its neck. If the horse made it through the twenty-four hours without any lameness or ailments, it was exercised at a light canter, followed by endless walking—up to two hours—under flannel blankets. It was allowed to drink freely but could only eat minimally.

The process gradually wound down until the fourth day after a race, when a recovering horse was finally allowed to return to its normal feedings of grain and hay. But, as cautioned by the *American Turf Register,* "if the horse had a hard race, a severe running of three or four heats of three or four miles each, he will need additional attention."

None of these protocols was followed for Lexington after the Great State.

Instead, Viley ordered the stallion's shoes to be removed and then turned him loose on a remote Louisiana pasture. For five days, Lexington gorged himself on grass. Idling away and unworked.

Whether Ten Broeck was immediately aware of the break in protocol is unknown. At some point, he did find out. Over the ensuing days, Lexington's two owners exchanged heated words about the horse's condition, as well as the possibility of a rematch at the end of the week. Despite the public's hopes of seeing the two horses face each other again, Viley wasn't bending. But Ten Broeck was always a man to back the merits of his horse. Especially when that horse was featured in national headlines. Many of the people who had traveled to New Orleans for the Great State were still in the city. That they would buy a ticket at the Metairie to see this new hero race again was an almost certainty.

In the end, Viley packed his bags and, with a $5,000 draft note from Ten Broeck to buy Lexington outright, set off to Kentucky and never looked back.

On Friday, one day before the Jockey Club Purse, Ten Broeck officially entered Lexington against Lecomte and another horse named Reube. When the *Picayune* announced the rematch, bettors at the St. Charles piled money on Lexington, favoring him evenly against Lecomte and Reube combined. At the Metairie, odds fell heavily on Lexington at 100 to 80 against the field, and separately, at 100 to 60 in favor of Lexington over Lecomte. As patrons tossed money on the betting tables, Time entered the pool. Fashion's record of 7:32 ½ for the fastest four miles ever run in America came up for speculation, setting off a whirlwind of bets. Defying decades of historical precedent—the thousands of attempts by horses who ran slower than Fashion—bettors nonetheless took those bold odds.

That same day, Lexington was hastily brought out of the pasture, reshod, and delivered to J. B. Pryor over at the Metairie. Pryor looked the horse over and hoped on a bygone fallen star that some stroke of luck would work in the unconditioned horse's favor. Worse, the grass bingeing had caused soreness in Lexington's feet. Overindulging on sugar-rich grasses can induce laminitis, a condition in which the laminae—the soft tissues connecting the hoof to the coffin bone—become inflamed, leading to varying degrees of lameness and, in some cases, death. Although the historical record is unclear to what extent Lexington suffered, the implication is that in the interval between the two races, his feet were temporarily affected by overeating. There seemed little chance Pryor could bring him race-ready to the post. The trainer said as much, strongly objecting to Lexington's start. While Lecomte had strengthened under the much-observed protocol and intermittent gallops, Lexington had been overindulged; he hadn't even cantered, much less walked under saddle, since the Great State in which he had given an arduous run. Whether the previous race and overindulging inflamed his good left eye again was never stated, but the factors that might bring it on were certainly there.

"Keeping a horse in condition is hard," wrote the *American Turf Register* in December 1831. "In bringing a horse around again after a severe race, good stable management and science are put to the test." By following the protocol, a skilled trainer should be able to bring a horse sound to run again within a week. Pryor had only twenty-four hours.

Saturday morning, April 8, 1854, the day of the Jockey Club Purse, the Metairie's mud-drowned track had dried and was nearly restored to its springy form. Ten thousand people filled the grandstand and turned the infield into a patchwork of blankets anchored by champagne bottles and picnic baskets.

At the Metairie's stables, J. B. Pryor draped a linen sheet over Lexington and opened the stable door. But the horse who usually sprang from his stall at race time firmly planted all four hooves and wouldn't budge. Pryor drove him forward under the whip's threat until the horse acquiesced, reluctantly following the trainer out to the track and through a curtain of applause, whoops, and whistles. Following closely behind was Henry Meichon. Pulling his orange cap firmly onto his head, he glanced nervously across the grandstand. A few yards away, Hawkins stood nearby, inspecting his whip with unfeigned interest while Hark walked Lecomte in circles, corralling his fraught energy, tugging now and then when the horse arched his neck too high or startled at the noise of the crowd.

When the bugle sounded "Bring Up Your Horses"—the signal played before races to send jockeys and horses to the post and to warn bettors to place their final bets—the trainers pulled the sheets from their horses and girthed on the saddles. Pryor hoisted Meichon up onto Lexington. John Ford, the renowned white jockey who had been hired to ride Reube, trotted the horse to the post, as Abe Hawkins settled into Lecomte's saddle and gathered the slack from the reins. Meichon, the youngest and least experienced of the jockeys, was on the favored horse. Only seven days earlier, he had ridden him to victory. Still, observing Lexington for the first time since then, he could tell there was much to be concerned about.

When the drum tapped, Lecomte drove to the front and onto the fastest path, along the inside rail. Lexington followed in the much deeper silt that cradled the outer track, his left and better eye fixed on Lecomte. Reube trailed. Lexington's usual easy, elastic stride had stiffened into a rigid, mechanized motion like a metronome hitching its swing. He didn't settle into a fluid run as he trudged through much heavier ground. Still, he charged after Lecomte until they were separated only by inches. Lexington tried several times to brush past him for the lead. Each time, Lecomte increased his speed and held his position. In the backstretch of the final mile, Meichon dug his spurs into Lexington, jolting the horse into a tremendous surge. The infield went wild. As Lexington moved up alongside Lecomte, Hawkins urged his horse, who responded—increasing his lead, first by one length, then two . . . three . . . four. Down the homestretch, Lecomte opened six lengths on Lexington, followed by Reube, and bounded across the finish line first, creating a rumble from the infield and grandstand that shook the Metairie. The horse had just lowered the chronometer's ticking hands to a number never seen before in American racing. Lecomte had run the heat in 7:26, defeating Fashion's twelve-year record.

The Knowing Ones, many of whom had bet in favor of Lexington, stared at their chronometers in disbelief. Ten Broeck likely glared at his own in shock, then turned his back to the track—as he had done in the past whenever he was unsatisfied with the result—pulling his hat down to further shield the disgusted expression that for once betrayed his poker-faced reserve.

At the cooling circle, Lexington blew hard, rapid, short, distressed breaths as grooms washed and rubbed him down. Pryor stood by exasperated, shaking his head, and no doubt mumbling curses about preparation and clocks. Meichon sat in the corner, mouth agape, chest heaving, and wide-eyed as the reality of the last four miles settled in.

Ten Broeck walked up; the cigar jutting out of his mouth was a chewed-up mass of frustration. The grooms glanced at him with serious eyes, then at the horse heaving for air, and finally at the young jockey slumped in the corner trying to rally. They wrapped Lexington in blankets and started walking him in large circles to slow his breathing. Whether Ten Broeck held Pryor's gaze is hard to say, but the conversation eventually settled around the young jockey who was desperately trying to catch his breath. If Lexington revived well enough to race a second heat, he would need a stronger rider to make the best of his energy.

In 1898, American historian Lyman Horace Weeks would write, "Jockeyship is an exacting profession and calls for more than the mere ordinary ability to keep a seat in the saddle. The courage, the vitality, the quickness of perception, and the rare good judgment of pace and of other details, are proof of something more than ordinary ability." The *American Turf Register* advised, "The strength of a rider should be sufficient to hold, support and assist the horse, otherwise the horse will exhaust his wind." Back then, American jockeys rode much differently than those in England. English jockeys had already adjusted their positions to tuck their knees up and hunch hovered over the horse's withers—the position for speed. American jockeys rode for endurance, with their seats touching the saddles and their legs draping the horse's sides. The journal's very specific advice to the rider is worth quoting:

A horse should be allowed to do what he needs to carry himself, even if it puts the rider out of ease. Give him all the support he requires in a smooth steady pull and do not increase it. If a hand is raised to keep him in, it will raise his head out of place. If a rider has to do this to keep a horse from running away with him, he is not strong enough. Neither must the [rider's] body be thrown out of center, nor feet planted forward to increase the pull. These operate to the disadvantage of the horse. You are to encourage, and it must be done without detracting from the horse—always to support the horse. Your hand must permit him to extend himself to the utmost when getting him to increase speed. Help him collect his haunches under him. Slack reins prevent a horse from bringing his legs close. If you yield your hand too much, you abandon the horse. If gathering him too much, he cannot extend [his stride]. The eagerness of the horse will cause him to extend himself as far as he can safely. The rider's strength should hold out with the horse.

As Ten Broeck scrambled to find another rider, Pryor thanked Meichon for his time and told him he was being replaced. The exhausted jockey jerked off the orange-and-black silks, handed them over, and walked off. The silks were then given to a Black jockey whose name, unfortunately, was never recorded.

After forty-five minutes of walking and rubdowns, Lexington's breathing had returned to normal. He was said by some observers to be "like his old self." With his horse revived and a fresh rider in the saddle, Ten Broeck walked over to the judge's stand and notified them of the jockey change. The judges nodded their consent and waved to the bugler to sound the horn. But just as Lexington's rider was receiving an earful of last-minute instructions from Pryor, the jockey's owner marched over and inexplicably had him pulled off Lexington.

Ten Broeck hurried to hunt down Meichon, leaving Pryor muttering as he walked Lexington again in circles. Ten Broeck soon returned, his hat pulled down even farther and his cigar now devastated to a pulp. Meichon trailed behind, working his way back into the orange-and-black silks. He was heaped up onto the saddle still tucking his shirttails into his breeches.

At the start of the second heat, Lexington charged to the lead and held the next two miles steadily. Lecomte trailed in his dust by two lengths. On the third mile, Lecomte made a rush and took the lead by fifteen yards. With Lecomte running as much as twenty-three feet per second, Lexington increased his pace, running into Lecomte's shadow, pushing him to run faster. Down the homestretch the two horses ran, head-to-head, completing the third mile in the fast time of 1:46. Reube followed. As Lecomte and Lexington entered the fourth mile, under neither whip nor spur, Lexington increased his speed, nearly passing Lecomte. From the crowd, Meichon heard "Pull up! The race is over!" The jockey, muddled and fatigued, pulled Lexington to a near standstill. Lecomte kept running. Hawkins looked back. Believing Lexington had broken down, he refocused, driving Lecomte into a fifty-yard lead. John G. Cocks, president of the Metairie Jockey Club, saw Meichon's mistake and pointed out the error to his colleagues. But by that point, Meichon had kicked into his horse. From almost a dead stop, Lexington dug into the silt and started walloping the ground, making up distance and chasing down Lecomte.*

In the backstretch, Lexington gained on Lecomte and was about to pass him when Meichon, peculiarly—his mind perhaps still swirling with confusion—pulled hard, slowing Lexington again. Then he dug his spurs in, asking the stallion for his most tremendous pace. This Lexington gave, ripping through ground to close Lecomte's lead to two lengths. But the finish line was too near for Lexington, whose speed was steadily increasing, to run down Lecomte. As Wells's horse crossed the finish leading Lexington by one length for the match win, Hawkins held the reins in one hand and waved his other triumphantly.

A correspondent later wrote to the *Spirit of the Times* that Meichon's errors were "fatal to Lexington's chance" to win the second heat. Meichon couldn't even keep his story straight on

---

* A horse stride is measured from the point where one leg hits the ground to where it hits the ground again. All four feet will touch the ground during a single stride. The greater the horse's stride length, the greater the amount of ground he covers. A horse with a large stride runs more efficiently than others. His strength is preserved because he does less work. The length of Lexington's stride was never recorded—J. B. Pryor never allowed the horse to reach his full stride; he was usually held back in reserve. Boston's stride was measured at twenty-six feet, one foot longer than Secretariat's. Lecomte's stride was measured at twenty-three feet.

what exactly had happened over that last mile. The jockey admitted to some people that he had erred in pulling Lexington, believing that the race was over. He then about-faced and denied he'd made any error.

The day after Lexington's loss, General Wells and his Red River friends roamed the streets of New Orleans, sauntering into the St. Charles's barrooms and then over to the gentlemen's sporting clubs, all the while aggrandizing Lecomte's success.

"I'll race Lecomte against Lexington at any time, for any money, and at any distance," Wells boasted.

On April 9, the *Picayune* wrote, "Well satisfied are we that we have witnessed the best race, in all respects, that was ever run; and that Lecomte stands proudly before the world as the best race horse ever produced on the turf."

That same day, Ten Broeck wrote a challenge to General Wells:

Dear Sir—I did not wish to run Lexington again this season, and believing you entertained the same sentiment in regard to Lecomte, I forbore making a proposal which you would have to decline or change your views in respect to your horse (though I believe Lexington's defeat was caused by his unskilled rider). As however, it was stated to me at a public assemblage yesterday, that you said that Lecomte stood ready to meet Lexington at any time, for any money, and at any distance, thereby inviting a proposal, I now say that I will run Lexington against Lecomte, four-mile heats, over the Metairie Course.

Ten Broeck rode out to Duncan Kenner's plantation, found Abe Hawkins, and paid him to ride Lexington in the proposed rematch. The turfman also hunted down Gilpatrick and retained him as well. Ten Broeck's retainment of both highly acclaimed jockeys signaled what many felt: that the race had been a jockeys' game; that Lecomte had won because of Hawkins's steady and assured drive, which allowed the horse to stretch further into his run than he ever had. Lecomte was a superb horse, but under the wrong rider, he might never have broken Fashion's record. Or beaten Lexington.

General Wells refused the rematch without explanation. Nor did he counter any terms.

In late April 1854, the governing minds in Albany granted lawyer S. J. Carter a charter for establishing a new racecourse on Long Island. The National Course, as it came to be known, ballyhooed its $8,000-purse offerings and a star-studded racing agenda that enticed turfmen from all over the West and South, as well as Canada. The *Spirit* published the news under the bold heading REVIVAL OF RACING IN NEW YORK! Given Wells's refusal to bring Lecomte out of his stall to rematch Lexington, Ten Broeck committed to racing his horse in the inaugural meet in New York. But homecomings and ribbon cuttings at a new racecourse were the least of the Northern turfman's ambitions for his prize stallion. New York was the springboard to England. At that time, no American had ever raced homebred horses in Great Britain, which was of course the originating country of horse racing. In 1853, Frenchmen had pulled off a victory in England's Goodwood Cup with the French-bred horse Jouvence. But Jouvence had been raised and trained in England under English racing methods, so his win wasn't a testament to foreign-bred horses but just another win for the English system.

For years there had been many fields of rivalry between America and England. Horse racing was one, and shipbuilding was another—the idea being to see who could build a seaworthy vessel fast enough to zip around coastal waters and outmaneuver its competitors for more efficient international trade. Spurred by American pride, John Cox Stevens, the owner of American Eclipse, requisitioned the renowned shipbuilder George Steers to design a three-sail gaff schooner that Stevens later christened *America*. On August 22, 1851, the last day of the Royal Yacht Squadron's regatta, *America* lined up against fifteen other yachts to race fifty-three miles around the Isle of Wight. *America* won by eighteen minutes.

Stevens's victory was an inspiring win for American sportsmen. Later that month, Benjamin "Ogle" Tayloe, an American diplomat as well as an astute and respected turfman, read about the *America*. Inspired by the accomplishment, he set about strategizing on the possibilities for a comparable victory on the racecourse. Tayloe wrote to the *Spirit,* "With the achievement of the yacht *America* on both sides of the Atlantic, now we should try our racehorses against the English. . . . Is there no gentleman upon the American Turf who can take up the gauntlet, and be delighted to do so?"

The answer was Richard Ten Broeck. The two-mile Astor House Stakes at Long Island's National Course was set for July 1854. He entered Lexington in the new track's inaugural race; then, as designed in Ten Broeck's untiring, striving mind, the horse would cross the Atlantic to England.

CHAPTER 9

TIME IS A MIGHTY GOOD HORSE

L EXINGTON ARRIVED IN Saratoga Springs, New York, no worse for wear. Under the care of William A. Stuart, a prominent trainer, the horse had been shipped by steamboat from New Orleans to Louisville, then by rail and a cargo boat—up the Hudson River to the summer resort, which was known for its healing waters. He would rest there a few weeks, nestled among the tall pines, before being shipped back down the Hudson to Long Island.

While Lexington idled in New York, Lecomte was shimmering as America's hero. The *Picayune* called his recent victory "a performance that has dwarfed and dimmed the luster of past renown" and labeled him the greatest of living horses. Even Ten Broeck conceded that Lecomte's win should be "blazoned in letters of light." The general's horse was so inspiring that poets wrote his name into verse, and he stood beside Wells as Louisiana governor Hébert awarded his owner and trainer medals to commemorate "Lecomte, the pride of America, the pride of Louisiana, the pride of Red River." T. S. Moise, the celebrated equine artist, felt similarly compelled. He committed Lecomte to oil on canvas, backdropped by the swaying oaks at Wellswood. Halls on Canal Street hung the painting prominently in its front wide window so that the whole of New Orleans could admire "Lecomte, the Creole of Louisiana." When the horse returned home from New Orleans, arriving during the dark hours near midnight, almost the entire population of Alexandria, the nearest town to Wellswood, crowded the banks of the Bayou Boeuf to see their champion disembark. Back at Lecomte's stable, grooms gathered to hear details of his great win. Then they danced into the early hours, playing banjos and tambourines, celebrating their racer.

A painting of Lecomte by Henri De Lattre, painted in 1856 toward the end of the horse's racing career at the Metairie. The original painting was once listed in the possession of the Jockey Club; however, its current whereabouts are unknown.

Lecomte's win had never squared right with Ten Broeck. He was not the type to blame himself, especially when there were so many other contributing factors at which to point: Lexington's failing eyes, the jarring and wrenching he had endured through every mud hole during the Great State, Meichon's fatigue and his confused mind, Abe Hawkins's masterful riding of Lecomte. People were now calling Hawkins "the Slayer of Lexington"! But the loss, Ten Broeck felt certain, also wasn't his horse's fault. Since

General Wells had scuttled away from any future contest, the man from Albany had to find another way to vindicate his horse against Lecomte.

On April 30, 1854, he wrote a letter to the *Spirit*. Temporarily sidelining any immediate plans for England, he offered a series of challenges as Lexington's valedictory to America. Wagering $10,000 a side ($10,000 from each party to the wager, for a total of $20,000), Ten Broeck proposed that his stallion race not against other horses but against Lecomte's record of 7:26. Alternatively, he wagered $20,000 that Lexington would beat *any named horse*. If either proposition was accepted, the match would occur the following year at the Metairie. The latter proposition—specifically aimed at Lecomte—put the question of the horse's abilities boldly on the general's shoulders. If Wells persisted in refusing to match Lecomte, Lexington would run to beat Lecomte's Time. Up to that point, records had been broken only by happenstance, when horses raced against other horses. No horse in the history of American racing had ever been matched solely against the constant Time.

Ten Broeck had taken a tremendous risk. If Lexington failed, his owner's credibility would be shattered. All the Knowing Ones and entitled gentlemen in the gambling circles would shun the man as a haphazard fool. Piling $10,000, plus all his credibility, on the back of Lexington was an all-in bet that those four legs would outrun Time itself. The proposition was sensational, and the absolute impossibility of the whole affair made it the topic of the moment. Overnight, throughout the North and South, everyone began talking about Lexington's chances.

But alongside the proposition's shock value was a legitimate goal: to break a record for Time over four miles, a victory that required not only speed but an unspoken hope that all the myriad of complications that could arise wouldn't.

To most of the population there wasn't much to guess about. Lexington was going to race against an immortal abstract. A competitor that couldn't feel pain, break down, falter in weather, run off course, or in any sense fail because of some unknown or unfactored condition. Time cannot be altered, and Time, in the proverbial sense, waits for no man or horse. Flesh and blood will always break down under Time. Beating it is the stuff of delusion.

Maybe that was why laughter rumbled through the smoke-filled mahogany rooms at the Boston Club, then down the street to the Orleans Club, where it settled smugly in the opinions of newspapermen from the *Picayune* and the *Crescent*. How much more, not even a year after Lecomte lowered Fashion's record, was Time willing to concede to another horse—if anything at all? "It is improbable that the best time ever made is to be beaten, except under very extraordinary circumstances," wrote the *Crescent*. "The best horse in the world might fail in such a trial—mishaps and dangers are all against him." Other pundits claimed that if Lexington beat Lecomte's 7:26, he "must be something more than a horse."

Ten Broeck's straight-faced proposal verged too much on a bluff. In June, two Virginia turfmen, Calvin Green and John Belcher, sauntered into Astor House in New York and deposited five thousand dollars as forfeit insurance to make good their intention to accept the bet in favor of Time, then walked away assured of inevitable success. Belcher, who had initially trained Boston for Old Nap Johnson, had seen Fashion lower Time in her race against Lexington's sire. So had Green. Since then, the two Virginians, along with the rest of the nation, had lived through the decades bereft of extraordinary happenings, and knew how nearly impossible it would be for a horse to achieve once again what so seldom occurred. The *Spirit of the Times,* whose offices occupied a room at Astor House, had its editor, William T. Porter, on hand with paper and pen to record the wager. "No match against Time, of such interest, has ever occurred in this country," wrote Porter. "Time is a 'mighty good horse' to bet on."

The sweltering temperatures of a June heat wave settled in about the time Lexington arrived at the National Course to begin training. Throughout Long Island people lazily waved their paper fans to cool their flushed faces, rocked in chairs under shaded verandas, and drank lemonade chock-full of sugar. A spell of stagnation settled over everyone, including those at work at the National Course. Blanketed exercising of horses made little sense in the dense air of the abhorrent, sticky sauna, where animals could easily overheat. Most of the work was pushed up even earlier to an ungodly pre-dawn time that made everyone who trained horses rethink their profession. But crack-of-dawn schedules did nothing to help Lexington. Although he had spent over a year training in the sultry climates of Mississippi and Louisiana and was better conditioned for that swampish heat than most, he was sidelined for graver reasons.

For several days Lexington had stood in the back of a dark stall at the National. A continual stream of liquid trickled from his left eye—the better one—which was now swollen closed almost entirely. The inflammatory pain had consumed his eyes again, causing him to shut out what light he could still see. Even the slightest ray of sunlight penetrating the gaps in the board planks of his stall irritated him. To isolate himself even more, the horse maneuvered himself to face away from the barn's aisle, where people were more apt to stroke his face while walking by. There were no medicines or groomsmen's miracle herbs at that time to alleviate the condition or ease his pain. Over the ensuing weeks, all that Lexington could do was rest inside the protective confines of his darkened stall. Every time the condition set in, as it did so randomly and viciously, it stole more of his permanent vision. The first time, it had claimed his right eye. Now he was slowly losing more sight in his left.

Ten Broeck withdrew Lexington from the Astor House Stakes, setting off a ruckus of criticism from the public that aggravated Ten Broeck no end. He shot back in the acerbic tone he so often defaulted to.

I learn from a paper of New York that there was great dissatisfaction because Lexington did not run at the last race meeting here. Lexington is, unfortunately, subject to inflammation of the eyes, which appeared before the last race, and I hope this apology will satisfy the dissatisfied; should it not, I will refer to a prevailing impression that this is a free country, in which opinion I accord. I have a vague idea that Lexington is my property, and that I will run him when and where I choose.

So much for anyone who dared question him! But what drove him to such rhetoric was his ultimate concern over his horse and the animal's future. Whether Lexington could recover to train against Time seemed uncertain. However great the horse might be, his physical limitations had set new parameters.

As Lexington stood in darkness, matters became even worse. Cholera had first appeared in America around 1832. The disease was then thought to be noncontagious—merely a congestive fever. Some people believed it was caused by insects, while others blamed it on the earth's electricity, or ozone, or carbonic acid, or atmospheric poisons. Even learned doctors claimed that fear of the sickness itself, along with sexual excess or gluttony, would weaken the system and predispose it to cholera. The gut-wrenching disease proved to be epidemical and deadly.

A month after Lexington arrived at the National Course, cholera swept through the nation, claiming, among many thousands of others, the life of Lexington's new trainer, William Stuart. But in the midst of this misfortune came a ray of light. The horse's left eye began to improve. The continual drainage stopped, his eye was less swollen, and he was soon facing the front of his stall, eager and sociable once more. Hopeful, Ten Broeck set his goal for the National's fall meet and scurried to hire another trainer. He found one in New Jersey.

Charles Lloyd listened to Ten Broeck's plight. Lexington hadn't been on a racetrack in nearly three months, and the progression of his blindness was unknowable. Still, Ten Broeck believed his horse to be one of the best America had seen, and he persuaded a reluctant Lloyd to take him on. Lexington moved from his stall at the National to Lloyd's Holmdel estate, where he was turned loose on the rolling pastures. With time and rest, Lexington regained some of the vision in his left eye.* His right eye remained blind. Once the horse had recuperated, Lloyd put him back to work.

While Lexington was rebuilding muscle on the trainer's private racetrack, the *Picayune* was wondering what had become of him. Just about every contender Lexington had previously faced had since raced in New York. The horses Madonna and Garrett Davis, Highlander from Alabama, even Little Flea, had competed at the National's inauguration. But Lexington was nowhere to be seen. The *Picayune* mused, "Ten Broeck must be holding Lexington up for something."

Ten Broeck had at long last publicly admitted his error in starting an unconditioned Lexington in the Jockey Club Purse against Lecomte. "For an owner to defend the defeat of his horse is an ungracious task," wrote Ten Broeck in the *Spirit*. His admission of fault said everything about what he considered his horse's capabilities to be. Others agreed. "I feel sure," wrote one racing fan, "that Mr. Ten Broeck will esteem it an injustice to his horse to take him to Europe until he has again attacked his rival in America. Should they meet, in good condition, the result will not be even doubtful. Lexington and Lecomte are like twin lions whelped in one hour, and Lexington the elder and more terrible!" The sentiment was shared. Many people felt Lexington had *pushed* Lecomte to break Time.

"Lazy" was a term often used to characterize Lecomte. In fact, the word was a gross understatement of the horse's blasé attitude toward racing. Jockeys had to spur Lecomte into caring, while

---

* The historical record is unclear how much of Lexington's vision returned to his left eye. According to what is presently known about ERU, every time the disease reoccurs, it can take away more of the horse's vision.

during his walks, grooms had to follow behind him shouting, "Giddy-up!" waving and cracking whips in midair just to move him along. According to one man who saw the horse in his paddock a few days after he beat Time, "Lecomte neither leapt nor bounded . . . showed no rash joy at his temporary freedom, and I failed to see the evidence of that hot courage and that high desire he might well have shown." Instead, the horse lowered his head and started grazing. In fact, it's a wonder, given Lecomte's disdain for exertion, that he was ever raced. Even Wells conceded his horse's apathy, quietly confiding to his small circle that he was indebted to Lexington for Lecomte's 7:26, "since no other horse could have forced [Lecomte] to the pace so far beyond all past performances."

As the months unfolded, Wells absorbed the sober realization that Lexington would race against Lecomte's record. The man from Red River had dodged every attempt to rematch his champion. In the wake of such avoidance, the boastful words he once spoke had been identified as the hollow vanity they were. Although he had refused to rematch his horse, the clamor over the inevitable fact that Lexington would race against Time rattled him. Doubling down, Wells backed his initial brag with something far more audacious. On August 19, 1854, the *Spirit* printed on page one: CHALLENGE TO THE WORLD! Finally, Wells had agreed to race Lecomte against any named horse from anywhere on the globe on any day, as long as the race occurred on any racetrack in the Deep South. The proposal sparked similar dramatic flair from Ten Broeck, who responded from New York, "General Wells can have a race with Lecomte when Lexington arrives at New Orleans in safety. If the mountain will not come to Mahomet, Mahomet will go to the mountain."

At the same time Ten Broeck was feeding the rematch fire, Lexington was galloping daily around Lloyd's track, once again exhibiting his commanding, far-reaching stride. But one morning, while wrestling to have his head, he snapped his bridle. With no

On Dits in Sporting Circles.

ACCIDENT TO LEXINGTON.
THE PROPOSITIONS OF LECOMTE AND RED EYE.

New York, Sept. 13th, 1854.

To W. T. Porter, Esq., Editor of the "Spirit of the Times."

Dear Sir—I regret to inform you that Lexington broke his bridle whilst exercising on his training track, and running through a field of standing corn, so bruised his legs as to make it necessary to stop his galloping, in view of his match against time next spring.

"*En passant*," I will reply, through your columns, to the proposals of the owners of Lecomte and Red Eye, (neither of whom were heard from though ample time was afforded), until Lexington had other engagements, which I thought he could easily win, and upon which I would have had to pay forfeit to bring about a meeting. Lexington's challenge to Lecomte was declined, when both horses were on the Metairie Course, at New Orleans, and when (according to the proof Gen. Wells adduced in an elaborate communication), the former would have had the disadvantage in condition. Subsequently, Lexington challenged Lecomte and his Time, either race to be taken, and if accepted on the part of the horse, $25,000 to $20,000 to be laid, if the race was run at New York or

Headline from the *Spirit of the Times*. Lexington so
enthralled the public, especially in light of his upcoming
match against Time, that any news about him was
widely reported and read with avidity.

hold on the horse, the jockey bounced, unsettled in the saddle, as Lexington bolted from the track into a nearby cornfield. Thickened stalks clothed in razor-edged leaves whipped against his legs, cutting deep gouges and bruising him badly. Back in his stall, he endured around-the-clock leg soakings and wrappings.

Ten Broeck once again withdrew Lexington from the National's races and, frustrated over the constant setbacks, packed up his horse in mid-December and sent him down the Mississippi to Natchez. Lexington was headed to the Pharsalia, back into the hands of J. B. Pryor.

There, he would prepare to face Time.

When Lexington arrived at Pryor's stables, his forelegs still bore the deep perforations caused by his wild charge through Lloyd's cornfield. He looked as if he had been to war in New York, and his weight had dropped during the nearly three-week journey to

Natchez. The animal looked far from ready to face and defeat an unfaltering constant.

Lexington had to run each of his four miles in under 1:51 ½ to beat Time and come a quarter second under Lecomte's 7:26. Back then, the fastest mile ever run by any horse was 1:45. That was Lexington's estimated time in one of his miles against Lecomte in their last race. But it was a speed he had summoned for just one mile. Having the stamina to maintain 1:51 ½ for each of four miles was entirely different. Even if a horse had the speed and bottom, everything had to work without error. One expert declared, "Lexington's condition must be perfect, and he must be ridden with the greatest skill. The track and the day, too, must be most favorable for making quick time. Should any of these requisites be wanting, the horse will lose, and Time will win."

To prepare Lexington to run against an abstraction, Pryor turned to the tried-and-true method of training him against other fast horses. Ten Broeck, who owned Arrow, withdrew the horse from his racing engagements and committed him solely to workouts with Lexington. Colonel Adam Bingaman, owner of the Pharsalia, also raided his stables and lent his horse Joe Blackburn, who had recently won a two-mile heat race over at the Metairie, and who had also been one of the few horses besides Lexington ever to challenge Lecomte's speed during a race. With Arrow and Joe Blackburn as training companions, Pryor set out to rebuild the tattered horse.

Over several months, Lexington continued to heal and put on much-needed weight. Then, mile after mile, Pryor raced him against one fresh horse after another. Each time, Lexington carried weights far beyond what he would ever be required to carry in a race. He strengthened, not just to run four miles but to run them faster than any horse ever had. Over time, the thundering hooves of Arrow and Joe Blackburn became distant, irrelevant echoes, as Lexington ran on alone, against the chronometer.

Monday, April 2, 1855, the day of the Time match, turned out to be warm and dry. The only sign of any weather was the occasional breeze that swayed the Spanish moss draping the oaks at the Metairie. The previous day's morning paper reported that the racecourse was in excellent order. In reality there was nothing excellent about the track at all. In preparation for the race, Metairie officials had hitched up two oxen to drag a plow across the surface to remove clumped debris, making it marginally more conducive to running. But in the process, too much of the top dressing of sand was removed. Compounding the lack of soft footing was the recent weather. Uncharacteristically for New Orleans, rain had been scarce for over a month. The whole region had shriveled up, parched as a desert plain. New Orleans's meteorological records for the days surrounding the match report a "great want of rain." There was an especially great want over at the Metairie.

With the Metairie's springy track now stone-hard, Ten Broeck and Pryor had to rethink running Lexington at all. Although the current dry ground resulted in a fast track as opposed to a muddy, slow one, the Metairie's extremely hard surface could have the detrimental effect of preventing a horse from fully extending. A horse will guard its run if it feels discomfort or pain. It won't run as fast. Worse, a horse could be injured by running several miles at high speeds over hard ground. Muscles and ligaments could strain, and hooves could crack, compromising the hoof wall surrounding the coffin bone and permanently laming the horse. The track was hardest along the inside rail, which was exactly where a horse should run to make the best time. With no rainwater to moisten the sand, the only means of possibly salvaging the track was to throw down sawdust or shredded pieces of oak bark to add a modicum of moisture. At Ten Broeck's behest, Metairie's officials laid tanbark along the inner rail and hoped for the best.

The New Orleans *Crescent* may have had an inkling that all was not well over at the Metairie. Slapping down a prediction in its morning pages, the *Crescent* wrote, "That which has been done may be done again, but it is not equally clear that the best that has ever been done may be excelled. It will take an extraordinary animal to come to 7:26, and a little more extraordinary one to cut under it." The *Crescent* was only mirroring what others felt. Almost all the bets placed—totaling half a million dollars (about $17 million today)—were against Lexington.

As bets were being cast around New Orleans and the nation, Ten Broeck sat down with his trainer and the race officials for a final meeting. There, Ten Broeck made a mammoth request. Lexington must, he argued, race the way he was trained. Fresh horses should be entered, just as they had been in training, at each of the four miles. This would, he continued, amplify the excitement for the ticket-buying crowd. He then made an even greater request. Lexington should be allowed to begin his run at the distance pole two hundred yards behind the starting line where Time would begin. With ten thousand dollars at stake on behalf of Time, Green and Belcher opposed both requests. The debate reached the stage of fervent finger-pointing and chest-puffing before being extinguished by the judges. No explanation ever found its way to the newspapers, but for whatever reason, they decided to grant both of Ten Broeck's requests. When the public found out, the majority felt that Ten Broeck wasn't out of line. If Lecomte had sprung from one stride to the next to claim his 7:26 victory, all the while with Lexington clipping at his heels, and Henry and Fashion had secured their victories over Time by running against other horses, how unfair was it for Lexington to have flesh-and-blood competition?

Whatever the advantage a running start was intended to give Lexington, his jockey's weight ended up negating it completely. After Lexington's loss to Lecomte, which was due in some respects to his jockey, Henry Meichon, Ten Broeck engaged the top jockey in the country: Gilbert Patrick, who had ridden Alabama's Highlander in the Great State. The man was universally regarded as the best of the best. If a horse was hailed as the next Great One, the public could be assured Gilpatrick had ridden that Great One in many or all of that horse's winning races. His success had given him a celebrity status that made even his most mundane activities interesting to just about everyone. Newspapers circled him like hawks: Gilpatrick is in Canada. . . . He is now in Louisiana. . . . He has turned down an engagement in New York to ride in Virginia. . . . Gilpatrick has broken a collarbone. . . . He has bought a new saddle. . . . He has donated a spur to charity.

Gilpatrick had all the know-how to carry a horse to victory, and in particular he was an excellent judge of pace. Hiring him was equivalent to deducting two or three seconds from a horse's time. Most important, Gilpatrick's character was above reproach.

But on race day, Gilpatrick, saddle in hand, sat down on the scales. Instead of resting at the desired 100 pounds, the hand swung to 103. He had done his best over the last few days of dieting and fasting and sitting for hours in sweltering saunas to bring down his normal weight of 110 pounds, yet he still hadn't lost enough weight to ride Lexington. Every extra pound a racehorse carries costs him theoretically one length: roughly a loss of one to two seconds. In this race, seconds—even *quarter* seconds—mattered, since Lexington had to run each mile in 1:51 ½ to come a quarter-second under Lecomte's 7:26. Gilpatrick had inadvertently added three to six seconds to the horse's work.

By early Monday morning of race day, five thousand people had managed to leave behind their work schedules to spend a few hours at the Metairie.

At three o'clock, as if by some malevolent force, the wind ushered up continual gusts that cut across the track. Lexington would be running into a heavy crosswind on the track's lengthiest stretches.

At half past three, the longshot walked in front of the grandstand followed by his training companions, Arrow and Joe Blackburn. When grooms removed Lexington's blanket, the crowd saw how the horse's form had improved in every way—the curve of his neck, the strength of his shoulders and hips. Lexington stepped forward, assured, head held high. His right eye was completely opaque. The left looked better. Although his true ability to see at that point was never mentioned by Ten Broeck or Pryor, both eyes had been compromised. Yet even though objects appeared to him as hazy and formless, Lexington never startled or swung his hips around quicky to face an uncertain noise. There was no nervous sidestepping, prancing, or fear of what was to come. Just a "consciousness of superiority," the *Picayune* would write. The horse appeared in such splendid condition that people tripped over themselves to make it to the betting ring to right their misjudgments in placing bets for Time. Before the bugle sounded, Lexington had risen as the new favorite at the Metairie's betting tables.

While cash was being flung around at the betting ring, the official timers, Duncan Kenner, William Minor, and Stephen Elliott, climbed the steps leading to the judges' stand, each holding one of the three chronometers that would be used to record Time. Gilpatrick trotted Lexington down the homestretch in the opposite direction of the start. About two hundred yards out, he turned the horse around and pressed his heels in. Lexington lowered his haunches and sprang forward. He reached the judges' stand at a run. The drum tapped and Time started.

As Lexington passed the starting line, Pryor released Joe Blackburn and his jockey. Lexington drew inside the rail, where the ground was hardest. He reached the half-mile post in 0:53. Behind, Joe Blackburn ran at full speed, but so much farther back that his competition was irrelevant. Lexington completed the first mile in 1:47 ¼.

Such an extremely fast pace was too great to maintain over four miles. Gilpatrick sensed as much and pulled back. Thirty yards behind, Joe Blackburn withdrew as Arrow entered. He never got close. Lexington was on his own again, circling the course on the inside rail. But then he started slowing. The tanbark and oak bark had provided little moisture to cushion his hooves from the hard ground. His feet burned and he swung out toward the middle of the track, where the sand was softer, but Gilpatrick pushed his right leg into Lexington, forcing him back to the inside rail. Again, Lexington veered back out toward the middle, and again Gilpatrick pushed him back inside. Lexington completed the second mile in 1:52 ¼.

Arrow kept running into the third mile and closed in on Lexington. Hearing him, Lexington increased his speed and held tight to the inner rail. He passed the third mile mark as the chronometer registered 1:51 ½, making his three-mile run in the fastest time on record, at 5:31.

As Lexington entered the final mile, Joe Blackburn replaced Arrow. Lexington never knew it. By now the ground was unbearable. Lexington made repeated attempts to take the middle of the track. Gilpatrick drew Lexington back inside. And back again. And again. The pushing and pulling, the wasted strides, worked in Time's favor.

Heat began swelling Lexington's feet, and pain spread throughout his hooves and up into his tendons, pressing against them so that it seemed his run might break or falter to an uneven pace. He rounded the final turn and into the homestretch in a time of 6:55. Into the quarter-mile stretch Lexington accelerated and, with Joe Blackburn far behind, crossed the wire to complete the four-mile run.

The chronometers stopped and froze Time.

The crowd was silent. Those in the stands with their own chronometers couldn't believe what they saw. To some, Lexington's run had appeared effortless. His ease of motion and suspended gait, even to the middle of the track on such a hard surface, made the actual battle against Time hard to detect from the stands. Others were unsure if he'd won.

Kenner, the official timekeeper, wrote the result on a piece of paper and handed it to a carrier. The boy ran the paper over to the telegraph room, and the operator dispatched the news up North to Astor House, where the Northern turfmen sat waiting. The telegrapher pinned the result to a bulletin board. From the press room down the hallway, William T. Porter rushed up and squeezed his way through the crowd that was gathered around the board.

Lexington—7:19 ¾.

Lexington had just broken the world speed record. Not only was he six and a quarter seconds faster than Lecomte, he was a quarter second faster than Britain's Matchem, the Godolphin Arabian's grandson, who had held the world record since 1755. It took exactly one hundred years for Lexington to come along and break it.

Covering the 2,122-foot length of the homestretch in 0:24 ¾, Lexington had run the final mile in 1:48 ¾. Although many of the betting populace had just lost their wagers on Time, they realized the magnitude of what had been accomplished. No one could truly have lost in the face of something so extraordinary. At a distance of four miles, Lexington was the fastest horse in the world.

When the result was announced at the Metairie, the crowd's silence was replaced by whoops and hollers. Gilpatrick paraded Lexington along the grandstand. The horse, still energized, stepped out with his buoyant stride, eager and supremely aware. "He could have gone another eight miles," some said. "And maybe at that same clip." Some in the crowd rushed toward him while others stood transfixed by the fantastic aura that always seems to radiate from champions.

Ten Broeck, taciturn even in that moment of greatness, said nothing. Before all the people who had doubted his audacious

proposal, he now stood vindicated. The *Picayune* wrote, "[Ten Broeck's] extraordinary self-reliance, based upon well-directed judgment and sound sense, cannot fail to place him in the estimation of true sportsmen as the leader of the host. He knew he had an animal of unflinching game, coupled with lightning speed, and bravely did his gallant ally respond to his call."

Benjamin Franklin Reinhart's painting of the pioneering Richard Ten Broeck, circa 1863.

After the race, Pryor lifted each of Lexington's burning hooves. In that moment, the force of the stallion's run became apparent. Half of the right side of one of his shoes had been mangled into an unrecognizable form. The other half had snapped off, thrown somewhere onto the hard, dry track. Lexington's left front shoe was missing entirely. His hind shoes were bent out of true. In that era blacksmiths used iron, heavier and stronger than the alloy used today. One news article from the time described a farrier's application of iron horseshoes as "the difficulty and tediousness of the manipulation of materials so unyielding as metallic substances." Yet they had been manipulated here by the horse over four miles.

More remarkable, two of the official timers had clocked Lexington's run at 7:19 ½. But Kenner, the head official, had timed him more conservatively at 7:19 ¾. Some in the crowd clicking their own chronometers timed Lexington at 7:19 ¼. The prevailing belief among older turfmen, the ones who had seen Boston and the other greats, believed Lexington could have run the match in 7:12. According to J. B. Pryor, because of the hard ground, Lexington never reached his full stride.

Late that afternoon, Lexington's figure of 7:19 ¾ was posted in the windows of the various banks and buildings on Royal Street in

New Orleans's business district. Word spread throughout the city like a firestorm. That evening and into the following night, the great celebratory fervor that was and is so uniquely New Orleans's own pulsed through every bar, hotel, and dwelling. Up the French side of Canal Street and down the American side, people toasted with anise-flavored liquor and frothy champagne, recounting the wondrous event. Lexington was not a Creole horse like their beloved Lecomte. But it was New Orleans, they said, that gave the new champion the opportunity, and so he belonged to them.

The Spirit of the Times.

NINE CHEERS FOR LEXINGTON!

7:26 BEATEN!

LEXINGTON WINS HIS $10,000 MATCH *vs.* **TIME IN**

7:19¾!

We had the pleasure on Tuesday last to receive two messages by Telegraph from New Orleans, announcing the astounding fact that Mr. TEN BROECK's *Lexington* (by Boston out of Alice Carneal,) won his Match vs. Time, the [day previous in SEVEN MINUTES, NINETEEN AND *three-quarter* SECONDS!

We quote the first dispatch that reached us, (from F. A. ABBOTT, Esq., who has our grateful acknowledgments for his courtesy) :—

THE GREAT RACE.

NEW ORLEANS, April 2nd.

Lexington won his Match of $20,000 to-day, running four miles against the fastest time ever made, which was by Lecomte, in 7:26.

Lexington won with apparent ease in 7:19¾—beating *Lecomte* six and a quarter seconds!

Our second dispatch gives the time of each mile, which we suppress, as great caution should be exercised in betting on time, as reported by telegraph. It was the remark of the celebrated Duke of Queensbury, that "a bet well laid is half won." Both reports give Lexington's time as 7:19¾.

This headline ran in New York's *Spirit of the Times* following Lexington's win against immortal Time on April 2, 1855.

Best Time ever Made.

Kentucky against the World—Lexington, the Kentucky Racer and Champion, Triumphant—Winner of the great Match against Time—Purse, $20,000—Four Mile Race.

TIME—7.19¾ !

The greatest event in the annals of the turf took place in New Orleans last Sunday, the 1st inst., over the Metairie race-course—the great match of Richard Tenbroek's Kentucky horse,

Newspaper headlines across the nation praised Lexington as the new world champion, like this one from the *Louisville Daily Courier.*

Three days after the race against Time, clouds formed into a dark, dense mass over New Orleans. They opened up to drop more than two inches of rain, drenching the ground at the racecourse, returning the track to its springboard form. The next day, the sun broke through a curtain of gray mist and transformed the Metairie into a lush brilliance.

Two horses had surpassed milestones. One had beaten the American record. The other had defeated the world's. They stood as near equals. For months the newspapers, the turfmen, and the rest of the people had spoken in glorious terms of greatness and pioneering achievements. The nation wanted a rematch. Back in December 1854, several months before Lexington's Time match, General Wells had decided to withdraw his proposed challenge to any horse in the world. Instead, he announced that Lecomte would run on April 14, 1855, in the Metairie's Jockey Club Purse for an inside stake of $2,500. The race was set to take place only twelve days after Lexington's victory over Time. In early March 1855, a couple of weeks before the Time match, the *Spirit* had reported, "Opinion is much divided as to which is the better horse, Lexington or Lecomte, and there is a universal wish . . . to see them meet again. . . . It is imperative on their owners after all the discussion concerning their respective merits to bring them together." Ten Broeck had always been willing to rematch Lexington against Lecomte. On March 31, 1855, two days before Lexington sealed his 7:19 ¾, he entered his horse in the Jockey Club Purse: the same race Lexington had lost to Lecomte a year earlier.

CHAPTER 10

THE WAVING FLAG
OF LEXINGTON

SEVEN DAYS AFTER Lexington beat Time, the Booker Tobacco Company in Lynchburg, Virginia, sent a package to Wills & Rawlins, the smoke shop on Gravier Street in New Orleans. Inside the package was "Lexington"-brand tobacco along with a note from Booker: "Lecomte's Time Beaten." Rawlins put the dried leaves up for sale.

Even in the most indirect ways, everyone wanted to be part of Lexington's victory. They craved that excitement. The radiance, the gloriousness, the uniqueness of the event spread through the streets of New Orleans—down its alleys, into its parlors, past the *marchands* on Esplanade Avenue selling their candied oranges and macaroons, and along Shell Road toward Lake Pontchartrain, flowing outward, entrancing much of the nation.

Although the horse's win had now electrified the populace, Ten Broeck hadn't made it easy for his country to behold its hero. Lexington had been entered to run in the Jockey Club Purse only fourteen days before its actual occurrence, leaving little time for people to make preparations to travel to New Orleans. Still, so much enthusiasm had been generated by the two horses' feats that people did their best to leave behind their daily obligations just to be present in the Crescent City, to see the horses battle for best. Amelia Murray, Queen Victoria's principal servant, who was visiting New Orleans, reserved April 14 specifically for the race. The *Picayune* wrote, "For several days our city has been filling up with visitors from all parts of the country . . . the great attraction being the great four-mile race between Lexington and Lecomte." They filed into New Orleans's grand hotels; attended its opera houses, concert rooms, and theaters; and patronized its coffee houses and all the shops along Chartres and Royal streets. The city began to tick like a metronome in time to the increasing joy and excitement, even more brilliant and glorious than all the colors and frenzy of Mardi Gras. Every moment added to what the *Picayune* called an "unequaled furor," a craze of breathless anticipation about the two-horse race. Every day, people continued to swoop in—despite the rampage of yellow fever that had claimed 2,425 lives in New Orleans in 1854 and was well on its way to passing that number in 1855.

Six days before the rematch, over one hundred thousand visitors had crowded into New Orleans, straining its seams and nearly doubling its population. The vibrant city lit up brighter than ever, operating without sleep. Everywhere people speculated, listened, predicted, read, and speculated some more. They waited for daily bulletins from the two stables, which they read, noted the *Picayune,* "with the same interest and avidity as though they announced the possible change of a dynasty, or the probable fate of a nation."

The *Picayune* reported,

There is not anyone to be met who [does not] talk of the race as if he had a personal interest in it. . . . It is the talk at street corners, on the Rialto where merchants most do congregate, in the private as well as the public circle, by all sorts and conditions of men, women and children. In brief, it is the ruling idea of the hour.

Nothing supersedes or stands beside it. The race, the whole race, and nothing but the race!

The talk came in all forms and from all of society. More Lexington-brand tobacco was shipped, then quickly sold. Every merchant tried to take advantage of the event, no matter how far-fetched the pitch:

> The great race between Lexington and Lecomte is now the main subject of conversation, and while all are anxious to know which is the fastest horse, we must not forget that COLEMAN'S UN-DULATORY MILL is the fastest mill in the world, making better meal and flour, in better time, than has ever been done by any other mill.

Puns abounded. Everything was now "run at a Lexington lick," had a "turn of speed like Lecomte," or "packed weight like Lexington." The excitement mounted to a mania as the day of the race approached.

Meanwhile, the *Picayune* was keeping a close eye on the two horses, reporting that Lecomte was running two-mile workouts on the Metairie with even more speed than he'd shown the previous spring. The *Picayune*'s reporters weren't the only ones standing trackside. English journalist Henry William Herbert leaned against the rail to study the horse's run, and to soak in whatever convictions escaped the mouths of Lecomte's team. "They reasoned," he reported, "that if Lexington could perform a four-mile heat in 7:19 ¾, there was no reason why Lecomte could not also do it, if required." Lecomte wasn't being prepared *merely* to run another four-mile heat race, he was being prepared to beat the fastest horse in the world. Hark worked the horse with unflagging ferocity, pushing him to Time's extreme. He had only two weeks to train such a magnitude of speed into Lecomte.

Over those same short weeks, word on Lexington's progress became nonexistent, despite the newspapers' efforts. Bulletins were no longer dispatched. Reporters were shunned on sight, close friends and allies pushed away. Even those in the know didn't know. The Lexington camp had fallen silent. All of New Orleans, *and* its thousands of continually arriving visitors, were left in the cold. Whatever predictions anyone wanted to make on the bay horse's chances against Lecomte would have to be conjectured from the overflow of unreliable rumors circulating throughout the hotels, churches, and bars. The betting odds didn't matter to Ten Broeck. He would cast his bet for Lexington on whatever terms he felt like. He had told the *Spirit,* "It is to me a matter of imperfect indifference if every man, woman, and child, think Lecomte superior to Lexington. This is not a national question, but a simple discussion concerning the superiority of two horses."

But, of course, it *was* a national question. "All over the sunny South went the word 'Lexington.' Far up into the North, even into parts where the race-horse was not known, traveled the word 'Lexington,'" wrote historian Charles E. Trevathan. Ten Broeck was playing to his audience; his silence only intensified the mystique surrounding his horse.

What Lexington was doing, or not doing, was irrelevant to General Wells. Though it was clear that the rival was capable of twenty-six-second quarter miles, it was not equally apparent that he could run those numbers after so brief a recovery. Lecomte, fresh and healthy, had that advantage.

Then, five days before the race, after several grueling days of training sessions, something happened to Lecomte.

In the early morning hours of Monday, April 9, while most of New Orleans still lay in bed, Lecomte, who had the appetite of a lion—eating up to twelve quarts of grain a day—pawed the ground demanding his breakfast, then ravaged the quart of feed that was poured into his trough. Afterward, Hark draped a heavy exercise blanket around the horse, cinched on a saddle, and hoisted up an exercise rider. Lecomte ran a quarter mile on the Metairie's track in twenty-six seconds. There was nothing at all unusual about anything the horse did that morning.

However, for the rest of the day Lecomte refused to eat, choosing instead to sleep. Hark sent word to General Wells. At four o'clock that afternoon, Wells checked in on his horse, accompanied by his friend William Minor—the prolific writer of turf opinions. Lecomte was drowsy, with cool skin and a heartbeat below the standard thirty-six to forty beats a minute. Whether General Wells or Hark took any remedial measures is unknown.

The next morning, Lecomte ate six quarts of grain for breakfast, then galloped a mile in the afternoon. On Wednesday, April 11, Lecomte continued to eat well and galloped both that morning and that afternoon. The *Picayune* reported that the "celebrated Lecomte" had recovered from whatever had ailed him.

By Thursday, April 12, two days before the rematch, Lecomte ate everything he was given. He ran two miles at a strong gallop and looked as if he could do two more, so General Wells told Hark to send him out again just to "ascertain in what time his horse could run a mile," Minor later wrote to the *Spirit*. Lecomte ran the last mile in 1:50. According to Minor, Lecomte showed no distress after the run. The *Picayune* reported in hyperbolic fashion that Lecomte had run in his workout in a way that "never was approached by any horse upon earth in a run of two miles. . . . Where will the watches stop?"

The Lexington camp had nothing to report.

Despite Lecomte's spectacular recovery and performances, and despite the sparse information on his competitor, Lexington turned out to be the heavy favorite. By April 13, the day before the Jockey Club Purse, betting was so profuse that "there was scarcely anyone who had not made himself a party to the race, by a wager of one or another kind," the *Picayune* reported. Women wagered gloves, bracelets, fans. Thousands of dollars were exchanged and freely promised. Even more people decided to cast bets when the *Picayune* announced that Captain Dollis of the steamship *Ben Franklin* had agreed to delay the ship's departure to Louisville until after the race, so that fans could not only see it but collect their winning bets.

The betting continued unabated, increasing Lexington's odds as the favorite. The general and his friends strolled into a downtown bar and offered 2 to 1 on Lecomte. Their bet went unanswered. Undiscouraged, Wells and his friends kept betting until Lecomte became the favorite. Wells reportedly dug into his pockets time and again until, as the *Picayune* put it, the dollars melted into air. But as soon as Wells and his entourage left, Lecomte's odds fell, and Lexington regained his favored position.

At nine o'clock on the eve of the race, Henry William Herbert shuffled to his bed and blew out his candle. Sleep didn't come quickly. The entire city resounded with race talk and hilarity. The next morning, "I found the excitement in no way decreased, everybody was inquiring about the starting of the trains, or making arrangements with hackmen to take them to the course."

Out on the clogged streets, carriages battled for space. The St. Charles dusted off its nine-passenger stagecoach—sending it out, as it had for the Great State race, packed to its seams with hotel guests. People who hadn't planned ahead faced enormous premiums for any means of thoroughfare, which on this day went for ten dollars or higher. The stiff fee placed many in the dilemma of staying home, walking the crunching five miles up Shell Road, or wedging themselves into the trains. The railroad made multiple trips throughout the day to the Metairie, each time packing its cars beyond regulation capacity. By two o'clock, the last of New Orleans trickled up Shell Road. By three o'clock, the city of two hundred thousand inhabitants and visitors was deserted.

At the Metairie, ticketless racegoers intent on seeing the great horses stood in lines wrapping the track, chiding themselves for not heeding the *Picayune*'s warning six days earlier to purchase tickets immediately. Inside the racecourse, the infield resembled an ill-formed jigsaw puzzle, with carriages parked wherever they could squeeze in. Ticket-holders packed the two public stands, while a few selected guests wore special badges allowing them the exclusive right to stand along the homestretch. Other patrons crowded inside the roped area of the betting ring to place their bets, while the more risk-averse sought out the array of other distractions: Creole dancers swirled, musicians swayed, and caged birds from faraway islands flapped their wings for the crowds. Henry William Herbert described the scene as "a most brilliant spectacle."

Just before three o'clock, grooms draped blankets over Lexington and Lecomte and walked them to the course. As the horses entered, people stood, stretching to peer around ladies' plumed hats. The crowd roared when grooms yanked away the horses' blankets to reveal their readied forms. Herbert wrote, "Even the gamblers in the alleys, underneath the public stands, undoubled their legs from beneath their faro tables, locked up their double card boxes, stopped the snap of their roulette to run upstairs and become innocent lookers on." From her reserved seat up high in the ladies' parlor, England's Hon. Amelia Murray looked upon Lexington as the horses walked the track.

> Though I have often been at English races, I never before saw a horse more graceful, or more beautifully formed, with such apparent gentleness and good temper, and yet with such an air of conscious superiority as this Lexington . . . and his firm, elastic, reaching step in walking, gave one confidence that it would hardly be possible for any other horse to match him. . . . His backbone is remarkably large; fifteen hands three inches high; one eye full and wild, but the right eye less convex, nostrils large; jawbone uncom-

monly wide; shoulder strong and oblique; he has not a long back or long legs, but his action is quite beautiful, so powerful, free and elastic, as if movement was no trouble to him. . . . I don't know that I ever took so much pains to describe a horse before, but really this one was worth the pains.

Even at a distance, as Murray was, the difference of his eyes was easily discernible. Despite his near blindness, his appearance and even his expression were noble. According to Herbert, who saw Lexington standing on the track, the horse displayed a "sedate and intelligent aspect, and looked calmly around, as if he felt that the sensation was quite what he expected and deserved."

General Wells was just as impressed with his own horse's form and shimmering chestnut coat. He stated so to several men hovering around him. The general's friends concurred, saying Lecomte had never looked better.

The sun had warmed the Metairie to an agreeable 78 degrees, and the winds had stilled to a calm. The track, having been restored by the heavy rainfall of April 5, was springy and soft. At long last the bugle sounded. Hark gave Abe Hawkins a leg up on Lecomte. Gilpatrick, who hadn't lost any weight in twelve days, put his foot in the stirrup and heaved himself up on Lexington.

Both horses advanced to the post and were steadied. Anchored by two grooms, Lecomte tossed his head wildly. Lexington stood still. A year had passed since Lecomte had beaten both the constant Time and Lexington in the same race. His rival now stood beside him as the new lodestar by which Time would be forever measured to mark a horse's greatness. The two sons of Boston, both remarkable for extraordinary accomplishments and abilities, stood abreast, in a unique moment. The crowd held its breath and the drum tapped.

Lexington ran inside and into the lead. Lecomte leaped with bounding strides until he caught up. "Around the turn they sped, like twin bullets, not a shade between them," wrote the *Picayune*.

At the first quarter pole Lexington edged farther ahead, his speed governed by Gilpatrick's strong hand. As Lexington held the lead, Hawkins stretched his horse into a fully extended run. Reaching the half mile in 0:53, Lexington held his lead down the backstretch, around the turn, and into the homestretch, still in Gilpatrick's regulating hold. Lecomte ran behind at full blast. Lexington led at the mile pole, with a fast time of 1:49 ½. Running into the second mile, Lexington kept the lead in the backstretch. "The pace was severe and steady," wrote the *Picayune*. Lecomte drove up the backstretch, closing in on Lexington, who shot forward around the turn and down the homestretch, completing the second mile in 1:51. Rounding the turn to begin the next mile, he opened a greater gap between them.

Hawkins sank his spurs into Lecomte. The horse bolted forward but struggled to maintain speed. Ahead, Lexington's hooves pounded into the Metairie's silt. Nostrils flared and wide-eyed, he ran the final turn of the third mile alone, extending, then pulling his strides back in. Coming into the homestretch, Abe pressed his legs into Lecomte once, then pressed again. Lecomte tried to answer his jockey's call, but "when his tail fell, as it did from this time out," wrote Herbert, "I could imagine he felt a sinking of the heart, as he saw streaming before him the waving flag of Lexington, now held straight out in race-horse fashion." Lexington completed the third mile in 1:51.

Entering the fourth mile, Gilpatrick kicked into Lexington, asking him for more. Down the backstretch for the last time, the horse increased his speed "as if running for the very fun of the thing," Herbert noted. Behind, Lecomte kept chopping away but never caught up. Lexington passed the wire in 1:52 ¼, running the four miles in 7:23 ¾—slower than his match against Time, yet two and a quarter seconds faster than Lecomte in his defeat of Time a year before. Refusing to relinquish his bit, Lexington continued to run around the turn, breaking free of Gilpatrick's pull. The horse finally relented halfway around the track.

Lecomte couldn't recover during the forty-five-minute cooling period. He had just run a race that was paced faster than any race he had ever run. General Wells and Minor met with the official judge. After a few minutes of deliberation, Judge Cox addressed the crowd and told them that in order to save the horse's life, Lecomte had been withdrawn.

Fans rushed to encircle Lexington as Gilpatrick guided him through the throng that opened to let him pass. "No one who saw Lexington walk quietly through the cheering crowd doubts that he has sense, memory, and powers of reflection," Herbert wrote. "And yet presumptuous mortals will aver that such an animal has got no soul!"

Lexington ran the race carrying 3 ¾ pounds more than Lecomte. Lexington was by 160 pounds the smaller horse.

Over the days following the race, the foyer of the St. Charles was lined with suitcases of mixed sizes that resembled the uneven jux- taposition of a city skyline. Packed away were all the one-button bottle-green gloves, Parisian hats from Olympe's, palm-leaf- patterned dresses, and flowered indigo vests, the gaiety and vi- brancy of such dress being best reserved for events of extraordinary moment. Maybe they would brighten the Metairie the next year, or somewhere at the other end of the coming decades of drought bookended by unparalleled spectacles. People returned home to England, New York, Kentucky, or wherever they came from dressed in more sedate clothes, taking with them a feeling that would be forever ingrained within them. They had seen great- ness.

Three days after the rematch, Ten Broeck contacted Francis T. Porter of the *Picayune*. The following day, the paper ran the news:

We speak by authority when we announce to the sporting world that the champion Lexington has been taken out of the training

Lexington's purse earnings of $56,600, about $1,724,000 today, accumulated in just seven races, were for that era unheard of as an aggregate for a single horse. Yet, as extraordinary a winner as Lexington was, his greatest achievements lay ahead. In the racing books his name was already immortalized, but paper isn't blood.

CHAPTER 11

THE FALL

GENERAL WELLS WAS bitter, brooding over his horse's lackluster performance while Lexington stood so brilliantly before the world. Gone were the titles and accolades. Even the shine of the medal once awarded to Wells in honor of Lecomte had dulled. The rematch had come at a great cost. Wells had reluctantly agreed to race Lecomte again in the Jockey Club Purse, knowing full well that Lexington would also race; and for what reason? In order to satisfy the nation's desire, he had sacrificed Lecomte so that *Lexington* could shine? He felt like a fool. Anger began to roil in the general's heart until it reached the level of unbridled resentment. Wells had coveted greatness for Lecomte as the nearly unobtainable thing it was, refusing to yield it to another until he was forced into it. But his mind rejected that reality. Instead, he felt there must have been some explanation for his horse's deplorable loss to Lexington. There must have been a reason that Lecomte had been off that one day, five days before the race. Wells's anger started spiraling into a twisted conviction that others had conspired against him.

And so, a month after the race, General Wells voiced his grum-

blings in a letter to his dear friend William J. Minor. Minor had
been one of the judges in Lexington's Time match, and the prolific
turf writer had also watched Lexington run at the Pharsalia on that
fateful day after the corn bingeing. One of the founding members
of the Natchez Jockey Club in 1835, Minor had made a life from
his love of horses. He could rattle off speed records, jockeys'
weights, and racecourse regulations in his sleep. He was well spoken and even better with a pen. Under the nom de plume "A
Young Turfman"—since, after all, he had not yet passed the age of
fifty and was much younger than his horse-racing companions—
he wrote numerous astute articles for the press. His theories on
horsemanship—breeding, bloodlines, and racing—were well researched or based on firsthand knowledge, and readers rarely questioned them.

Wells's grumblings distilled to a belief that Lecomte had been
dosed with a "pizen," or poison, of morphine. There was no per-
suading him otherwise. The general obsessed over the thought of
horse tampering, claiming it as the reason Lecomte fell ill five days
before the race, and why his horse had lost to Lexington. Wells
ascribed the foul play to George Graves—a trainer employed by
Duncan Kenner, who was one of the most respected men in horse
racing and was in fact a close friend of Wells. Wells could offer no
motive as to why Kenner's trainer, who had nothing to do with
either horse, would drug Lecomte. Nor was there any proof.

A few days passed . . . then a couple of weeks. Hearing nothing
from Minor, Wells wrote down his accusations, omitting the part
about Graves, and shot them off to the *Picayune*. In the letter, he
also attacked Lexington.

Wells argued in the pages of the newspaper that Lexington's
Time win was a mockery of all the previous horses who had lowered Time's record. Lexington had won, he claimed, *because* of the
Metairie's concrete-hard track, not in spite of it. But the contention made no sense, and everyone knew it. The day Lexington
raced Time, the track had been in its worst state. In addition to his

proffer that the concrete-hard track had aided Lexington, Wells also astounded the reading public by claiming that, on the day of the Jockey Club Purse, Lecomte had not been in racing condition. Worse, he alleged that Lecomte had been drugged a few days before the race. The *Picayune* responded incredulously, admonishing Wells on his lack of sportsmanship. The *Spirit* reprinted the *Picayune*'s words verbatim.

William Minor eventually responded to Wells's incessant barrage of complaints, dismissing the accusation of dosing. "I can hardly think Graves would do such a thing," he wrote, "especially, as he knew Kenner was betting on Lecomte. When I first told Kenner Lecomte had been dosed, he said he could not believe it for he could not see how it could be done. That he and I had been racing for fifteen or twenty years and we never had a horse dosed." If anything, Minor said, Duncan Kenner and George Graves believed Lecomte was given too much work prior to the race.

Wells brooded some more. He had never fit well within society, often awkward in polite company. And his writing to the *Picayune* making excuses for his horse only further eroded his credibility. Since Lecomte's loss to Lexington, chatter circulated that Wells and Hark were fools to subject Lecomte to merciless overtraining before the race. This response was more than Wells could bear.

He implored Minor to bring the issue of Lecomte's prerace condition to the forefront. Minor was Wells's friend, and he had also seen Lecomte lying lethargically on the ground of his stall on that fifth day before the Jockey Club Purse. He agreed to help outline information to set up the charges in the national press. Minor wrote to Wells,

I shall endeavor to draw that Lecomte was made unsound by drugging, and that he was not knocked off by too much work, as asserted by some. To do this, I wish you to give me a letter and schedule of Lecomte's training at home; the work he took, the quantity he ate, the date of his arrival to New Orleans, the state of

the course when he got there, what work he took on account of
the hardening of the course, the extent of the work he took and
its affect upon him.

More important: "After your Red River friends came down
and bet their money, you decided to bet your money. . . . I wish to
know all about this because I will be asked why you put up your
$2,500 if you thought the horse not all right." Minor added that
he happened to be on the same boat—most likely traveling from
Natchez to New Orleans—as Ten Broeck, who never mentioned
the race at all. For him, it was over.

When Minor later saw Ten Broeck in downtown New Orleans,
he told him, "Wells believes Lecomte was dosed. That's why he
lost to Lexington." Ten Broeck retorted, "That's a lie!"

The scandalous accusation of dosing spread like Southern grassfire.
Supported by the *Spirit* and the *Picayune,* the public doubted the
claim. A correspondent identified as "Kentuck" wrote in the *Spirit,*

> When Lexington was beaten by his rider pulling him up prema-
> turely, did his backers make mockery of it and claim pizen or
> unfairness? No. They let it stand as it was. An accident. As you
> exchange ink with the N.O. Picayune folks, cannot you get them
> to send our trainers some of that "drug," the rumor of which sets
> the odds against a horse, and then palliates a defeat, though en-
> abling him to run with an extra year's weight in 7:23 ¾. . . . I think
> the managers of Lecomte highly blamable to encourage his back-
> ers to up the start of the race when they knew him to be chock
> full of pizen.

Minor sifted through Wells's letters, then coiled for the attack.
In a letter to the *Spirit,* he argued that Lexington's 7:19 ¾ should
be increased a full twelve seconds because of his running start—

a start that Minor would later concede only gave Lexington at most a two-second advantage.

Replying to Minor's letter, the *Spirit* reminded readers that Minor was one of the three official timekeepers of Lexington's Time match and clocked the horse at 7:19 ½, *not* 7:19 ¾. Yet he said nothing then of any advantages of the hard track or Lexington's running start. Nor did Minor say anything about the track's springy, soft condition when, twelve days later, Lexington beat Lecomte in the Time of 7:23 ¾, nearly three seconds faster than Lecomte's record of 7:26. No running start. No fast track.

The *Picayune* was even less forgiving and wanted to know what was driving all this anger.

General Wells had since shifted his dosing suspicion from Duncan Kenner's trainer, George Graves, to Lecomte's jockey, Abe Hawkins. Wells wrote to Minor, who wrote back in vain, trying to temper his friend's paranoia. Minor cautioned, "What I am now going to state I wish you to consider *strictly confidential*." Graves had paid Minor a visit and told him that he had heard rumors that Wells believed Hawkins had dosed Lecomte. Graves told Minor that there was no reason the jockey would cause his horse to lose. Minor responded, "Wells believes Abe betted against Lecomte." As proof, Minor told Graves that after the race, Hawkins had waved a hundred-dollar bill around while on the steamboat.

Graves told Minor that Hawkins had no money other than the fee Wells paid him for riding Lecomte. He pointedly declared that Lecomte wasn't dosed, but that instead, the horse had been overworked. Minor had heard that assessment before. During the week in question, he had been told that Wells was working Lecomte to death. But Minor had defended Lecomte's training schedule, claiming that the horse could stand as much work as a team of mules. Graves continued on with Minor, arguing that if the horse had been drugged, the likely culprit was Hark, or any of a number of men who were seen entering and exiting the stables to play cards with him on the day the horse fell ill. On his way out the door, Graves told Minor, "Wells has no right to a fine jockey like Abe."

In a final moment of candor, Minor wrote to Wells that he had asked Lecomte's stable grooms about Hawkins. They corroborated the jockey's innocence. Yet, in spite of all this evidence to the contrary, Minor stood by the general.

Hawkins was a scapegoat. He was the wrong color and was "owned" by another man, unable to even earn an honest dollar without the insinuation that he had made it the wrong way. He had earned a profession through skill. That part came easy: the feel of horses, the knowing of when to ask, how much to hold back, and how much power was still there. The harder part was climbing out from under the suffocating reality of the identity to which he had been born. He was a man with a title, most assuredly—just like some men were called respectable things like "colonel" or "sir." But his title—that word, "slave"—was too heavy for any man. So he wore a solemn expression, as if everything he had seen and lived had sunk his soul to an unfathomable depth. But climb he did. He had a sense of loyalty and deference, which he backed with ability and an incisive mind. To those men he rode for, Hawkins was the paradigm of trustworthiness, a jockey in whom they could put their faith. So much so that he was awarded the best horses to ride and was paid accordingly, a man who could provide a coveted skill to a select group of men whose success depended on his know-how. Hawkins had no reason to delve into bribery or ill deeds—to intentionally sink himself back down into that blackened hole—for money he could easily earn the next day on the back of a horse. Wells's suspicion was misplaced. Graves knew it, and so did everyone else. Assessing the truth in his own heart, Minor must have known it too.

Nevertheless, seven months after the match race, in November 1855, Minor set out to prove General Wells's conviction that his horse had been drugged. Although Lecomte was lethargic on April 9 and 10, by the 13th, the day before the race, he had eaten all his feed and looked in perfect health. Even Wells had conceded to the public that because of lethargy, Lecomte had missed one training gallop at most. Recovery aside, Minor contended that at race time, when his blankets were stripped off, Lecomte was sweating profusely and trembling on all legs. Still, Wells, having seen his horse's shaky condition, didn't withdraw him. Minor wrote to the *Spirit,* "We are now quite sure, Mr. Editor, that Gen. Wells and his experienced friends committed a great error of judgment in starting Lecomte in doubtful condition against such a horse as Lexington." He added, "Now, with due deference, we submit that a horse that was decidedly off on Tuesday the 10th, could not be in condition to run on Saturday the 14th, let the *friends* of Lecomte and the *Picayune* say what they want. For that paper has asserted that the *friends* of Lecomte admitted on his starting that his condition was unexceptionable." As for Wells's betting $2,500 on Lecomte, "where his friends are, there Genl. Wells always is, to save or to suffer." From these accounts, "Mr. Editor . . . we are forced to believe that, in some way, a large dose of morphine was administered to Lecomte late on Sunday night, or early on the morning of the 9th of April, 1855."

Absent was any reference to Hawkins. Nor was there any inference as to which person or persons might have done the alleged drugging. Neither did Minor offer a motive. His vague conclusion established nothing, and eventually the matter dwindled. Still, the accusation left a cloud over Lexington's wins.

Eight months after Lecomte's loss to Lexington, the five-year-old stallion Arrow dug in and beat Lecomte in a three-mile heat race on the Metairie. Wells, through Minor, wrote the *Picayune* and *Spirit* accusing the Metairie Jockey Club of deliberately causing Lecomte's defeat. James Valentine, secretary of the Metairie, wrote in reply: "The idea of ploughing the track to give Arrow an advantage over Lecomte is the coinage of a silly brain." The day that

Lecomte competed against Arrow, the track had been in perfect condition and Wells had made no complaints.

Ten Broeck had always thought highly of Lecomte, naturally considering him the horse most comparable to Lexington. Despite the rancor, as he assembled his stable for England, he approached Wells about a purchase. Wells, in a surprising move, tossed his horse aside with apparent ease, selling Lecomte to Ten Broeck for $12,500. Ten Broeck dug deeper into his pockets and also bought from Wells a leggy, dark bay filly whom he renamed Prioress.

Wells had named her Poison.

PART II

CHAPTER 12

THE KING'S HORSES

ENGLAND CREATED THE Thoroughbred horse over the span of centuries. Strongly supported by royal edicts, it was a calculated experiment that had been undertaken solely to improve the breed. King Henry VIII had a penchant for field sports and desired a horse more refined and agile than the large, thick-limbed steeds occupying his stables. Around the same time, Francesco II Gonzaga, an Italian aristocrat, began importing Barbary horses from North Africa and breeding them at his farm in Mantua. As a diplomatic gesture, Gonzaga gave several of them to Henry, who rode the Barbs and, as history tells it, fell in love with the breed. He began importing more Barbs from Italy.

Along with the Barbs, the wonderfully agile Andalusian jennets from Cordova, Spain, were also bestowed upon Henry, so that soon, Barbs and Andalusians overflowed the King's Kent and Hampton stables. The surplus was stashed in stables spread throughout his kingdom, which became known as the royal studs. Yet, though the Barbs and Andalusians were refined and adroit, they lacked endurance.

After King Henry, British royals continued to improve the breed by creating a specialized post termed "master of the horse." The posts were filled by noblemen from all over the British Empire who were knowledgeable about equine breeds and what it would take to better Britain's horses. The masters were sent to scour foreign lands for horses that could add speed and heart to Britain's emerging breed. But the imports didn't rest solely with the masters.

Lexington's sire line, as noted earlier, ends with the Byerley Turk, a horse that Captain Byerley had imported to England in 1690. There, the horse was bred with the mares in the royal studs. Then twelve years later, in 1702, Thomas Darley, serving as counsel to Queen Anne in modern-day Syria, shipped an Arabian horse from Aleppo to his father in East Yorkshire, and Francis, the second Earl of Godolphin, did the same with his Arabian horse in 1727. The Byerley Turk and the Darley and Godolphin Arabians, along with numerous other horses from the Arabian Peninsula and the Barbary Coast, provided the heart and endurance—the *bottom*—that now courses rampant through these "thoroughly blooded" animals.

Although the British royals initiated the drive to improve the quality of horses they rode, they were amenable to sharing their animals with the not-so-royal—provided they could pay the price. And so the royal studs began offering annual sales of their yearlings. Not only were these colts bred from the new blood crossings, they were raised with no expenses spared. Horsemen who bought them were also men of wealth—lords, dukes, marquises, and other notables—who likewise continued the colts' top-quality conditioning. They purchased the best lot to run races sponsored by the monarch, called king's plates—four-mile races offering the winners great sums of money. The incentive behind the plates was to encourage breeding distribution, lifting the burden from the royals and onto those wealthy families who cared enough to keep advancing the blood horse.

But with breeding distribution came the need for regulations.

Initially, British horsemen had no self-regulated body to act in the interest of horses and themselves. The government of racing fell into Parliament's dominion until horsemen were able to form their own governing body. The Jockey Club, founded in 1750 and headquartered at Newmarket, was comprised of members elected from Britain's growing class of racehorse men. They wrote rules and regulations, supervised them, and, if necessary, issued judicial verdicts along with penalties.

Along with establishing rules to govern racing, British horsemen regulated Thoroughbred breeding, distilling it to a system of exact and proven blood crosses. Details about matings, offspring, and the pedigrees of all involved were meticulously recorded in the royal stud books and, in 1791, consolidated in an official stud book under the auspices of James Weatherby, secretary of the Jockey Club.

Weatherby's *General Stud Book* reads like the painstakingly detailed investigation it undoubtedly was. The job for Weatherby was to sort out an altogether confusing assemblage of similarities piled upon other similarities, which was particularly difficult when it came to the horses' names. There was Snip, son of Snap, along with Hornet sired by Matchem, Hornet sired by Blank, and Hornet sired by Drone. There was also a Highflyer and a Young Highflyer as well as a Hip by the Curwen Barb, a Hip by Childers, a Hip by Herod, a Hippo, a Hippogriff, and so on with various spin-offs of Hip. The English mares weren't spared either, with names that often reflected the misogyny of the era. The Bloody Buttocks mare existed on Weatherby's pages, along with a Slut mare (who in fact was a high-bred mare and mated with only a small number of horses!), the Snake mare, twelve different Snap mares, *only* three Snip mares, four Squirrel mares, and finally, a Young Hag.

With the aid of Weatherby's book, the benefits of certain blood crossings became more apparent, and the decisions as to who should be bred to whom more carefully thought out. Among the highly successful results were horses such as the record-breaking speed horses Flying Childers, son of the Darley Arabian, and Matchem, grandson of the Godolphin. There were also Eclipse, Regulus, and Fearnought. All these eighteenth-century horses ran incredible distances in king's plates while carrying heavy weights. Regulus, a chestnut son of the Godolphin Arabian, won eight king's plates before retiring undefeated.

By 1780, the king's plates at which Regulus so excelled started to fall into disfavor as an antiquated test of horses. Races were cut down to one-mile and sometimes two-mile "dashes" called derbies and oaks. Although plate racing continued, lucrative purses sponsored by racecourses and often paid for by subscribers—those men who paid a fee to enter a race—were withdrawn from the distance races and put toward the single-mile sweepstakes instead. British horsemen followed the money.

By the early nineteenth century, racecourses like Newmarket offered four-mile races only once or twice a year and were hard-pressed to fill those. Although the British still raced horses under high weights, from 120 to 140 pounds, the concept of *bottom* was approaching irrelevancy. "The most important quality in a horse is speed," one forward-thinking American noted, "for those who say bottom, they are greatly erred. . . . The 'plate' horses in England have almost uniformly failed as stallions. A good stallion needs speed. Bottomed horses are slow." To meet the increasing demand for speed, the British breeding studs began to alter their focus, eroding bottom in the process.

By the mid- to late nineteenth century, this change of emphasis had had a reverberating impact on horse breeding in general. In 1873, the respected English turfman Admiral Henry Rous testified before a parliamentary Lords committee on the deterioration of racehorses:

> My firm belief is that there are not four horses in England now
> that could run over the Beacon four-mile course at Newmarket
> within eight minutes, which in my younger days I used to see

constantly done. You can hardly persuade gentlemen to run four miles, because they can win large sums in running shorter races, and their horses can come out oftener. I am afraid that it is more a question of winning money than it used to be eighty years ago, when there were a vast number of persons who took a great pride in breeding horses of a different stamp. I dare say that at Goodwood for the past ten years there have not been more than three horses entered for the Queen's Plates [four miles], and these have walked half the distance.

Along with the deterioration of bottom, another issue had arisen. There was a growing awareness that all horses should no longer compete together. Some simply outperformed their competition. Whether the losing horses were short on bottom or speed was debated, but to the extent it was bottom, reintroducing stamina through the breeding process seemed a task as impossible as "reproducing long whist in good society," as equine historian Samuel Sidney jested. British racing was becoming a matter of "I'll take my ball and go home." Owners of these inferior horses didn't want to race unless they actually stood a chance. They also wanted to compete in the big payday races.

To satisfy everyone, in 1851, the year after Lexington was foaled, the Jockey Club contrived a new system of handicapping races. Now an assigned handicapper, usually a horseman of some repute and knowledge, adjusted the weights to be carried by each horse to make it more equal to the rest of the field. As one correspondent explained it, "Horses carry weight according to their adjudged racing ability. Thus, by giving or taking weight, horses of every grade or character and worth are placed as nearly as may be on an equality in their principal sweepstakes, and also in their most important matches."

Consequently, the best horses were always handicapped to a disadvantage. The unintended result was that the ones that kept on winning would eventually become so handicapped they would lose, thus ending a potentially lengthy career. As one horseman wrote in the *American Turf Register* in 1838, handicapping "unfairly taxes the qualities of a good horse and lessens his real value." Admiral Rous agreed, saying the system was "too unjust and unpredictable and any horse with a semblance of a pedigree can run against a true racehorse." Many felt handicapping to be yet another form of deteriorating the *bottom* the British had sought to instill over centuries.

In America, early Thoroughbred breeding was much less planned out. About twenty years before the Jockey Club was formed at England's Newmarket, Sir William Gooch, governor of Virginia, began to enforce the Tobacco Inspection Act of 1730, which had the anticipated consequence of draping Virginia in prosperity. The act required tobacco to be inspected before it was shipped abroad. The result was a high-quality product in limited supply. Tobacco prices soared. Now, wealthy Virginia farmers who coveted Britain's blood horses could afford to buy them and ship them to America.

Also in 1730, Bulle Rock, a descendant of both the Darley Arabian and the Byerley Turk, was imported by Samuel Gist into Virginia. The fantasy of owning a Matchem or a Regulus was suddenly a reality for a handful of privileged Americans. Bulle Rock was followed by Jolly Roger, Morton's Traveller, and so many others that by the 1750s, British Thoroughbred blood was well established and thriving in Virginia.

Owning a Thoroughbred was a coming-of-age for American horsemen, a "badge of civilization," noted Virginia historian Fairfax Harrison. Americans now put themselves on equal footing with the British by importing *their* blood horses. But it wasn't just about owning blooded stock. The bigger part of the honor was maintaining it, preserving that blood that the British had spent countless years scrutinizing, testing, and bettering. It meant breeding the blood horse properly and not diluting the blood with lesser stock—blood that wasn't thoroughly bred. It meant breeding only to horses and mares that could be traced, on both paternal and maternal lines, back to a British blooded animal. Even more, it meant continuing to improve the breed just as Henry VIII had.

Early Virginia families understood the importance of blood—well enough to pay plenty to import it. Yet they needed good lineage for reasons other than racing. Virginians intended not only to improve the blood horse but to breed the Thoroughbred to their common horses too.

Among these first Thoroughbreds that arrived on Virginia's shores, two stand out as crucial to the development of the American bloodstock, and particularly in the lineage of Lexington. The first was purchased by John Baylor, a Virginian educated in England and son of a wealthy tobacco exporter. In addition to his education, Baylor became schooled in the British traditions of horse racing at the Newmarket Racecourse, and in the history of blooded horses. When he returned to Virginia, he inherited his father's wealth and named his plantation Newmarket. He then applied his shrewd understanding of bloodstock to enhance his own net worth.

In 1764, Baylor sent a letter to John Backhouse, his bloodstock agent in Liverpool. Baylor wanted Backhouse to secure for him

a most beauti'l strong bay at least 14.3 hands high, as much higher as possible, provided he has beauty, strength and spi't with it, and one that has won some King's plates with a pedigree at full length and cert. of age under a nobleman's hand, as most of the list belong to noble'n.

Baylor wrote separately to Thomas Hales, a horseman who was to advise Backhouse: "I should be sorry to see any but a Kgs. Plater come as I am in want of strength for our small Virginia mares." He then listed twenty horses he felt satisfied his exacting specifications. Number nine on the list was Fearnought.

A striking deep bay, Fearnought was fifteen hands, three inches high. Foaled in 1755, he was sired by the aforementioned eight-time king's plate winner, Regulus, the undefeated son of the Godolphin. Consistent with Baylor's request, Fearnought had won three king's plates in 1761 and two other races in 1762, carrying the high weight of 143 pounds. In 1764, as close as we can tell, Fearnought arrived at Baylor's Virginia stud.

Baylor bred Fearnought with the "small Virginia mares," mares who more than likely weren't pedigreed Thoroughbreds. The resulting offspring were considered "half-breds": dilutions of the pure blood. Fearnought provided a fortunate infusion of stamina to the common Virginia horse but was a damning stain on the American-bred blood horse's credentials. Britain would later hold over Americans questions of the quality and authenticity of this "lesser" stock.

Despite Fearnought's dalliances with nonpedigreed mares, he was also put to imported blood mares who fit the bill. Through him and the imported mares, Britain's racing stock made significant inroads in America. Fairfax Harrison praised Fearnought's exceptional contribution:

> Fearnought holds the first claim prior to the day of Medley, and is therefore entitled to the palm in preference to any stallion that had preceded him in giving the Virginia turf stock a standing equal to that of any running stock in the world. The blood which flowed in the veins of old Fearnought must have been peculiarly rich in those qualities that make up the conformation of the race horse, as not only the whole stock got by Fearnought ran well, but also his sons and his grandsons were remarkable for generally getting good running stock. There was also strength and stamina universally pervading the Fearnought stock, to which may be added good size, that made them the best distance horses of their day. The fact is that the Fearnoughts ran well at all distances, and the old horse stood higher than any other horse on the continent for

getting racers; and he got more of them than any other—he also was the sire of more fine stallions than any other horse of his day.

A few miles from Fredericksburg in northern Virginia stood a plantation founded by a colorful ex-military Englander named Alexander Spotswood, who reportedly was once shot in battle with a four-pound cannonball and survived. On February 8, 1710, Queen Anne commissioned Alexander as lieutenant governor of Virginia. For the next twelve years, he served in that capacity while also building the state's first ironworks, a highly profitable business in which his son John continued.

Like most prosperous Virginians, John Spotswood became interested in the British blood horse. In 1757, he began importing Thoroughbreds from Britain—notably, a mare named Diana I, also known as the Cullen Arabian mare, who was the second foundational import supplying the Thoroughbred blood to Lexington's lineage.

While Spotswood was busy importing British mares, another plantation, Chatham Manor, arose on the eastern shore of Virginia's Rappahannock River. Owned by William Fitzhugh, a longtime friend to George Washington, Chatham had housed the future president on many occasions. Washington once wrote to Fitzhugh, "I have put my legs oftener under your mahogany at Chatham, and have enjoyed your good dinners, good wine and good company more than any other." Washington, likely through Fitzhugh, was somewhat of a fixture on the American racing scene, even becoming one of the managers of the Alexandria Course.

Fitzhugh purchased Diana I from John Spotswood and bred her to Fearnought to produce Diana II—beginning a line that would eventually lead to Lexington's dam, Alice Carneal. Fitzhugh's acquisition of Diana I, and his breeding of her to produce Diana II, set off a decades-long breeding and ownership of Dianas—five in all.

While the Virginians made headway importing the blood horse

and had made an effort to breed blood to blood, they lacked a recording system that would provide authenticity to the American
Thoroughbred. There was no reliable way to know if the resulting
cross was in fact thoroughly bred. Although some matings were no
doubt recorded in private stud books—now lost to history—the
majority of breed-crossing knowledge existed simply by oral tradition. It was a system subject to dishonesty, embellishment, and just
plain error. In 1819, in an attempt to provide a recording method,
the American attorney John S. Skinner began publishing pedigrees of Thoroughbreds in his periodical *The American Farmer*. But
as its name implied, the magazine was primarily devoted to agri-
culture. The multiple uses of the rutabaga plant tended to grab
the headlines in that journal, so in 1829, Skinner began publishing a separate magazine titled *American Turf Register and Sporting
Magazine*—devoted almost entirely to the blood horse.

Despite Skinner's good intentions, most of the pedigrees he
published were based on earlier, often faulty oral tradition or on
advertisements not checked for accuracy. J. H. Wallace, who compiled his own stud book in 1867, wrote that Skinner's *American
Turf Register* contained pedigrees that were "very badly expressed,
and some of them ingeniously arranged to cover defects; and it is
to be greatly regretted that Mr. Skinner did not give more attention to this department of his magazine, as it appears to have been
his custom to publish whatever was sent him in the shape of a
pedigree, and just as it was sent." Given this lack of accountability,
imaginative horsemen could and often did borrow from the lineage history of famed stallions or mares to enhance the pedigrees
of their own horses.

Many of the pedigrees that appeared in Skinner's publications
were submitted by Patrick Nisbett Edgar. Edgar was a friend of
many American breeders and had accumulated a great amount of
oral testimony. In 1833, he published volume one of *The American
Race-Turf Register, Sportsman's Herald, and General Stud Book*. He
never published the second volume, the one about mares, thanks

to financial disputes and his irascible temperament. Believing no one appreciated his work, he burned all the material that would have comprised the second volume, forever extinguishing information that may have proved conclusive for many questionable pedigrees. Pride and arrogance weren't his only flaws. He also showed unquestioning favoritism to his friends and damning condemnation of his enemies. Consequently, many of the pedigrees that he published were incorrect, prejudiced, or fantastical.

Because of this lackadaisical method of documentation, the British, as well as a few Americans, denigrated many of the Virginia-bred horses as "cocktails" or inferior half-breds. This view of the American horse, however, wasn't altogether just. Although the British had engendered the Thoroughbred meticulously and for the purpose of improving the stock, they too had crossed that new breed with lesser ones, and indeed their own half-breds raced. The difference was that only horses pedigreed as Thoroughbreds could race as such in Britain; half-breds were restricted to separate events. American racing wasn't so specific. At least not yet.

In defense of their respective countries' breeding efforts, Britain and America began a decades-long debate over who bred the better horse. Every horseman or equine antiquarian, it seemed, had an opinion and was eager to share it with the entire sporting world. What it all distilled down to for Americans was *bottom* versus speed. They maintained that going the distance was the only way to test a horse; they viewed those eighteenth-century dashes of one and two miles run at Newmarket as ridiculous little races. Child's play. Since the British had eroded bottom in breeding, there was no way their horses could now compete in any semblance of a heat race. Americans viewed this deficit as a kind of character flaw—as a lack of the heart and spirit that were so deeply ingrained in their own national identity. But though British horses ran shorter-distance races, they carried about thirty pounds more than American horses. If there was any question of bottom, the British believed it was satisfied by weight. American horses could run farther, but carrying only a feather's weight.

The matter of weights raised another debate about the British handicapping system. In America, horses ran carrying weights designated by their age, and in distances according to ability. Not every horse could run a four-mile heat race. Some only ran two-mile heats or even shorter distances. That caliber of horse would never run against the likes of Lexington and Lecomte. And, according to American horsemen, there was no reason to handicap a great horse like Lexington. Let him run against horses of like quality; distance and time would sort out the better. Handicapping detracted from the merits of a horse and made racing more of a jockey's game.

The fact that Americans clung to bottom as the sine qua non of a good horse justified their homebred version of the Thoroughbred. Questionable lineage aside, American racehorses looked like Thoroughbreds and ran like them. Test enough was the four-mile heat system—a bottom-breaker type of racing derived from the king's plates. No horse could endure that type of extremely strenuous repetition unless it originated from the stamina-based crossings once practiced by the British. While Americans lacked an accurate recording system, they were nonetheless racing the best of the breed.

Yet, though American horses ran like Thoroughbreds, credibility still mattered. Without it, the young country's Thoroughbreds would continue to be a lesser breed in the world's eyes. The only way to obtain this integrity was by maintaining meticulous standards and written documentation—and by continuing to breed horses that ran as fast and as well as British Thoroughbreds. In the more than one hundred years since 1730, when the British horse had first been imported to Virginia, America had failed to develop the sort of exactitude that authenticated a breed.

But all that was about to change.

CHAPTER 13

ROBERT ALEXANDER'S PURCHASE

IN 1856, RICHARD Ten Broeck landed in Liverpool, England, to race Lecomte, Prioress, and another horse named Pryor against the British speed horse. From the first time he walked along the cobblestone streets, the American turfman fascinated Britain's racing elite. This was due largely to his introduction to one of the country's most esteemed members of racing, Lord William Wentworth-FitzWilliam, the sixth Earl FitzWilliam. In a short time, dukes and lords were elbow-jamming their way to the front of ballrooms to gain Ten Broeck's attention. The Duke and Duchess of Badminton hosted a party for him, and the Earl of Derby raised a toast at a Jockey Club dinner to Ten Broeck's health and success. There was scarcely a social soirée that didn't include his name on its roll call of attendees. In England, Ten Broeck was making much more of a splash than he ever did in America.

While navigating Britain's long-established and complex world of racing, Ten Broeck met a man from America who, like himself, was in the United Kingdom because of horses. Robert Aitcheson Alexander was searching for an extraordinary animal and thought he might find one there. They crossed paths at the Goodwood Racecourse in Chichester, near England's southern coast.

While Ten Broeck needed no introduction to any American horseman and was quickly gaining approval with the British, Alexander was an unknown. His name had been published once or twice in an obscure part of the *Spirit of the Times* reserved for news about cattle breeding and other agricultural particulars compressed into narrow columns next to advertisements—hardly the big-bannered racehorse promotions about Ten Broeck and Lexington. But Alexander was in England with a plan, which he and his friend Nelson Dudley proudly outlined for their new acquaintance.

Alexander owned close to 3,200 acres of Kentucky bluegrass in Midway, which his father had named Woodburn Farm. Alexander knew next to nothing about racing but had spent a good deal of time learning about Thoroughbred pedigrees and breeding. He dreamed of turning Woodburn into a farm styled after the British method of authenticated pedigrees, annual auction sales, and a deliberate system of mating the best mares and stallions. Nothing like that yet existed in America. Setting up a breeding operation and offering the result to the buying public at large would be no small task. He needed a stallion with a strong pedigree. He had already bought an unraced English stallion named Scythian but was looking for another. He asked Ten Broeck if Lexington was for sale.

Ten Broeck must have thought the idea bravely presumptuous. And seeking to involve Lexington, no less! It was just the type of risk-taking and boundary-pushing he would have done had breeding been his greater interest. Undoubtedly, he felt an appreciation for the kindred soul standing before him, but that was about as far as he was willing to concede. Ten Broeck told Alexander that he had never considered selling Lexington. He was perfectly content to allow the horse to graze his days away in Kentucky's lush and fertile fields. In fact, the stallion was there now, servicing a few mares at General Abe Buford's Bosque Bonita Farm—coincidentally, the neighboring farm to Woodburn—and enjoying his well-earned life of leisurely retirement. General Buford, a connoisseur of horses who had been one of the Kentucky men on Lexington's Great State team, had chosen Ten Broeck's bay as the best stallion in Kentucky—a fact that was surely dropped into his owner's conversation with Alexander.

Ten Broeck went on. Lexington was now so valuable as a celebrity horse that he was worth more than any racehorse in America or even Great Britain. Alexander could become Lexington's new owner for $15,000: a high price, most assuredly, but Lexington wasn't just *any* horse. He was the most extraordinary horse in the world. Ten Broeck named his price without as much as a sideways glance. Alexander thanked him for his time and walked away.

Although a nationally adored champion and the favorite of General Buford, Lexington was an unproven stallion. Since he had been retired less than a year, any foals he'd sired were so young they hadn't been raced. Lexington might be a reasonable risk for a *small* sum, but not the absurd asking price of $15,000. No one had ever paid that much for an American racehorse, let alone a sire who had yet to produce a winner. Alexander had just paid $800 for the blue-blooded Scythian.* And Ten Broeck had bought Lecomte, still regarded by some turfmen as a better racehorse than Lexington, for $12,500. Lexington's price was high, but after their meeting at the Goodwood races, Nelson Dudley urged Alexander to think again.

Robert Aitcheson Alexander—R.A. to just about everyone—was a wisp of a man who looked as if he might be taken away by a gust of wind. Since childhood he had suffered ailments that, over time, had weakened him. He was unimposing—so small and frail—and ghostly pale. Like Ten Broeck's, his standout feature was his deep

---

* Historical sources differ on the price Alexander paid for Scythian, an untrained and unraced Thoroughbred. According to some, he paid $7,500, but in a letter from Alexander to his brother, he estimated the price in American dollars to be $700 to $800.

blue eyes, but R.A.'s were a good deal warmer. Alexander often dressed simply and in black, with a felt hat pushed high up on his forehead. One observer said he resembled a Quaker. He was as honest as one too, his handshake being sufficient to bind his word.

Much like Ten Broeck, Alexander came from a long line of prestigious ancestors. He was the namesake son of a British citizen whose lineage traced to parliamentary members and a lord provost of Edinburgh. Robert—R.A.'s father—had graduated from Cambridge with a law degree, then donned a white wig and black robe to practice as a London barrister. His astute mind and cultural refinement, as well as his family's Anglo-French connections tracing back to Louis XVI, paved the young lawyer's way to a meeting with Benjamin Franklin, who, in 1776, was in Paris to gain support for American independence. Franklin chose Robert to serve as his personal secretary throughout his nine years of diplomacy on America's behalf, including his negotiation of the 1783 Treaty of Paris, which ended the Revolutionary War. When Franklin left France to return to America, Robert followed, eventually purchasing two thousand acres of wooded land in Woodford County, Kentucky. Because the land bordered Elkhorn Creek, Robert named his acreage Woodburn—Scottish for "wood creek." Far back among Woodburn's rolling hills, he built a modest log-and-stone house and moved there.

Robert then set out to distinguish himself among Kentuckians by serving a lengthy stint as director of the Bank of Kentucky while moonlighting as a member of the Kentucky Legislature in Frankfort. It was there that he met and married Elizabeth Richardson Weisinger, the daughter of an inn-and-tavern proprietor. On October 25, 1819, Robert Aitcheson Alexander was born.

Young R.A. lived the early years of his life at Woodburn in what was to him a sublime existence—bantering with siblings, cradled by his mother's love and acceptance of him for all that he was, for he was hardly robust. R.A. fatigued often and never had the physical abilities of other boys his age. There was always that awareness within him—that he didn't measure up all the way. Despite his poor health and his love of home, R.A.'s uncle, Sir William Alexander, a Parliament member knighted by King George III, had summoned him to England. Great things were expected of him, and to bear it all with stability and humility, R.A. would require the same grooming that had been bestowed upon his father.

When R.A. turned eighteen, Robert told him to pack his bags. He was headed to Scotland to visit Sir William. Robert handed his son a letter, sealed tight by melted wax, and told him to deliver it to his uncle. Then Robert accompanied R.A. from their humble home to the nearby train depot to say goodbye.

In New York, R.A. shuttled from the train to a ship bound for Scotland, where a stranger met him at the port and took him to Sir William's home, Airdrie House—a castle-like expanse of cold gray stone. Once inside, R.A. was led to a large room to meet his father's brother. R.A. handed him the letter, which Sir William took and sat down to read in silence. At William's request, his brother had sent him an heir. William told R.A. that Airdrie was his new home, and he was escorted to a chilly room that would become his for the next several years. He took out a piece of paper that very afternoon and wrote a letter to his father.

It would be the first of many that went unanswered. Robert merely collected them and stowed them away. He never discarded them but, for whatever reason, deemed them not suitable for response. Sir William even admonished his brother, the eloquent and able scribe of Benjamin Franklin, "to shake off in favor of your son, your habitual indolence in writing. It is material to him to be engaged in frequent correspondence and you cannot expect it from him unless you set him the example."

Still, nothing came.

Sir William became fond of R.A. and, over time, filled the fatherly role vacated by Robert. Everything regarding R.A. became his uncle's driving concern. Especially the boy's health. Worried that R.A. wouldn't be able to pursue the rigors of a secondary education, his uncle packed him off to London to visit a round-table of notable physicians. But after days of physical examinations, the doctors scratched their heads and prescribed a concoction of medicines and a summer of sea bathing. Nothing helped.

As if R.A.'s poor health wasn't enough, Sir William took to saving the boy's soul, writing to Robert that he was incredulous that his son hadn't been baptized according to their Protestant faith. Having provided the boy what spiritual guidance and medical care he could, Sir William eventually enrolled him in a London boarding school, while also initiating him into the intricacies of English society. Uplifted by his uncle's fatherly influence and interest, R.A.'s spirits improved, but he remained frail. He was always bent over somewhere at his spine, as if the upper half of his body were incorrectly hinged to the lower.*

The reason for all the refinement, soul saving, and education was Airdrie. The Alexanders had built Airdrie House in the small town of Airdrie, thirty-five miles west of Edinburgh. There, R.A.'s ancestors had constructed a lucrative ironworks foundry. Because Sir William was childless, R.A. stood to inherit his uncle's portion of the house and business and was being steadfastly groomed for that purpose. He was never expected to return to Kentucky. There was nothing there for him anyway but a farm in the woods. Perhaps for this reason, Robert—knowing his son's ardor for Woodburn—purposely ignored him in order to keep him away. Still, despite his father's absence, R.A. persisted, writing to his father about his ideas of clearing Woodburn for its lumber, selling the wood, and then farming the land. R.A. couldn't shake his love for his Kentucky home. But knowing what his future held, he dutifully adhered to the family plan, even becoming a British citizen so he could legally inherit the Scottish estate.†

---

* Though undiagnosed, the descriptions of Alexander's physical condition and ongoing ailment indicate that he possibly suffered from muscular dystrophy.
† Whether Alexander renounced his American citizenship is unknown. Two Woodburn historians claim that he did not hold dual citizenship, that he renounced his American status to become a British citizen. See William Preston Mangum II, *A*

In February 1841, Robert was thrown from a carriage and died surrounded by family at Woodburn. A man of wealth, he'd naturally had the foresight to prepare a will wherein he bequeathed the whole of his portion of the Scottish estate to R.A. But he left Woodburn Farm to his three other children in equal parts. One year later, Sir William followed his brother, Robert, in death, and in that moment, Robert Aitcheson Alexander stood as sole heir of the family's Scottish estate and ironworks. At the age of twenty-three, he was wealthy in the extreme.

Loyal, even when he no longer needed to be accountable, Alexander completed his studies and, in 1846, graduated from Trinity College at Cambridge. He remained in London for a few years, leaving periodically to tour Europe, but the one place that continued to captivate him more than any other was Woodburn Farm. In 1849, he chose a farmer's life and returned home to Kentucky. Still a British subject, Alexander could not own property within the United States. He petitioned the Kentucky Legislature to allow him an exemption, which was granted—most likely because he was native-born. He then bought out his siblings' interest and cleared the land, just as he had suggested to his father, and bought back some of the acreage his father had sold, restoring the farm to its expanse of 3,200 acres—more than three times the size of Manhattan's Central Park. In 1851—about the time Ten Broeck bought the Metairie—Alexander started importing England's Durham and Alderney cattle, along with Southdown sheep. He bred them at Woodburn and sold them for high prices. News of his efforts to improve Kentucky's livestock caught national attention in the *Spirit*. While Alexander still owned and operated the Airdrie ironworks from afar, his reputation and skill as a Kentucky livestock breeder was growing.

By the time Woodburn was profitably producing cattle, Alexander had set his eyes on the American racetrack and its horse. In

---

Kingdom for the Horse (Louisville: Harmony House Publishers, 1999), 9; Dennis Domer "Inventing the Horse Farm," *Kentucky Humanities,* October 2005, 6.

his youth, Alexander had sat at his Trinity College desk trying his best to block out the alluring distractions of the Newmarket race-course nearby. Although a respected British sport, racing involved gambling—an aspect disdained by, if not outright repulsive to, his deeply Protestant family.

Religious thoughts aside, to Alexander, racehorses were un-yielding animals who powered through to reach extraordinary feats of endurance, while for him, even the simple task of sitting upright was becoming more painful as he aged. Perhaps it was his own physical frailty that made him choose an animal known for its strength and stamina. About the time Harry Lewis was training Lexington to run his maiden, Alexander bucked off his family's religious stranglehold, bought a colt named Ruric from his friend Nelson Dudley, and started dabbling in racing. Soon, he was booking tickets to board steamships to England, France, and Germany to educate him-self about equine farms and the methodical British system of breeding the racehorse. The course of self-education took him two years. By 1856, he was ready to purchase a stallion on which to build his stable.

Jean Édouard Lacretelle painted this only known image of the burgeoning horse breeder.

Alexander and Nelson Dudley had been friends since child-hood. Valuing Dudley's years of horse-racing experience, Alexander took him to England to hunt for stallions. While Ten Broeck's asking price was too high to tempt Alexander, it sparked an interest in Dudley. He told his friend that it wouldn't do to buy English bloodlines and leave behind "the best racehorse in the world." So Alexander hunted down Ten Broeck, shook his hand, and with that bond, sealed an agreement to buy Lexington for the asking price.*

Within days, news of Lexington's purchase and price hit the American press. *The Louisville Daily Journal* reported,

> Mr. Alexander, of Woodford, has purchased the celebrated horse Lexington. He met Mr. Ten Broeck in England, and the purchase was made there. The price paid was $15,000. This, we believe, is the highest price that was ever paid for any horse in the United States.

The news flashed quickly around the nation, from the *Boston Herald* to the *Picayune.* Opinions flew about, just as they had when Ten Broeck proposed Lexington would beat Time, painting an unflattering assessment of Alexander's judgment. The *Cleveland Plain Dealer* skeptically called the purchase price "a good deal of money to invest in horseflesh." Incensed at what seemed a public shaming of his dreams, Alexander made a promise to himself, and a public vow, that one day he would sell a son of Lexington for more than $15,000.

After Lexington's sale, Ten Broeck gave notice to General Buford to deliver the horse to Alexander. Reluctantly, Buford obliged.

When Alexander returned home from England, he found his pricey new horse at Woodburn, rubbing his muzzle along the paddock fence the way a blind person reads Braille. In the parlor of his log home, Alexander found a letter from Ten Broeck, who was perhaps now feeling a little regretful about losing Lexington.

"Have you seen him?" Ten Broeck wanted to know. "Do you like him? There is no such horse in the world."

---

* Lexington's purchase price equates to about $460,000 today.

CHAPTER 14

WOODBURN FARM

A good gait makes for speed. A strong heart makes for gameness. Combine the two and you have a good race-horse. The
trick is to know when they are combined. The fellow who can
fathom it is the winner in a horse deal.

—SAMUEL C. HILDRETH AND JAMES R. CROWELL,

The Spell of the Turf

MIDWAY, KENTUCKY, WAS a train town: a cluster of buildings
propped up near the railroad tracks that bifurcated the main
street. The town was built in the 1830s as a way station on the
Lexington and Ohio Railroad. Its sole purpose was to refuel loco-
motives and route passengers to their next stop. No one disembarked at Midway, unless their destination was Woodburn Farm.

Woodburn's acreage bordered what is now known as the Old
Frankfort Pike. The Pike, canopied by blue ash and Ingleside oaks,
cuts through a secluded paradise of blue-hued grass fields and
wildflower vines. It's the kind of road that invites travelers on a
detour to see its beauty. For a few months, back in the early 1850s,
the serenity of the road had been disrupted by carpenters, brick-
makers, and Irish immigrant stonemasons employed by Alexander.
They labored sunrise to sunset over many months to cut five-
hundred-million-year-old limestone into hundreds of thousands
of bricks. Then they dry laid them one by one, five feet high and

doubled in width, to enclose Woodburn's 3,200 acres. The wall stopped at Woodburn's entrance, abutting two stone-cut columns that heralded another tree-lined thoroughfare, this one leading to Alexander's home—the simple single-story log-and-stone structure he grew up in.

Alexander built the limestone wall pursuant to KRS Chapter 256—Kentucky's fence law—enacted in 1780 to encourage farmers to build strong barriers to prevent livestock from roaming the lands. But the wall also kept out feral horses that might contaminate the thoroughly bred genetic pool that Alexander was determined to preserve. The wall was a trademark in many respects, an emblem of what one Woodburn visitor would eventually call "an immense breeding operation, the largest in the world for breeding Thoroughbreds."

Alexander's limestone fence surrounding Woodburn Farm can still be seen today.

That visitor's observation was in no way exaggerated. Inside Woodburn, post-and-rail oak fencing stretched over the hills, creating a jigsaw-puzzle maze of fifty-acre divisions that separated animals by breed. The Thoroughbred operation consumed one section. Seven or eight hundred Southdown sheep were quartered in another, and Shorthorn cattle further along. An emerging breed, the Standardbred or trotting horse—the kind that pull buggies in races—grazed in an entirely different area. Within the fifty-acre divisions, animals were grouped according to purpose: Broodmares and their foals roamed in one section, stallions in another, and yearlings in race training in yet another. Each section contained a series of European-style barns with center aisles and paddocks. There were houses for each of the six distinct farm superintendents and their teams. Many of them were Irish and Scottish horse trainers and stud farm employees who knew how to work the British system of equine breeding. When it came to his racehorses in training, however, Alexander turned to the skilled services of a Black man named Ansel Williamson.*

Prior to the Civil War, Woodburn, like many Southern estates, utilized the work services of enslaved labor—men and women whom Alexander's father, Robert, had previously "owned." Some writers claim Alexander purchased slaves, but this author has found no primary source that corroborates those contentions. The Alexander family papers do contain an 1857 contract showing that Alexander leased the services of an enslaved man and paid money not only to the man's owner but to the enslaved man as well. Kentucky, a neutral state at the Civil War's onset, was not bound by the Emancipation Proclamation of 1863, so it is unclear when Woodburn's enslaved were freed. According to Alexander's estate ledgers, many of Woodburn's enslaved, when freed, remained under his employment earning wages that were equal and fair. It was the only life they knew.

Woodburn's workforce was, therefore, diverse, and Alexander sought his workers for their skill and expertise, no matter their

---

* One historian wrote that Ansel Williamson was freed by the time he started employment with Alexander. There are other sources that state that Alexander "bought" Williamson as a slave. This author has found no primary source that corroborates either scenario. What is clear is that the Alexander family papers contain estate ledgers showing wages paid to Williamson as well as Lexington's groom, a Black man named Jarrett.

country of origin, race, or social standing. Woodburn was possible only because of their work and effort. In all, Woodburn employed on average 150 people, all of whom lived on-site and kept Woodburn running with ceaseless precision.

In addition to the stone-cut barns and homes, Woodburn contained dairy houses, hay barns, carriage houses, a blacksmith shop, a ring for breaking horses, a show ring for annual auction sales—which were modeled after those at England's royal stables at Osborne; there were loading docks at the nearby train depot to ship the purchased stock out afterward—and, yes, even a Protestant church with a Scottish minister.

On a high hill next to Alexander's home—presiding over the whole of Woodburn—was the stallion barn, with Lexington as its star resident. On an adjacent hill lay the racehorse training stable, and next to that stretched not one but three training tracks, each perfectly graded, each one mile in circumference. Further down, the trotter stable housed Alexander's Standardbred horses.

Long before geneticists started fractionating specific traits according to an exacting science, breeders had to deduce for themselves what type of cross might work the best. There were no genome sheets of X and Y traits, no calculations of cardiac capacity and breathing, no biomechanical analyses of a particular horse's motion or stride length. Nor were there reams of computer-generated findings of everything a horse or mare had ever done or produced, or which bloodlines drew out the best of other bloodlines. Instead, breeders had a stallion's racing record in one hand and the racing records for a host of broodmares in the other. In theory, like begets like. Alexander sought mares that were proven racehorses, or that had already produced proven racehorses. He sought soundness, good temperament, gameness, and speed. It was a method of breeding that came down to that old saying of guessing at half and multiplying by two. Nothing was precise, and things didn't always turn out as they should. Breeding was based on the known and the probable, a keen sense of foresight, and a whole lot of luck. But guesswork and crossed fingers aside, the odds that Alexander would be able to breed horses to produce champion colts were already favorable. "I have now," Alexander wrote to his brother Alexander John "A.J." Alexander, "the most remarkable horse in the U.S. as a native bred stallion."

Lexington exemplified every essential quality in a racehorse. He had never come up lame. His ability to withstand various types of racing surfaces correlated to his hocks and slightly upright pasterns, located directly above his hooves. "The most elastic pastern that we remember to have seen on a horse," wrote one journalist. His sire's conformation was similar. "Boston never slipped in mud," said Uncle Ned Blackburn. "His foot set on like a hook; where it struck, it stuck." Thanks to those genes, Lexington powered over surfaces that would have broken down most horses. Francis T. Porter, editor of the *Picayune's* sporting pages, wrote, "His feet, though mostly white, are excellent, as are his legs, with good bone, clear, strong tendons, and good proportions, uniting in their motion great ease and correctness. His action cannot be surpassed; bold, free and elastic, full of power; and with his elegance of action, and a remarkable racing-like form throughout, he unites great beauty and grandeur." He was fast, and temperamentally even-keeled, but above all, "his gameness was unquestionable," wrote turfman Charles J. Foster. "For when his feet were burning hot in the time-race, and both the fore plates were badly twisted, he no sooner heard Arrow approaching than he shot away like an arrow from a bow." Lexington was the embodiment of bottom.

Selecting the right mares to breed to him would be *everything*. Sanders D. Bruce, who later compiled the *American Stud Book,* wrote, "The establishment of reputation by a stallion depends on his having good mares, at first, for if he has only bad and indifferent ones, the produce will be in low form and a disappointment, and the horse condemned as a failure."

To find the best broodmares, Alexander looked not only at what they might have accomplished on the turf; he stepped back a generation and took a look at their sires. Then he employed what is now known in breeding as a "nick."

Nick breeding involves putting a selection of mares sired by a particular stallion to an unrelated stallion, such as Lexington, for example. If those crosses consistently produce winners, a nick is created. It is a type of cross that brings out the good. In the case of Lexington, the nick would eventually come in the form of brood-mares sired by the small but powerful chestnut stallion named Glencoe.

A champion British Thoroughbred, Glencoe was the youngest horse ever to win Britain's coveted Goodwood Cup—a holdover from the old king's plates distance races. A mere day after winning the cup, he ran in Goodwood's Racing Sweepstakes and cantered home for the trophy. He followed those victories with wins in the Garden Stakes at Newmarket, as well as the Ascot Gold Cup and the Whip, at England's Ascot Racecourse. He retired as a champion at the age of four in 1835, spurring *The Sporting Magazine* of London to write, "Glencoe has shown himself the best horse in the world. Where is there one to be found to meet him at weight for age? Not in England, assuredly."

The following year, Glencoe was imported to America and, starting in 1848, stood several stud seasons in central Kentucky.

Alexander surmised that mares sired by Britain's proclaimed best racehorse might produce a champion foal when crossed with America's greatest horse. He started buying up Glencoe mares throughout Kentucky—paying whatever was asked—to build his broodmare pool at Woodburn. With six Glencoe mares in his stable, he put them to Lexington and hoped for the best.

While Lexington's foals were in gestation, Alexander set the second phase of his visionary quest in motion. He opened Lexington's breeding rights to any man who could pay the hundred-dollar stud fee *and* produce an authenticated pedigree for the mare he desired to breed to his stallion. Although stud farms of the past had offered stallions to outside breeders for a fee, none of them had required the hefty condition that the mare's pedigree be provided in writing, under what was tantamount to a sworn oath under seal.

In that era, just as in the present day, Thoroughbred foals were produced by a live cover in order to quell rumors of fraud. There was no artificial insemination. A stallion was put to a mare in season with the hopes that, eleven months later, a healthy foal would be born, that it would survive those often tumultuous initial days of life, and that it would eventually mature into a healthy horse. But to get that foal, live covers were the only accepted method. Thoroughbreds, as the breed's identity implies, must be thoroughly bred from a stallion and mare whose lineage traces to recognized British Thoroughbreds. The temptation of selling a half-bred foal by passing it off as a thoroughly bred one was far too great for some breeders and horse owners. Alexander aimed to correct this danger by recording the information of all the mares put to his stallions, whether they were his own broodmares or those of a horseman who supplied a mare and paid the stud fee to breed her. A live cover witnessed by his breeding staff was testament to the union, and thus recorded in Alexander's records. Those records eventually served as the basis for the *American Stud Book,* now maintained by the Jockey Club.

To entice other horsemen to bring their mares, in 1857, Alexander published the first breeding-farm catalog ever offered in America. In those pages he explained Woodburn's purpose:

> In introducing this establishment to the notice of the public, I may say that I have been actuated not only by the interest I feel in all sort of good stock, which has induced me to attempt myself the breeding of thoroughbred horses, but by the desire of affording to those who have the same taste as myself . . . the opportunity of having stock properly kept . . . and with the view of giving every facility to these breeders who are disposed to avail themselves of

the opportunity here offered, I have purchased of his late owner, Mr. Ten Broeck, the celebrated horse Lexington. . . .

Of Lexington little need be said, as the public are fully aware of his performances as a race horse, which render him probably the most remarkable horse of his time; and my strong conviction of his superior merit, combining as he does, speed and bottom in a most remarkable degree, cannot be better illustrated than by stating the fact that I purchased him whilst in England, at a high price ($15,000) after having seen and inquired into the character and performances of almost every horse of note in that country.

Soon, every sporting paper worth its salt trumpeted the news that with a quality mare and a hundred-dollar banknote, any turfman, breeder, banker, farmer, or baker—*any* person who so desired—could own a Lexington. The horse hadn't even produced any proven racehorses yet—a fact irrelevant to anybody who had ever dreamed of greatness. Horsemen from all over the nation started sending their mares, along with their legally stamped pedigree documents, over to Woodburn Farm. Even Richard Ten Broeck sent his mare Martha Washington to be bred to Lexington. In December 1857, leaving England for a short trip to Kentucky, Ten Broeck likely stopped by Woodburn to see his new colt, naming him Optimist. The horse would later run for Ten Broeck in Great Britain, winning the 1861 Ascot Stakes, Palatine Cup, Royal Stand Plate, and Stamford Cup—all two-mile distance races.

Within no time, Lexington-sired foals began dotting the pastures of respectable estates, and small farms as well. His get carried the power, heart, and courage of their sire. Many of them stood as his mirror images in conformation, springing their steps and stretching easily into their strides. But it was the foals out of Woodburn's Glencoe-sired broodmares that would forever seal Alexander's breeding acumen as ingenious. One turf historian called these foals the most fabulously successful colts ever produced. Alexander began auctioning them off at his annual sales.

In those days, equine auctions in America were unheard of. No one bred horses specifically to sell, but rather to enhance their own stable. Uncle Ned Blackburn's farm didn't breed Boston to produce a systematically thought-out cross of racehorses that were then sold to anyone interested in racing. None of the stud farms did, until Woodburn. Once Alexander advertised his annual auction in the press, deep-pocketed turfmen booked trains to Midway to buy up Lexington's foals. Each year, the sale's grand finale was the exhibition of Lexington in the auction ring.

But in 1858, the success of Lexington at the stud stood in a precarious balance. Although Woodburn was attracting turfmen to its auction for his foals, the question still remained whether the offspring would perform like their sire. The first foal crop had barely matured to racing age. Some of them were making their debut at the Pharsalia. "Report speaks well of them," noted William T. Porter in the *Spirit*. But these were early days.

Alexander had already sunk a wincing amount of his fortune into turning his aspirations into reality. His success entirely depended on Lexington. In 1859, St. Louis, Missouri, was in the throes of hosting its state fair. Latticed orchard pies and elaborately pieced quilts would soon turn the fairgrounds into a paradise for the eyes and palate. But the prime ticket-selling attraction would feature the crowning of the best Thoroughbred sire. Alexander paid the entry fee and shipped Lexington over to St. Louis to contend.

On Saturday, October 8, 1859, twenty thousand people filed toe-to-heel in a line that wrapped around the St. Louis amphitheater. Earlier that day, the *Spirit* had advised that anyone interested in seeing Lexington should head directly there. Competing for the title alongside Woodburn's horse was a stallion named Revenue, already acknowledged nationwide as a sire of champions. As if the horse needed further endorsement of his credentials, only a few months before, Kentucky's state fair had awarded Revenue its own Best Stallion title. When Revenue wasn't traveling around the country winning blue ribbons, he stood as a sire at General Abe Buford's Bosque Bonita Farm, just a few miles down the road from Woodburn. Although Bosque Bonita did not breed foals specifically to be sold at auction, the farm did offer Revenue as a sire to outside breeders. Turfmen could choose to breed their mares at either farm, but the blue ribbon would hang at only one of them.

As multitudes filled the amphitheater, the contest's judges settled into their seats and awaited the announcement of Revenue's entrance. He paraded the ring, walking with a grace that displayed symmetrical perfection. This was a horse whose purse winnings totaled a laudable $38,000 (about $1.35 million today); a horse whose get were proven racehorses—like the mighty Planet, a champion racer who had already elevated the laurels of his sire.

As Revenue stood perfectly still for inspection, a raucous scene erupted alongside the trees outside the amphitheater. The cacophony of the fair made Lexington rip away from his groom and gallop frantically, perilously close to the trees. He abruptly skidded to a stop and stood erect, facing the building, trembling and lathered in sweat. Two other grooms approached him and calmly took him in hand. Here, in this place, were all the sounds of the racecourse, and he twitched his ears trying to decipher the noise from the shadows that appeared before his eyes. He called out in a whinny that vibrated through his body. Then he stiffened up. As the grooms started to tug against him, urging him closer to the arena, Lexington tossed his head and shuffled sideways to evade their hold. He pivoted and turned on his haunches, churning up dust and flinging the men around.

When he finally came within view and his name was announced, the crowd rushed to their feet—shattering the arena with a resounding ardor. They chanted his name. Lexington stilled, quivering, then bounced forward into the arena, springing his steps, and edged ahead of the two men holding his reins. Author Joseph Cairn Simpson was on hand at the ring. He wrote, "I saw Lexington in the show ring . . . and was struck with the grandeur of his appearance, heightened by the darkened orbs." The horse walked alone in his magnificence as flowers cascaded onto his path. He startled only for a moment, when a young woman tied a garland of florets around his neck. Then Lexington continued his walk, decorated as he was with the adoration of his fans.

Revenue was awarded the blue ribbon. The judges cited Lexington's failing vision as the reason, as if he had a fallible gene that would impair all future generations. Over the following weeks, his loss sparked a fury. People shouted about the wrong of bestowing the ribbon on what they felt was the inferior horse. Some made wagers that Lexington's get would someday beat that of Revenue. One man went so far as to propose a match race for that purpose to occur at some future date over the Metairie. Another man, identified only as "GERF," was so moved by the injustice that he appeared in *Wilkes' Spirit of the Times* bemoaning the loss in verse.

> Lead him forth, the sightless hero!
> Round him group the noblest steeds;
> He will match the proudest horses
> Of the famous racing breeds.
> Now he hears the hum of voices—
> Voices blended in his praise;
> And he longs to meet the glances
> Of the eyes that on him gaze.
>
> Flowers are scattered in his pathway,
> Ruby lips repeat his name,
> Twice ten thousand hearts are throbbing
> With the mem'ry of his fame.
> They recall the day of triumph,
> When he flew with lightning speed,

Fleeter than the wind of winter,
Or the fabled winged steed.

Still unbroken in his spirit,
Matchless still his noble form,
And his neck as proudly arches
As the rainbow of the storm.
Yet the prize is not awarded
To the Champion of the Turf,
Though he stands among his rivals
Like a prince beside a serf.
Let another wear the honor—
Lexington has higher fame,
For upon the roll of races
Foremost stands his glorious name. . . .

Lead him back—his muscles quiver
At the sounds that round him rise;
And he longs to know the meaning,
Hidden from his sightless eyes. . . .

Alexander never again entered Lexington in a contest where subjectivity triumphed over results. From then on, Lexington's record as a sire depended on whether his foals won their races. In 1861, a mere two years after losing the title of Best Stallion at the St. Louis Fair, Lexington was recognized as the leading American sire. The recognition was not determined by a committee of judges but based on the number of races and purse money won by a stallion's get. Lexington's sons and daughters had won more races that year than the offspring of any other sire.

Meanwhile, America was crumbling.

In March 1861, newly elected president Abraham Lincoln arrived in Washington, D.C., to try to soothe an angry nation. Seven Southern states had already seceded. One month after his arrival, artillery shots arched over Charleston Harbor and bore down on Fort Sumter, igniting the American Civil War. An additional four states seceded. Kentucky, a slave state, remained neutral. But war was coming there, nevertheless.

CHAPTER 15

WAR

M EN ON BOTH sides believed the war would be over in three months. Yet, as the months unfolded, the enormous consequences resulting from the conflict became more apparent. General Ulysses S. Grant later called the war a stake of life, property, and every claim for protection granted by citizenship of the United States. Not every state was willing to risk those constitutional protections and rights. Kentucky chose to remain neutral.

As soon as the war began, Washington and Richmond both bombarded Kentucky with bureaucratic pleas to join the Northern or Southern cause. But Kentucky—fiercely independent and desiring to remain that way—commenced on a stubborn and emphatic refusal to provide troops for the Union, citing "wicked purposes of subduing her sister Southern States," the deplorable notion of having to "hold together a Union by a sword," and, not sparing the South, dramatic censuring of the Confederate states for failing to consult Kentucky before they seceded.

But inevitably, after several months of the state's general assembly rejecting all the Northern and Southern presidential requests for support, the war moved itself into Kentucky. On September 4,

1861, Confederate major general Leonidas Polk stuck his foot across the Tennessee border and planted it firmly in Columbus, Kentucky. The very next day, Brigadier General Ulysses S. Grant responded more emphatically by moving his massive army deeper into the state and occupying the western town of Paducah. The distance between the two armies was equivalent to a day's march by either side to what would surely be a cavalry-charging battle on Kentucky soil.

On September 11, amid incoming pleas from Tennessee and Ohio imploring Kentucky to honor her neutrality, the state's general assembly—incensed by the South's brazen aggression in invading its territory—voted for its governor to order the Confederate troops to withdraw. No such order was sent to General Grant. From that point on, Kentucky was no longer neutral. She became a Union-friendly, federally entrenched state. But not all its citizens were willing to kowtow to the Union way of thinking. And therein lay Kentucky's problem.

At dusk on September 20, 1861, Captain John Hunt Morgan gathered his ragged group of Lexington Rifles, a volunteer militia he'd organized in 1857 because of the escalating territorial tensions. The general assembly had just issued the order for all private militias and state guards to disarm and to relinquish control to the Union army. But Morgan wasn't about to honor a government with views different from his. He decided to take Kentucky into his own hands, eventually engaging the state in a battle of opposing interests within a larger war over nationality and freedom. Kentucky's quagmire was deepened by divided citizens who no longer stood unified on any subject except, perhaps, the value of a good horse, and who sometimes flip-flopped between sides because of emotional outrage at one injustice or another. Kentucky's goal of maintaining peace was never so disrupted as by those living within her borders. No one was safe. Nor was their property.

Despite the cataclysmic events taking place across the nation, and particularly in Kentucky, Woodburn Farm was thriving. By late 1861, Lexington had been at stud for five years and had sired 183 foals. That number only accounts for the foals that survived gestation and birth. So many complications can arise—infection, malformation, poor bone growth, premature birth and consequent low weight—causing a foal to die in birth or shortly thereafter. Whether any of Lexington's get succumbed to such birthing and foaling complications was never recorded. That it happened in the course of his stud career is likely.

Even in those days of rife division within the state and entire country, Woodburn was selling horses not only to local turfmen but to those from as far away as New York. Potential buyers piled into Woodburn's annual auctions to snatch up Lexington's progeny, as well as those of Alexander's other stallions, the British Thoroughbreds Scythian and Australian. Not only were horsemen paying cash for the chance to own Lexington's bloodline, they were also getting horses whose schooling had already been started by Alexander's roster of talented trainers and jockeys.

Three years earlier, Alexander had answered a knock at his front door and discovered a small, rawboned teenage French boy standing on his doorstep, saddle in hand and speaking broken English phrases. The boy had no résumé listing Great Ones he'd ridden, nor could he recount any race of consequence in which he'd held the reins. He had only the backing of Richard Ten Broeck, who'd discovered the boy's father, a French jockey named Napoleon Belland, while racing in England and thought the New York tracks could use his talent. Swayed by Ten Broeck's proposition of seeing America, Belland packed up his family and set off for New York. His son, his namesake, was only a boy, and hobbled by the barrier of the unfamiliar English language. Yet he had a gift for riding that had been polished under his father's tutelage. Alexander hired Belland, Jr., on the spot and put him to work starting Woodburn's colts under saddle and exercising them.

It wasn't long afterward that Belland was told to take his saddle to the stallion barn and tack up Lexington for his daily fitness walks.

Having retired from the racetrack only three years before, Lexington could likely make out shadows with his left eye, but his vision was, for the most part, gone. Even so, Daniel Swigert, Woodburn's foreman, refused to relegate the horse to a vacuum of hollow existence. The stallion could still be ridden at the lower gaits. For three hours every morning, Belland rode the eight-year-old horse over hills that had been etched into the land. Despite living in a nearly blacked-out world, the horse was strong, driven even more now by his will, which had not succumbed to his blindness. Yet, thanks to his courage, the horse remained untroubled by the strange noises and feel of the unseen world surrounding him—a world that moved and snapped, shrilled and rumbled, in a way that could very easily spook sighted horses into a crazed bolt.

But Lexington, Belland believed, had intelligence that bolstered his great confidence. "Riding him was a thorough pleasure," he said. During those early years at Woodburn, the young rider gave Lexington compassionate guidance, allowing the nearly blind horse a rare freedom. "Lexington on his walks at Woodburn was a sight worth seeing," recalled painter Thomas J. Scott. "At such times, with his head carried level—the neck slightly arched, and a long, light, feathery tail gracefully carried, his rich golden tinge of bay in contrast with his white markings, together with the look of power and grace in action—made me then, and still, think him the handsomest horse I ever saw."

Scott's admiration of the horse was widespread. Years before Lexington ever registered on the national scene, even years before he was ever conceived in the mind of Dr. Warfield, the Swiss artist Edward Troye had spent a number of years in America painting every racehorse, horse trainer, and turfman of note. Later, two months after Lexington left the Metairie for Kentucky, Ten Broeck commissioned Troye to capture the horse in his racing form.

Two years later, Alexander invited the artist to visit Woodburn and to bring his oils and brushes. Troye readily obliged and, in 1857, unpacked his charcoals and easels at the farm's stallion barn, where he began reconnecting with Lexington and sketching him in his blind state. Troye also painted many of Lexington's get before packing up and heading to Syria. There, he painted the Arab horses of the Damascus desert, standing regal under white tents alongside men in red cotton thobes. But it was Lexington who kept on drawing Troye back to Kentucky. The stallion became his lifetime study. Troye sketched and painted the horse a minimum of seven times—possibly more, according to Troye biographer Alexander Mackay-Smith.

Lexington's ability to reel in admiration wasn't confined to Belland, Scott, and Troye. Although the horse had been tucked away on Woodburn's pastures for a few years, the nation still regarded him as *its* horse.

About the time Belland was riding Lexington over the hills of Woodburn, a man from California mailed Alexander a large rack of antlers taken from an elk killed in a hunt, along with his written wishes that Alexander would "please hang above Lexington's stall." The idea came from the great Mississippi steamboat races, in which the fastest boat on the river was awarded gold-encrusted antlers that, by tradition, were nailed above the door to the wheelhouse. There they remained until the next fastest boat claimed them, or "took the horns," as the saying went. Alexander affixed the antlers as requested, along with a banner underneath that read, "7:19 ¾."

By 1862, the Lexington Rifles had grown to over eighteen hundred men. In the wake of the Partisan Ranger Act of that year—an act passed by the Confederate States Congress to recruit independent militias into its army—the Confederate army commissioned John Hunt Morgan into its ranks. Now a Confederate regiment, Morgan's Rifles flew the flag of the Second Kentucky Cavalry. Even though they could now officially be called soldiers, Morgan's men were still a motley group whose uniforms consisted of whatever happened to be on their backs when they enlisted. The only commonality among them—indeed, considered an absolute necessity to the ensemble—was a large black ostrich plume that dangled from every store-bought or stolen hat. Other than this one adherence to common rule, Morgan's men did what they pleased under their leader's laissez-faire direction. In any case, for Morgan to have kept his ranks under even a modicum of military decorum would have been a near impossibility. As Basil Duke, Morgan's right-hand commandant, noted, these were men of spirit "young and wild, and inclined, when they could evade the vigilance of camp guards, to rove nocturnally and extensively." Discipline, according to Duke, would render soldiers fearful of punishment and turn them into "unreasoning machines."

Morgan marched his cavalry through Tennessee, daringly up into Ohio, and back into Kentucky on so-called Confederate expeditions. Because of his unwavering belief in his own abilities and destiny, things usually ended up the way Morgan had planned. He had also to thank his gifted telegraph operator, George "Lightning" Ellsworth. Ellsworth relished sending official-looking dispatches to the Union army stationed in Kentucky, marching them all over the state on false orders. While the Union clumsily fumbled around like Ellsworth's string puppets, Morgan's Second Kentucky Cavalry burned bridges and trestles along the Kentucky Central Railroad and ripped up rails on the Lexington & Frankfort line, derailing trains carrying valuable Union supplies. Near the northern Kentucky town of Cynthiana—a town that had already seen its share of musket-firing skirmishes—Morgan's cavalry hijacked three trains loaded with Union horses and rolled them off the track, killing the animals. The Second Kentucky then burned much of the business portion of Cynthiana. They even pointed guns at a Mrs. Hamilton, who had chosen that day to ride her horse into town to deliver baked goods to injured Union soldiers. Morgan's Second Kentucky took her jewelry, watch, money, *and* her horse. Then they headed toward Morgan's hometown of Lexington, where the Union had stashed substantial supplies.

Morgan gave the order, "Light up the town!" The Second Kentucky proceeded to fire their Enfield rifles into stores and homes, then dragged Lexington's citizens out, lined them up in the town's center, pointed their guns at them, and demanded they turn over money, watches, rings, wallets, and anything that *might* be worth something. Morgan's men kicked the doors open to the Branch Bank of Kentucky, pointed their guns again, and stole $10,000 in federal currency. Meanwhile, down the street at the Union cavalry stables, others from the Second Kentucky opened the gates and whipped frenzy into two thousand Union horses, stampeding them out of town and toward Morgan's base of command. Captain George H. Laird, the Union quartermaster in Lexington, later reported that the actual number of horses stolen was 2,528. After the horses were driven away, the wayward cavalry grabbed logs and wrapped torn strips of linen around them. They drenched the rags in turpentine, ignited them, then threw the fiery torches into the empty Union cavalry stables and any other Union-occupied building. As fire ravaged Main Street, Morgan and his men rode out of town, engulfed in the dust raised by the Union's charging cavalry horses. Behind, they left the city of Lexington in flames, haloed by a dark cloud of smoke.

Morgan and the Second Kentucky headed in the direction of Versailles. Roughly seven miles away, north of Versailles, was Woodburn Farm.

Alexander had taken precautions. With the pillaging of Kentucky's deposit banks, not to mention the $80,000 in gold, silver, and federal banknotes that Morgan's men stole from the Farmers Bank of Kentucky's bank vault in Mount Sterling, people had to turn to other means of protecting their assets. Furthermore, every possession was at risk, because everything was potentially valuable enough to be stolen. There was no guessing what a Union or Confederate soldier might find appealing enough to take for his own: wallpaper, mattresses, Venetian blinds, hoop dresses made with twelve feet of costly Parisian silk, sheet music, novels, chess sets, birdcages, Bibles, pianos, and, of course, those commodities that held their value in sentimentality, beauty, and monetary significance— silver and gold. Deemed trophies of war, any item had potential value by the very fact it came from a battlefield, a civilian on the wrong side of the war, or even a civilian on the right side. Although both armies carried scrolls of military regulations that forbade pillaging and plundering, with penalties up to death by hanging, theft happened routinely, and with such an abounding frequency and unapologetic amorality as to nullify the existence of the regulations in the first place.

Alexander had plenty worth protecting. In June 1860, he'd commissioned Tiffany & Company to create a silver competition vase for the Woodlawn Association Stakes, a four-mile heat race in Louisville. Tiffany's, earlier known as Tiffany, Young & Ellis, had already gained a reputation for excellent silver craftsmanship, as well as for selling diamonds, jewels, and other "fancy articles," as one advertisement promoted. But, for the vase, Alexander envisioned something of pure silver in the form of a cup, to be passed annually to the winners of the Woodlawn Stakes. Tiffany's created something far more priceless, and more unique. The pure-silver Woodlawn Vase, as the cup came to be known, stands forty-three inches and weighs twenty-nine pounds and twelve ounces. At its base are four projections containing a horseshoe, a racing saddle, a whip, and a jockey's cap. Above the projections is a lawn, divided

into fields by a planked fence. A stallion stands in one field, a mare and
foal in the other. The scene is from
Woodburn Farm. On top of the
Woodlawn Vase is Lexington in full
figure under saddle and jockey. After
Tiffany's completed the vase, Alexander paid $1,500 for the commis-
sioned work.*

At Woodburn, Alexander summoned Nugent, his Irish gardener
and a trusted worker, and asked the
man to go to the flower garden and
dig a large hole, as deep as a grave
and about as long as one. Alexander
then took the Woodlawn Vase and
other family silver, wrapped them in
cloth, placed them in the hole, and
asked the gardener to fill it and re-
plant. With the Woodlawn Vase
buried, Alexander focused on what
he had to do to make Woodburn a
safe haven for horses.

The Woodlawn Vase, crafted by
Tiffany & Co. in 1860, on
commission from R. A.
Alexander. The base of the vase
contains a stallion opposite a mare
and foal. The setting is Woodburn
Farm. Lexington under saddle
surmounts the trophy.

Alexander didn't subscribe to the
Confederate ideology. All his business operations were conducted in
New York, where his lawyers, financial directors, and banks were
located. Everything pertaining to the ironworks business at Airdrie
was likewise directed to his New York agents. Midway- and
Versailles-based horse farmers didn't have much to fear from the
Union. Their concern was for the Confederate-minded guerrilla
raiders. Alexander's only chance of surviving a raid was to de-

---

* The Woodlawn Vase has reached an estimated value today of $4 million.

emphasize the rumors of his Union-bent beliefs. Since he had never relinquished his British citizenship, he still held fast to this symbolic loyalty to Great Britain.

The South had long believed that Britain would join her cause. That erroneous conviction primarily had to do with cotton. Southern cotton was by far the most exported American commodity between the 1820s and 1840s, topping tobacco, flour, and sugar. As much as 20 percent of Britain's population was said to rely on imported cotton for clothing. In 1824, $15 million worth of Southern cotton was exported to the British Isles. By 1825— one short year later—that value had doubled to $30 million. Over the next five years, the number of bushels of cotton exported to Britain rose by 82 percent. The 1830s through the 1850s saw continued demand. New plantations were purchased, and heavy investments funneled into enslaved labor, horses, and plows—all in a speculative, gold-rush-like attempt to cash in on America's leading export. With cotton being so highly sought, the South believed in its own destiny. Southerners were convinced that Britain would back them, should ties be severed from the North.

Even as late as 1864, the Confederacy still grasped onto those vanishing hopes. Anything British was therefore considered pro-South, and anything Southern was considered hands-off by Confederate-minded raiders. War-torn Kentucky was home to a large community of Confederate sympathizers centered primarily in and around Bloomfield, a small city located in a rural area halfway between Louisville and Lexington. Outside of Bloomfield, pockets of Confederate supporters huddled in different areas; however, Versailles and Midway, where Woodburn Farm was nestled, were known to be more Union aligned.

Opening his chest of drawers, Alexander dug through his linens in search of the one thing he thought might save Woodburn: the Union Jack.

Lightning Ellsworth's Thoroughbred, Maud, was worn-out. Morgan supplied him with a replacement named Fleetfoot that, despite his name, moved with such slowness and trepidation that Ellsworth was forced to abandon him. Ellsworth always suspected the reason to be that Fleetfoot was, after all, a Yankee horse.

Having a slow war mount was no small problem. A good horse was more valuable to a soldier than the Navy Colt revolver strapped in his holster. A horse with stamina, speed, and courage could carry a rider through a hailstorm of bullets, take several hits, and oftentimes keep going. It could make the difference between a cavalryman's life or death. At the Battle of Shiloh, Colonel James B. McPherson's horse was shot with a musket ball that entered its flank and traveled through its body, exiting the other side. The horse delivered McPherson to safety, then collapsed dead. In the Battle of Williamsburg, General Jubal A. Early's horse was shot in the eye. Partially blind and undoubtedly bleeding profusely, the horse carried the general for the duration of the battle. At the Battle of Gettysburg, Captain H. C. Parsons wrote of the horses that ran in Farnsworth's Charge, "Running low and swift, as in a race . . . and guided at the slightest touch on the neck; never refusing a fence or breaking from a column . . . they carried their riders over rocks and fallen timber and fences that the boldest hunter would hardly attempt to-day." Of his own horse Parsons wrote,

How he sprang into the charge! How he leaped the four walls! How he cleared Farrington's horse as it rolled over in the rocks! And how gently he carried me from the field, although blood spurted from his side at every step. Four better horses passed him in the race, but only to fall or carry their riders to death! And when I was lifted down into unconsciousness, my last recollection was of his great eyes turned upon me as in sympathy and reproof.

In his memoir, *Hardtack and Coffee,* Union private John D. Billings wrote, "Those who have not looked into the matter have the idea that actual combat was the chief source of the destruction of horseflesh. But, as a matter of fact, that source is probably not to be credited with *one-tenth* of the full losses of the army in this respect. It is to be remembered that the exigencies of the service required much in the line of hard pulling, exposure, and hunger, which conspired to use them up very rapidly."

Billings's assessment was in no way understated. The reports listed in *The War of the Rebellion: A Compilation of the Official Records of the Union and Confederate Armies* from May through August 1864 are replete with the tribulation and deterioration of military horses. On June 15, 1864, the Fourth Iowa Cavalry reported, "Forage was very scarce. . . . The animals were not supplied with more than half rations of grain and the last two [days] none was secured, though the labor of the horses was exceedingly severe." Seven days later, the horses in the Fourth Iowa were "starved and exhausted and having difficulty dragging the artillery and wagons. It is impossible to find forage." On July 8, 1864, the Thirty-seventh Kentucky Infantry informed its headquarters, "The horses have already traveled nearly one thousand miles. They were broken down; only having received eight ears of corn, subsisting on bushes, weeds, and a little white clover." The devastation only worsened. On July 24, 1864, the Third Iowa Cavalry advised, "Due to lack of forage, for three days the horses were scarcely fed. These facts combined with intense heat, dustiness of roads, and severe labor accounts for the great deterioration of the horses." During a march by the First Ohio Heavy Artillery Regiment, "many horses fell by the roadside due to fatigue and breaking down. We were compelled to leave them on the mountains where they fell." On average, a thousand-pound war horse should receive eighteen to twenty-one pounds of hay and ten to twelve pounds of grain daily. To preserve muscle and flesh, the horse should not march more than 150 miles a week. But such niceties were impossible in war.

With fresh horses being in such heavy demand, the armies on both sides began taking them from anywhere they could be found.

The taking was called "impressing," and, for the most part, was done of necessity. Although receipts to the owners were supposed to be issued by both the Union and Confederate armies, they rarely were. Most of the time, the impressing by both sides was more akin to outright stealing—justifiably, the men felt, because the civilized way of life had become so hard to honor. Horses were different from gold and silver. Soldiers needed fresh and healthy war mounts to better their chances of staying alive.

Morgan's cavalry marched throughout Kentucky, sometimes for twenty-four hours without rest. When the horses could go no farther, they were abandoned along the way. Morgan often issued one-week furloughs so his men could, as Ellsworth put it, "recruit" new horses. Racehorses were ideal cavalry horses because of their stamina and speed. If the horse was sired by Lexington, all the better. It was likely faster and more courageous, and had an endless supply of bottom. By the time the war started, Woodburn had already amassed a reputation, according to Ellsworth, as "the well-known Thoroughbred stock farm of Robt. A. Alexander." But when it came to horse recruitment, Morgan insisted that his rag-tag and unyielding soldiers follow two rules. First, they must never procure horses from Confederate-friendly farms. Second, on Morgan's stringent orders, the Second Kentucky Cavalry must never confiscate Robert Aitcheson Alexander's racehorses at Woodburn Farm. "And the men," Ellsworth later wrote, "although very anxious for fresh animals, never offered to molest the property of this British subject."

But in times of unfettered self-indulgence and desperation, precautions and orders eventually serve little purpose.

On Friday, June 10, 1864, an untold number of men from the Second Kentucky rode down the Old Frankfort Pike. They followed the limestone wall that stretched over endless acres of rolling grassy hills, ending at an imposing fortress-like iron gate. The posse swung the gate open with surprising ease and walked their horses down a dirt road canopied by blue ash and oaks. At the road's end lay Alexander's home. Attached to a pole anchored to the roof flapped the British flag.

Finding no one at home, the men rode to the racehorse training stables and pointed their revolvers at a horse groom named Henry Granison. They demanded, "We need fast hosses and appreciate a good hoss as well as anybody."

Further details of the raid are lost to history, but what is known is that four horses were stolen from the training barn that day. Two of them were Lexington-sired mares. The other two were Thoroughbred geldings, one of which had also been sired by Lexington. The posse rode away at a fast clip past the miles of stone wall and back out onto the Old Frankfort Pike. Then they turned in the direction of Cynthiana to rejoin the rest of Morgan's cavalry.

According to Alexander, who wasn't present at Woodburn during the raid, men under Morgan's direction stole his horses. Lightning Ellsworth later denied the accusation. But when Alexander's farm superintendent, Daniel Swigert, returned to Woodburn, he and Granison rode ninety miles to Cynthiana. There, they paid ransom in an unspecified amount to Morgan himself for the return of the Lexington mares. But Alexander's two Thoroughbred geldings were never seen again.

Morgan's theft of Woodburn horses showed just how accessible the farm was to anyone who might not go there with good intentions. Commodities formerly protected by beliefs and affiliations that no longer held significance in a crumbling society lay helplessly open. Three of Lexington's Foals had been stolen and never recovered. At the time, the question lingered: How many more of his foals would succumb to the same fate, not only from Woodburn but from other farms where they had been sold? To most, a horse looked like any other and would do just as well, especially in the hour of need. But some men claimed to know a Lexington colt when they saw one—the build, the high-set pasterns. They knew the quality of Woodburn's horses and what trophies they were. Already the raid had impacted Woodburn's sales. Alexander said as much to his brother. Horsemen who might otherwise be interested in buying the farm's horses were too wary of traveling in the South and especially of buying pricey racehorses that could be so easily stolen.

In September 1864, John Hunt Morgan was killed by a Union soldier. His regiments, scattered, were left to fend for themselves in a land that was quickly turning Union blue. But Kentuckians were not to be spared further torment by lawless roughriders. One of his own cavalry riders rose up to take his place.

Marcellus Jerome Clarke wore his hair loose in love knots that hung in waves around his shoulders and answered to the name of Sue Mundy. Already a war veteran at the age of nineteen, he tried to leave behind his disruptive days with Morgan and live his life right. He took up work as a farmhand and, on Sundays, squeezed himself into an uncomfortable wood-backed pew at the local church. But it was there where he was called out for who he was. "He's one of Morgan's," they mumbled.

On July 5, 1864, President Abraham Lincoln proclaimed martial law throughout Kentucky, suspending the writ of habeas corpus— the common law safeguard of the inherent right of freedom and the right to due process. Even before the suspension, the president had stationed a tyrannical general, Stephen Gano Burbridge, to watchdog over Kentucky. With his Morgan affiliation potentially exposed, Clarke knew he wasn't safe. But his Kentucky roots ran deep. He vowed he would never leave his Kentucky home, as long as he could first find a fast horse.

CHAPTER 16

THE SHE-DEVIL

Marcellus Jerome Clarke galloped his horse out of Springfield, Kentucky. Wrapped snugly around his shoulders was a woman's fur stole. The mink's beady eyes peered out, black and lifeless, from its head. Clarke wore a black velvet hat with a black ostrich plume streaming off the back, intertwining with the mass of his long dark curls. On the hat's front, an upended crescent moon sparkled, for good luck. Strapped to Clarke's belt were as many as four Navy Colt revolvers—loaded. He had just used one of them to fire three shots from horseback into the back and side of a man named Thornton Lee, and now the unfortunate wagonmaker crawled across the ground to the momentary protection of a fence. Lee rose from beside the fence gasping, then staggered around to the back of a house. Clarke charged after him, firing again. Lee was eventually killed—shot twice through the temple by another man in Clarke's posse—in retaliation for firing a musket at Clarke.

Earlier that day of November 25, 1864, Clarke and twelve men, dressed in a mismatched concoction of Confederate uniforms and red roundabout jackets, had galloped into Springfield, shooting their pistols in the air, riding their horses into homes, firing up through ceilings, and yelling at people to line up in the town square. One brave fellow, Grandison Robertson, a livery stable keeper who resisted the order, was told to line up or his "damned brains would be blown out." Robertson quickly stood in line.

Then Clarke and his twelve men turned loose their mayhem. They kicked open front doors to homes, tossed aside furniture, and pulled out bureau drawers, spilling their contents and rifling through them for keepsake items. One victim had his hand splayed against the wall and a revolver pointed at his ring finger, along with a demand to turn over the ring or lose his hand entirely.

Over on Main Street, Hugh McElroy, president of Springfield's bank, stood up from his desk, trembling and raising his hands defenselessly, when gun-wielding men marched into the bank's counting room and demanded he open the vault. When he did, out tumbled a set of silverware, $150 in greenbacks, $600 in Confederate money, and the local church's silver sacramental pitcher and cups—a jumbled pile as distressing as the angry expressions crinkling across the looters' faces. A man in Clarke's gang named Henry Magruder rubbed the heated barrel of his pistol across McElroy's forehead. Magruder told McElroy he'd better goddamn tell him where the balance of the money was or he would "blow out his brains," apparently the favored threat of Clarke's men. McElroy told him to go ahead, there was nothing left to take.

Meanwhile, another man grabbed the church's sacramental silver pitcher and cups, only to discard the pitcher when he learned it belonged to God. Keeping the less clunky but equally God-purposeful cups, he dashed out of the bank and onto his horse. Then, for unknown reasons, Clarke's men shot and killed the local cobbler. Seeing the horror, other townspeople readily turned over pocket watches, money, and fur stoles—anything the men wanted. One of Clarke's twelve men was Jim Davis, alias Harvey Welles, alias William Henry. After having fired shots at the wagonmaker, Thornton Lee, Davis grabbed a copy of *The Louisville Daily Demo-*

crat so he could read about his recent escape from the Union. Then Davis, who frequently decorated himself in war paint to resemble an arrow-shooting warrior of the Western plains, may have blown into his bugle, as he was known to do. Whatever the signal, Clarke and the others kicked spurs into their horses and galloped out of Springfield with their treasures, leaving behind a terrified and devastated town. Grandison Robertson, the livery stable keeper, said he was "a good deal frightened about the matter. They were the first guerrillas we had with us, and we expected they would murder every one of us." What frightened him more, he recalled, was the fact that the gang of men kept referring to their leader as "Sue Mundy."

The name had struck terror in the hearts of Kentuckians ever since this mythical bandit had first arrived in October of 1864, wielding her guns and threats. She was vile, greedy, a she-devil completely devoid of compassion with no qualms about taking a human's life for a horse. The idea to create her had come about earlier that month along the potholed route of the Harrodsburg Road.

At dusk on Friday, October 7, a stagecoach negotiated the uneven road leading to Harrodsburg, Kentucky, jostling its passengers uncomfortably with every wheel-jarring dip. Suddenly, a guerrilla band on horseback, dressed in Confederate uniforms, emerged out of the woods and surrounded the coach. The men pointed their revolvers at James Saffell, the stagecoach driver, and told him to stop. Saffell rested the reins on his lap, then slowly raised his hands in the air. A man with one arm jumped off his horse, pointed his gun at the coach door, and ordered everyone to step outside, hold their hands up high, and line themselves along the road. The passengers stared wide-eyed as the guerrillas gutted mailbags, ripped open envelopes, and stuffed money into their pockets. Their eyes grew even wider when one of the thieves, an androgynous young beauty with long, curly brown hair dangling out from underneath a decorative black hat, unhitched one of the coach horses and galloped it down the road to "try it out." The rider returned the wheezing horse back to Saffell, complaining that the animal was too slow. Then the marauders—their pockets heaving with cash— jumped on their horses and tore off. In their dust they left a cluster of heightened heartbeats and confusion over the striking person underneath the black hat. Someone in the group referred to the marauder as "Lieutenant Flowers."

The following morning, George D. Prentice, a steely-eyed, Machiavellian wordsmith, sat behind his editorial desk at the downtown Green Street offices of *The Louisville Daily Journal*. He picked up a telegram, freshly translated from the signals speeding along the miles of wire connecting the *Daily Journal*'s offices to smaller towns throughout Kentucky. Reading about the thievery of the beautiful brazen raider, Prentice conceived a plan.

Although a Whig and a friend of President Lincoln, Prentice had become agitated by the Union army's inability to police John Hunt Morgan, as well as the many camps of roughshod, silent riders who had sprung from Morgan's faction of the Confederacy. Worse, to Prentice, was the man President Lincoln had placed at Kentucky's helm, Major General Stephen Gano Burbridge. General Burbridge was an unreasonable absolutist.

Long before Lincoln's proclamation of martial law over the state, Burbridge had wielded unfettered punitive authority in levying hefty fines and confiscating the property of those Kentuckians who weren't Union. Even Union-friendly citizens feared retaliation for perceived violations of any of a number of his arbitrary codes of loyalty. In 1864, it was reported that Burbridge had imprisoned a number of Union women in Louisville for no specified reason. And, significantly to Prentice, Burbridge forbade any newspaper in Louisville from reporting about the major general's government overreach.

Then, just eleven days after Lincoln's July 5 proclamation, Burbridge issued General Order No. 59, which stated, "Whenever an unarmed Union citizen is murdered, four guerrillas will be se-

lected from the prison and publicly shot to death at the most con-
venient place near the scene of the outrages." Five days after
Burbridge issued the order, the Union army started shooting imprisoned Confederate soldiers on the spot, or transporting them to
the scene of a guerrilla attack to execute them there. Rather than
slowing down guerrilla warfare, the order inspired the guerrillas to
fly their black flag higher.

General Burbridge had become a ruthless dictator, but so far,
the leadership in Washington didn't seem interested in replacing
him. Prentice felt he had to get the attention of Abraham Lincoln.

A few days after the Harrodsburg Road stagecoach robbery,
Kentucky's citizens awoke to sip their coffee and flip through the
pages of Prentice's early edition of *The Louisville Daily Journal.* Underneath the paper's logo they read about a "desperado female
guerrilla" named Lieutenant Flowers, alias Sue Mundy—a name
Prentice purportedly borrowed from the arrest record of a woman
named Susanna Munday. Young E. Allison, a former editor of the
Louisville *Courier-Journal,* wrote,

> The real woman who bore the name of Sue Mundy seems to have
> been a notorious courtesan, living in the vicinity of Bloomfield,
> in Nelson County. She was a large woman, with the face and fig-
> ure of an Amazon, piercing black eyes and a profusion of black
> hair.

In crafting Lieutenant Flowers, Prentice put his creative pen
into overdrive. "She dresses in male attire, generally sporting a full
Confederate uniform," Prentice wrote. "Upon her head she wears
a jaunty plumed hat, beneath which escapes a wealth of dark-
brown hair, falling around and down her shoulders in luxuriant
curls. She is possessed of a comely form, is a bold rider and a dash-
ing leader."

Back in the deep woods of Nelson County, Clarke and his gang
no doubt read about their stagecoach robbery so colorfully told in

the October 11 edition of the *Daily Journal,* laughing to tears over Clarke's "comely figure" and "luxuriant curls." But to Clarke, gender confusion was a form of manipulation he knew well.

Gifted with dark features that jumped out against his beardless face and china-doll complexion, Marcellus Clarke was a young man people had always called handsome. His narrow waist and long hair—ringlets worn loose—added a touch of femininity to his otherwise masculine and, as some expressed it, "remarkably well-built" form. Clarke had learned to embrace this image if not become enamored with it entirely. He frequently sat unshakably still in a swaggered pose for the five minutes or more it took a camera to sear his likeness onto a glass or silver plate. Every photographer in a fifty-mile radius of Nelson County, it seemed, had set Clarke's figure to some photographic medium. Daguerreotypes abounded of him in oversize military uniforms that clumsily overhung his shoulders, or flouncy blouses, compressed under dark leather jackets, maybe with a revolver or two jutting butt-end forward out of a holster, with dark, teasing eyes—or sometimes tense ones hovering over a smirk, or no smile at all.

It was no secret that during his days with Morgan's brigade, Clarke masqueraded as a woman so he could infiltrate the Union lines to learn about upcoming operations. On one occasion, he squeezed into a blue dress and petticoat and seduced an entire uniform off a Union post guard, leaving the man completely naked, heartbroken, and wondering, Who exactly was this femme fatale to whom he had succumbed?

To complicate matters, Clarke hired a local tailor to outfit him in the most outlandish military-style getups. Lace, decorative gold buttons, and gaudy gold tinsel accented his coal-black waist-length cavalry-style jackets, worn with shocking apple-red shirts and pants—the blood color chosen to signify his ruthlessness. He buckled spurs in the shape of daisies around the heels of his knee-high riding boots, and sometimes wore a brown leather jacket buttoned tightly over the blue dress, girthed with a holster

Marcellus Jerome Clarke mustered this menacing pose wearing an oversize Confederate uniform. In other daguerreotypes, Clarke outfitted himself in laced blouses and velvet roundabout jackets decorated with elaborate buttons—always wearing the black hat—and a much more welcoming come-hither smile.

full of revolvers. That same blue dress embellished Clarke's frame the day Burbridge's army chased him across the hills—the dress flapping mockingly as he rode his horse at lightning speed away from a volley of carbine balls, and into the arms—literally—of his true love, a girl named Mollie. But the one consistent item in his ensemble—whether red pants or blue dress—was the black velvet hat, toppled crescent moon, and black ostrich plume that sat atop his enviable mane of tresses.

Rather than shun the association with Prentice's demoness, Clarke embraced everything about the editor's fictional Sue Mundy. He took the name and encouraged his men to refer to him as Sue in public. On raids, as Clarke stripped gold rings, watches, and other valuables from frightened citizens, he delighted in revealing that he was none other than Sue Mundy. During this time, the blue dress likely saw more appearances than usual to help ratchet up the hysterical gossip that began whirling through Kentucky. The theater in Louisville sold out several performances of the play *Bel Demonio,* based on the novel by Paul Féval, since Kentucky's own gorgeous demon had become so widely known. To Clarke, the nom de guerre likely provided a welcome shield for his true identity. He pressed Sue Mundy heavily into service to keep fueling the fire of Prentice's generally exaggerated reports of the comings and goings of the "wife of the Devil"—the "Terror of Kentucky."

In Prentice's *Daily Journal* pages, the cold months of 1864 and 1865 became heated by the horror suffered at the hands of the "woman" guerrilla. Every train derailment, all robberies of pedestrians, trains, stores, homes, banks, stables, and stagecoaches—as well as murder—were supposedly orchestrated by the vixen Sue Mundy.* According to Prentice, Mundy was a *she*-devil so evil that men shook in their boots at the sight of her shadow. Women ran terrified into their homes and hid their furs, silver-backed hair combs, and beaded purses. Farm owners took their fine horses out of their barns and hid them in the cellar. Sue Mundy walked into a home and, without provocation, drew her pistol and shot a man point-blank between the eyes. She shot sons in front of mothers and took the lives of Union soldiers who were home on furlough to bury their fathers. She burned down the Masonic Hall in Bloomfield, Kentucky, and a train depot at nearby Bardstown. Sue Mundy was a "tigress," driven by an unquenchable greed, with no loyalty to anything or anyone but herself. She stopped at nothing to take what she wanted, and always seemed to vanish at just the right moment. The bumbling Union army, still in a tailspin over John Hunt Morgan, could never trace Sue Mundy's whereabouts. She had been *somewhere* and had already gone. All that was left were the smoldering remains of her campfire pit and one or two haggard horses who could no longer keep up.

Sue Mundy was a born leader, accompanied by as many as twenty of "her murdering band of male cohorts," as *The New York Times* called them. In a span of six months, Prentice's woman guerrilla had stolen enough gold and silver to live comfortably into her elder years. But it was horses that were foremost in Sue Mundy's never-ending pursuit of fine acquisitions. She always rode a

---

* Prentice always addressed the bandit using the feminine pronoun to embarrass the Union army for being duped by, of all things, a woman!

thoroughly blooded horse, freshly stolen from some unfortunate farmer who had just sunk his life savings into buying the animal in great hope of owning the next Lexington.

Lexington was by now completely blind. Napoleon Belland was pulled from the stallion's riding schedule and shuffled off to Canada's racetracks, taking with him a string of Woodburn's horses to compete there. The stallion, robbed now of what little independence he had previously enjoyed, found new ways of expressing his dominance. If his groom Jarrett was late with a feeding, Lexington pawed the ground and kicked the gate. The horse still romped across his paddock, sometimes bumping smack into a tree, stunned on impact, as if in disbelief that such a thing would dare impede his path.

By 1864, Lexington had been recognized three years in a row as America's leading sire, an astounding feat given that during those three years of war, easily half of his offspring had been stolen from their owners and pressed into war service by both sides. The *Cleveland Plain Dealer* published a touching story about a string of one hundred war horses, which the reporter had witnessed tied to a fence in Nashville: beaten-down horses with protruding bones and dead eyes, destined for death. A man whose name is lost to history, wanting to purchase one of them to rehabilitate into service, walked along the line, surveying the sad specimens. He stopped abruptly at one of the tied-up horses, then continued walking. Reaching the line's end, he asked to see that horse again. Examining him carefully, the man affirmed, "This is a high blooded horse, and worth money, five times over, than the entire troop beside. Still, he is a mystery to me. He is certainly a Lexington horse. . . . There is no such horse in this country and yet here he is!" The horse was taken off the line of dying horses and inquiry made. According to the *Plain Dealer,* the horse had indeed been sired by Lexington, captured in Kentucky, and thrown into Confederate service. The man purchased him and attempted to nurse the horse to health. Whether the horse ultimately survived was never reported.

But not all of Lexington's war foals fell into such disuse. Nor were they all stolen. In January 1864, after Ulysses S. Grant won the Battle of Chattanooga, he hurried to St. Louis to be by the bedside of his eldest son, Frederick Dent Grant, who was gravely ill. While in St. Louis, General Grant received a telegram from a man unknown to him but who went by the name of S. S. Grant. The man lived in St. Louis and insisted he had something important to tell the general. Intrigued by the name similarity, General Grant obliged. When the general called on S. S. Grant, he found a bedridden and deathly ill old man.

S. S. Grant told the general that he greatly admired him for his Vicksburg success and wanted to give him the most valuable thing he owned, "a true son of the magnificent Lexington." The dying man had evidently bred his mare to Lexington back when the horse was contending for the crown of Best Stallion at the St. Louis Fair. S. S. Grant's only stipulation was that General Grant care for the horse its entire life. The general agreed and, according to historian Frazier Hunt, "thus came into possession of possibly the most perfect battle horse ridden by any officer in either army."

Grant named the three-year-old stallion Cincinnati. Lexington's son quickly rose in the general's esteem to outplace his other horses. He carried the general to the front lines at the battles of the Wilderness, Spotsylvania, and Cold Harbor, where Cincinnati weathered the hailstorm of bullets and exploding shells with the same undaunted courage as the general. Grant so loved Cincinnati that he permitted no one else to ride the horse—except for President Lincoln.

Those of Lexington's foals who were not in the war raced on the small number of tracks that still operated in the South and in the North, where interest in horse racing had reawakened. Wherever they raced, be it Louisville or New York, Lexington's sons and daughters were supremely fast and bold. His 1857 filly Idlewild beat some of the nation's top horses on a hard and difficult track, charging to the lead from dead last—as the *Spirit of the Times* put it, "strong and elastic as the Saxon bow that strewed the field of Cressy"—to win by two lengths.

But it was Lexington's 1861 foal crop that was exceptionally strong. Perhaps the greatest of them all was the colt Asteroid, whom Alexander kept and raced in order to promote the qualities of his sire's get. As with all his racehorses in training, Alexander turned Asteroid over to his Black trainer, Ansel Williamson. Under his training, Asteroid raced throughout Kentucky and Illinois, garnering Woodburn's blue-and-white silks a pile of wins. By 1864, he had never been defeated. Entreaties to buy the colt flooded Alexander's desk. Convinced that Asteroid was better than any living horse—better even than Lexington—he refused them all. That belief wasn't based just on opinion; it was backed up by the chronometer.

Most mornings, when Alexander was physically able, he joined Williamson to stand along the rail of his training tracks to clock his colts as they circled the course. Bent over and physically frail, he had taken to wrapping his body tightly with bandages to hold himself more upright. But his physical discomfort did little to tamp down his joy in seeing how his colts were maturing. It was on one of those mornings that the chronometer recorded Asteroid running four miles in 7:23 ½ over a track that wasn't primed for speed. On that occasion, the horse carried eleven pounds more than his sire had during the match against Time. That being the case, Asteroid was deemed faster than Lexington by about ten seconds. Writing to his brother A.J., Alexander offered, "I think [Asteroid] the best race horse in the U.S. by long odds and that if I keep him well and right, I can beat Lexington's time by several seconds under similar circumstances. I ran him four miles in better time than was made except in Lexington's time match." Alexander added, "You see what I think of this horse Asteroid and in some measure, I have shown you why I think so well of him; as it is possible that our Yankee friends may desire to try his mettle, I wish this to be kept quiet, indeed, I wish you to burn this on receipt after reading it." Not only did A.J. *not* burn the letter, he archived it in the family papers.

Though, due to the war, only half of Lexington's get made it to a racetrack, those that did were successful enough for the New York sports pages to be singing the stallion's rightful praises. *Wilkes' Spirit of the Times* wrote, "This king among horses has more than paid for himself, and we hope his days will yet be long on the land."

As the fourth year of the war dragged on, Clarke and his men continued to terrorize Kentucky. From his desk in Louisville, George Prentice crafted more words to his devoted readers, knowing those sentiments would certainly make their way to the president's advisors, and eventually to him. "How very strange that [Sue Mundy] isn't caught," wrote Prentice. "She has no reputation and probably deserves none for military sagacity or tact. Nevertheless, she goes wherever she pleases and does what she pleases and none of our military leaders seem to have the ability, if they have the disposition, to lay their hands on her. We can't imagine what the matter is. Surely, they are not afraid of her. To permit this she-devil to pursue her horrid work successfully much longer will be a military scandal and shame."

President Lincoln would soon address the situation in Kentucky.

CHAPTER 17

THE UNDEFEATED ASTEROID

O N OCTOBER 27, 1864, the sun was at high noon as Henry Grani-son, a groom at Woodburn's racehorse training barn, mucked out stalls. A few hills away, hoofbeats resounded on the dirt road as five horses bearing men dressed in Confederate gray approached the estate. Belted with an arsenal of guns, they trotted toward the training stable as if they knew the place by heart. Sensing something, perhaps feeling the reverberations, Granison eased up from his chores and leaned on the tall handle of his rake. Looking out at the terrain, he wasn't expecting to see anything, but then he spotted the riders. He couldn't figure who they were. They could be from the main house. But that didn't seem right, and the urgent pace at which they rode troubled him. Behind him in the stables were five Lexington-sired horses—Ansel, Norwich, Bay Dick, an unnamed colt, and Asteroid.

As the group approached, Granison surely recalled that day not too long ago, when he was staring into the barrel of a revolver as Morgan's men ordered him to give them "good hosses." Certainly, these oncoming riders knew that it was here, in this training stable, that they would find the most perfect horses—not only in Kentucky but in the nation. They didn't look like the type of men who would leave without first claiming such a prize. An unwelcome pang of uneasiness set in. Granison was going to have to live it out.

When the Confederate men rode up, Granison faced them and waited for them to speak. They never raised a gun and never yelled. They just told him calmly, "Show us some horses." But he could see that these men were used to fighting and had armed themselves for whatever might come. The revolvers holstered around their waists might hold 120 rounds altogether, he reckoned. Twenty-four rounds per man.

A mile away, Alexander had just sat down for lunch with friends at his dining room table and laid a napkin across his lap. The equine painter Edward Troye happened to be visiting Woodburn to paint another portrait of Lexington. The artist, already so well known to American horsemen, was no doubt an honored guest at the table. Alexander was surely pleased to show him off and to have him recount for the group, through his trained and knowing eyes, the wonderful symmetry of Lexington.

But it was Asteroid, perhaps, that aroused the group's attention. Troye must have fussed excessively over Lexington's undefeated son, for it was that horse who was at the moment the subject of his brush. The artist had already planned to honor Asteroid by placing him next to his trainer, Ansel Williamson, and his talented jockey, the young Edward Brown. But the painting wasn't yet finished; it was merely sketched, yet fully vivid in rich colors in the artist's mind. And as he described the scene with increasing excitement, those at the table would have nodded, saying, "Yes, yes, you *must* add that. . . ." Suddenly, in the middle of this reverie, the kitchen door slammed wide open and an elderly maid ran down the hallway shouting, "Somebody is after the horses!" Gasping for breath, she said it again: "Somebody is after the horses!"

For a moment, Alexander smiled slightly, befuddled at the old woman's excited talk. It strained credibility that such a thing could occur in broad daylight. But then a sober realization sank in. Only a few days earlier, Alexander had written to his brother A.J., telling him the latest news that was circulating around Kentucky. Word had it that Louisville was an agitated beehive of swarming guerrillas who thought it their daily obligation to rob tollgates and steal horses. Louisville wasn't that far from Midway; maybe a day on horseback at most. Woodburn had already been robbed once. Lightning couldn't strike twice . . . could it?

Alexander abruptly rose from the table and hurried to his dining room window. Somebody was running across the field. Again, the kitchen door slammed open, and this time a boy ran in, yelling, "Men are taking the horses!"

A field hand then came hurtling over the hill on a horse still encumbered by a plow harness. Alexander rushed out to meet him as the man repeated the cry, "Somebody is stealing the horses!"

Alexander turned to his friends, telling them to gather as many of Woodburn's workers as they could. He went back inside his house, grabbed his rifle, and loaded it.

Down at the training stable, the men in Confederate uniforms ordered Granison to tack up the Lexington horses, including Ansel, Norwich, and Bay Dick. The fourth man remained on his own horse, perhaps a favored or proven mount, while the fifth directed Granison to saddle the large bay. Granison looked at Asteroid, hesitated, then reluctantly girthed the saddle on Lexington's prized son. That last man jumped off his own horse, pulled himself up on Asteroid, and gathered the slack from the reins. Granison was ordered to saddle the unnamed Lexington colt and get ready to ride. The men, with Granison as their hostage, dug their spoked spurs into the horses' sides and galloped them across the fifty-acre fields and out the gates of the limestone fortress.*

---

* The facts of this event are taken from the testimony of Henry Granison and R. A. Alexander in the court-martial trial *United States v. Jim Davis*. Granison's testimony never made it clear how the men left Woodburn—specifically, whether they rode the stolen horses away or tethered them by lead while riding the horses on which they arrived. There is testimony that can support either conclusion. The most logical scenario, given the facts, is that at least four of the men and Granison rode the Woodburn horses away.

Alexander, his friends—possibly Troye too—and Nugent, the Irish gardener who had buried the Woodlawn Vase, raced their horses from the main house to the training stable. Alexander glanced around. Granison was gone. So were five of the Lexington horses, most notably Asteroid.

Alexander told his men that he was going after the thieves and asked which of them would join him. Six of them came forward, and, garlanded with seldom-used pistols and rifles, the men spurred into their horses. At the time, none of these gun-firing neophytes knew that they were chasing Sue Mundy's gang. But such tall tales wouldn't have stopped them.

Galloping one of the stolen horses down the road, Marcellus Clarke led his posse, his hair whipping wildly from beneath his hat. For ten miles they rode swiftly through forests, jumping over fallen timber, and back out onto the ragged road that headed north. Clarke stopped near a blacksmith's shop and huddled with his men for a brief rest. A few hundred feet ahead, around a sharp corner, the road forked to the left and led to the white rapids of the icy Kentucky River. A quarter mile wide at certain points, the expanse was a tiring swim for man or horse. The road to the right avoided the river but would lead to a sea of Union blue at Frankfort. As the men debated which danger was worse, Granison scanned the group, wide-eyed.

For over three hours the groom had held white-knuckle tight to the reins of the Lexington colt. Riding under the watchful eye of Clarke's men, he knew those reins were the tether to his only chance to live. He had been threatened at gunpoint and made to become an unwilling accomplice to robbery, and not only from Woodburn. During their escape through Woodford County, Clarke and his men had aimed their guns at a team of horse drivers and demanded they turn over a stout gray mare. Then they swapped Granison onto the mare and told him to secure the Lexington colt to run alongside.

Granison eyed the revolvers weighing down the circle of men.

Then he noticed the sprigs of pokeberries tucked snugly beneath their hatbands. If cautiously used, pokeberries could be a source of mind alteration, a high. But if heavily ingested, pokeberries would cause certain death. Granison wasn't sure which purpose these pokeberries served, and he grew worried that once these men no longer needed him, he would be forced to consume them to end his days.

For miles, Alexander and his men saw no trace of the stolen horses or Woodburn's groom. When they reached a farm known as the Nichols's place, they noticed an elderly enslaved woman standing in front of the old Grecian-styled house. Alexander slowed his pace and asked her if she had seen any men with horses. "Yes," she said, and pointed north. They rode on.

Within a short distance, Alexander spotted hoof tracks that turned in the direction of Frankfort and the Kentucky River. But by now it was late afternoon, and darkness would soon mask the thieves. He worried his horses were gone forever.

As Alexander obsessed over his lost horses, an excruciating pain shot up his spine. Riding at top speeds for hours at a time required an exceptional seat that relied on a strong abdominal muscle core to prevent the body from falling too far forward or too far behind the horse's motion. The group had zigzagged at a gallop through forests and crossed undulating landscapes of rough-grown grass with occasional unseen holes burrowed by moles and rabbits. Alexander had been jostled unmercifully in the saddle, and the bandages wound tightly around his body did little to guard against the grueling travel. He felt his body weakening. Still, he and his team pressed on.

As Alexander's group neared the fork in the road, he spotted some men gathered near the blacksmith's shop. Among them he saw Granison sitting on the gray mare, holding the reins of the unnamed Lexington colt. Next to him was Asteroid. Alexander's other horses were there too.

Just as the marauders noticed them, one of Alexander's men raised his rifle and fired. A carbine ball sliced through Clarke's group, narrowly missing them, and burrowed into the dirt somewhere beyond. Another ball zoomed through. And another. Clarke and his men hunkered down behind the necks of the horses, reached for their revolvers, and shot back. Alexander yelled for his men to stop shooting, fearful they would kill his horses. But the firing continued. The racehorses jumped, reared, frantically sidestepped, and lifted their heads in a fighting posture that made them much harder to control. Clarke and his men kicked into the prized horses, redirecting their energy into a full run. Up the road they galloped, a percussion of hooves that reverberated with the futility of pursuit as they disappeared around a sharp corner. Granison, now the least of their concerns, rode the gray mare safely in a different direction.

By the time Alexander and his men rounded the corner, Clarke and his gang were gone. At the place where the lane forked, hoof tracks could barely be made out in the waning light. They veered to the left, the route leading to the Kentucky River. Within a few hundred feet, Alexander saw one of his racehorses running, crazed and abandoned. They slowed down and trotted around the horse to herd it into capture. Securing the colt, they continued, following the lane around its curved path. On rounding the turn, Alexander saw three more of his horses running free, stirrup irons dangling from their saddles and flopping against their sides. Asteroid was nowhere to be seen.

Reaching the Kentucky River, the thief slid Asteroid down the soft dirt of the bank and plunged him into the dark rapids. Asteroid carried his rider into the wide river, swimming strongly against the current. He lifted the man out on the far bank and charged up a hill dense with trees. The other guerrillas soon caught up with them.

By the time Alexander and his group reached the river, there was no sign of Asteroid or any of the thieving gang. Studying the river's massive width of white-foamed rapids in the darkening light, Alexander estimated that crossing would be a strenuous twenty-minute feat. He surveyed his small group of friends and Nugent, the gardener. It was almost nightfall, and the late October air was sharp. The river's water was even colder. The men debated whether to return home or to continue the madness of crossing the rapids. Five of Alexander's friends shook their heads over the risky proposition, apologized to him, and said they were turning back. But the sixth said he would stay and ride into the river with him.

Before the men could leave, one of the guerrillas came down the hill on the other side of the river. Taunting childishly, he yelled in a sing-song voice, "We have your racehorse. Come across and get him!" He took out his revolver and launched several bullets across the river that fell short with plunking splashes into the water. Nugent aimed his rifle across the river and fired several shots. Taking out his revolver, a second guerrilla slid down the hill to join the shooting. In rapid succession, six to eight bullets soared close to Alexander. Jumping off his horse, he ran to a fence and knelt behind it. The day had taxed what little reserves he had, and he rested momentarily at the fence as bullets continued to fly. Catching his breath, he took out his carbine, aimed, and fired four shots across the river. "They did not appear to mind my shots at all," he later said, "which surprised me a little." As firing continued between the thieves and Alexander's men, a third guerrilla started descending the hill. Spotting him, Alexander took aim. He fired, hitting the guerrilla's foot and downing him. A bellow of cries pierced the cold air. Abandoning the fight, the guerrillas slid down the hill to help their man.

As darkness fell, the situation was hopeless. Alexander and his men climbed on their horses and turned toward home, leaving behind Asteroid, and all of Alexander's hope.

Within a couple of days, the incident was being reported around the country. The *Chicago Tribune* wrote,

> Sue Mundy's gang entered the stable of R.A. Alexander, in Woodford County, on Thursday afternoon, and stole six of his fine horses. The gang, it is said, have possession of the celebrated Asteroid. Mr. Alexander offers $1,000 for the return of Asteroid, and $5,000 for the capture of Mundy.

Wilkes' Spirit of the Times in New York reported,

> Guerrillas lately made a raid upon the farm of Mr. Robert Alexander in Woodford County and carried off six of his horses. Among them was the famous colt Asteroid, who has won some very notable races, and never suffered defeat. This is the second time that Mr. Alexander's place has been plundered by the predatory hands who carry on their work in Kentucky.

The New Orleans *Times-Democrat,* Washington, D.C.'s *Evening Star, The Baltimore Sun,* and *The Detroit Free Press* wrote similarly, but clarified that the actual number of horses stolen was five, and that Alexander's reward for Sue Mundy was $500; the extremely large $5,000 amount had been a typographical error.

Despite all the clarifications, the newspapers didn't report the latest developments. By the time those articles were being read at breakfast tables across the nation, Alexander, who at the time was feeling "dangerously ill," had already accepted the assistance of his neighbor, Major Warren Viley, the son of Captain Willa Viley, who years before had co-purchased Lexington with Ten Broeck for the Great State. The morning after the raid, Major Viley had set off through Versailles with his friend Colonel Zach Henry, an imposingly tall, muscularly built man. In addition to his revolvers, Viley was armed with Alexander's full authority to ransom the colt back.

Riding out to the far side of the river where the guerrillas and Asteroid were last seen, Viley and Henry spent the next three days following hoof tracks and pressing passersby about whether they had seen or heard of a striking bay colt. Their journey eventually led them some forty miles to Nelson County, a land "infested with murderous bushwhackers," Viley would later report. This was an area where guerrillas tucked themselves away for safety. It was the type of territory that disgusted the likes of George Prentice, the Union generals, and any Union-favoring Kentucky citizen. But it was also the place where Asteroid would most likely be found. Viley and Henry rode deep into the woods until they encountered some men on horseback quietly observing them. To gain their trust, Viley told them he was the uncle of the man who had been wounded by gunshot at the Kentucky River shootout. He was there to help if they could tell him where to find the man. The men pointed Viley down a wooded road and told him to look for two men; one of them would be riding a large bay.

Viley and Henry rode a few miles through what was described as a "lonely and unfrequented spot in which guerrillas and robbers are said to swarm." Eventually, they saw two more men on horse-back. One of the horses was Asteroid. As Viley and Henry approached, the bandits drew their revolvers, aimed, and told them to halt. Viley rested his reins on his horse's neck and raised his hands slowly. He told them he was here for the bay horse, his favorite pet. Henry dismounted, lumbered toward Asteroid, and seized him by the bridle.

Asteroid's rider looked down at Henry's immense size and then measured the man's determination. Holstering his revolver, he told Viley that he had recently lost his own horse valued at $250. He would agree to part with this horse for that sum if Viley would also give him a horse of equal quality to this bay. Viley agreed and handed him the money. Satisfied, the guerrilla swung off Asteroid, leaving him to Henry. As a final thought, the man told Viley, "This is the best horse I've ever ridden."

Foolishly, Viley agreed. Incredible as it sounds, he added that the colt was none other than Lexington's undefeated son. The guerrillas looked at Viley in disbelief and expressed their doubt. "No three-year-old horse is this fast," the man countered. But Viley assured them the colt was indeed Asteroid. Folding the money into his pocket, the guerrilla stored Viley's name in his unforgiving memory.

Viley and Zach Henry rode to Woodburn and delivered Asteroid. For their bravery, nearly one hundred people from Versailles gathered to crown them with a gala celebration, complete with music and home-baked goods from local farms. Alexander offered to pay Viley the reward, which Viley refused because Alexander

Edward Troye started *The Undefeated Asteroid* at Woodburn, but his work was abruptly halted due to Asteroid's theft by Sue Mundy's gang. Upon Asteroid's return, as a final touch Troye depicted the thieving guerrilla squad in the background, firing their revolvers as they quickly approach Asteroid; his trainer, Ansel Williamson; his jockey, Edward Brown, and an unidentified groom.

"had done so much for the stock interest of the state." Henry, however, did accept Alexander's $1,000 reward. Besides Alexander, none was happier, perhaps, than Edward Troye, who reportedly had been angry that his inspired painting had been disrupted by Asteroid's theft. Now able to complete his vision, Troye painted Asteroid standing regally beside Ansel Williamson and Edward Brown. As a final detail Troye painted Sue Mundy and his gang off in the distance, firing their pistols and galloping their horses toward the unsuspecting trio. Troye named the painting *The Undefeated Asteroid*.

As accolades continued to shower Viley over the ensuing days, he settled back at his Stonewall Farm in Versailles, just off the Old Frankfort Pike—basking in the sublimity of his heroic deed. The promises he had made the guerrilla had receded far back in his thoughts. There was no need to honor, much less concern himself over, token words he'd made to a thief.

But a few days later, that very man startled Viley at his kitchen door. The guerrilla and his men pushed their way in and sat down uninvited at the dining table. They asked for supper. As Viley's staff prepared the meal, the man questioned him. "Have you found me a colt of equal value to Asteroid?" Viley assured the guerrilla that his word was honorable, and he'd deliver a colt as promised. After the meal, the guerrillas left Stonewall. Viley later said that the man who'd sold him Asteroid was Sue Mundy.

Within a matter of days, the guerrilla squad traveled to Nantura, the Versailles farm of brothers John and Adam Harper. Dressed now in Union overcoats, they told John Harper they were there to press for horses. "On what authority?" inquired Harper. Marcellus Clarke pointed his revolver at Harper, saying "This is our authority." When Adam tried to resist, he was shot and killed. The bandits fled without horses.

In the wake of the October 1864 guerrilla raid, Alexander intensified precautions at Woodburn. He installed locks on all the stables and placed armed guards at each end of the training and stallion stables. He hired additional watchmen and armed his laborers with pistols and rifles, issuing orders to use them as necessary. A sense of renewed order settled over the farm.

Camped in the woods of Nelson County, Jim Davis, Henry Magruder, and the rest of Marcellus Clarke's guerrilla band continued dressing in red flannel jackets, accompanied by Clarke in his blue dress, to rob trains, plunder towns, and raise hell. All the while, Clarke kept remembering that day in the woods in October 1864. The day he lost Asteroid for a paltry sum.

News of the infamous Marcellus Clarke / Sue Mundy gang spread throughout Kentucky and across the border into the charred territories of Missouri and Kansas. But for the past two years, Kansas had endured evil from its own marauder in the form of a light-auburn-haired, blue-eyed devil. He had ripped through the state, leaving hundreds of dead men and wreckages with fire-smoldered buildings. He claimed he murdered because Kansas was filled with too many "jayhawkers"—Union-sympathizing men who had no tolerance for slavery. The truth is that William Clark Quantrill* needed no pole on which to fly a banner of justification. He liked to kill.

Quantrill had read about the beautiful and brazen Sue Mundy and thought he might join her. Gathering a band of his trusted Raiders, a group that included Frank and Jesse James and Cole and Bob Younger, he shielded them in Union uniforms. They rode out of Missouri and crossed the Mississippi River at Devil's Bend, twenty-five miles from Memphis. From there, Quantrill's Raiders worked their way through Tennessee and passed into Kentucky.

It was New Year's Day 1865, and the snow lay thick.

---

* Quantrill's assumed identity of "Clark" has been spelled differently in history. The name appears as "Clark" and "Clarke" in *The War of the Rebellion: A Compilation of the Official Records of the War of the Rebellion*. To avoid confusion with Marcellus Jerome Clarke, the spelling of "Clark" will be used in reference to Quantrill.

CHAPTER 18

SMOKE SCREENS

SNOW HAD FALLEN to the height of men's knees. It made for difficult passage for Quantrill and his Raiders, cutting through the woods to avoid the main roads. William Quantrill was a man running from himself, from the emptiness and pain that twisted his heart.

As a boy in Canal Dover, Ohio, Quantrill nailed live snakes to trees. He maimed dogs and cats to hear them cry and stuck his knife into the sides of cows and horses as they grazed. He once shot a pig through the tip of its ear from over two hundred yards away and was seen laughing as the animal squealed in pain.

Quantrill's bizarre lust for torture soon turned to people. He derived pleasure from inflicting pain and psychological distress on others. On one occasion, he locked a girl up high in the belfry tower of a church in town, then watched from a distance as towns-people tried for over twenty-four hours to pry open the door. She was found lying on the floor facedown, insensible from fright.

That vein of cruelty continued into Quantrill's early manhood, taking odd forms. Unable to control him, and afraid of his vio-lence, his mother sent him away to Kansas in the charge of a traveling companion. En route, the escort discovered him in the middle of the night standing quietly over the body of another man, holding a twelve-inch Mexican dagger as if he was going to plunge it into the sleeping man's heart. The companion screamed in terror, then intervened, caning young Quantrill mercilessly before forcing him out on his own.

The source of his cruelty was unknown. It could've been over a whipping he had received from his father. Quantrill was said to have "return[ed] to the room pale, tearless, trembling, and with the look of a demon." Whatever the source, torment lay behind his hard-cut eyes. The only way to ease his torture was by making other living beings feel pain much more acutely. But that crazed way of subduing his inner turmoil never provided him lasting solace. His mind was constantly plagued. He had once written to his mother, "I think everything and every body around me is happy and I alone am miserable, it seems man is doomed to aspire after happiness; but never in reality to obtain it; for God intended that this earth should *be earth* and not *heaven* for mortal man."

Out of the woods Quantrill and his Raiders rode, into the town of Canton on the Kentucky side of the Cumberland River. Disguised in Union blue, they eased through the main street and toward Robert Hall's blacksmith shop. Quantrill's war mount, Old Charlie, had a hind shoe dangling and in need of replacing. For four years the horse had carried the devil through hell, culminating in the early morning of that dreadful day in August 1863 in Lawrence, Kansas, when Quantrill and his Raiders cracked open the early morning with gunfire, killing over a hundred men because they were jayhawkers. At the end of that morning's carnage, Quantrill and his gang rode their horses over the blood, dust, and gore—dragging red, white, and blue strips of an American flag that had been shredded and tied to their tails. How confidently Old Charlie had carried Quantrill then as the Raiders fired irreverently at the sun, hollering victoriously while whipping their horses forward. How gallantly Old Charlie had led the Raiders in that pell-mell frenzy out of the hell they had created, and on down the Osawatomie Road, leaving behind the smell of burning flesh and Lawrence burning to ashes.

As Hall started to work on Old Charlie's shoe, Quantrill ventured into Canton under the guise of Captain Clark of Colorado, a name he had taken from a Union man he had killed months earlier. While inquiring if anyone knew anything about the whereabouts of Sue Mundy, Quantrill was summoned back to Hall's. When he returned to the blacksmith, Old Charlie was standing on three legs, with his fourth leg, his hind, drawn up high underneath his belly. A steady stream of blood trickled from his hoof, pooling in the dirt. In Hall's hands, Charlie had unexpectedly jerked his foot away, causing the buttress knife the smith was wielding to slip, severing the horse's digital flexor tendon that supported his leg. Charlie was permanently lamed and unserviceable. Quantrill said, "It is fate. So be it." Word quickly spread. A sympathetic woman from Canton, thankful to these Union soldiers for their service, provided Captain Clark with another horse, but one that was green, skittish, and unbroken to gunfire and the horrors that surround it. Quantrill saddled the new horse and left town.

By dusk the Raiders spotted the rugged outline of Greenville, Kentucky. Still wearing their blue overcoats, they rode into the Union-controlled town. Stopping at Greenville's Federal livery stable, they untacked their horses and talked with the commander, passing themselves off as cavalry beaten down by travel and hunger. The commander invited them to join his officers for dinner, and afterward, Quantrill paid the tab with government scrip, signing his name as Captain Clark.

After dinner, Quantrill's men retired to the barracks while he joined the officers in their quarters, listening to their lively stories of the she-devil Sue Mundy and the bugle-playing Jim Davis. These guerrillas were impossible to catch, the officers said. Amused,

Quantrill told them guerrilla warfare was something he knew a great deal about. He would be glad to help them capture these marauders the following day if their hosts would kindly point the way.

The next morning fourteen Federal soldiers saddled up at the livery stable, excited about accompanying Captain Clark on his guerrilla-catching expedition. Quantrill and his Union-disguised Raiders were already saddled and waiting. They exchanged handshakes and jovial banter as the Union soldiers readied their horses and loaded their carbines. Sue Mundy's haven in Bloomfield was about 150 miles away, they said. But she could most likely be found anywhere along their route.

The men left Greenville and rode out into the flatland, where the snow's crystalline reflection amplified the light. As they rode a little farther north, the woods began to overshadow the plains, and in a seemingly haphazard way, two Raiders placed themselves on either side of each Union soldier. They talked to them of irrelevant matters in a calm tone, with faraway eyes. As the main column marched on, the Raider team farthest back steered its soldier deep into the woods, feigning the need to investigate a noise or something seen. Under thickly fringed branches weighted with snow, the Raiders slit the life from the soldier's throat. Then they cut the reins from the bridle of the soldier's horse and tightened them around the animal's neck until it fell dead. They left horse and rider there and rejoined the rank. One after another, a Raider team lured a Union soldier to the back of the line, then led him deeper among the trees, never to return. The ensemble continued through the forest until all fourteen Union soldiers lay slain in the snow. Quantrill's sole motive was that the men were Union.

Minus their escort, Quantrill and his men continued their search through Kentucky, arriving at Hartford in the late afternoon on January 22, 1865. Sue Mundy was rumored to be in the vicinity. Earlier that day, Marcellus Clarke and his gang had fired their revolvers head-on into a locomotive engine, running it off the track. They'd then proceeded to burn down the Lebanon Junction railroad station in nearby Bullitt County, first shooting and killing two Union soldiers and robbing the railroad hotel's patrons. Throughout this latest rampage Clarke, dressed head to toe in a shirt and pants colored blood-red and accented with gold tinsel, had answered to the name of Sue Mundy.

Seventy miles away in Hartford, Quantrill and his men rode their horses at a walk, clopping down the road that bifurcated the town. Blue overcoats still covered their backs, and they tipped their hats amicably to those who eyed them from curtained windows. At the Union headquarters, Quantrill informed Colonel Shanks that he was Captain Clark, this time of the Fourth Missouri Cavalry. He was there to hunt Sue Mundy. Quantrill's hypnotic words of assurance and eagerness worked their magic. So entranced was Colonel Shanks that he was prepared to do just about anything Quantrill asked, later saying in an official report that he regarded Clark as a "true Federal captain."

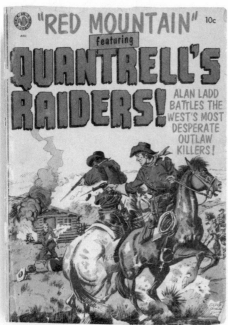

William Quantrill and his Raiders, including Frank and Jesse James as well as Bob and Cole Younger, were so notorious that they became the epitome of gunslinging, murderous outlaws. Any romanticism or mythologizing by comic books was not too great of a stretch from the gang's real-life deeds.

Quantrill asked for a guide to lead his team to the vicinity of Sue Mundy's rumored location. Shanks summoned Lieutenant Andrew Barnett, who knew the area well, and asked him to escort the Fourth Missouri Cavalry and Captain Clark. Along the way, Quantrill and his Raiders beat and shot Barnett and cast his lifeless body aside on the snow.

On January 28, Marcellus Clarke stopped at a house off the turnpike road near Bloomfield. Always vigilant for potential enemies, he asked a woman there if she had seen any Union men. She told him she had seen about twenty of them headed toward Bloomfield. Clarke had heard rumors that Ed Terrell was in town. Turned out, he was right.

Edwin Terrell was menacing and maniacal. His cold stare did nothing to camouflage his deranged mind. Born in Harrisonville in Shelby County, Kentucky, Terrell had assembled a small militia of Home Guards from his town when it became apparent the Union army couldn't contain Kentucky's guerrilla problem. His authority, though self-appointed, received nods from Governor Thomas Bramlette, who had a habit of firing off hotheaded letters to President Lincoln about the ineptness of the Union army stationed in Kentucky. The Home Guards, the governor argued, were his state's only chance for peace. They were more equipped than the Union soldiers with the know-how and brawn required to fight guerrillas. Under Governor Bramlette, Terrell's little band began to cut through the heart of Nelson County, the land where—no matter how much they were needed—the Union army *wouldn't* go. But for Terrell, Nelson County offered prime pickings. He shot guerrillas on the front porches of what they thought were safe havens and sneered as he said, "Another damned Rebel gone to hell." With his tally growing exponentially, Terrell's name became etched into the consciousness of every Confederate-minded guerrilla slinking through Kentucky.

The last thing Marcellus Clarke wanted to hear was that Terrell was in Bloomfield. Only the day before, editor George Prentice had informed his reading public that, according to a very reliable source, Sue Mundy was a hermaphrodite. The implication made Clarke hopping mad. He was either a man or, only when he chose to be, a woman, but definitely not both simultaneously. And, as if that weren't enough, Prentice had already said that the she-devil was, without a doubt, Marcellus Clarke, son of Hector M. Clarke of Simpson County, Kentucky. Worse yet, Prentice wrote that Clarke assumed the name of Sue Mundy so he could woo John Hunt Morgan, the Confederate general who, according to Prentice, had lost his senses over Clarke's striking features.

As the innuendos and name associations piled up dangerously on top of one another, Prentice's gender-questioning shocker rocketed throughout the entire *Louisville Daily Journal*–reading populace—including President Lincoln, Secretary of War Edwin Stanton, the editors of *The New York Times,* and every living soul in Kentucky and the surrounding states.

Compounding this setback was Clarke's new worry about dodging the aim of Terrell's carbine. Rather than wait to be caught, Clarke gathered a team of sixty guerrillas and, on January 28, rode to Bloomfield to confront Terrell. During the shooting spree that transpired—at a full gallop, over miles of territory—one of Clarke's gang shot Terrell. Clarke didn't stick around long enough to see Terrell rise, or to hear him yell at a doctor that he was a "damned liar" when he told Terrell that his prognosis was death. As Terrell fought to live, Marcellus Clarke rode out of Bloomfield southward down the Perryville Pike toward Danville, Kentucky.

The next day, Quantrill and his men, still disguised in Union-blue overcoats, traveled to Danville, raided the town, and gutted its Union telegraph office to stop the news about their wrongdoings from spreading. But one message got through:

TELL YOUR MEN TO BE VERY CAREFUL.

THE GUERRILLAS ARE ARRAYED IN FEDERAL UNIFORM.

SHOOT TO KILL.

William Quantrill and his Raiders hurriedly rode out of Danville northward on the Perryville Pike, their blue coats flapping behind them. Riding southward down the same road at an equally frenzied pace was Marcellus Clarke, racing to further his distance from the Terrell shooting. At any moment, the Perryville Pike would become a collision course.

The coming together of the two marauders became a savage union; their common aim appeared to be theft at whatever the cost. To operate as one force, Clarke and his men followed Quantrill's lead, stealing Federal uniforms and wearing them as disguises.

On February 2, 1865, in the early evening, Midway was closing down when about twenty-five men dressed in Union overcoats rode in. They dismounted and, cocking their revolvers, walked into the train depot. They found the safe, broke it open, and stole the contents. Then they pointed their guns at the surrounding people and took their money. One man inquired of his robber, "To whom am I giving my money?"

"To Sue Mundy" was the reply. Other citizens overheard some of the bandits refer to one of them as Quantrill.

While Midway's citizens were surrendering their valuables, another Raider lit a flame and threw it into the depot's telegraph room. As smoke curled out of the windows, the thieves walked along the street, aiming their revolvers at people and taking their watches, money, purses, and jewelry. The men took whatever else they wanted, then left town. Although his pockets were replenished with money and gold, William Quantrill still lacked a reliable horse. The young colt given him to replace Old Charlie had failed to provide that measure of security that a good horse should. And Warren Viley still had not given Clarke a colt equal to Asteroid.

Leaving Midway, the gang rode in the direction of the Old Frankfort Pike. Along the way, they stopped at Stonewall Farm, the home of Major Viley. Although Warren Viley wasn't home, his father, Willa Viley, was. They seized the aged man in his nightshirt, bound his hands, and forced him to ride behind the saddle of one of the Union-dressed men. With Willa Viley in tow, the men rode down the Old Frankfort Pike toward Woodburn Farm.

CHAPTER 19

THE HEIST OF WOODBURN

THE SUN SANK. The Old Frankfort Pike was weighted with mud and unforgiving to travelers. Undeterred, twenty-five riders in faded blue overcoats plodded through the rain and the wet snow.

When the men in blue reached the road leading to Woodburn, they turned, entering through the limestone gates, and proceeded under the leafless canopy of blue ash. They rode in a double-breasted formation, smelling of mildew, smoke, and dried blood. Some of the guards spotted them, took them for Union soldiers and reported them as such to Alexander.

Assuming the worst, Alexander ordered his staff to bar the windows and doors while he assembled guns and ammunition. Woodburn foreman Daniel Swigert escorted his wife, Mary, who was holding their baby, and the household's children to the dining room where they were told to wait in silence. Alexander shoved a pistol in his belt as a worker went out the back to spread word throughout the farm.

In they came, sullen vestiges of men on blank-eyed horses worn to bone. They swelled through the kitchen yard as Alexander watched from a small window. He'd been warned that he'd be raided again, and that this time he'd be kidnapped and forced to pay his own ransom. But these men were in Union blue. Alexander stepped to the front door and called for them to halt. They stopped and maneuvered their horses to face him.

"What will you have, gentlemen?" Alexander asked.

One of the men said, "We want provender for two hundred horses."

"That is a pretty large order. I have provender in various places but I have no place to feed so many horses."

A different man said, "We are out pressing horses."

"Show your order to press horses."

Some of the men in blue drew pistols. One of them said, "This is our order."

"Well, I suppose if you are bound to have horses there is no necessity to fight about it," Alexander said. "But if you are disposed to have a fight, I have some men here and we will give you the best fight we can."

Hearing Alexander's words, Willa Viley, shivering in his night-shirt, his hands bound by rope, spoke up from behind one of the riders: "Alexander, for God's sake, let them have the horses. The captain says he'll be satisfied if you'll let him have two horses without any trouble."

Seeing his neighbor, Viley, Alexander replied, "The thing can be very easily arranged. Who is the captain?"

Either Clarke, Quantrill, or a third guerrilla, Bill Marion, announced he was the captain and assured Alexander that what Viley said was true.

"Then you shall have two horses," Alexander said, "and as I am a man of my word, you may consider the matter settled. Let us shake hands on the bargain."

Alexander stepped down from the doorway. The soaked ground

was uneven, and Alexander stumbled, then righted himself. The captain waited on horseback. The two men shook, then the captain said, "March out your men and deliver up your arms."

"We've made a bargain and I am to give you two horses. You shall have the horses, but I will neither march out my men nor give up my arms."

"Well, deliver up your arms anyhow."

"Captain, I have these arms for my own protection. You said that if I would give you two horses without a contest that you would be satisfied. I'm going to keep my arms but I assure you that a gun will not be fired. However, to assure you that I am acting in good faith I will send my arms into the house."

"Do so then and if a gun is fired, I will burn up your whole place."

"If a gun shall be fired, it will be your fault."

Alexander walked inside, through the kitchen and down the long passage to the dining room. There he unarmed himself and handed his weapons to his servants and guards. He asked them to remove their own guns and hide the weapons in one of his stables. Except for Nugent, who Alexander said retained his gun and then hid himself. Alexander returned to the kitchen. The captain, on horseback, was waiting for him at the door. "Where are those horses? I'm in a hurry."

Alexander pointed to his riding stable, the closest one to his house. The captain questioned Alexander, "Is the horse a good one?"

Alexander assured him, "As good as any horse can be."

"Do you have a horse called the bald horse?"

"I have several horses answering that description."

"No, I mean a horse known as the 'bald horse.' I must have him."*

★   The bald horse may have been Alexander's trotting horse, Bay Chief, foaled in 1859 and sired by the famed trotter Mambrino Chief II. Bay Chief had raced half a mile in 1:08, a good time for that era. Bay Chief had a white face that made him appear bald. It's possible that the captain was referring to Lexington, who also had a pronounced white blaze running down his face. However, the Lexington scenario is unlikely. Lexington was a racehorse, not a trotter for pulling buggies. The captain

"The horse is a good trotting horse," Alexander said, "one that has value to me, but of comparatively little value to you. I have twenty horses better suited."

"I must have him," the captain insisted.

"The horse is valuable only as a trotter," Alexander repeated. "He is quite unsuited to your use."

"If the horse is valuable to you, he is valuable to me. I must have him."

Alexander offered the captain $10,000 to allow the bald horse to remain at Woodburn. The captain shook his head.

Conceding, Alexander said, "The bald horse is in my trotting stable on the opposite hill. My man Hull has the key." Alexander volunteered to get him. The captain allowed him to go.

Alexander hurried to the stable barracks and found F.V.R. Hull, an Albany native who superintended the trotting stable, pulling on his boots. Alexander told him about the men and the captain's demand for Bay Chief. If there is any chance, Alexander stressed, Hull must switch out the bald horse for a lesser one before the men arrive at the stable. Hull assured Alexander he would do whatever he could and set off in haste toward the trotting stables. Alexander then rushed back to his house.

The captain waited, but when Alexander did not return with Hull, he rode to where the trotters were stabled. Hull had just arrived there. The captain pointed his revolver at the superintendent and demanded, "We must have a few horses. Good ones, and if you have any objection, I'll kill you." Hull opened the stable doors. The Raiders pulled out some straw and set fire to it. As flames jumped higher the excited horses ran out into the night. In the herd was Bay Chief. The captain spotted him.

When Alexander arrived at his house, two Raiders were sitting

---

was likely looking for a serviceable horse. Lexington's blindness—making him unreliable as a war mount—was known worldwide. Still, it is possible that the guerrillas planned to capture Lexington. He would have been taken for the purpose of ransom: a sum that would easily have exceeded $15,000.

on horseback outside the kitchen door. They held two riderless horses, and on seeing them, Alexander assumed that the other two men had gone into the kitchen for water. But the men weren't there. Alexander walked up the long passage to the dining room, where Mary Swigert was hiding with her baby and the other children. Standing in the room with her were two Raiders dressed in Union overcoats. One had his back to the door and was pointing a cocked revolver at Mary and the infant in her arms. The two Raiders had gathered some of the guns in the house, and the one who was pointing the revolver told Mary to get the rest of the arms.

Alexander held up his hands. "The captain says if I will give him two horses without any trouble I can keep my arms, and I'm going to keep them."

The Raider turned to Alexander and pointed his pistol. The man's eyes were red, maddened and inflamed by liquor and smoke. Alexander approached him and tried to knock the pistol away, but the man held it tight. Alexander grabbed the man and, throwing all his weight into the Raider's right shoulder, swung him toward the passage door. Incensed by the fight of this small, hunched-over man, the Raider shoved back. Alexander didn't budge.

The two men fell into the passage, crashing on the floor and rolling in a disproportionate grapple. Alexander weighed into the man underneath him, pinioning the Raider in a strong hold. The Raider yelled to his friend: "Shoot him! He's killing me!"

The other Raider stared wide-eyed in disbelief at the struggle, then said, "He's not armed. He can't hurt you much."

Alexander tightened his grip on the Raider's arms. The man writhed and twisted but couldn't free himself. Again, the trapped Raider yelled, "Shoot him!"

The other man, still cradling the guns, called out, "Let him go, Mr. Alexander."

Alexander yelled back, "I won't let him go. He'll shoot me."

The Raider jerked against the hold, rolling hard against an iron safe. He cried out, "He has broken my arm!"

"Let him go," the other Raider said to Alexander. "I'll protect you."

"Do you promise me on the word and honor of a gentleman that you will protect me?"

"Yes," the second Raider answered.

Alexander relinquished his hold and rose breathlessly from the ground.

The second Raider stepped forward, still holding the stolen guns in his arms, and maneuvered his drunken friend out of the dining room and down the passage toward the kitchen. Alexander rushed after them and threw the bolt. He told Mary not to open the door. "If any of the Union men come looking for me, tell them I'm gone," he said.

Alexander left through a side door. From the garden he saw the trotting stable on fire and his horses scattered.

His first thought was for Lexington. Ransom had been the word foremost on his mind in those compacted minutes since he became aware these men wanted only his best horses. He was a man worth plenty, but in these war times, maneuvering funds was especially difficult, and he might not be able to gather sufficient cash quickly enough to save his prized animals. The stallion would make for a high ransom. If Alexander couldn't pay it, these men would not hesitate to kill Lexington. A blind horse whose ransom could not be paid would be only a nuisance. Braced by his bandages, Alexander quickened his pace toward the stallion stable on the opposite hill.

The men in blue had not found Lexington by the time Alexander arrived. He ordered one of the grooms there to hide Woodburn's most valuable horses, while telling another to rush to the racehorse training stable and tell Ansel Williamson to hide all the best horses there.

Alexander never stated what occurred next, but the following scenario is likely.

That cold February night, the rain felt like shards of ice. Wrapping a flannel blanket snugly around Lexington, the groom slipped on a halter and lead, then nodded to Alexander that the horse was ready. The woods lay beyond the stallion's paddock, and there he hoped to shield Lexington from danger. The two men walked the blind horse across the open field and into the thicket of trees, negotiating through fallen saplings and dodging the branches that reached out from every direction. The night had gone horribly wrong. Much had been lost. When they reached a point in the woods where Alexander believed no soul would hear Lexington's whinnies, they stopped. There, in the silence and rain, the future of his prized horses and his entire farm seemed in the balance.

At the training stable, Marcellus Clarke and some of the Raiders were already pointing their guns at Williamson, telling him to bring forth Asteroid.* The trainer walked into the unlit barn, candle in hand, and emerged with a big bay that he saddled in the dim light. Clarke jumped off his horse and pulled himself up on the bay. Holstering his gun, he pressed his spurs into the animal, and rode off into the night. Williamson watched them go. Then he returned to the barn, haltered Asteroid, and walked Lexington's famed son deep into the woods.

That night, the guerrillas left Woodburn on fifteen stolen racehorses and trotters with an estimated value of $32,000—more than $500,000 today.

At Cane Spring, a neighboring farm, Willa Viley either fell from his horse or was thrown off by one of the Raiders. They left him lying there in the cold, shivering and defenseless. He was later

---

★   The identity of the guerrilla in charge at the training stable was never identified by Alexander. Since historical sources place Sue Mundy and William Quantrill together at the Woodburn raid, it is likely that Mundy took the lead at the training stable, given his previous raid there and his knowledge of Asteroid.

found, nearly frozen, and taken home. The elderly Viley never recovered from that night and died within the month.

On the night of the raid, the Union army headquarters in Lexington received word that some of Alexander's horses had been stolen and that Midway was burning down. Brigadier General Edward H. Hobson coordinated the Union army's chase, summoning his forces from all four cardinal directions. But confusion ensued. The whereabouts of Quantrill and the guerrilla identified in the dispatches as "Sue Mundy" was unclear. Hobson ordered troops to move in various directions and told them to be on the lookout for both gangs.

While Union army dispatches were giving mixed signals, sowing uncertainty all around, the Woodford County Home Guards, a self-organized militia of local farmers and townspeople that operated under the auspices of Governor Bramlette, succeeded in homing in on Marcellus Clarke, Quantrill, and the Raiders. Twelve miles from Woodburn, the thieves stopped to rest in a farmer's field next to the Kentucky River. Circling in, the Home Guards saw the guerrilla group and took aim. Under fire, the guerrilla captain jumped on the bald horse and kicked him into a gallop. The Home Guards galloped off in pursuit. Some of them slashed sabers at Bay Chief and the captain whenever they got close. But Bay Chief outran them until one of the Home Guards pulled the trigger of his revolver, launching a ball that passed through Bay Chief's muzzle. A second ball struck one of the trotter's hocks. A third ball lodged in the horse's left thigh, and a fourth in his right thigh. Still Bay Chief ran, carrying the captain down the road. After two miles, weakened by blood loss, the horse's stride broke into a faltering footfall. As Home Guards overcame them, the captain jumped out of the saddle and fled on foot. Bay Chief was left standing, blowing hard, his blood pooling in the road.

Back at the farmer's field, the rest of the guerrillas took off in a different direction, forcing the stolen horses to swim across the

Historical marker at Midway, Kentucky, telling of Sue Mundy and William Quantrill's burning of Midway and robbery of Woodburn Farm on the night of February 2, 1865.

Kentucky River, then kicking them to run the fastest race of their lives. Among those horses was Abdallah, one of Alexander's famed trotters. Unshod and unconditioned for work, he had been forced to swim the river with the other horses, then gallop another twenty miles.

As the guerrillas headed north, the Union army was nowhere to be seen.

By the predawn hours, General Hobson was holding a batch of puzzling dispatches from his officers stationed throughout Kentucky. Some claimed they had seen Sue Mundy and Quantrill. Others said they were chasing an entirely unrelated guerrilla band who had also burned down a train depot, elsewhere in the state. Then Hobson received a dispatch from a colonel of the Fifty-fourth Kentucky Cavalry reporting that he had chased Sue Mundy's gang northward, but that they had to halt their pursuit. "Our horses are worn out; can't do anything without fresh horses. Please send some, if only fifty. Quantrill is with the gang." For whatever reason, Hobson didn't send orders for help.

The Union army failed to catch Marcellus Clarke or Quantrill that February night. General Hobson had bungled the pursuit, failing to investigate the most promising leads received from his commanders in the field. The only group who even came close to seizing the guerrillas was Governor Bramlette's Home Guards. But the Home Guards, who were trying to aid the Union army, had fired erratically, mortally wounding Alexander's beloved Bay Chief without capturing any of the Raiders.

Abdallah was found where the Raiders had abandoned him,

twenty miles from Woodburn. Too broken to be moved, the stallion died there of exhaustion and hard use. Other Woodburn horses were found abandoned with Abdallah and were returned to Alexander. But Edwin Forrest, another of Alexander's trotters, believed to have been stolen by Frank James, was never found.

Alexander and Lexington survived the raid. Because of the Union army's inability to handle the guerrillas, Alexander worried endlessly about the safety of his champion stallion. Writing to his cousin, he described the horrors of the February 2 raid. He told him that his worst fear was the potential loss of Lexington. "Matters have at length become so unsatisfactory, and life and property so unsafe in my part of Kentucky that I have at last come to the determination of leaving my place, taking with me such stock as is likely to be stolen."

In the dark of a February night not long after the raid, Woodburn stable grooms walked Lexington and fifty Thoroughbreds along the back side of the farm to the Spring Station rail depot. There, in the quiet of that hour, they carefully loaded each horse onto the train, securing them in stalls configured for cattle. On the platform, Lexington stood, neck stretched high, twisting his ears toward the steam hissing out the engine's exhaust valve. The rattle of the planks under his hooves registered what his eyes could no longer see: a large monster, deeply exhaling and rumbling with a belly full of fire. As grooms attempted to lead Lexington aboard the train, he reared and sidestepped, turning his haunches swiftly to clear anyone who tried to get near him; then he coiled up, poised to buck and kick out to defend his ground. Grooms moved in and cautiously surrounded the stallion. Hugging their bodies close to his, they shuffled and pushed Lexington onto the car.

At the Kentucky border, Woodburn's men led Lexington and the other Thoroughbreds off the train and walked them quietly and unnoticed to the bank of the Ohio River. There, several barges were waiting, bobbing softly in the water. Lexington and his progeny rode the Ohio River to the safer grounds of Springfield, Illinois, where Alexander owned another farm.

A few days after Lexington left Woodburn, Alexander moved forty-two more trotting horses to yet another Illinois farm he owned, this one in Montgomery. His racehorses in training were moved to his farm in Cincinnati.

By early March 1865, Woodburn Farm was effectually gutted of its livestock.

Quantrill and his Raiders continued their travels through Kentucky, hell-bent. Marcellus Clarke and Henry Magruder accompanied them, no longer caring that their associations belied any future claim of operating under a rebel flag. Their flag was black.

CHAPTER 20

LOUISVILLE

Pᴿᴱˢᴵᴰᴱᴺᵀ Lᴵᴺᶜᴼᴸᴺ ˢᴬᵀ in his office chair, a towel wrapped around his neck. His barber puffed shaving cream over his cheeks, then, using a straight razor, slowly scraped away whiskers and foam, bringing the president's beard down to below his prominent cheekbones.

Five days after the February 2 Woodburn raid, Union general Burbridge, the commander in charge of Kentucky, had issued an order for the Home Guards to lay down their guns and to stop interfering with the job of the Union army stationed there. Governor Bramlette viewed the situation differently. Nearly a week after the Woodburn horses had been stolen and the Midway depot reduced to ashes, the guerrillas remained at large. Some of the horses still had not been found. To complicate matters, William Quantrill was now raising havoc in the state, treating innocent citizens with the same contempt he held for jayhawkers. Bramlette had fired off more provocative letters to Washington. The president had to do something, so he summoned his friend General John M. Palmer to his office.

John Palmer, a staunch abolitionist who hailed from Illinois, had successfully led the Fourteenth Illinois Infantry against a guerrilla faction that loomed over Missouri, Quantrill's haven. Lincoln told Palmer that Burbridge had made a mess of Kentucky. Now the populace feared for their lives and property. Some were leaving the state. Lincoln was appointing Palmer to step in for the Union to finish what Burbridge couldn't—a job, the president explained, that was about as difficult as containing a raging fire. He told Palmer, "Go to Kentucky, keep your temper, do as you please, and I will sustain you." Palmer left Washington with a no-fail directive, boarded a train, and headed for a land spiraling into chaos.

As Lincoln met with General Palmer, two hundred guerrillas were spotted hovering again near Alexander's farm in Midway. Some of them were even ordering dinners at Cunningham's Restaurant in nearby Paris. In broad daylight. At General Hobson's Lexington headquarters, dispatches rolled in, apprising him of the increasing number of guerrillas and their locations. All he could manage was to order his lieutenant to send dispatches requesting more horses and men to hunt down and kill the guerrillas. But Hobson's army never captured any of the wayward, thieving bands.

Palmer arrived in Louisville on February 17, 1865. After meeting with Governor Bramlette that afternoon, he issued General Order No. 1, taking command of the Department of Kentucky. By February 22, General Burbridge had been relieved of command. Editor George Prentice wrote, "Thank God and Mr. Lincoln."

Palmer's presidential orders mandated that he turn Kentucky's army men back into disciplined soldiers and rid Kentucky of its guerrilla infestation. Putting his order into words, Secretary of War Edwin Stanton wrote, "These parties, it is said, are accustomed to making raids in different portions of the State, plundering and murdering peaceable citizens who are obnoxious to them. All such persons are to be treated as enemies of the human race, and no effort spared to root out and destroy them in the most prompt and effectual manner." Lincoln instructed Palmer to protect all persons and property of Kentucky. Extinguishing the guerrillas was crucial.

Sizing up the Bluegrass State's Federal troops, Palmer instituted an off-the-books approach to catching the guerrillas. He hired Edwin Terrell, who had survived his near-fatal gunshot wound from the Bloomfield fight with Marcellus Clarke. Since then, Terrell's contempt for rebel guerrillas had seethed even hotter. Paying him fifty dollars monthly, Palmer commissioned Terrell captain of the Shelby County Home Guard and unleashed him and his militia upon Kentucky to hunt guerrillas for the Union. Then Palmer turned to his enlisted Union soldiers to do what they could to break up Mundy's band and catch Quantrill.

Marcellus Clarke and Henry Magruder eventually separated from Quantrill and his Raiders over what was said to have been Clarke's disdain for Quantrill's extreme violence—too much for even the young Kentucky gunslinger. On March 3, 1865, Clarke, Magruder, and fellow gang member Henry Metcalf were riding south through Kentucky when they received the news that the war was going to end. General Grant had cut off supplies to the Confederacy's capital. The populace in Richmond was starving and about to fold—as were most of the people in the South. The Confederacy was now ordering all its officers and soldiers out of Kentucky. Those who remained in the state risked being reported to Union authorities as guerrillas.

While attempting to flee the state and head to friendly Tennessee, Magruder was shot in the chest—the bullet burrowing into his right lung. As he lay on the ground, he begged Clarke and Metcalf to take him to a doctor he knew in Meade County. They agreed and secreted their companion inside a tobacco barn at the Cox farm in Webster, Kentucky.

But somehow, word got out.

General Palmer received a report that Sue Mundy was isolated in a beaten-down barn, forty-five miles away. Turning again to his off-the-books approach, Palmer met secretly with Cyrus J. Wilson, a retired major of the Twenty-sixth Kentucky Infantry, and told him to go after Mundy. To help him, Palmer placed Captain Lewis Marshall and Company D of the Thirtieth Wisconsin Infantry under Wilson's command.*

As the dawn broke on the morning of March 12, fifty soldiers of Company D surrounded the dilapidated barn housing Sue Mundy. They readied their carbines and held a steady aim at the structure. One of the soldiers knocked on the door. Hearing no response, Wilson ordered the doors forced open. Taking a large stone, soldiers heaved it into the door, breaking the handles. They kicked the doors, swinging them open. Someone inside fired a revolver. Company D shot back, showering the inside of the barn with forty carbine balls. Shots cracked rapidly from inside the barn, hitting four of Company D's soldiers and wounding them. Other soldiers sank back into the protection of the trees. Wilson told Company D to stand down—Sue Mundy must be taken alive.

After a few minutes of silence, Clarke called for Major Wilson to enter. Wilson lowered his firearm and walked alone to the barn door. He stood at the entrance and raised his arms.

Clarke stood a few feet from the entrance, pointing a revolver at Wilson. He asked Wilson how many men were in his command. Wilson told him fifty infantrymen and one hundred cavalrymen. Clarke lowered the revolver, motioning for Wilson to come in and sit down. He asked Wilson for some tobacco. They rolled and smoked.

Wilson asked, "Are you Sue Mundy?"

---

* The roster of the Thirtieth Wisconsin lists Lewis O. Marshall as a captain of Company D. However, in the court-martial trial of Sue Mundy, Captain Marshall testified that he was captain of Company B of the Thirtieth Wisconsin. The trial transcriptionist might have misheard Marshall and written Company B instead of Company D. In addition to being charged with acting as a guerrilla and outlaw, Clarke was also charged with shooting and wounding soldiers of the Thirtieth Wisconsin. The specifications never mention the military company to which they belonged. Their names do not appear on the rosters of Companies B or D.

Clarke nodded. Wilson asked for his surrender.

"Major, if I surrender to you, will you kill me?" Clarke asked.

"No. Not at this time."

"Your men will do it."

"No. Not at this time."

"Where will you take me?"

"To Louisville," Wilson said.

"There is enough published about me to kill me. Some of those publications are true. Some are false. George Prentice has done me a great injustice." Clarke spoke of the publications that claimed he was a hermaphrodite and disguised himself as a woman to woo Captain John Hunt Morgan. "That was all damn stuff. There was nothing of it," Clarke said. Then he continued, "You will kill me in Louisville."

"I have no doubt of that at all," Wilson said, "but it will give you a few more days to live. We came to take you, and we will take you dead or alive."

"I'm not ready to surrender."

From his bed on the barn floor, Magruder called out for Clarke to surrender. Metcalf remained silent. Clarke refused.

Wilson told Clarke he would give him five minutes. "If you don't surrender, we'll open fire."

Minutes passed. Wilson, fearing he would lose more of Company D's men to gunfire, approached Clarke again. "There might be a chance of your escape. One chance in a thousand or in ten thousand. Turn over your revolvers."

Clarke remained silent. Magruder again insisted that he should surrender.

Clarke had escaped from the Union prison at Camp Morton, Indiana, by feigning drowning while bathing in the river. This he accomplished while soldiers were guarding him at gunpoint. So shocked were they by his perceived drowning that they dropped their rifles to go in and look for him. Meanwhile, Clarke had swum underwater to the opposite bank, climbed out, and fled naked through the trees. On another occasion, he reportedly jumped from a moving train to escape capture by the Union. Clarke had reason to believe in his capability of pulling off another escape.

Finally, Clarke said, "I have only one object in surrendering— life is sweet to any man. I have always said I will not surrender, but there is one chance in a thousand to get away."

Wilson called for Marshall to come to the barn. He introduced Clarke to him as "Sue Mundy" and told Marshall of the surrender.

"Are you Sue Mundy?" Marshall questioned, incredulous.

"I am the man they call 'Sue Mundy,'" Clarke said.

Marshall took Clarke, Metcalf, and Magruder into custody. Patting down Clarke, he found four hidden revolvers. Wilson tied Clarke's hands behind his back, then chained him to Metcalf and Magruder. Company D escorted the trio to Brandenburg, where they boarded the steamer *Morning Star*.

Traveling against the currents of the Ohio River, the steamboat docked in Louisville on a Monday morning. Sue Mundy had been captured. *She* had been a figment of many imaginations, a rapture of a thousand descriptions from Prentice as well as from her countless victims. To most, she was a maniacal phantom, but to many, she was a legend. Kentuckians, including the *Daily Journal*'s editor, George Prentice, wanted to see her.

Prentice later wrote, "Sue Mundy is a rosy-cheeked boy, with dark eyes and a scowling brow. He is beardless with small hands and feet. He has a soft feminine voice but bore himself as a man of culture and gentlemanly refinement." The *Daily Democrat,* which had previously taken the stance that Prentice's "Sue Mundy" was an exaggerated fiction, naturally saw Clarke differently. "He is six feet tall, muscular, of swarthy complexion, with high cheek bones. He has a devilish wicked eye and the appearance of a wild Indian. He had a self-possessed air but when he spoke, he gave himself away. He is Sue Mundy, alias, Marcellus Clarke."

Before the water had dripped dry from the paddle wheel of the *Morning Star*, General Palmer had signed papers instructing Judge Advocate William Coyl to bring Sue Mundy to trial without delay. The one-day trial consisted of testimony from various witnesses who had been robbed by Sue Mundy, whom they described as looking a lot like the man sitting at the defense table. Clarke was denied the request to call his own witnesses, and the military commission found him guilty.

On March 13, the day before Clarke's trial, General Palmer had signed an order to have Clarke hung. On March 15, Palmer sent a telegram to Secretary Stanton.

I HAVE CAUGHT SUE MUNDY; TRIED HIM BY MILI- TARY COMMISSION. HE IS TO BE HANGED AT FOUR O'CLOCK TODAY.

The Union army stationed in Louisville had hung guerrillas be- fore, always behind the walls of the military prison.

But this was Sue Mundy.

The day after Clarke was summarily tried and convicted, a group of men assembled in a public square on the corner of Eigh- teenth Street and Broadway. They roped up oak beams and con- structed a crude platform of planked wood. Curious people stopped to watch. The men nailed a large crossbeam on top of the oak posts, then swung a hemp rope several times around the beam, measuring it downward to an exact length. A noose was affixed. Underneath was a trapdoor.

During the ensuing hours, people stopped to stare at the hastily constructed device. Rumors started. Gawkers began arriving, el- bowing aside others for a spot to see Sue Mundy hang. By three o'clock that afternoon, four thousand people had amassed around the gallows, the crowd swelling up and down Broadway.

At noon that day, Father Jeremiah J. Talbot visited Clarke in his prison cell. Talbot asked him if he had heard the verdict. Clarke had not, and said, "I suppose I shall be shot, since the court-martial would not hear any witnesses from my side."

Talbot asked him when he thought he might be executed. Clarke said in a few weeks. "Who knows," Talbot said, "that it might not be in a few hours. But you will not be shot."

"Hung, then?" asked Clarke.

Talbot nodded.

"*Oh!*" Clarke remarked.

Clarke immediately knelt beside his bed and prayed. He asked to be baptized in his cell.

At twenty-five minutes past three o'clock, four Union soldiers outfitted in parade dress came to Clarke's cell and told him it was time to go. Still bound in chains, he shuffled down the corridor and out of the military prison. Soldiers placed him in an open-top carriage next to Father Talbot. Clarke slid into the seat, slumped down, and leaned his head against the carriage. Four companies of Union soldiers in uniform raised up their polished bayonets and pushed through the crowd, leading the processional down Broadway. The Thirtieth Wisconsin band played the "Dead March" from Handel's *Saul.* A wagon carrying a pine coffin traveled past Clarke's horse-drawn carriage and headed toward the scaffold. Clarke put his baptismal handkerchief over his eyes. He never raised his head.

The carriage stopped at the steps to the left of the scaffold. Assisted by Talbot, Clarke climbed the stairs. The two knelt on the platform and prayed. At the scaffold, soldiers stood Clarke atop the trapdoor facing the massive crowd. He still did not look up. They wrapped rope tightly around his wrists and ankles and removed the chains.

Clarke paid no attention as the commission's charges and order of death were read out. Instead, he muttered over and over, "Lord, have mercy on my poor soul." The black velvet hat with Clarke's good luck charms—the upended crescent moon and black ostrich plume—was taken from his head and tossed underneath the platform. A white sheet was pulled over his head, covering the face that had so intrigued Prentice. The noose was cinched tightly around Clarke's neck. Talbot backed away. Captain George Swope counted out loud to three and the trapdoor dropped from under Clarke. He fell only three feet—to the end of the rope's length. His neck didn't break, and he writhed to the point of nearly ripping the ropes that bound him. After three long minutes, Clarke's convulsions broke several of his neck bones. Then all struggling stopped.

After twenty minutes, the Company D soldiers cut the rope from Clarke's neck. His body dropped to the ground, the sheet still covering his head, his bound wrists and ankles deeply cut from his struggle to live. As Clarke lay dead, three men brawled over his black velvet hat. Union soldiers broke apart that fight, then arrested and imprisoned the men. The hat was turned over to Captain Swope and later meandered its way to unknown whereabouts. "Green & Green," the finest milliners in Louisville, was stamped inside.

The James and Appomattox rivers comingled at a muddy juncture, then channeled to the banks of City Point, Virginia, headquarters for the Army of the Potomac. A river steamer carrying President Lincoln churned its way along the currents. A hundred feet ahead lay the wharf. On most occasions, hundreds of stacked guns lined the perimeter of the planked dock, ready to be outsourced to some distant battlefield. On this day, General Ulysses S. Grant and his staff officer, Horace Porter, stood on the dock, waiting.

When the boat was moored, Lincoln descended the stairs, grabbed the general's hand, and wrung it vigorously for an exaggerated length of time. This was the president's first visit to Grant at his office on the battlefield, and Lincoln was about to inspect the Army of the Potomac from horseback.

Grant himself hoisted the president up on the general's favored horse, Cincinnati. Lincoln adjusted his black trousers and frock coat to sit better in the saddle. His high, black top hat made him appear to touch the sky. But Cincinnati was strong and seventeen hands high, and the president was well seated on the horse's large frame. Grant rode beside them on his little pony, Jeff Davis, accentuating the president's six-foot, four-inch frame and Cincinnati's immense size. Lincoln, apparently unaware that he would ride horseback, had failed to bring riding straps to wrap his ankles and prevent his trousers from creeping up his legs. Yet, despite the irritation of his bare legs rubbing against Cincinnati, Lincoln retained his smile and engaged the traveling party in banter, recounting humorous anecdotes.

By the time they reached the troops, the president appeared as a "country farmer riding into town wearing his Sunday clothes," his trouser legs worked up high around his shins, baring slender legs that presumably were now rubbed to a painful red. Lincoln was covered head to toe in a fine film of dust that made him look "Confederate gray," Horace Porter recalled. Ignoring what Porter described as the president's almost comical appearance, the troops rushed to Lincoln, cheering him, calling him "Uncle Abe!"

Lincoln so loved Cincinnati that he became the only horse to

General Grant's favorite war horse, Cincinnati, sired by Lexington.

carry the president when he visited Grant's armies. On March 26, 1865, in preparation for another troop inspection, this one of the Army of the James, Grant told Porter, "I shall accompany the president, who is to ride Cincinnati, as he seems to have taken a fancy to him." Lincoln's inspection of the Army of the James astride Cincinnati was the last time he rode Lexington's son.

In the early morning of April 9, 1865, Grant sat in the back of a sick wagon nursing a migraine that had stubbornly settled in the night before. He braced against the siding as the wagon jostled over the Virginia hills. From across a field, a Confederate rider galloped up, waving a white flag and carrying a communication from General Robert E. Lee. When Grant read the note, his headache vanished immediately. Bypassing his two other war mounts, he ordered Cincinnati to be saddled and rode him to Appomattox to sign a letter outlining the terms of Lee's surrender.

On April 15, 1865, the day President Lincoln died, William Quantrill and his Raiders relaxed on the porch at the home of Judge Jonathan Davis, a Confederate sympathizer in Spencer County, Kentucky. Leaning back in his chair, his legs propped up on the porch railing, Quantrill ordered Davis to bring rounds of toddies to him and his men. They soon became liquored up and began laughing and shouting hails to the Confederacy. Not long after, Davis's wife and her friends entered the porch, prompting Quantrill to stand, remove his hat, and bow. "Excuse us, ladies," said Quantrill. "We are a little in our cups today, the grand-daddy of all the greenbacks, Abraham Lincoln, was shot in a theater in Washington last night." Marcellus Clarke's friend, One-Arm Berry, was with Quantrill. Raising his glass high, Berry added, "Here's to the death of Abraham Lincoln. Hoping that his bones may serve in hell as a gridiron to fry Yankee soldiers on."

Ed Terrell had been on General Palmer's payroll for nearly two months, and he'd been earning every dime. On May 10, 1865,

Terrell stopped to visit a relative in Bloomfield. It was from there, seated on the relative's porch, that Terrell spotted a group of men dressed in Union blues riding toward Taylorsville. The scene didn't look right. Terrell hadn't heard of any Union troops in the area. Terrell gathered his men and pursued. He didn't know he was following William Quantrill and his Raiders.

Near Smileytown, as the skies darkened above Quantrill, he and his men rode off the turnpike and cut half a mile through a field to the home of James Heady Wakefield, a Confederate supporter. They arrived at Wakefield's place in the afternoon, hitching their horses underneath a shed near the barn. Rain began falling, breaking hard on the shed's roof. Quantrill lay down on a pile of hay and closed his eyes. In the corner of the shed sat a burlap sack full of corncobs. To pass the time, his men started pelting them at one another, howling from the stinging impact.

A few miles back, Terrell and his Home Guards followed horse tracks that led to Alstead Jacobs's blacksmith shop outside Smileytown. They stopped there to ask Jacobs if he had seen any guerrillas. He replied, "Boss, there was a gang just went in that gate not more than ten minutes since." Through the gate was a large grass field and then a fence surrounding the Wakefield home.

At the end of the field, Terrell spotted the Raiders and their horses at the shed. He shouted, "Give 'em hell, boys!" Terrell's men pressed low against their horses' necks and called on them for speed. At the shed, one of the Raiders, chased out by a spiraling corncob, ran into the rainy darkness. The ground thundered, and he looked up to see nineteen men on horseback headed toward him at a gallop. He yelled, "Here they are! Here they are!" Within fifty yards of the barn, Terrell's men unleashed a hail of carbine bullets.

According to one account, Quantrill awakened and jumped from the hay pile. He grabbed his horse, but it was young and unaccustomed to excitement. The horse skittered across the ground and reared as Quantrill struggled to mount. Quantrill defiantly placed his foot in the stirrup and swung his leg over the horse, but the stirrup leather snapped apart, and Quantrill lost his balance. Frightened, the horse ran from the shed with Quantrill unsettled in the saddle.

Other accounts vary slightly. According to eyewitnesses, in the frenzy of ambush, Quantrill tried unsuccessfully to catch his excited horse. He then fled the barn on foot, running to the grassy field. Terrell spotted Quantrill and aimed. A ball rocketed from the chamber of his Spencer carbine rifle and sliced into Quantrill's left shoulder blade, traveling down and lodging in his spine. Quantrill fell, instantly paralyzed from his waist down. Terrell rode to Quantrill, who was trying hopelessly to right himself. Looking down at him, Terrell aimed at Quantrill's head and fired again. The ball struck Quantrill's right hand, which he may have raised to deflect the gunfire. Quantrill's trigger finger and thumb were shot off. He pleaded with Terrell to spare his life.

"If you give me a parole," Quantrill said, "I'll give you two hundred fifty dollars out of my pocket, and another two hundred fifty in a week."

"What's your name, rebel?" Terrell asked.

Relying on his usual alias, Quantrill told him, "Captain Clark of the Fourth Missouri Cavalry."

"Well, Captain, I'll just check that out myself," Terrell said.

He then took the money offered and the gold watch from Quantrill's wrist.

As Quantrill lay paralyzed on the ground, bargaining his way back into life, his Raiders broke away in haste. Some were shot and killed by Terrell's men; others, including Frank James, escaped into the woods surrounding the Wakefield home. Terrell's men moved Quantrill inside the house and left him there to die.

By the following morning, Ed Terrell had reviewed the war reports and concluded that Captain Clark of the Fourth Missouri might indeed be William Quantrill. On May 11, Terrell and his Home Guards returned to the Wakefield home with a wagon pulled by two mules. Terrell found Quantrill lying on a chaise lounge looking like hell. The Home Guards swooped him up, took him to the wagon, and placed him on top of a feather mattress. Surrounding the wagon and readying their rifles for whatever might come, they escorted the wagon out of the Wakefield gate through which they had galloped a day earlier. Riding up to the wagon master, Terrell told him to take the paralyzed man to General Palmer's headquarters in Louisville. He suspected the man he had shot was the butcher who had slaughtered his way through Kentucky.

Terrell delivered Quantrill to Palmer's headquarters on May 13. Palmer ordered Quantrill to be taken to the military prison's hospital. There, he was placed in a bed and given the little comfort the Union afforded to Confederate men who were going to die.

When death was near, Quantrill was transferred to St. Joseph Infirmary in Louisville. The Sisters of Charity took over his care. On June 4, Father Powers of St. John's Catholic Church in Louisville visited Quantrill. Whether he ever achieved his mind's peace during those last few bedridden days is unknown. Instead, Quantrill may have handled death the way he had everything else in life: by shortcutting honesty to achieve his desired goal. According to one of his biographers, Quantrill gave Father Powers $800 in gold, supposedly to build a monument over his grave. According to John Harmon, a friend of Quantrill's from boyhood, Quantrill meted out over $2,000 to Father Powers and the Sisters of Charity for absolution, which Harmon claimed the priest granted.

Father Powers buried Quantrill in the Portland Cemetery in Louisville. He erected no monument. Instead, he instructed the Sisters of Charity to level the ground so that no mound would show, and to throw slop water over the grave. No marker or other insignia bore Quantrill's name in that final resting spot. Father Powers claimed he feared the grave would be vandalized if Quantrill's burial site became known.

On July 26, 1865, Quantrill's remaining Raiders surrendered to the Union army in Kentucky. Because of their cooperation, they were treated as prisoners of war and paroled. General Palmer allowed each man to leave with the horse on which he rode, and to retain possession of two revolvers and whatever ammunition was loaded in them. The Raiders had dropped in number to sixteen. Frank James was among them. Whether he was still riding Alexander's trotting horse Edwin Forrest is not known. According to Frank, his brother Jesse accompanied the Raiders throughout Quantrill's days in Kentucky and was also present at the surrender.

After the war, Alexander returned to Midway. Woodburn Farm was now a vast wasteland of decay, its barns partly burned, its land left barren.

The war and the guerrilla invasions had severely affected Alexander's health and the farm's financial profits. He questioned the viability of Woodburn. But he held fast to his dreams, knowing that his farm would stand a better chance now that the war was finally over. He brought back Lexington and the other horses, and soon the farm was once again operating, trying to restore its former glory. Above Lexington's stall door, the elk's antlers remained nailed and intact.

CHAPTER 21

THE BEQUEST

A MERICANS WERE PINING for enjoyment, for good-natured rivalry in place of the hatreds of war. During the previous four years, New York had taken the baton from the battle-damaged South and was now regarded as the country's horse-racing mecca. Eastern racetracks were on the rise. By the end of the war, the number of New York racecourses had nearly doubled. Southern tracks such as those in the ravaged land of Kentucky were in shambles. Deeply plowed gouges from wagon wheels crossed their infields, and the remnants of pedestrian stands—long torn down for firewood—stood along the homestretches like ghost ships with tattered sails.

Yet when it came to producing quality horses, the South still reigned.

John Hunter was about as savvy as they come. Raised in Westchester County, New York, he was an aristocratic sportsman who had been racing horses under his red-and-orange silks since he had reached the age of maturity at twenty-one. By the time of his thirtieth birthday, in 1863, he was, as historian W. S. Vosburgh put it, "a young man with the racing experience of an old one." Using his knowledge of horse racing, Hunter convinced his friend William R. Travers, along with famed prizefighter John Morrissey, to join him in a grand venture. Together, they carved out a one-mile oval track amid swaying pines in Saratoga Springs, New York, and formed a racing association. In 1863, during the heartache of the war, the Saratoga Race Course opened, promising a happier future. Hunter's timing couldn't have been better.

Turfmen were weary of racing in the war-battered South, but they still owned racing stables bustling with high-dollar racehorses. The town of Paterson, New Jersey, also hosted a race meeting in 1863, and the venue enticed turfmen from both North and South. Among them was Senator Henry Clay's son John M. Clay, who had recently purchased a son of Lexington from Alexander, a bay colt named Kentucky. The horse won Paterson's one-mile sweepstakes and was then sold while still up North. Changing hands again, Kentucky eventually found his way into the stables of John Hunter.

The following year, Hunter sent Kentucky back to Paterson to enter the Jersey Derby, a one-and-a-half-mile sweepstake spectacular named in honor of the Derby at Epsom in England. But Kentucky ultimately ran a disappointing fourth-place finish. Hunter was little discouraged. In fact, two months later, he doubled down on Kentucky, entering him in the inaugural running of the Travers Stakes at his own Saratoga Race Course. To make an eye-catching show of it, he retained Lexington's former jockey, Gilpatrick. Still, despite the horse's illustrious connections, the Knowing Ones considered him a negligible entry. The most anyone was willing to risk was thirty dollars in a five-hundred-dollar asking pool. After the final bets were cast, Kentucky won the Travers by four lengths while pulling hard against Gilpatrick. The horse continued to race carrying Hunter's sunset-colored silks, winning every contest with such ease that it seemed there was no horse on the Eastern tracks who could defeat him. Kentucky's reputation soared, and he was soon glorified as the king of the Eastern turf.

One of the horses that defeated Kentucky that day back at Paterson was another of Lexington's sons, Norfolk. Although the day had gone miserably for Hunter and Kentucky, it was a most serendipitous one for Alexander. A curly-haired Californian named Theodore Winters, who'd made a fortune freighting gold out of the Sierra Madre, had made the lengthy journey to scout for a Thoroughbred to take back. After the Jersey Derby, he bought Norfolk on the spot, paying Alexander not only his $15,000 asking price but an extra $1 to help the breeder make good on his promise to one day sell a son of Lexington for more than his own original purchase price. Winters shipped Norfolk to California to contend against the great Thoroughbred Lodi, whom Norfolk duly defeated. Norfolk continued to dominate his West Coast competition, earning Winters a pile of purses.

With Norfolk committed to the San Francisco and Sacramento tracks, there was no chance he would race Kentucky again. That left only one other horse possibly capable of defeating Kentucky, and that was Asteroid. In 1864, Asteroid had been racing in Ohio, tallying a roster of wins that would reach the double digits. But then, in October of that year, Marcellus Clarke stole the horse from Woodburn.

In 1865, after Asteroid was ransomed back, none the worse for the ordeal, he started seven times in St. Louis, winning each race. He won two additional races in Cincinnati. Two of those nine races he won by a walkover after all the other horses were withdrawn. "He so completely outclassed his contemporaries that owners would not start their horses against him," wrote Vosburgh.

Asteroid's winning streak may not have been the only factor that provoked other owners' fears. Intensifying their apprehension and angst, *The New York Times* had released a bombshell: "[Asteroid's] private trials had been so high that it was confidently asserted that he would beat the four-mile time record made by his immortal sire, Lexington, which has never yet been equaled or approached." If the press's insider confidences were correct, and Asteroid was equal to and quite possibly better than Lexington, no other horse stood a chance. Unless, of course, that horse was also sired by him.

With so much commotion, so many predictions and grand forecasts, now circling around Kentucky and Asteroid, the *Spirit of the Times* wrote in June 1865 that there was an enormous national interest in seeing the two horses compete. A possible venue, the paper offered, was at the 1865 Saratoga Cup, just two months away.

The *Spirit* was right about the nation's enthusiasm. People wanted to know which of Lexington's sons was faster, and indeed, whether either one of them was faster than the king sire himself. They wagered plenty of cold cash on the two horses in hopes they would meet on the turf. The *Spirit* warned: Woe to Alexander should he fail to deliver his esteemed colt to New York.

Alexander did nothing.

His chronic illness had worsened. By the time he returned to Woodburn at war's end, he had taken to treating his condition by flinging himself at hopeless remedies, including endless cold-water baths and ingestions of enormous quantities of potassium carbonate. The treatments had no effect on his cycles of misery. He required a regime of round-the-clock care. Only on rare occasions did he feel well. Even then, he had to muster everything within himself just to tackle the ordinary happenings of life.

Alexander's health wasn't his only concern. The war and guerrilla travesties that ravaged Kentucky had struck a severe blow to Woodburn. In November 1865, only eight months after the Quantrill–Sue Mundy raid, Alexander wrote to his brother-in-law that Woodburn was struggling to turn a profit, despite his concerted efforts to revitalize its operations. Finances were so bad that he had done the unthinkable: He'd put Asteroid up for sale—along with his entire Woodburn stud. Most astonishing, Lexington too was up for sale to the highest bidder. To keep Woodburn afloat, Alexander continued to race his horses in local Kentucky and Ohio meets, hoping to catch the eyes of turfmen with full wallets.

Compounding the problem, Alexander's brother's excesses fell on him. "My pockets," wrote Alexander to A.J., "have been pretty well drained to meet the calls made on the big purchases made by you. . . . [I] shall feel far more satisfaction in being quite free from such a thing as a 'bill payable' staring me in the face when I open my diary!" He added, "I am not well. I have a bad feeling about my eyes, hands and feet caused by deranged circulation." About Woodburn Alexander expressed unrelenting concerns, saying that if he could turn out another Norfolk, Woodburn would stand in better finances. "I have quite enough animals for sale to bring me in more money than that, *but the question is shall I find buyers.*"

John Hunter sent out a bugle call: Kentucky versus Asteroid in a match race at a New York track. Alexander still refused Hunter's challenge—not because of his health, he claimed, but because of his Protestant faith. Match races, he said, required "more gambling than I like." Setting aside his personal animosity toward excessive gambling, Alexander offered a compromise: He agreed to race the two horses provided the *racehorse* Kentucky come to the *state* of Kentucky. Hunter ignored the proposal and a venue standoff ensued.

Then, in January 1866, Alexander, who had gone to great lengths to thumb his nose at Hunter, jabbed it at him provokingly. Alexander wrote to the secretary of the Saratoga Race Course, informing him that Norwich, another Lexington colt who had been stolen twice by Marcellus Clarke and twice recaptured, would be sent to his track to compete for the 1866 Saratoga Cup. He also promised to send several other horses to compete for the Saratoga Stakes and the Travers Stakes.

Asteroid was not on the list.

Instead, in March 1866, Alexander entered Asteroid in the Woodlawn Stakes at Louisville's Woodlawn Race Course. Ever hopeful that Asteroid would face other contenders, Alexander watched instead as his undefeated horse walked the course uncontested to win the Woodlawn Vase, recently unearthed from the garden at Woodburn and polished to a sheen. But even though the vase once again decorated Alexander's fireplace mantel, Asteroid had inexplicably injured a tendon. Alexander shipped Asteroid back to Woodburn and turned him out to heal in a small grass pasture.

That summer, feeling in better health, Alexander left Woodburn and traveled to Saratoga Springs to see Norwich compete for the Saratoga Cup. Although his name was now known as an important horseman, Alexander had not personally frequented the new Eastern tracks. He was an ever-deepening mystery. Saratoga buzzed with talk—not about Kentucky, Asteroid, Norwich, or the Saratoga Cup but about Alexander. Racegoers sat in the parlor of Saratoga's Grand Union Hotel sipping Congress Spring water, which, according to the editor of the *Turf, Field and Farm,* "ain't half so good as the Mississippi River water," or played croquet in one of the city's numerous wooded parks. All the while, they watched Alexander meander through the hotel and its gardens, tipping his hat to ladies and otherwise comporting himself in a calm and cheerful manner. According to the *Turf, Field and Farm,* people speculated:

"Is he Scottish or English?"

"Any man with a grain of sense ought to see that Alexander is a native of England."

"He was born in Woodford County, Kentucky!"

"Why, he looks like the rest of us fellow Christians!"

While hotel guests amused themselves with similar speculations, Napoleon Belland—the young French jockey who'd ridden Lexington on his morning walks at Woodburn—paid a visit to Alexander. Having returned from Canada, where he had taken a string

of Woodburn's racehorses to compete with and hopefully sell, Belland had come back with only three of the original thirty-four
horses unsold. "During all that time," Belland said later to historian
John Hervey, "no settlement of any kind had taken place between
Mr. Alexander and myself and he knew little of how I had fared.
As a matter of fact, I had done remarkably well." The Woodburn
horses were superior to all the others, enabling Belland to sell them
for high prices. Astonished tears filled Alexander's eyes when Belland told him that he had earned a profit of $334,000. The breeder
reportedly said, "You have saved Woodburn Farm!" Alexander offered the Frenchman perpetual employment at Woodburn, but
Belland refused, choosing instead to stay in New York. He later
rode for August Belmont, Sr., the financier who would contribute
so richly to New York's racing community, and for whom the
Belmont Stakes—the third leg of the Triple Crown—would be
named. Belmont's son later founded the Belmont Park racecourse.

On cup day, July 27, 1866, New Yorkers filled the grandstand at
Saratoga. Some meandered around the booths near the gambling
tables, where Edward Troye's most recent portrait of Lexington
stood on an easel for all to view. "It is the only picture we have
seen which does justice to that renowned horse," wrote the *Spirit*.
The prizefighter John Morrissey, mistakenly believing it was *his* day
at his co-owned racecourse, sidled up to reporters, trumpeting his
bygone boxing match with John Heenan—claiming, "If Heenan
hadn't been such a coward, he could've whipped me." Reporters
nodded, all the while training their eyes on the graceful, quiet Kentuckian. They even noted how Alexander knelt during a race so he
wouldn't obstruct the view of the ladies behind him. Then they
watched him focus his attention on Kentucky as the horse won the
Saratoga Cup for the second straight year.

"He's praying for Asteroid to be here," reporters whispered, or:
"He's thanking the good Lord, you can be sure, that Asteroid is *not*
here."

Asteroid was, at that time, back in Kentucky, walking a gangplank from the platform at Spring Station onto a railcar. Asteroid's exercise in Woodburn's paddock—moving with caution, sensing his own limitations—proved miraculous in healing the strain of the tendon in his right foreleg. Over time he was taken to Woodburn's track and slowly cantered around the course. He showed no signs of lameness. Still, his veterinarian, Dr. Herr, instructed Alexander to leave the horse alone in his paddock for another seven months— a precaution to make sure that the tendon had fully healed.

Despite the warning, on September 8, 1866, a mere month later, Asteroid and Lexington's champion mare Idlewild were loaded into box stalls in the cargo section of a railcar—destined not for Saratoga but for New York's Westchester County.

Jerome Park was built in 1866 in Fordham, New York, in what is now the Bronx. Leonard W. Jerome, the maternal grandfather of Winston Churchill, fashioned the park after the Newmarket Racecourse in England. A larger future now loomed for the turf. Saratoga held its own in an America roughened and raw from bitterness and hurt, a country clawing to regain her stature. Having served as a springboard from that bitterness to better times, Saratoga seemed destined to forever remain a racing mainstay. But Jerome Park was something different. The course was a unified endeavor of turfmen from the North and South; something new: a postwar coming together, and a sign, perhaps, that America, with a deeper sense of self and a more seasoned view, was ready to realign with the world. It made sense, then, that Alexander finally agreed to race Asteroid against Kentucky on this racecourse unified by hope.

With news that the long-awaited match race would finally take place, people from "New Orleans, Mobile, St. Louis, Cincinnati, Cleveland, and other Western cities [came] East purposely to witness the race between Asteroid and Kentucky," wrote *The New York Times*. "Once more," wrote Vosburgh, "the racing world was aroused as it had not been since the Lexington-Lecomte races in 1855."

While Jerome Park's manager hastened to finalize preparations for the Inauguration Stakes, Asteroid was on a train, tucked away in his box stall, riding the gyrating sway over one thousand miles of rails. The trip provoked an unwelcome tension to his healing foreleg. Two weeks later, he arrived at Jerome Park. On September 22, during a deluge of rain that saturated the track, Asteroid galloped over fetlock-deep mud, the kind of track surface his sire would have trounced. But for Asteroid, the workout was injurious. He walked off the track with a limp. That night, the tendons of his right foreleg began to swell. Grooms worked through the night's hours to massage and wrap the horse's leg with herbs and heated woolen towels. By morning, Asteroid walked unhindered, and the decision was made to exercise him one last time before the race.

Late that afternoon, John Ford,* the celebrated jockey from New York, waited for Asteroid at the track. The rain hadn't stopped in the last twenty-four hours and was still falling at what the *Times* called "a very unpleasant and most suggestive rate." The ground sloshed higher than Ford's ankles as he inspected the track on foot. Whether Alexander's confidence in his racehorse had shifted is not known. Asteroid had traveled the distance to New York not only to compete against Kentucky but to prove his speed over Lexington's. Ford had heard the talk, and he had no reason to doubt that under normal conditions, Asteroid was capable of defeating his sire's record.

As Ford waited trackside, grooms cinched a saddle on Asteroid and walked the horse away from his stall, out under the canopy of a storm-darkened sky. He moved without a trace of pain, and when Ford saw the horse walk steadily toward him in the rain, he surely felt renewed hope. After he was given a leg up into the

---

* Historical references mention only "Ford." The jockey was most likely John Ford, who, along with Gilpatrick, accompanied Richard Ten Broeck to England to showcase American horses. John Ford had raced alongside not only Gilpatrick but also Lecomte's former jockey, Abe Hawkins of New Orleans. It's likely a jockey of John Ford's reputation and skill was placed on the talented Asteroid, especially for a race as anticipated as the one between Lexington's sons. Richard Ten Broeck's former jockey Charles Littlefield had been retained to ride Kentucky.

saddle, Ford grabbed the reins and eased Asteroid into his work. He then asked the horse to sprint. But he soon pulled Asteroid up, dropped the reins loose on the horse's neck, and, reportedly, broke into tears. Asteroid's fluid glide had broken to a hobble. His right foreleg tendons had completely given way.

Alexander withdrew his champion from the upcoming Inaugural Stakes, entering the mare Idlewild in Asteroid's place. Idlewild, foaled in 1859 out of one of Alexander's Glencoe mares, was considered one of Lexington's best daughters. She had won in Memphis, New Orleans, Philadelphia, New York, and all throughout Kentucky, and would later retire with a record of twenty-six starts and nineteen wins. She was fast, running some of her race miles in a highly respectable 1:47 ¾. Although the mare was more talented than most Thoroughbreds, *The New York Times* reported, "The withdrawal of Asteroid in consequence of his breaking down, naturally deprived the race of a great portion of its interest, as he was generally looked upon as the only horse on the turf that stood a chance of plucking the laurels from the mighty Kentucky."

Asteroid was eventually returned to Woodburn and retired. His race record remained intact: twelve starts and twelve wins. Between Kentucky and Asteroid, Alexander had always considered Asteroid the better horse. Before Asteroid broke down at Jerome Park, Alexander had refused the astounding offer of $50,000. Many sportsmen believed he had been determined to save the best of Lexington's triumvirate for himself.

Despite *The New York Times*'s prior warnings that the rain would close Jerome Park, race day opened to a sun-brightened warmth. Still, as if distrusting their eyes, racegoers scurried to Astor House, the Jockey Club's headquarters, to note whether its flags were hoisted at half-mast—a sign to the public that Jerome Park's races had been called off due to stormy weather. But the flags flapped high that day.

At the track, the crowds bustled into the grandstand—filling all nine thousand seats that it accommodated—and out to the infield, toting their picnic baskets. Some funneled past Kentucky's stall in hopes of catching a glimpse of the champion. Since his arrival at Jerome Park, hundreds of racing fans had paid him a visit.

The first race scheduled that day was a hat tip to Britain's shorter-distanced sprint races. At one and a quarter miles, the dash showcased six horses, three of whom were sired by Lexington. Alexander retained Lecomte's jockey, Abe Hawkins—who Alexander said was better than any European rider he had ever seen—to ride Baywater, a son of Lexington. Hawkins rose to the occasion. To aid Baywater's speed, the jockey altered his riding position from the American style of bandy-legged saddle straddling to the speed position that had been in use for years by British jockeys. Crouched over the saddle, knees tucked up by the withers, Hawkins rode Baywater to claim the win.

But it was the second race—the much-anticipated Inauguration Stakes—that had lured not only the masses but celebrities as well. General Ulysses S. Grant arrived slightly late—just after the dash race—at about one o'clock. His attendance had been ballyhooed in advance, and his throngs of admirers were quick to spread updates of his approach. As Grant made his way to the grandstand, the racecourse band struck up "See! The Conquering Hero Comes." The crowd started clapping in rhythmic time, cheering the general as he maneuvered through the stands, shaking every other hand and offering an occasional salute. At the top of the grand stairway, Grant turned to face his audience and waved his hat before being escorted away for a luncheon featuring, as *The New York Times* noted, "champagne and cigars."

After stomachs were filled and good cheer imbibed, five-year-old Kentucky, along with three other horses including his half sister, seven-year-old Idlewild, were brought to the post for the Inauguration Stakes's first four-mile heat. With Hawkins in the saddle, Idlewild took the lead at the first turn, running two lengths ahead of Kentucky. The other two horses followed. The mare maintained her lead through the third mile, driving a steady pace, with

Kentucky closely trailing her tail. Entering the fourth mile, jockey Charles Littlefield asked for more, and Kentucky pressed forward. Passing Idlewild, Kentucky led for the rest of the way, winning the first heat while pulling hard against the reins. The second heat proved equally easy for Kentucky. He led wire to wire. As he crossed the finish to win the Inauguration Stakes, his ears pricked forward: an indication that he was barely spent. Like Lexington during his great runs, at no point in the race was he ever extended by Little-field into his full run. Kentucky clocked 7:35 for the first heat and 7:41 ½ for the second.

On the heels of that success, Leonard Jerome purchased Kentucky from the horse's owner at that time, William R. Travers, paying $40,000. Kentucky was now in a class all his own. No other horses could defeat him. Jerome decided not to even try to enter the horse in any other races, feeling that it would spoil the sport if he did. Instead, he set his eyes on breaking Lexington's 7:19 ¾.

The match against Time took place a year later, on October 17, 1867, at Jerome Park. When the chronometer started, Kentucky dug into the dirt and rocketed into a tremendous speed. As he ran the backstretch, Time trailed far behind. Kentucky held that speed over the next three miles. But coming into the fourth mile, the horse slowed, and his breathing became labored. He jogged in a swerving, offbeat pattern. Drained of bottom, Kentucky lost to Time by 11 ¾ seconds. In accordance with Britain's practice of saddling their horses with higher weight, Kentucky had carried fourteen pounds more than Lexington had when he'd beaten Time over the Metairie, twelve years before.

There was nothing left for Kentucky on the turf. A year after he faced Lexington's Time, he was brought to the auction ring at Jerome Park. Stripped of his blankets, the seven-year-old champion looked in his prime, his coat shining over his muscled form. He stood proud, gazing out over the horsemen, two of whom had once owned and cherished him when he brought them mounds of accolades. But his racing days were over. The bidding started cautiously at $5,000. The auctioneer's quick tongue rambled about days gone by and Kentucky's grandeur. The bid rose slowly to $7,000. Feeling a dedication to the horse, John Hunter eventually raised his hand, offering $14,500. He refused to raise even $500 more and allowed an anonymous bidder to win Kentucky for $15,000. The high bidder was August Belmont, Sr., who retired the racehorse with a record of twenty-three starts, twenty-one wins, and one loss each to Norfolk and Time. Kentucky went into Belmont's breeding shed to sire horses for his private stable, producing several champions who were singled out for their unique stamina. But he could never replicate his sire's list of leading horses.

Kentucky by Edward Troye. The horse, painted at Jerome Park, is considered one of Lexington's best colts. Kentucky won the inaugural runnings of the Travers Stakes, the Saratoga Cup, and the Inauguration Stakes at Jerome Park. He was retired with twenty-one wins and two losses.

The Inauguration Stakes and Kentucky's match against immortal Time had each pulled together an audience of twenty thousand Americans. North and South had joined, if only for the short hours of those days at a racecourse. Decades later historian Charles E. Trevathan would write,

The War had swept away the racing institutions of the South, the breeding studs were broken up, and the bloodhorse bridled and made to do service in the army . . . [but then] the performances of the three great sons of Lexington roused sinking courage and directed attention to the turf. It was a theatre on which men of all political opinions could meet in social enjoyment; it called the thoughts from the harrowing scenes of the past and gave a silver lining to that dark cloud which overhung the future. The people were sick of war and the wrangles growing out of it, and they turned to the turf with eagerness. It was the only practical means of reunion at the time.

In the afternoon of November 26, 1866, Alexander sat down at his desk to write to his brother A.J. Earlier in the day, Alexander had driven a carriage over the hills of Woodburn seated beside Nugent, his former Irish gardener, who was now head of the General Improvement Bureau for Woodford County. Throughout the tour, Alexander had pointed out the various roads and byways that had been added since Nugent left Woodburn's employment. But the tour's real purpose was to request that he construct a new route on Woodburn that led to the land where Alexander hoped to resettle. A few months before the tour, Alexander had hired architects to remodel a Greek Revival mansion consisting of thirty-three rooms—larger than George Washington's Mount Vernon—a home that Alexander had acquired in buying additional acreage. It would be a residence worthy of the king of the bluegrass.

As he wrote, Alexander heard his cook Betsy in the kitchen, clanging the cast-iron skillet down on the stove lid. Soon the smell of mutton chops searing over the fire wafted into the room. It had been a warm day, "beautiful," wrote Alexander. He was overjoyed by the familiar aroma of Betsy's cooking and the hopes of finalizing Woodburn's numerous construction projects with a grand new home for himself. "I expect to eat my Christmas dinner with you. Am receiving some turkeys," he wrote to A.J. Then he went on to advise him about Woodburn's business matters.

A few days later, the *Turf, Field and Farm* published a letter from Alexander informing the racing world of his retirement from the turf. The stress of the Civil War, racing horses, and maintaining a breeding operation were too much, he wrote, saying he was increasingly unwell. He told horsemen that Woodburn Farm would never close her gates, and that he would continue to breed racehorses for the remainder of his life.

The farm was then averaging an income of about $5,000 a month in sales of racing colts—roughly $92,000 in today's dollars. Sales weren't slowing down. Everyone wanted a Lexington, or at least something like him—a Norfolk, a Kentucky, or an Asteroid. But with his stallion being in such extreme demand, Alexander decided to curb Lexington's stud services in a judicious attempt to not overbreed him. By 1865, Alexander was offering the horse's stud services to outside breeders on a limited basis only, and for five hundred dollars—a staggering price tag, though reportedly equal to fees charged in Great Britain at the time for the top sires. Lex-

This drawing of Lexington, made during his prime as a stallion in 1866, appeared in New York's sporting magazine the *Turf, Field and Farm*.

ington was in his prime as a stallion. His most fertile year had been in 1859, when, as a result of servicing eighty-three mares, he got fifty-two foals. But amazingly, at the late age of sixteen in 1866, he covered forty-nine mares with a resulting thirty-seven live births. Lexington's potency continued well beyond that age, with on average about half of the mares serviced producing live births. Of those foals born post–Civil War, nearly all would race to success, earning Lexington recognition as America's leading sire year after year.

No mention was ever made of Alexander's desperate long-ago advertisement to sell his prized stallion. If he still had any buyers as late as 1866, he may have politely closed the door, realizing, as he must have, that without its king, the empire would fall. In May 1867, Alexander sold six colts and fillies to M. H. Sanford of England. Sanford named one of them, a bay colt by Lexington, Preakness—after his Preakness Stable. Preakness would later become the namesake for the second race in America's Triple Crown series. In June 1867, Alexander held his annual auction of stock. He sold sixty-six colts, the majority sired by Lexington. The average selling price per colt was $4,000—about $74,000 today.

In early November 1867, a reporter from New York and his entourage took a small wagon a mile from the Spring Station depot to the old log-and-stone house where Alexander still lived, work on his mansion having not yet begun. Alexander met them on the front lawn and extended his gaunt hand. He was bent at the waist and pale, and his "face was at a compromise between humorous and grave." Alexander was dressed in plain black trousers and jacket and wore his black felt hat resting, as usual, high up on his forehead.

He had organized a tour of Woodburn's expansive 3,200 acres. As the visitors rolled across the hills in Alexander's carriage, he entertained them with stories of Lexington and Asteroid—all the while pointing to various fields, informing the men of famous horses. He then spoke of his own heritage, and how he had bought

Woodburn from his siblings. Later, he introduced the entourage to Betsy, whom the reporter described as "a mulatto woman who raised [Alexander] from birth and who gained freedom from slavery." He then escorted them to the room where he had wrestled one of Quantrill's Raiders to the floor. Edward Troye's portraits of Lexington and Asteroid hung on the walls. There was "nothing of chaotic order associated with bachelors," the reporter opined. Everything was tasteful, not ornate, and had its place. Surrounded by the enormity of Woodburn, Alexander's life was, in most respects, simple.

The New York reporter later wrote of Alexander and Woodburn as only one would who had been enchanted by his brief stay. "Even the famous breeding operations of England sink in comparison to Woodburn. It is a princely domain and the small, plainly dressed man with a kind smile is lord and master of it all."

Less than a month later, at the age of forty-eight, Robert Aitcheson Alexander was dead. Shortly after the New York reporter left Woodburn, Alexander had a relapse of his mysterious illness and was bedridden in his log home for three weeks with acute jaundice. On the morning of December 1, 1867, he whispered words about a prismatic brightness appearing before his eyes and said, in finality, "There is nothing true but Heaven."

Alexander's numerous obituaries and tributes painted a picture of a man of genteel manners and kindness, a man who seemed aware his days on Earth were short in number; and one who used every ounce of energy his frail body possessed to pack his dreams into that brief time. He built Woodburn into a world-renowned breeding farm in just ten years. Soon after Alexander's death, the *Turf, Field and Farm* wrote, "He bred with judgment and care, and the prosperity and high standing of the American Turf today are largely due to his influence. He labored earnestly and hard to elevate the condition of the best types of the animal kingdom, believing that their elevation would have a refining influence upon mankind." In a later publication, B. G. Bruce wrote that Alexander's "knowledge of stock was clear and accurate, but the Thoroughbred horse was his greatest love."

Back in 1860, when Woodburn was beginning, Alexander had instructed his lawyers to draft a will. Alexander never married, feeling that it would be unfair to impose his weak health upon a woman. He left Woodburn Farm and all its assets to A.J.

Racehorses had never been A.J.'s passion. And Alexander's bequest, written so early in Woodburn's existence, stipulated nothing regarding his farm's continuance. A.J. loved his brother and knew that what he had accomplished was nothing short of extraordinary. He retained Daniel Swigert, Woodburn's foreman, and asked him to continue in service. Swigert took over the breeding operations of Woodburn Farm, continuing them in the same manner Alexander had done.

Eventually A.J. moved to Woodburn and remodeled the mansion of Alexander's dreams. One morning, dressed in a fine suit, he strolled out of the house and down the new route constructed by Nugent. Along the way he encountered a carriage of visitors, who stopped to ask if he could give them directions to certain Thoroughbred horses they wanted to see.

He responded courteously and honestly. "I regret my inability to do so. I am not familiar with the racehorse department."

PART III

CHAPTER 22

THE FOUR-MILE HORSE

J. M. WOMACK was treasurer of the Louisville Jockey Club in 1874. The club had leased land from John and Henry Churchill on the southwest outskirts of Louisville and was in the final stages of building a new racetrack. They scheduled the track's inaugural race meet for May 17, 1875, and planned to name the main stake for three-year-old horses "the Kentucky Derby"—a one-and-a-half-mile race.* All the club needed now was a president to preside over the illustrious board of members. Womack knew just the man who could add prestige to what he felt was to become a legendary track. He took a carriage out to the Hurstbourne mansion on the outskirts of Louisville, the home of Richard Ten Broeck.

Ten Broeck sat there in his West Room, surrounded by stained-glass windows that cast an array of gold and purple onto Italian marble statues dotting the parlor, and listened patiently as Womack and his entourage expounded on the track's near completion and the plans they had to host great races and offer generous purses. Something this grand should draw every horse in the nation. Ten

---

* The Kentucky Derby was shortened to one and a quarter miles in 1896.

Broeck nodded his agreement, then said, "I've been a very active man my whole life. I feel like I've earned a rest." He was sixty-two and had been racing on and off in Great Britain, losing and winning fortunes, since he had retired Lexington nearly twenty years earlier.

Womack left Hurstbourne crestfallen, having grudgingly accepted the turfman's refusal to lend his celebrated name. He later filled the club's presidency with Colonel Meriwether Lewis Clark, Jr., a nephew of John Churchill. In 1872, Clark had traveled to England, where he attended the Epsom Derby, thereupon becoming enthusiastically involved in racehorse mania. Clark offered his name, willingness, and deep pockets to promote Kentucky's horse-racing and breeding industries. Clark took over as the Louisville Jockey Club's president and helped establish Churchill Downs, marshalling it toward its grand opening.

While Ten Broeck may not have had any interest in becoming a figurehead for a racetrack, he remained interested in Thoroughbred breeding. He'd imported the stallion Phaeton from England and set him up as a sire in Hurstbourne's elaborate bricked stables, which had engraved bronzed nameplates affixed to each stall and an equine Turkish bath heated to 110 degrees by steam pipes concealed beneath a floor—a spa for horses. It was a small-scale enterprise, hardly Woodburn, but Ten Broeck hoped his stallion, a son of England and Ireland's leading sire, King Tom, would produce quality American racehorses.

"Old John" Harper of Nantura Stock Farm in Versailles had been breeding racehorses for his personal stables for years. He'd bred Loadstone, a horse Marcellus Clarke tried to steal, and Longfellow, who beat Lexington's famed colt Harry Bassett to win New Jersey's Monmouth Cup. It wasn't just his stallions that won races. Old John's mares were equally talented. His broodmare Fanny Holton, sired by Lexington, had won twenty-three of thirty starts. So, when Old John chose Phaeton as his breeding choice for Fanny Holton, few questioned his judgment. In 1872, after her visit to

Hurstbourne, Fanny Holton produced her fifth and last colt. Harper named him Ten Broeck.

When Old John died, Ten Broeck changed hands by inheritance to Frank Harper, John's nephew. Harper kept the colt in training until age three. On May 10, 1875, he raced Ten Broeck for the first time in the Phoenix Hotel Stakes in Lexington. Ten Broeck won—defeating, among others, a three-year-old named Aristides. A week later, stable boys walked Ten Broeck onto a cargo railcar and shipped him to Louisville. There, he faced Aristides again in the inaugural running of the Kentucky Derby at Churchill Downs. While Aristides ran into the history books as the Kentucky Derby's first winner, simultaneously setting a world record for running one and a half miles in 2:37 ¾, Ten Broeck trailed fifth out of fifteen contenders. Not even his bloodline containing Lexington's powerful drive made a difference. Eleven of the fifteen horses in the Kentucky Derby's first running had either been sired by Lexington or were descended from him within one generation—including Aristides, whose dam, Sarong, was Lexington's daughter.

As if the Kentucky Derby loss weren't enough to demoralize Frank Harper about his inherited colt, Ten Broeck continued his downward spiral—coming in last or next to last every time he raced that year. After several losses, turfmen decided that Old John Harper's choice of Phaeton as a sire had, after all, been an error.

Then, in the last three months of 1875, three-year-old Ten Broeck started winning. He closed out the season with six victories and set a new world record—one that would stand for nearly a decade—by running one and five-eighths miles in 2:49 ¼. Over the next two years, Phaeton's colt won eighteen of nineteen starts. He also broke more records, lowering the two-and-five-eighths-mile record to 4:58 ½ and, a week later, the three-mile record to 5:26 ½. Impressive feats, but not the sorts of records that would immortalize him.

The race that would set him apart was still to come.

On August 20, 1874, a year before Ten Broeck started racing, one of Lexington's grandsons, a horse named Fellowcraft, tore into the dark-brown sand covering Saratoga's track and ran four miles against the constant Time. He lowered Lexington's record by a quarter of a second, for a running time of 7:19 ½. However, turfmen everywhere knew that Fellowcraft had possibly only *matched* Lexington's actual time. Lexington's historic run over the Metairie was clocked separately by three official timers. Two of them, Captain William Minor and Stephen Elliott, timed Lexington at 7:19 ½. But Duncan Kenner, the head official timer and the one whose reading counted, clocked the run conservatively at 7:19 ¾.

Four days after Ten Broeck lowered the three-mile record to 5:26 ½, Frank Harper challenged him at four miles against Fellowcraft's 7:19 ½. Harper then enlisted the one man who knew how to beat Time. It was a brisk morning when Richard Ten Broeck led his namesake onto the track at Churchill Downs. Although he had turned down management of the racecourse only a year before, his agreement to oversee Harper's horse during the timed run brought him a renewed joy. On September 27, 1876, at Churchill Downs, Ten Broeck lowered Time to 7:15 ¾, without question beating Lexington's record by four seconds. He had carried 104 pounds, one pound more than Lexington's official weight of 103 pounds, in his match against Time.

Over the decades, across the North and South, thousands of horses had run not merely to beat another horse but to conquer an unseen constant. "Time waits for no man, nor horse" had been repeated in all the pundit chatter leading up to Lexington's Time match. Time had been lowered by only a rare few: Henry, Fashion, Lecomte, Lexington, and Fellowcraft. Ten Broeck was the last horse to whom Time conceded the test of four miles; the record stands today in his name. With Ten Broeck's win against the constant Time, the grandson of Lexington effectively closed out the era of the great four-mile horse.

When Lexington's Time was bested, the ribbon bearing 7:19 ¾ was removed from the elk's antlers that hung above his stall. But the antlers remained.

"Them horns have never been sent," Frank Harper told a reporter from the New York *Sun*. "They were to be sent to the horse that wiped out the old score." Pointing to the antlers above Ten Broeck's stall, Harper continued, "That pair of horns were from a buck killed by Mr. Weyman Dickson of Yazoo, Mississippi. But them are not the horns that should be over Ten Broeck's door."

The next day, the New York *Sun* reporter visited Woodburn Farm. He met Woodburn's new foreman, Lucas Brodhead, at what he later described as his "commodious cottage," surrounded by a dense cluster of oak trees. There they discussed race records, Lexington's progeny, and whether English racehorses were faster than those in Kentucky. "English horses have been bred so fine for speed that their stamina for long distances has departed. Those in Kentucky gain bone, muscle and strength, while they lose none of their fleetness," declared Brodhead.

After hitching a pair of horses to his wagon, the foreman drove the reporter to Lexington's stall. The large antlers hovered majestically over the stallion's door. Brodhead explained the old custom of nailing a rack of horns on the wheelhouse of the fastest boat on the Mississippi. For the two decades that those antlers had hung above the stallion's stall, the assumption had always been that only a son of Lexington would be capable of lowering his Time. In that sense, any of his descendants who beat his record would not take away his laurels but merely add another. Although antlers on the Mississippi routinely pass to the next fastest boat, Lexington's antlers remained at Woodburn.

CHAPTER 23

CATALOG NO. 16020

FIVE YEARS AFTER Alexander's death, Woodburn continued to dominate the breeding world, with Lexington producing more champion colts than any other stallion. By 1872, he had been listed as America's leading sire for eleven consecutive years. The distinction did not even take into account the incredible wins of his grandchildren, such as Aristides and Ten Broeck. Woodburn was acknowledged in those days as the best breeding stud in America.

Lexington now spent most of his days outdoors, rolling on the ground to stretch his back or running under the shade of the giant oaks scattered throughout his paddock. Over the years he had learned the placement of each tree, mapping them into his memory, so that now he negotiated his paddock unimpeded. He still looked robust and continued year after year as Woodburn's head stallion. "His deeds," noted the *Turf, Field and Farm*, "have made the name of Lexington famous in all quarters of the civilized world."

Turfmen, and people who aspired to be, still came to buy his colts and to visit their hero. A few years before General George Armstrong Custer traveled to Montana to lead the Seventh Cavalry Regiment into battle at the Little Bighorn, he paid a visit to

Woodburn—ostensibly to purchase a colt to race. Before he left, he asked to see Lexington. Brodhead took the general to the stallion's barn and introduced him to Lexington's groom. The groom threw the bolt and opened the stall door, allowing Custer and those with him to enter. Unlike most horses, Lexington did not turn his head to ascertain the cause of the disturbance. He stood still in his straw-bedded stall, covered with a blanket in the November chill, pricking his ears—as if, Custer would write, "by his intent listening he could determine by the sounds of the voice who we were and the occasion for our visit." The presence of Lexington—that aura of greatness that captivated the emotions by evoking grand memories of who he had been and who he was—stunned Custer, who admitted that his every act thereafter was in awe. Custer wrote,

> As his groom drew back the bolt and opened the door which admitted us into the distinguished presence of this famous horse, we involuntarily felt like lifting our cap, and with uncovered head and respectful mien approach[ed] this great steed as if we were in the sacred presence of royalty.

The groom led Lexington out into the barn's aisle and removed his blanket. At the age of twenty, the stallion still carried the build of a racehorse except for his back, which had sunk down a little. His limbs were still strong and unaffected by the ailments that twisted bones and made joints crackle. Custer marveled at his appearance, thinking him "[the] greatest horse, whether on the turf, or in the stud, which this country has yet produced." It was only his eyes, the general noted, that "seem to appeal for sympathy and pity." Custer later bought a horse, thought to be a grandson of Lexington, named Victory, and rode him in his last stand at the Little Bighorn.

Lexington had earned admiration from Custer and throughout the world. The *Turf, Field and Farm* wrote,

Nothing commands so much respect in the great, busy world as success, and through success piled upon success we have learned to speak the name of Lexington with a feeling akin to reverence. We count the beats of his pulse with anxiety, and when he languishes in sickness millions hold their breath, and feel within their veins a mysterious, tingling current of sympathy.

On the morning of July 1, 1875, a stable hand told Lucas Brodhead that Lexington was having difficulty breathing and had refused his feed. By the time the foreman arrived, concerned stable boys had circled his stall. Brodhead wedged through them and strode toward Lexington, who pinned his ears sharply to warn Brodhead away. The foreman inched closer, and Lexington stood still, too ill to follow his threat with a kick or abrupt pivot and snap of his jaws. He held his head erect and shifted his hindquarter weight while making a horrible wheezing sound as he struggled to breathe. Yellow mucus streamed steadily out of his nose. Brodhead looked down at a large bulge underneath the horse's throat.

A few months before, Doctors Herr and Harthill, Woodburn's veterinarians, had taken a carriage ride out to the farm to examine Lexington. They felt the bulge and then probed his nose with their fingers. Discussing the matter, they shook Brodhead's hand, then shook their heads and said they'd be in touch. They wrote a letter to A.J., who was then in England, telling him Lexington had a catarrh causing the nasal drainage. There was no cure. The mass that had formed underneath the horse's jawline was enormous.

About the same time the vets visited, Lexington's digestive tract had become compromised. His teeth had been worn down through the years, making it harder for him to chew. Like his old rival, Lecomte, Lexington began to endure episodes of colic—the painful gut strangulation that can kill horses. To aid his ability to eat and to ease his digestion, stable hands began feeding Lexington porridge mashes of oats.

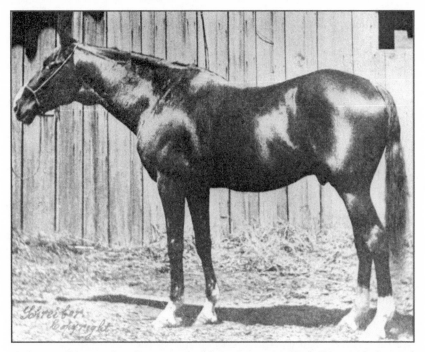

Only two photographs of Lexington are known to exist. The photograph depicted
here was taken in 1872 by George Francis Schreiber. A print exists in
the Woodburn Farm papers at the Kentucky Historical Society. Note the
bulge or catarrh located underneath Lexington's throat.

Despite the nasal drainage, enlarged throat, and digestive trou-
bles, Lexington had continued to breed, and to give his groom
gate-kicking and hole-pawing hell whenever the man was inatten-
tive to his needs. But on this morning, the horse had no stamina
for temperamental antics. Lexington continued to stand, his head
facing the darkened corner, straining to breathe. Sensing the worst,
Brodhead led Lexington out of his stall and placed him in his four-
acre paddock to expose him to clearer air.

On July 1, as time's hands ticked away the hours, minutes, and
seconds of that day, Lexington stubbornly stood on his feet through
his discomfort, refusing to lie down in his paddock. Word of his
condition spread among Woodburn's grooms, stable hands, trainers, cooks, and handymen. Throughout the day they gathered
around the horse they so fondly referred to as "Jack," a humble

endearment they had chosen, while others called him the King of Time, or the Blind Hero of Woodburn in honor of the blind seventeenth-century poet John Milton.* Nearing twelve o'clock that night, Lexington finally lowered himself to the ground. By midnight, he was gone.

Lexington was twenty-five years old in 1875. He had held the distinction of being America's leading sire for fourteen consecutive years.

Lexington's death was widely covered by the press. Articles appeared not only in the sporting papers but in *The New York Times,* the *New York Herald,* the *National Republican,* the *Hartford Daily Courant, The Patriot* of Harrisburg, *The Cincinnati Daily Gazette, The Indianapolis Sentinel,* and *The Evening Post.* They called him "King of the Turf" and "King of Sires." The *Turf, Field and Farm* wrote, "The hero of 7:19 ¾ lives in the forms of his children and grandchildren. They will long keep his memory green. . . . In the years to come thousands who have heard of his deeds will uncover their heads when they tread near his grave. Alas! Where shall we find another Lexington!"

Lexington's former trainer, J. B. Pryor, had written:

No horse was ever his match or ever could race with him after a half mile. . . . Lexington, when right, was a distance better than any horse I ever saw run in America [at] four-mile heats, and I have seen all the best horses run in England for five years, and there is not a horse there that he could not beat [at] four miles. There are horses in England that might beat or race with him two miles, but none four. He could go faster at the end of four miles than most horses can a half mile. I have been training horses thirty years, and am positive that Lexington is the best race horse I ever saw in any country. When he ran against Time in New Orleans, he could have run in 7:10. When he beat Lecomte, the next week,

* Reporters had taken to comparing Lexington's accomplishments through blindness to those of John Milton.

he could have beaten him three hundred yards, and I doubt if you could have beaten Lexington that day. . . . I never allowed him to run his best in any trial.

The *Kentucky Live Stock Record* wrote,

We need not, we are sure, make any apology to our readers for the space devoted this week to the memoir of *Lexington,* the most remarkable horse this country, if not the world, has ever seen. He was not a passing meteor that rushes through the air, dazzling our eyes with its brilliant light, leaving little or no impression, but a blazing sun whose influence interpenetrated and has been identified with all our stock. No horse was his equal upon the American turf, and none can be compared with him as a stallion.

In the hours following Lexington's death, an assemblage of men from Woodburn constructed a casket and dug a hole eight feet into the ground opposite his barn. While men prepared his grave, Brodhead stationed a trusted worker as a sentinel over Lexington's body, instructing him to permit no one to touch the horse. Still, against the sentinel's protest, a couple of men managed to clip locks of Lexington's mane as keepsakes. When the grave was prepared, a harness was attached to Lexington's body and hooked behind a wagon. Two horses pulled his body 150 feet to his grave. Presumably with ropes and slings, men painstakingly placed Lexington inside the casket and lowered it into the ground. The *Kentucky Live Stock Record* only briefly described Lexington's burial. It is unknown whether there was a ceremony, or how many were present. All that was mentioned was that Lexington was laid to rest by those who loved and had taken care of him through the years. After he was buried, the elk's antlers were removed from above his stall door.

Years before, as the stallion aged, A.J. had started receiving applications from numerous individuals and institutions requesting

Lexington's bones upon death. A.J. refused, saying Lexington was too valuable and dear to Woodburn Farm to be "cut up by uncaring hands."

But shortly after the burial, the Smithsonian Institution reached out, and A.J. began a correspondence with a physician and medical historian acting on its behalf. In November, four months after Lexington's death, Professor Spencer Baird, the Smithsonian's first curator, wrote A.J. to memorialize an agreement. A.J. agreed to donate Lexington's skeleton to the Smithsonian, and also for the bones to be exhibited at the upcoming Centennial Exposition in Philadelphia. Professor Baird acknowledged A.J.'s request that Lexington be prepared "in the best manner and suitably exhibited in the National Museum." Baird added, "We shall prize very highly the remains of this remarkable animal and . . . the stipulations made on your behalf shall be faithfully complied with. We have entrusted Professor H. A. Ward of Rochester, New York, who is the accomplished preparer of skeletons in the country, to personally visit your farm and superintend the disinterment of the remains."

Henry Augustus Ward must have had his bags already packed. Within days of the news that Lexington had been donated, Ward and a team traveled from Rochester to the barn of the great stallion to dig up his grave. Specifics of the disinterment were not recorded.

One must imagine how, on a brisk November day, Ward and his men thrust shovels into the ground until they hit wood. They hoisted scallops of dirt to the side until they defined the edges of the box. Ropes, pulleys, and slings would have been used to lift Lexington's casket into the Kentucky sun. Ward pried open the top and unleashed the foul musk of four months' disintegration. According to Lucas Brodhead, who attended the exhumation, a quart of masticated food was found under the left side of Lexington's skull, near the eye socket. This location was where Brodhead had observed a cushiony bulge, separate from the diagnosed catarrh. The food had seeped inside Lexington's cranial cavity through an opening in his jaw where he had lost a tooth. Brodhead surmised the masticated food may have caused the mucus drainage from Lexington's nose and led to his death. Lexington was reported to have had a jaw that ached constantly for several months before he died.

Satisfied that he could salvage the remains, Ward placed Lexington's body on the back of a buckboard wagon and took him out through the gates of the limestone fence.

On November 20, 1875, the *Spirit of the Times* reported:

LEXINGTON—The bones of this grand old racing king have been exhumed, and shipped from Kentucky to Professor H. A. Ward, of Rochester, N.Y., who will prepare and set up the skeleton for the Smithsonian Institution, at Washington. The skeleton will form one of the features of the Centennial, as it will be exhibited there, under the direction of Professor S. F. Baird. After the world has gazed upon the remains of former greatness, the horse will be placed permanently in the National Museum at the Capitol.

With Centennial celebrations happening the very next year, H. A. Ward had little time to spare. When Lexington arrived in Rochester, the professor began immediate work on the skeleton. The Smithsonian's archived file doesn't mention the method Ward used to prepare the remains; nor do his papers, housed at Rochester University, make any mention of the process he used on Lexington.

In 1894, William T. Hornaday, who worked under Ward at his Natural Science Establishment, published *Taxidermy and Zoological Collecting: A Complete Handbook for the Amateur Taxidermist, Collector, Osteologist, Museum-Builder, Sportsman, and Traveller.* He wrote that the two most common methods for cleaning bones were boiling and maceration. Of the two methods, maceration was the better process to rid the bones of fat. According to Hornaday, "A greasy bone in a mounted skeleton is an unpardonable offense."

Based on Hornaday's book, we can surmise how Ward would have gone about his work. To begin, he would have sketched and measured every inch of the horse's frame, its natural curvatures, the position of the shoulders and hips, and the location of smaller bones whose placement might not make sense later. There were a lot of bones to keep track of—Lexington's body contained 205 of them.

Then Ward would have divided Lexington into several parts by separating him at his primary joints. Smaller, indistinguishable parts were kept separate, labeled, and placed in dishes. The next step would be to thread a thick string through holes he bored in the horse's vertebrae and ribs—linking them in the correct order, then tying the string at both ends to secure them throughout the maceration process that was to come. If any of Lexington's organs hadn't decomposed, they were removed and discarded.

The bones would now be ready for maceration. "Maceration of a skeleton," wrote Hornaday, "is a question of time as compared with eternity." For large animals like Lexington, the process could take up to a year. It would take Ward two years, starting in 1884, to prepare P. T. Barnum's Jumbo, the elephant. Jumbo was twelve feet high, fourteen feet long, and weighed six and a half tons.

Over the maceration period, Ward would have had to contend with a daily affront of foul, reeking odor brought on by flesh disintegrating to a pulp. Maceration was a rank job, guaranteed to bring on the heaves in less sturdy stomachs. "But," warned Hornaday, "if you're going to study bones you must not mind that." Evidently Ward learned not to.

To begin, Lexington's bones would be placed in tightly sealed kegs of warm water. In this case the temperature might have been raised to cause tissue to fall more rapidly from the bones. To avoid their being discolored by blood and tissue—turning Lexington into a shocking blackish-purplish color—the water had to be changed frequently, until all the tissue dissolved. It usually took several months.

At this point Lexington's bones would be glistening. Next came the process of articulating the horse, or putting him back together in the most harmonious, physically logical, and eye-pleasing position. Ward would have started by pulling out his meticulous notes, taken upon Lexington's initial presentation at Rochester. The next step would be to position Lexington's bones by following the natural curves of the equine body. Ward most likely then consulted one of Troye's paintings or brought live horses into his workshop to observe their natural stance.

The entire process inevitably involved an infinite supply of iron rods, brass wires, brass pins, pliers, and patience. Since the electric drilling machine hadn't been invented, Ward likely bored holes into each bone by using a drill press powered by steam or water, or with handheld tools—a tedious and time-consuming task requiring precision and strength.

After lining the vertebrae along an iron rod for support, the keel on which the whole skeleton was based, Ward would have attached the ribs with copper wire. Approximating Troye's painting of Lexington may have had more to do with ease of articulation and available time than artistic homage. A walking equine skeleton is much easier to articulate. A rearing one requires additional iron rod to bolster the hind leg bones that bear the weight.

Lexington's head would be the last of the skeleton to be articulated, by fastening the mandible to the skull and the skull to the cervical column.

When Ward had finished, Lexington stood as perfectly as he had that day so many years before at Woodburn when Troye first sketched him with bold strokes of charcoal.

The Centennial International Exhibition of 1876 encompassed 236 acres in Philadelphia's Fairmont Park. From May 10 through

November 10, an estimated ten million people from around the world thronged the exhibition halls and pavilions flanking the Avenue of the Republic and Belmont Avenue. They traveled to see President Ulysses S. Grant pull the valve lever of the colossal Corliss steam engine that thrust power to the numerous buildings throughout the grounds. They came to see a gumming-and-folding machine for envelopes; inventions created by women to improve sewing machines; an apparatus for printing brightly colored wallpaper; and Thomas Edison's automatic roman-letter telegraph machine. A plaster cast of Rameses II stood at the Egyptian exhibit, while at the Agricultural Hall, "Old Abe," the war eagle who rode the shoulders of the Wisconsin Volunteer Infantry's Eighth Regiment for three years during the Civil War, perched on his dais eyeing and squawking at passersby. Elsewhere at the park, the Statue of Liberty's arm and torch, which would later be used in the statue, sprouted oddly from the ground, towering over a one-story ticket booth that charged visitors a small fee to ascend a portion of the arm up to the torch's platform. Assembly of the rest of the statue was set to commence on Liberty Island in September of that year, supplemented with proceeds from tickets sold at the booth. In that six-month period, admission receipts for the Centennial totaled nearly $4 million.

At the Centennial's Main Exhibition Building, encompassing almost twenty-two acres, Professor Baird showcased H. A. Ward's articulation of the famed horse. To some, Lexington must have seemed a surreal vision of death's aftermath: stark, frigid, and barren, with a blankness of emotion. Soulless. A framed edifice unfinished.

To others, his rebuilt form was a memorial of an extinct era, or a structure of osteological perfection. Whether the beholders saw him as Lexington at a time when memories still summoned his living, moving image is hard to say. Even to them, his skeletal form might have seemed a mere mechanized manipulation held together by iron rods and pins.

That same year, 1876, Lexington was posthumously recognized a fifteenth time as America's winningest stallion based on his get who were still living and racing to victories on racetracks across America. The distinction was again posthumously bestowed upon him in 1878, making a total of sixteen times Lexington was recognized as the leader among stallions. "Lexington holds a record," wrote the *American Racing Manual* of 1936, "unequaled by any other sire in the history of the Thoroughbred horse." As of this writing that statement still holds true.

After the Centennial celebration ended and the onlookers dispersed, Professor Baird returned Lexington to Washington, where the skeleton entered the Smithsonian's National Museum. Smithsonian personnel pulled out their paper catalog of exhibits naming the objects that had been so fervently acquired at the museum's behest. They located the next number in line and handwrote it beside the horse's name—"Accession No. 121040, Catalog No. 16020." Lexington stood on display until the middle of the twentieth century in the Smithsonian's National Museum of Natural History.

Then the extraordinary horse went missing.

CHAPTER 24

STANDING ON ALL FOURS: NINETY-FIVE YEARS LATER

Lexington belonged not alone to the turfmen.
He was the heritage of the nation.
—CHARLES E. TREVATHAN, "The Last Race of
Lexington," *The American Thoroughbred*

IN 1970, GERALD Strine, the horse-racing editor and columnist for *The Washington Post,* wondered what had ever become of Lexington's bones. No one had seen the horse at the Smithsonian since the 1950s and his name hadn't appeared in print or any other media form in over twenty years. The Smithsonian hadn't reported the skeleton as stolen, so where was it? The Bone Hall at the Smithsonian Institution's National Museum of Natural History seemed like the place to start.

With the same meticulous mindset that he would later use to write about Secretariat, Seattle Slew, and the Affirmed versus Alydar rivalry, Strine went looking for Lexington. Setting out on his new quest, the reporter opened the front door of the *Post*'s office and headed northwest a couple miles to where Tenth Street and Constitution Avenue converge at the Smithsonian's array of red sandstone buildings.

Inside the Natural History Museum, Strine ignored placards

pointing the way to the Smithsonian's prized attraction—the deep-violet-hued 45.5 carat Hope Diamond. Instead, he walked up two flights of stairs to the Bone Hall. Row after row of glass cubicles encased the bones of exotic saber-toothed tigers, kangaroos, chimpanzees, and a gray whale—all poised as if they were about to pounce on prey, swing from trees, or swoop down to the bottomless depths of the ocean. Strine quietly walked the rows, surveying the world's greatest osteological assemblage of creatures. He finally stopped in front of an articulated skeleton labeled EQUUS CABALLUS. High above Strine's head arched the skeletal framework of a rearing horse striking its leg out aggressively to defend its turf. Nothing on the plaque identified the animal as anything other than a horse. Strine looked around, but there were no other equine skeletons. No evidence whatsoever of Lexington.

Back at the Post, Strine made a series of phone calls to the Smithsonian, resulting in mumbled handoffs to one employee after another who might know something about the location of the missing bones. The chain of calls ended with Frank Greenwell, taxidermist for the museum's Division of Mammals and the very man who would help prepare the remains of the tremendous Fénykövi Elephant that stands under the rotunda of the institution's Museum of Natural History.

Strine found Greenwell on the first floor of the museum. He explained that he was looking for the bones of the century-old horse. Greenwell listened, blinking now and then behind thick black-framed glasses that magnified his eyes considerably. Greenwell invited Strine to follow him. They walked down a corridor that led to a stairwell. "I don't know why he's up here instead of being in the Osteology Hall downstairs," the taxidermist told Strine. "Maybe it's because the horse skeleton on display down there is more dramatic in appearance. That one's rearing up on his hind legs." Strine trailed Greenwell up four narrow flights of stairs to a large open-floored attic. A maze of gangplanks stretched across steel beams connecting various platforms with artifacts scattered over them, weighted in dust. Looking around them, Greenwell commented, "Subjects seem to be picked for what they are, not what they were."

Walking toward one of the plywood gangplanks, Greenwell motioned for Strine to follow. Above the planked corridor ran a highway of steel pipes funneling an unknown substance in an array of directions across the ceiling. Three floors below—and one wrong step—was the *Life in the Sea* exhibit and the gargantuan rib cage of a humpback whale. As Strine negotiated the gangplank, he passed a horde of antlers on his left, resting beside bones of an okapi and a blackfish. Not far from them, propped against the row of windows along the attic's outer wall, stood the mortal remains of Lexington.

To the naked eye, there was nothing special about these bones. This skeleton stood on all fours, head cocked slightly to the right—almost as if straining to hear something in the distance. "This horse was a very healthy specimen," Greenwell noted. "He obviously was a good-sized animal with no flaws in the bones. Museums are like everything else," Greenwell explained sympathetically, regarding Lexington's placement in storage. "They have trends."

It turned out that Strine's idea of getting Lexington out of the attic and back on display in the Bone Hall was wishful thinking. In 1956 there was an initiative at the museum to renovate the exhibits, and the skeleton didn't fit with whatever the curator was trying to say. Fourteen years later, it still didn't. "But don't worry," Greenwell assured. "There's no chance Lexington's bones will be destroyed. Everything that is donated here is kept unless, say, the skin of a mounted animal becomes eaten."

If the Smithsonian wasn't willing to take Lexington out of the attic and display him, Strine believed the legendary horse should be moved somewhere that would. Over the next few days, he flipped the wheel of his Rolodex and made a list of contacts who said they'd help. Saratoga's National Museum of Racing and Hall of Fame wanted the bones. So did others. Gerald S. Smith, then a

Frank Greenwell and Lexington in the Smithsonian's attic in May
1969. The King of Time stands surrounded by antlers.

trustee of the New York Racing Association and a member of the
Jockey Club, said he'd showcase the bones behind glass under Belmont Park's rotunda. "That would be a magnificent spot for it,"
Smith said. "Think of the thousands of racing fans who could see it
set off in a setting it deserves." Ted Bassett, president of the Keeneland Association—the parent company of the Keeneland Race
Course in Lexington—was also gathering artifacts for a museum
devoted to horse racing and wanted the horse to return to the state
of his birth, "where he had made his great reputation."

But moving Lexington anywhere wasn't going to be resolved
over a handshake and good intentions. His bones had been gifted
to the Smithsonian at the institution's request; not to Saratoga, nor
Belmont Park, nor Keeneland. Lexington was United States government property.

"The policy here," said Helena Weiss, the institution's registrar,
"has been that once something like this is part of a collection, it is
not easily released. It becomes part of the Smithsonian." She directed Strine to Dr. Richard Cowan, the museum's director, who
offered no hope. "We have almost a sacred trust feeling for objects

that have been donated to the national collection. We have, in fact, a legislative responsibility in that regard." The more Cowan talked, the more Strine felt Lexington "had a 100 to 1 shot of getting out of the Smithsonian." Then Cowan offered a glimmer of hope. "Perhaps a long-term loan could be worked out, if it turns out Lexington is not in our plans for future showings. We do constantly rotate exhibits. Have the racing museums write to us, to make a formal request for Lexington, to request consideration to display the skeleton." But it was only a glimmer.

Meanwhile, Lexington's bones remained in the attic. Over the following months, more writers walked the same gangplank, noted Lexington's unchanged location, and wrote more articles about the layers of dust he was collecting. In response to mounting pleas from racing fans who learned about the situation, the American Horse Council got involved, as did other equine groups. Kentucky congressman John B. Breckinridge picked up the phone and spoke to the Smithsonian. Racecourse presidents and directors of racing museums also phoned and wrote letters promising to give Lexington a better display. But the Smithsonian turned down all offers.

Then, in 1974, turf writer Peter Chew visited Lexington, walking with Greenwell out on the same precarious gangplank. The horse's bones were still there, propped against the windows, rising above the horde of antlers that formed his dais. Chew wrote an article emphasizing Lexington's triumphs, and his location in the attic, then sold it to none other than *Smithsonian* magazine for that year's May edition. The editors' decision to publish the piece created a stir within the museum itself that sent internal memoranda flying back and forth. According to one of those, "Since Lexington's present disposition was discovered by reporters several years ago, we have gotten much bad publicity and a continuing barrage of requests for transfer of the skeleton to various race tracks for exhibit." The memorandum continued, "Our response was a statement of the skeleton's value to us and a loan policy which was restrictive enough so that no one has taken us up on it. Rather than

protest this mischief in our own camp, it occurs to me that there is
a simple and inexpensive way to end the problem once and for all,
to the satisfaction of everyone concerned: the Museum, the *Smithsonian* magazine, and the racing public."

One year later, in June, members of the Smithsonian's Department of Osteology climbed up into the attic. They removed Lexington's head from his spine and carefully shuffled him along the
gangplank. They lifted him down four flights of stairs and then
carried him into a room where he was cleaned and reassembled, his
wooden stand conditioned, and his commemorating plaque polished to a sheen. After a few more memoranda between decision-
makers over what exactly to say about him, a new label was prepared:

SKELETON OF THE RACEHORSE LEXINGTON, SIRE OF MANY
CHAMPIONS. HE LIVED FROM 1850 TO 1875.

Finally, on July 29, 1974, the Thoroughbred Racing Association
issued a long-overdue press release. "In response to increased public interest . . . Lexington will be placed on permanent exhibition
back in the Bone Hall in the Smithsonian's Natural History Building."

How to showcase the undramatic Lexington became the Smithsonian's next perplexity. Curators eyed him indecisively and
scratched their heads in puzzlement. He was a forgotten horse, and
he had no place in a narrative about oceans or the Jurassic age.
With the exception of the Hope Diamond, the Museum of Natural History had not spotlighted individual pieces in its collection.
Ever since the Smithsonian acquired Lexington's bones, he had
been placed in a group of displays designed to attract curious eyes.
He'd stood inside glass cases with kangaroo lizards, a dinosaur, lla-
mas, and an ostrich. Visitors were left to draw their own conclu-
sions: Was it possibly about which animal could run faster?
Smithsonian officials had even discussed disassembling the bones
and rearticulating Lexington "in a graceful galloping posture," ac-

cording to a memorandum. But this was never done—most likely either because the bones were too fragile to manipulate without breakage or because the Smithsonian felt it necessary to honor one of the last existing works of H. A. Ward and to leave the skeleton as he had envisioned. Instead of reworking the bones, the curators took down the rearing horse labeled *EQUUS CABALLUS* and replaced it with Lexington, standing on all fours. There he stood quietly for decades, once again among the other skeletons in the Bone Hall.

Then, in 1999, Timex came knocking. The Smithsonian decided to place Lexington in the watchmaker's sponsored exhibit named *On Time*—a study of clocks, calendars, and timing devices. The four-thousand-square-foot exhibit showcased Mickey Mouse's gloved hands circling 360 degrees, and an eighteenth-century four-faced clock that not only told the location of the planets but chimed out "God Save the King." Museum technicians lumbered Lexington out of the Bone Hall and moved him across the street to the exhibit's showplace at the National Museum of American History. There, the King of Time stood as an example of why men needed stopwatches that split minutes into fractions of seconds. Whether visitors realized who Lexington was and what he had actually accomplished is hard to say.

Kentuckians, however, knew their iconic horse. In 1974, when Lexington was taken out of the Smithsonian's attic, they intensified their efforts to reclaim him.

In 1978 the State of Kentucky acquired 1,224 acres of grass in Fayette County near the city of Lexington. There the state opened the Kentucky Horse Park, dedicating the facility to "man's relationship with the horse." Inside the park is the International Museum of the Horse, dedicated to the same proposition of uniting people and equines. There was no better place to showcase Lexington. Kentucky congressman Breckinridge picked up the phone and made his request again.

In no uncertain terms, the congressman was denied. Lexington was too fragile—"invaluable and irreplaceable" as a resource, Smithsonian officials said. He was a step in the evolution of a breed and an "outstanding example of the Thoroughbred at its best." Lexington was too important for research purposes to loan to just *anybody*.

Refusing to acquiesce, the International Museum of the Horse called upon the power of First Lady Pat Nixon and First Lady of Kentucky Lucy Breathitt Winchester. The two women campaigned alongside Bill Cooke, curator and director of the museum. Cooke believed Lexington was "the horse who definitively assured that Lexington became the horse capital of the country, if not the world," he said. Lexington didn't belong in Washington inside cages with dinosaurs.

In August 1988, the City of Lexington's Urban Council decided to lend its name and voted to ask the Smithsonian to "return the great horse Lexington to his bluegrass home." After all, the Council said, "his genes were in 14 of the first 20 [Kentucky] Derby winners."

The Smithsonian denied Kentucky again. Lexington, it seemed, was doing just fine standing in the Bone Hall next to tigers.

Then, in 1996, the Smithsonian established its affiliations program to share its mass of resources and acquisitions with like-minded organizations and museums. To be recognized as a like-minded organization worthy of borrowing the nation's treasures, piles of forms had to be completed—along with, seemingly, sworn oaths and what must have felt like signatures written in blood. In a renewed effort, Bill Cooke picked up his pen and created those mountains of documents and proposals, outlining in depth the exemplary qualities of the International Museum and promising to promote Smithsonian artifacts—particularly Lexington—for the benefit of the viewing public. Cooke mailed the thick package of documents and sat back to wait. He felt the International Museum had acquired enough panache and presence to pique the interest of the Smithsonian.

Cooke was right. In 2006, the Smithsonian approved his proposal, and the International Museum of the Horse became an affiliate. That same year, the Smithsonian ended its seven-year Timex exhibit. Officials carted off all the fancy clocks and stored them away. Back at the Bone Hall, Lexington's display spot had been filled by a zebra skeleton, and the Smithsonian wasn't keen on removing the zebra. The museum tagged Lexington and placed him in a wooden crate in a storeroom at the National Museum of American History.

Bill Cooke contacted the Smithsonian.

In the back of the storage room, Smithsonian conservators pried open the crate containing Lexington's bones. They discovered a fragile skeleton. The horse had been moved many times throughout the years, and the less-than-refined tools Ward had used to drill holes had left the skeleton fractured in many places. Nearly all of Lexington's teeth were on the brink of falling out, and many of his ribs had undergone earlier renovations to wire them back in place. Decades of dust had settled into nearly every crevice of the skeleton, flooding the delicate bones with swarms of microscopic bone-eating bacteria. Years of storage in the attic's heat had only advanced the deterioration process.

After Lexington's condition was documented, he was vacuumed and gently cleaned with soot-removal sponges. His teeth and ribs were secured with resin, failed iron rods were replaced with sturdy new ones, and a stand was created to better stabilize and support the skeleton. His delicate head was carefully secured on a new armature running through his spine. "It's a lost art. No one does this today," one Smithsonian official said about skeletal articulation. Lexington was treated with a solution to help minimize dust, and recommendations were given to store the bones henceforth in a climate-controlled room. Conservators cautioned that future movement of the skeleton should be minimized because Lexington's bones were so susceptible to displacement from vibration. The skeleton was put back inside the crate, and they wrote their report.

In late August 2010, the Kentucky Horse Park was deep in the throes of preparing to host the Fédération Equestre Internationale Games—the first time the games had been held outside Europe. While the park was constructing a cutting-edge six-thousand-seat indoor arena for the events, a truck rumbled past the crews of hard hats and headed toward the back side of the International Museum of the Horse. Bill Cooke and his team were waiting. The truck slowed to a stop, and a large wooden crate was carefully lifted onto the loading dock. Inside the crate, separated by rows of heavy rubber shock absorbers, was another crate. Inside that crate were two platforms separated by a thick cushion of more rubber shock absorbers. Standing upright, wedged between two plywood support frames, was the Styrofoam-buffered skeleton of Lexington. His head had been removed and wrapped separately. "He arrived in very good condition, and the packaging was just amazing," Cooke said. "It was a huge bureaucratic mess. It took twenty-five years to the day to get him back to Kentucky."

Smithsonian conservators and collections personnel, along with employees from the International Museum, assembled Lexington as the centerpiece of its permanent *Thoroughbred in Kentucky* exhibit. The skeleton's base was placed atop a larger platform, and the stallion's commemorative plate was buffed and polished. A vitrine was built around him, with a life-size reproduction of Edward Troye's 1868 painting of the horse displayed as a backdrop. On the walls of the display room, surrounding the skeleton, hung reproduced paintings of Dr. Elisha Warfield and Robert Aitcheson Alexander, as well as facts about Lexington's breeding career— all commemorating how Kentucky became the Thoroughbred-breeding capital of the world.

Lexington's homecoming was banner news. His name once again filled the newspapers; most were stories of sentiment, with an occasional objection by some who felt his remains should be interred. Once again, the city's citizens adopted him as their own— reverently showering him with respect.

To celebrate Lexington's return, the city of Lexington adopted the stallion as its mascot. The city named him "Big Lex" and used Troye's painted image of him—but in the University of Kentucky Wildcats' team color of shocking blue. Big Lex appears throughout the city of Lexington on historical markers and parking meters, and on the city's website. To this day, his blue image directs visitors around town and is found on T-shirts, coffee mugs, cellphone covers, vehicle decals, and much more—all in a blue-horse push to promote the city of Lexington. His blue image even greets visitors at the city's Blue Grass Airport. Although some citizens found the color disrespectful to his memory, as the *Lexington Herald-Leader* noted in an article titled "Logo: Blue Horse Doesn't Please All," Big Lex is a constant reminder that Thoroughbred horse breeding and horse racing are legacies deeply rooted in the history of the vibrant city.

On any given day, visitors can see Lexington at the International Museum of the Horse—a skeletal homage to that early golden age of Thoroughbred racing. Lexington is now only a shell, absent the exceptional bottom so ingrained in his very being. But the long slender bones still serve to embody an extraordinary horse.

Adjacent to the *Thoroughbred in Kentucky* exhibit is the Calumet Farm trophy display. Shimmering racing trophies line shelf after shelf of mirrored glass, filling the room with an extreme brilliance. Whirlaway's Triple Crown trophies are there, along with hundreds of metallic vases and plates won by other descendants of Lexington. Horses whose victories were obtained by that undeniable drive and courage buried somewhere in their souls. Horses who then passed down those attributes to the next generation before themselves being committed to history.

From the display shelves, slices of silver and gold reflect off the mirrored glass and refract prisms onto the walls.

EPILOGUE

I N THE PROCESS of writing this story, I've often been reminded what a powerful metaphor Lexington was, not only to society at that time, but to his two owners: Richard Ten Broeck and R. A. Alexander. Both men had been sent away by their fathers. In turn, both shunned their familial expectations, and the straight and easy paths their families had so deliberately secured for them: the right schools, the right inheritance, the right family. Instead, Ten Broeck and Alexander purposely chose the much harder, somewhat unrealistic route of following their dreams, turning the lives they imagined into concrete reality by trusting their intuition and seeing it through. Things didn't always go smoothly, but their unfailing directive to themselves—bottom, if you will—and their acumen and love of horses drove them to the grandest of accomplishments. It only makes sense that with everything they had to overcome to reach success, both men would own the one horse whose accomplishments were achieved through his sheer will to surpass his own limitations. As undeniable a sire as Lexington was, his races are where we see his courage—his bottom—acted out.

Lexington was the backbone and blood of Alexander's empire,

siring an estimated 543 foals out of approximately 940 covers of mares. That number only accounts for his get that eventually raced, not the dozens claimed by the Civil War, or those lost for other reasons during those violent years.

In today's pedigrees, one has to scroll back through a hundred or so years to find Lexington. But he exists in a staggeringly high number of them, reaching into the tens of thousands, and he doesn't appear only once in a given pedigree, but usually multiple times. In contemporary horses, like the 2018 Triple Crown champion, Justify, Lexington appears significantly throughout his pedigree, to the point that correctly identifying all the crosses—the times he appears in the pedigree—would take hours of painstaking research. But the closer in time a horse is or was to Lexington, the stronger the blood or qualities assumed from him. While Seabiscuit contains seven crosses to Lexington, Man o' War, born sixteen years earlier, traces to Lexington only one time, in the fifth generation of his pedigree. Still, Man o' War carries a greater percentage of Lexington's blood than does Seabiscuit. And Seabiscuit carries a greater percentage than all the incalculable crosses in Justify's pedigree.

Lexington was also what breeders call a "broodmare sire," meaning that his daughters were more successful in passing along his lineage than his sons. Although both sons and daughters carried the potent Lexington lineage, his daughters were able to be put to a greater number of highly regarded sires that existed at the time: Australian, Eclipse, Bonnie Scotland, Phaeton, and so on. Conversely, Lexington's sons had a limited number of high-quality mares available to them, except for their own sisters, and they were intentionally not interbred to them. The daughter side of Lexington, therefore, carried on further than his sons, and Lexington is seen more predominantly on the dam sides of pedigrees.

Yet Lexington's prepotency as a sire is undeniable. Thoroughbred bloodstock consultant Alan Porter has said that "Lexington's influence on the foundation of pedigrees is incalculable. Without him, the breed we know today would be totally different." Without Lexington, Porter told me, there would be no Northern Dancer, or Mr. Prospector, or Domino, or any of the very significant sires that have created the modern Thoroughbred. It can therefore safely be said that Lexington's contribution to the American Thoroughbred has been beyond extraordinary. In that sense, he enters the pedigree, in varying degrees, of nearly every American horse who ran after him, or who will ever run.

As of this writing, going back to 1919, thirteen Thoroughbreds have won the Triple Crown:

1919	Sir Barton
1930	Gallant Fox
1935	Omaha
1937	War Admiral
1941	Whirlaway
1943	Count Fleet
1946	Assault
1948	Citation
1973	Secretariat
1977	Seattle Slew
1978	Affirmed
2015	American Pharoah
2018	Justify

Lexington appears in the pedigrees of all but Citation.

Of the first twenty runnings of the historic races listed below, the following number of winners traced their direct lineage to Lexington within one to three generations:

The Kentucky Derby: seventeen of the first twenty winners
The Kentucky Oaks: nineteen of the first twenty winners
The Belmont Stakes: thirteen of the first twenty winners
The Preakness Stakes: fifteen of the first twenty winners

The Travers Stakes: fifteen of the first twenty winners

The Saratoga Cup: seventeen of the first twenty winners

The Jerome Handicap: seventeen of the first twenty winners

Over the last decade, Lexington enters into the pedigree of *every* horse honored as the National Turf Writers Association Horse of the Year:

2009 Horse of the Year: Rachel Alexandra

2010 Horse of the Year: Zenyatta

2011 Horse of the Year: Havre de Grace

2012 and 2013 Horse of the Year: Wise Dan

2014 and 2016 Horse of the Year: California Chrome

2015 Horse of the Year: American Pharoah

2017 Horse of the Year: Gun Runner

2018 Horse of the Year: Justify

2019 Horse of the Year: Bricks and Mortar

2020 Horse of the Year: Authentic

2021 Horse of the Year: Knicks Go

2022 Horse of the Year: Flightline

"All America's best racehorses will one day trace to Warfield's Darley." Elisha Warfield's bold words, spoken at an uncertain time in that horse's future, were tossed aside then by all who heard them merely as sentiment for his dear colt. Yet, how prophetic they were.

In honor of his racing accomplishments, Lexington was inducted into the National Museum of Racing and Hall of Fame in 1955, its inaugural year. Boston was inaugurated alongside his son. In turn, numerous get of Lexington have been inducted throughout the years, Tom Bowling being the most recent inductee in 2020. Both Lexington and Boston's jockey, Gilbert W. Patrick, widely considered America's first great jockey, was inducted into the Hall of Fame in 1970. Despite the fact that other Black jockeys and trainers have been inducted into the Hall of Fame, Abe Hawkins has not been so honored. William "Old Nap" Johnson was inducted into the trainers' Hall of Fame in 1986. Ansel Williamson, Woodburn Farm's trainer and the trainer of Asteroid—as well as Aristides, the first Kentucky Derby winner—was inducted in 1998. Horse racing's Hall of Fame carves out a category for racehorse owners under what it calls "Pillars of the Turf." Expectedly, those honored include August Belmonts I and II; Cornelius Vanderbilt Whitney; Harry Payne Whitney; the prizefighter John Morrissey, who was a driving force behind the Saratoga Race Course's inauguration; Elias J. "Lucky" Baldwin; Hal Price Headley; Penny Chenery; and Ogden Mills "Dinny" Phipps—just to name a few. Neither Richard Ten Broeck nor Robert Aitcheson Alexander has been so honored.

Lexington is also recognized annually by the Keeneland Race Course. Every spring, Thoroughbreds line up to run the distance of one and one-sixteenth miles in the Keeneland Race Course's Lexington Stakes, a Grade III race for three-year-old horses. The race is named in honor of the great horse.

Lexington's rival, Lecomte, has also been recognized by the Fair Grounds Race Course in Louisiana, the track that replaced the legendary Metairie. The Lecomte Stakes, also a Grade III one-and-one-sixteenth-mile race for three-year-old horses, runs every year in January, in honor of the only horse who ever defeated Lexington.

Over time, American breeders and turfmen reshaped the American Thoroughbred to favor speed, a change that in many ways started with Lexington's and Lecomte's historic runs against Time. Handicappers today look to Beyer Speed Figures—a figure comprised of three variables: a horse's final race time; the distance of the race; and the track variant, a measure of the inherent speed of the racetrack—to assess a horse's likely performance in upcoming races. Today's horses run a furlong, about one-eighth of a mile, in an average speed of twelve seconds. That number would equate to roughly four miles at a speed of 6:24, compared to Lexington's 7:19 ¾. Whether today's horses could maintain that speed over four miles raises another question. Horses today aren't trained, nor are they bred, to run that kind of distance. There is no need for it. Generally, horses no longer serve as the right arms to humans, as they did in the nineteenth century. To subject horses now to such a demanding test as a four-mile heat would be senseless if not outright cruel.

Still, bottom has lingered as an important test for racehorses, separating, now as in the nineteenth century, the extraordinary from the exceptional. Every year, horses compete for the Triple Crown. There is a reason only thirteen horses have ever won the Crown in its over one-hundred-year history. The three races are packed close together on the calendar and spread hundreds of miles apart, making recovery difficult, so that it is nearly impossible for most three-year-olds to compete effectively in these highly competitive races. The horse who wins all three is truly extraordinary.

On June 6, 2015, on a warm day at Belmont Park, American Pharoah won the Belmont Stakes by five and a half lengths to claim the Triple Crown, ending a thirty-seven-year drought that had lasted since Affirmed won the Crown in 1978. American Pharoah made running look easy. He was a fantastic glider. Smooth. He covered ground more efficiently than other horses. But that was only part of American Pharoah's magic. The other part was his drive and courage, his staying power. That's what the Triple Crown really is: a test of bottom. American Pharoah's pedigree traces to that great racehorse and sire Domino, and through him to War Dance, a horse sired by Lexington out of the mare Reel, the dam of Lecomte.

In 1905, the writer Charles E. Trevathan described his favorite portrait of Lexington—one painted not by Edward Troye but by Thomas J. Scott:

There are many portraits of Lexington in existence, but the most impressive one is that painted by Scott, representing him led by Black Jarrett, his groom. The head is turned outward, and we have a full view of the dull, sightless eyes. The right fore-foot is thrown out haltingly, as if feeling for clear, firm ground upon which to place it. The whole attitude of the picture speaks the infirmity of the animal, and one loving a hero cannot look at Scott's production and recall the brilliant triumphs of the horse it represents without a shade of sadness stealing into one's heart.

Scott's painting is not displayed publicly. If it exists today, it likely hangs in a private collection, or perhaps is lost to history in an attic or basement as merely another horse painting once owned by someone's ancient relative.

Besides the other known paintings of Lexington that hang in galleries or racecourse clubhouses, there exists another tangible thread to the horse. At the International Museum of the Horse, inside the Kentucky Room where Lexington's bones now stand, Dr. Elisha Warfield's stud book is propped up under a Lucite box. The stud book is a rarity. Somehow, Dr. Warfield's book meandered into an antiquarian bookstore in Virginia. The Keeneland Race Course purchased the stud book for its library, which then loaned the book to the International Museum.

I have had the good fortune to review the stud book—to hold the book in my hands, gaze upon Dr. Warfield's scrawled writing, and turn its delicate pages, glimpsing into a long-ago world. On the page he numbered "nine" is the stud entry for Alice Carneal. Her sixth foal: "Darley by Boston. Sold to Viley and Ten Broeck." She foaled seven more by 1857, at which point, her page ends. Dr. Warfield died two years later. He lived long enough to revel in Lexington's exploits at the Metairie, though not to witness his prophecy's truth.

ACKNOWLEDGMENTS

T HE FIRST TIME I ever became aware of Lexington was on a
Sunday afternoon—October 28, 2012, to be precise—while
reading *Man o' War*, a book on the racehorse Man o' War. "Big
Red," as the chestnut was known, was mighty indeed: one of the
best that ever ran and a horse that *BloodHorse* magazine had rated
the top racehorse out of one hundred champion horses of the
twentieth century. The authors of the book went a step further,
comparing him to another great horse from the antebellum era,
one that was arguably better than Man o' War. His name was Lexington and he ran races of four-mile heats. "Both horses," wrote
the authors, "had that indescribable quality of greatness which
lifted those who saw them out of their ordinary lives and made
them conscious that they had witnessed something that would stir
their memories as long as they lived." I wanted to know more
about the nineteenth-century horse.

When I began researching Lexington's story, very little had been
written about him. His history had been distilled to less than one
page on Wikipedia. There was no book on Lexington—anywhere.
A few magazine articles about him existed here and there, and

through interlibrary loans I began to understand a little more about the reasons for Lexington's legendary status. About two months into my quest, I managed to find on eBay an 1860 London publication, volume one of *Baily's Monthly Magazine of Sports and Pastimes,* containing a write-up on Richard Ten Broeck. So it was with that I started: a half-blank Wikipedia page, a handful of magazine articles, and *Baily's Monthly*. Discovering Lexington's story ultimately led me on a nearly decade-long endeavor to unearth everything I could about this phenomenal horse and his owners. I found his history scattered in four different states and in uncountable libraries and historical societies, and pressed deeply into the rag pages of long-ago-published books as well as in the scribbled memories and thoughts contained in the private letters of his owners.

Anyone who writes about a racehorse must sift through the rich repository of turf history housed at the award-winning Keeneland Library at the Keeneland Race Course in Lexington, Kentucky. It is only there, not on the Internet or through a library loan, that the nineteenth-century pages of not only the *Spirit of the Times* but the *Turf, Field and Farm* and the early publications of the *Kentucky Live Stock Record* can be accessed. It was at Keeneland where the bulk of my research was conducted. The wealth of information compressed into each volume of those nineteenth-century periodicals can be learned only by turning one page at a time, and is not accessible by a computerized database keyword search. But, after all, we are talking about the nineteenth century, and turning those ancient pages was for this author an incredibly delightful way to really understand the sporting world of that era. The multiple weeks I spent at the Keeneland Library are a treasured memory. My heartfelt thanks to Becky Ryder, the library's top-notch director and a racehorse afficionado who not only runs a world-class library but is an expert who can wisely direct researchers to sources within both the library and the community. Thanks also to Ms. Ryder's assistant, Kelly Coffman, for scanning various information and sending it to me during the Covid-19 pandemic. As one can imagine, a decade-long research endeavor means that helpful guides come and go. My research at Keeneland was benefited greatly by Cathy Schenck, who was always ready to answer my questions by placing the correct book in my hand. Thanks as well to Betsy Baxter for returning more than one phone call to read to me verbatim from a page I no longer had access to while sitting at my desk in Albuquerque, some thirteen hundred miles west of Lexington.

Besides Keeneland, I owe special thanks to the National Sporting Museum and Library in Middleburg, Virginia, where I conducted research into Lexington's pedigree as well as the work of equine artist Edward Troye. I am especially grateful to Claudia Pfeiffer, the museum's director, for opening the library doors on a Saturday morning and for showing me Troye's truly wonderful sketches of Lexington. Thanks also to Lauren Kraut for assisting with image rights of Troye's depiction of the racehorse Kentucky.

I spent a considerable amount of time at the Kentucky Historical Society in Frankfort, poring over Woodburn Farm's bank and estate ledgers, stallion and mare brochures, newspaper clippings, photographs, and the handwritten letters of R. A. Alexander, including those sent to him from Richard Ten Broeck. My thanks to the Historical Society's staff, who assisted in my numerous trips there. I would like to especially thank Alyssa Ollier, digital archivist, for taking the extra step to research the background of one of the only known photographs of Lexington, a copy of which is contained in the Woodburn Farm papers, and for assisting with the rights to use that photo in this book. Thanks as well to the Woodford County Historical Society for opening up their files on Woodburn Farm and the Alexander family.

The Filson Historical Society in Louisville was generous not only in providing its archived photographs and eyewitness accounts of some of the colorful happenings in the life of Marcellus Jerome Clarke, alias "Sue Mundy," but also in taking extra time and care to retrieve a segment of the hanging rope and a lock of Mundy's famous brown curls—still richly dark and shining—from its warehouse for my viewing. I greatly appreciate Filson's efforts. Thank you as well to the Simpson County Historical Society, housed in Simpson County's old jail, which also contains a wealth of information on Marcellus Jerome Clarke. Their research file on Clarke holds information that simply cannot be obtained anywhere else.

West Point Military Academy approved my application to conduct research in its archives room provided I leave the library at the hour of "Taps." Although I did not find a smoking gun as to whether Richard Ten Broeck was forced to resign or chose to leave on his own accord, I did find other material, maps, diaries, and a doctoral thesis that were so helpful in understanding the life of a nineteenth-century cadet. Farther north of Highland Falls, the National Museum of Racing and Hall of Fame in Saratoga provided access to several portraits of Boston, Lexington, and some of the people surrounding our hero. Special thanks to Stephanie Luce, who oversaw my requests to reproduce these images.

Microfiche saved the day on more than one occasion. Thankfully, the Louisville Public Library and the Lexington Public Library (Kentucky Room) have archived many valuable old newspapers in that format. Considerable time was spent reviewing George Prentice's *Louisville Daily Journal,* the *Daily Democrat,* and *The Kentucky Statesman,* all of which were relied on heavily in this book.

I want to thank Ann McCrory, a writer from my "250s" group at Kenyon College's workshops, who drove from Baton Rouge to New Orleans to escort me to the Metairie Cemetery so that we could walk the old racecourse.

Separate from on-site research, I became an avid collector of first edition books and periodicals on nineteenth-century horse racing in America and Great Britain, as well as the American Civil War. Those sources were invaluable in understanding the two early systems of British and American horse racing and training as well as that era's modes for transporting horses. Thank you to Robin

Bledsoe of the now permanently closed Bledsoe Books in Boston and to Glover's Bookery of Lexington, Kentucky, who sold many source books to me and recommended others.

I also requested and received information from the Virginia Historical Society; the Smithsonian Institution Archives, with particular thanks to Ingrid Rochon, Heidi Stover, and Deborah Shapiro; the U.S. National Archives, with particular thanks to its staff for photocopying the couple thousand pages of trial transcripts from the Marcellus Jerome Clarke guerrilla band court-martial proceedings and forwarding them to me; the Library of Congress; Louisiana State University for providing access to William J. Minor's handwritten letters to T. J. Wells about their Lecomte conspiracy theory as well as for providing documentation about New Orleans's weather conditions leading up to and at the time of Lexington's great match against Time. Yale University's Beinecke Library provided additional records from the personal files of William J. Minor, which contained his several drafts of T. J. Wells's "pizen" allegations that Minor outlined in the national press. Thanks also to the Kansas Historical Society and Lisa Keys for information on William Quantrill and the Lawrence, Kansas, massacre, as well as for the rights to use the Quantrill comic book image. Thanks also to the Kentucky Weather Bureau; the New York Public Library; Dr. Sharon Cregier for providing me with her doctoral thesis on equine transportation; Anne Peters, pedigree historian, for reviewing an early draft I had written about Lexington's pedigree; the late Ellen Parker, a pedigree analyst; bloodstock agent Alan Porter for answering the key question: "What impact has Lexington had on the modern breed?"; Howell Perkins and the Virginia Museum of Fine Arts for the rights to use two of Edward Troye's poignant paintings: *The Undefeated Asteroid* and *Richard Singleton;* Dr. Michael Peterson, professor of biosystems and agricultural engineering at the University of Kentucky, who explained racecourse surfaces to me in plain English; Steven Smith of Rolling Dog Farm, a sanctuary for blind horses, who answered several questions

I had about the care of these animals; Dr. Claire Latimer, equine ophthalmologist at Rood & Riddle Veterinarian Clinic in Lexington, Kentucky, for answering questions on what might have caused Lexington's blindness; Bryna Reeves of Calumet Farm for assisting when I inquired about their one-eyed racehorse, Patch; Genevieve Baird Lacer for informing me about the unknown whereabouts of Thomas J. Scott's painting of Lexington and his Woodburn groom, Jarrett; the late Bill Cooke, who spoke to me about the very lengthy process of acquiring Lexington's bones for display at the International Museum of the Horse; the International Museum of the Horse for graciously providing their files on Lexington as well as for research conducted by them about the history of Black horsemen; Melissa Mead at Rochester University for reviewing their collection of H. A. Ward's papers to ascertain the process for preparing Lexington's skeleton; and Ed Bowen, turf historian and writer, for his support and gracious review of parts of the manuscript and for putting me in contact with Alan Porter. Thank you to Roger Rosenblatt, my instructor at Kenyon College's workshops, who believed in the concept of this book from the beginning; the "250s" at Kenyon who read and commented on some of my earliest writings about Lexington, particularly Dona Bolding for all her years of support; and the late Bill Mooney, two-time Eclipse Award winner and turf writer, who took an early interest in my research and edited a very early partial draft. My heartfelt thanks to Eve Claxton of Unfurl Productions for her insightful guidance and her valued assistance in preparing a book proposal to submit to publishers; Tom Jenks for his editorial services and also for lending his horse-racing knowledge in those edits; photographer Crystal Heis for meeting me at the Keeneland Library to photograph several of the images that are in this book; and Athena Lark for her authenticity and sensitivity reading of the completed manuscript.

My deepest-felt thanks to my family, who have not heard those words enough over the years. Thanks to my mom and dad, Terri and Charles Vrabel, for their encouragement. My utmost love and thanks to my husband, Mike, who has always believed in me; to my son, Connor, who at the current age of twelve has only known a mom who locks herself within her office for stretches of time to write about an ancient horse; and to my grandfather, the late Mayo Boucher, who immersed me in the world of horses and books.

This book would not have existed without Lou Ann Walker, founding editor of *The Southampton Review,* who was my editorial guide over the course of a few years as I continued research and chapter drafts. Thank you for allowing me to find my voice and ask the right questions, and, most important, for instilling confidence within me to keep going.

I am most grateful to my agent, Emma Parry, a thoughtful and elegant woman who has an uncanny Ten Broeck–like feel for society's pulse. I believe that assumptions are often made about the author being the sole idea-maker behind the story. But sometimes authors can overlook factors of interest or importance, which can be the case if that writer is too close to the story. In this instance, Emma asked many questions and raised subjects of interest that pushed my research and analysis further. The book is a richer and deeper account as a result. I wish to also thank Emma's assistant, Ali Lake, who saw something appealing in this story and helped to usher it through. Thank you as well to the Janklow & Nesbit agency for everything done on behalf of this book and myself.

My deepest appreciation to Ballantine Books and Penguin Random House and the terrific team who worked behind the scenes on this book, from the beautiful cover design to publicity and marketing. There are so many people involved in making a book come together, and I am thankful to all who made this happen. Special thanks to Kim Hovey, Kathleen Quinlan, and publicist Sarah Breivogel for getting this book written by an author unknown to readers into the hands of those readers; Jessie Bright for her beautiful and eye-catching book design, especially her wonderful treatment of Lexington's revered image; Caroline Cunningham for her beautiful design of the book and image placement; Mimi Lipson, my copy editor, for the very keen and insightful edits and fact-checking; production editor Luke Epplin; my proofreaders who read this book critically for errors; and editorial assistants Anusha Khan and Sydney Shiffman for guiding this book through production.

In his book *In Cold Blood*, Truman Capote reserved his final, "but really foremost," thanks for his editor, "whose judgment stood me in good stead from first to last." Susanna Porter, my editor at Ballantine Books, courageously took on this debut author. Her penciled notes in the various drafts of the manuscript were encouraging when needed, but most important—and I truly appreciate this—challenging and honest. She is another maker behind the ideas, and a gatekeeper to the unnecessary "We already know" followed by lines through the sentence(s). She has championed this magnificent horse through the pages of drafts, the image selections for the book, and the multiple meetings with untold numbers of Penguin Random House personnel. And she did it while kindly guiding an author through her maiden. My deepest appreciation and gratitude to Susanna for helping bring to life the extraordinary Lexington.

NOTES

PROLOGUE: BOTTOM

3   **When prizefighter James Ambrose:** "The Late Prize Fight: Sullivan v. Morrissey," *Spirit of the Times,* October 22, 1853, 421.

4   **Besides politics and religion:** John L. Hervey, *Racing in America: 1665–1865* (New York: The Jockey Club, 1944), 1:247–48.

4   **Per nineteenth-century racing regulations:** "Rules and Regulations of the Metairie Jockey Club of the State of Louisiana," *Spirit of the Times,* February 21, 1852, 3–4.

5   **Cooling periods:** Ibid.

5   **Some riders fainted:** "New York Races: Second Spring Meeting, Beacon Course, Hoboken, N.J.," *Spirit of the Times,* June 9, 1838, 133.

6   **Generally, it took at least two jockeys:** "A Duel to the Death: First Written Account of the Great Race Between Boston and Duane," *Kentucky Live Stock Record,* August 4, 1894, 65–66.

6   **Fifty-nine tracks operated:** Hervey, *Racing in America,* 2:378.

6   **News of the results:** "The Great Match Race," *Spirit of the Times,* May 28, 1842, 150.

6   **On race day, those people:** "Postscript! Boston Distanced by Fashion, in 7:42–7:48!," *Spirit of the Times,* October 30, 1841, 414.

7   **It took two equally pioneering:** Charles E. Trevathan, "The Last Race of Lexington," *The American Thoroughbred* (New York: The Macmillan Co., 1905), 305.

CHAPTER 1: REBIRTH

11   **He enjoyed the misimpression:** "Exploits of a Famous American Sportsman," *Thoroughbred Record,* October 11, 1913, 173.

12   **In 1663, Dirck Wesselse Ten Broeck:** Emma Ten Broeck Runk, *The Ten Broeck Genealogy* (New York: The De Vinne Press, 1897), 11–16.

12   **Born in 1812:** Hervey, *Racing in America,* 2:190.

12   **To enhance Richard's chances:** "Laws of the State of New York," fiftieth session, Albany, January 1827, Chapter 335.

12   **In 1829, rebellions aside:** Richard Ten Broeck, "Some Personal Reminiscences, Incidents and Anecdotes," *Spirit of the Times,* December 27, 1890, 872.

12   **But in less than a year:** United States Military Academy West Point Archives, West Point, NY, "Richard Ten Broeck." U.S. National Archives, Washington, D.C.; "Ten Broeck's Great Coup," *The Thoroughbred Record,* November 30, 1918, 254; "Reminiscences of a Busy Life: Richard Ten Broeck Tells of Men and Horses," *San Francisco Call,* November 2, 1890.

12   **Instead of polishing:** While hazing was considered a rite of passage at West Point, other regulations were strictly enforced, and an accumulation of offenses could result in dismissal. Card playing, drinking, and absence without leave, many times to Benny Havens Tavern in nearby Highland Falls, occurred regularly. Incidents of fighting were more problematic. Fighting with a superior meant mandatory expulsion. Outbursts against superiors were understandable. West Point officers and professors had carte blanche to prevent a cadet's advancement. Holdbacks were theoretically based on academic performance, but the system was subjective, with no recording of daily grades. A cadet's mastery of a topic was as good as his professor deemed it. Personalities could, and did, lend themselves to favoritism. Although the school was designed on a four-year plan, the number of years a cadet spent at West Point was entirely out of his hands. A cadet could remain at West Point six or more years: an abysmal setback in a once promising life. See James L. Morrison, "The United States Military Academy, 1833–1866: Years of Progress and Turmoil" (PhD diss., Columbia University, 1970), West Point Library. Ten Broeck's name does not appear on West Point's disciplinary records. However, by his own admission, he felt snubbed by superintendent Thayer—leading to, according to one of Ten Broeck's friends, the alleged duel. Such a challenge would certainly have caused the no-nonsense Thayer to expel the cadet.

13   **His political pull worked:** U.S. National Archives Record Group 94: Records of the Adjutant General's Office, Entry 212: Correspondence Relating to the Military Academy, 1819–66, dated January 10, 1830, #977.

13   **Although the family's honor:** Hervey, *Racing in America,* 2:190–91.

13   **No longer was he:** "Military Academy at West Point," *The American Farmer,* August 5, 1825, 158–59.

13   **The Mississippi and all it had:** George Ward Nichols, "Down the Mississippi," *Harper's New Monthly Magazine,* November 1870, 835–45; T. B. Thorpe, "Remembrances of the Mississippi," *Harper's New Monthly Magazine,* December 1855, 25–41; Ben Lucien Burman, "Mississippi Roustabout," *Harper's New Monthly Magazine,* May 1940, 635–43.

14   **So much so that nineteenth-century:** Thomas Ruys Smith, *Blacklegs, Card Sharps, and Confidence Men: Nineteenth Century Mississippi River Gambling Stories* (Baton Rouge: Louisiana State University Press, 2010), 1–30.

15   **"I back my opinions":** "Reminiscences of a Busy Life," *San Francisco Call.*

16   **But gambling on horses:** Kenneth Cohen, "The Entreaties and Perswasions of our Acquaintance: Gambling and Networks in Early America," *Journal of the Early Republic* 31, no. 4 (Winter 2011): 599–638.

17   **One memorable day:** Ten Broeck, "Some Personal Reminiscences," *Spirit,* 872.

17   **By post time:** "American Eclipse," *American Turf Register,* October 1831, 58; "The Great Match Between Henry and Eclipse," *Porter's Spirit of the Times,* May 28, 1859, 198–99.

18   **In 1807:** Hervey, *Racing in America,* 2:77–88.

18   **His whole ensemble:** Charles Stewart, ed. Annie Porter, "My Life as a Slave," *Harper's New Monthly Magazine,* October 1884, 732–33.

19   **His dear friend John Davis:** Alexander Mackay-Smith, *The Race Horses of America, 1832–1872: Portraits and Other Paintings by Edward Troye* (Saratoga Springs: The National Museum of Racing and Hall of Fame, 1981), 26.

19   **The place had notoriously reformed:** "Visit to Oakland, Residence of Col. W. R. Johnson," *American Turf Register,* June 1832, 521.

19   **Stallion advertisements often quoted:** John L. O'Connor, *Notes on the Thoroughbred from Kentucky Newspapers* (Lexington, Ky.: Transylvania Printing Company, n.d.).

19   **His supreme confidence:** Ten Broeck, "Some Personal Reminiscences," *Spirit,* 872.

20   **Boston was christened not:** "Old Boston's Early Life," *Spirit of the Times,* November 19, 1859, 486; "Boston, the Sire of Lexington," *Spirit of the Times,* December 18, 1875, 441; Hervey, *Racing in America,* 2:214.

21   **Many speculated that Boston:** "Kendall Course (MD) Fall Races" and "Camden (NJ) Fall Races," *Spirit of the Times,* November 10, 1838, 306–7.

21   **The horse packed grandstands:** "The Best Race Ever Run in America!," *Spirit of the Times,* May 14, 1842, 126; "To Readers and Correspondents," *American Turf Register,* April 1842, 174; "On Dits in Sporting Circles," *Spirit of the Times,* November 20, 1841, 450.

21   **a New York–based:** "New York Races, Union Course," *Spirit of the Times,* June 2, 1838, 124.

21   **His rival was a sensational mare:** Hervey, *Racing in America,* 2:157.

22   **By the age of four:** "The South v. the North," *American Turf Register,* December 1841, 685–86.

22   **By 1839, Boston had been sold:** "Memoir of Boston," *Spirit of the Times,* March 7, 1840, 6.

23   **In December 1841:** "The North v. South," *Spirit of the Times,* December 4, 1841, 474.

23   **On May 10, 1842:** "The Best Race Ever Run in America!," *Spirit,* 126; "The Fashion and Boston Match," *American Turf Register,* July 1842, 368; "The Great Match," *Spirit of the Times,* June 4, 1842, 162; Hervey, *Racing in America,* 2:164; "On Report of the Boston and Fashion Race," *Spirit of the Times,* August 27, 1842, 306.

25   **Outside the Union Course's gates:** Ten Broeck, "Some Personal Reminiscences," *Spirit,* 872.

26   **Though he'd been beaten:** "The Best Race Ever Run in America!," *Spirit,* 126; "Sporting Intelligence from Kentucky," *Spirit of the Times,* May 28, 1842, 147.

26   **Boston was worth more:** "Reflections upon the Great Match," *Spirit of the Times,* June 18, 1842, 186.

26   **The following day at the Union Course:** "New York Jockey Club Spring Races," *Spirit of the Times,* May 14, 1842, 127.

26   **The horse mattered to the people:** Hervey, *Racing in America,* 2:220.

CHAPTER 2: WARFIELD'S PROPHECY

28   **By this point in his career:** George Washington Ranck, *History of Lexington, Kentucky: Its Early Annals and Recent Progress* (Cincinnati: Robert Clarke & Co., 1872), 363; John L. Hervey, *Life of Lexington,* unpublished manuscript (Lexington Public Library, n.d.), 59.

28   **Warfield also taught:** Ranck, *History of Lexington,* 45.

28   **Therefore, Warfield became:** Hervey, *Racing in America,* 1:229–30, 233.

28   **His most beloved mare:** Stud Book of Dr. Elisha Warfield, unpublished document (Keeneland Library, n.d.).

28   **The celebrated stallion:** "Some Facts About Boston," *Spirit of the Times,* July 26, 1879, 619.

29   **There Boston entered the wood-planked:** "Boston and American Eclipse," *The Thoroughbred Record* 67, n.d., 9.

29   **As Boston walked:** "On Dits in Sporting Circles," *Spirit of the Times,* March 23, 1844, 42.

30   **The horse belonged to an ancestral line:** C. M. Prior, *The Royal Studs of the Sixteenth and Seventeenth Centuries* (London: Horse & Hound Publications, Ltd., 1935), 83.

30   **Boston's dam was a full sister:** Hervey, *Racing in America,* 1:182, 2:10.

30   **Alice Carneal, named in honor:** Stud Book of Dr. Elisha Warfield.

30   **Out of the mare Rowena:** "Turf History: Imported Sarpedon," *Turf, Field and Farm,* September 23, 1865, 113.

30   **In one of his many books:** It is unknown which depiction of the Darley Arabian Warfield relied upon, or if in fact it was more than one. John Wootton, the famed equestrian painter, had painted a well-regarded likeness of the Darley Arabian. So had artist John Nost Sartorius, an engraved reproduction of which appears in *American Turf Register,* September 1830, 1.

31   **Warfield liked the little foal:** Ten Broeck, "Some Personal Reminiscences," *Spirit,* 872.

31   **Over the next two years, Darley indeed grew:** Hervey, *Racing in America,* 2:311–14 (assimilation of descriptions of Lexington's build); "The Horse: Horse Portraiture," *Turf, Field and Farm,* April 27, 1867, 258 (observation of Lexington walking off a railcar, description of build and broad jaw like a squirrel with a mouthful of acorns; resolute look).

32   **By the time Darley was born:** Kent Hollingsworth, "Street Names Only Reminder of Famed Breeding Nursery," *Lexington Herald-Leader,* August 24, 1960; Kent Hollingsworth, *The Kentucky Thoroughbred* (Lexington: The University Press of Kentucky, 1976), 19–22; Hervey, *Life of Lexington,* 62–63, 71, 73; "Kentucky Association Records, 1907–1932 (Historical Note)," Filson Historical Society, September 5, 2014, filsonhistorical.org/research-doc/kentucky-association-lexington-ky-records -1907-1932/ (all sources used for historical background on Elisha Warfield).

34   **He went further on one occasion:** "How Lexington Was Saved to the Turf," *Turf, Field and Farm,* February 1, 1884, 75.

34   **Deeply serious about his work:** Equine artist Edward Troye painted Harry Lewis saddling the famed racehorse Richard Singleton, the horse he trained. The artist's depiction of Lewis was used here to portray the trainer.

34   **Kentucky turfman Captain Willa Viley:** Mackay-Smith, *The Racehorses of America,* 55.

34   **Although the date is unclear, by possibly 1853:** Katherine C. Mooney, *Race Horse Men: How Slavery and Freedom Were Made at the Racetrack* (Cambridge, Mass.: Harvard University Press, 2014), 90.

34   **Lewis had crossed a forbidden barrier:** The history of the enslaved and freed Black horse trainers and jockeys has been heavily researched and written about by Edward Hotaling in *The Great Black Jockeys: The Lives and Times of the Men Who*

Dominated America's First National Sport (Rocklin, CA: Form, 1999), as well as by Katherine C. Mooney in *Race Horse Men*. The International Museum of the Horse in Lexington, Kentucky, which showcases the wonderful exhibit *Black Horsemen of the Kentucky Turf*, was also helpful in providing this author with research conducted by many other historians, documenting the struggles and, at times, the very unusual "high" societal status these men seemingly held, though in reality never attaining freedom. Especially interesting is the account of the enslaved and later freed jockey and trainer Charles Stewart, as relayed to Annie Porter and told in *Harper's* October 1884 publication.

36 **He asked to lease Darley's racing rights:** Hervey, *Racing in America*, 2:281.

37 **Books of the era expounded:** S. Sidney, *The Book of the Horse*, 3rd ed. (London: Cassell & Company, Ltd., 1884–86), 557.

37 **To break Boston:** "Old Boston's Early Life," *Spirit*, 486.

38 **"Her nerves were as delicately tuned":** "The Death of Lexington," *Turf, Field and Farm*, July 9, 1875, 31.

39 **Back at The Meadows:** Hollingsworth, "Street Names Only Reminder."

CHAPTER 3: THE METAIRIE

40 **Bishop Henry Benjamin Whipple listed:** Henry Benjamin Whipple, *Bishop Whipple's Southern Diary, 1843–1844* (Minneapolis: University of Minnesota Press, 1937), 119–20.

40 **On any given week:** James E. Winston, "Notes on the Economic History of New Orleans, 1803–1836," *The Mississippi Valley Historical Review* 11, no. 2 (September 1924): 220–26.

41 **Open to all comers:** Grace King, *Creole Families of New Orleans* (New York: The Macmillan Co., 1921), 23.

41 **The Eclipse Course:** Hervey, *Racing in America*, 2:181–84.

41 **Not to be outdone:** King, *Creole Families*, 23–66.

42 **Metairie's track was something:** Michael Peterson, PhD, Professor, Biosystems and Agricultural Engineering, Race Track Surfaces, University of Kentucky, telephone call with author, May 12, 2021; Hervey, *Racing in America*, 2:180; "The Extraordinary Time Made at New Orleans," *Spirit of the Times*, April 16, 1842, 78.

42 **By the mid-1840s:** "Prioress and the Cesarewitch," *The Thoroughbred Record*, June 1, 1895, 347.

42 **But in May 1837, a financial panic:** Hervey, *Racing in America*, 2:154.

43 **Managers were often hired:** John Dizikes, *Sportsmen & Gamesmen* (Columbia: University of Missouri Press, 2002), 133.

44 **Three thousand people:** "Bull and Bear Fight at New Orleans," *Spirit of the Times*, June 12, 1852, 194.

44 **In 1845, Ten Broeck stood:** Ten Broeck, "Some Personal Reminiscences," *Spirit*, 872.

44 **In 1847, the New Orleans Jockey Club was sued:** "Interesting to Turfmen," *Spirit of the Times*, April 3, 1847, 66.

44 **Racehorse trainer William Day:** William Day, *Turf Celebrities I Have Known* (London: F. V. White & Co., 1891), 251.

44 **Ten Broeck's typist:** "A Machine Talk. Queer Odds and Ends of a Typewriter's Life," *San Francisco Call*, December 18, 1892.

45 **Yelverton Oliver had also lost money:** Hervey, *Racing in America*, 2:188–89.

46   **Impermanence inspired little:** Dizikes, *Sportsmen & Gamesmen*, 133.

46   **After forming the Metairie Association:** Hervey, *Racing in America*, 2:239.

46   **He started by enlarging:** Ibid., 2:240; Dizikes, *Sportsmen & Gamesmen*, 144–45.

48   **Ten Broeck tripled:** Dizikes, *Sportsmen & Gamesmen*, 145; "The Racing Season at New Orleans," *Spirit of the Times*, November 23, 1850, 474; "New Orleans Spring Races," *Spirit of the Times*, March 22, 1851, 54.

48   **He also insisted that horses:** "Rules and Regulations of the Metairie Jockey Club of the State of Louisiana," *Spirit*, 3–4.

48   **In February 1852:** "On Dits in Sporting Circles," *Spirit of the Times*, February 7, 1852, 606.

49   **Since masquerade balls:** Albert E. Fossier, *New Orleans: The Glamour Period* (Gretna, La.: Pelican Publishing Company, 1998), 458–60.

49   **Now, on various occasions:** "New Orleans Races," *Spirit of the Times*, April 12, 1851, 90.

49   **"The Metairie Course":** "On Dits in Sporting Circles," *Spirit of the Times*, April 1, 1854, 78.

50   **Talk of a multistate race:** "The Most Brilliant Sporting Event of the Age," *Picayune*, February 12, 1854.

50   **He gave the race:** "Advertisement: Great State Post Stake," *Spirit of the Times*, February 18, 1854, 10.

50   **"The most brilliant":** "The Most Brilliant Sporting Event," *Picayune*.

CHAPTER 4: OUTMANEUVERED

52   **Darley was the least-bet colt:** B. G. Bruce, "Memoir of Lexington," *Kentucky Live Stock Record*, n.d., 8.

53   **As rain assailed the track:** "Lexington (KY) Races," *Spirit of the Times*, June 4, 1853, 186.

53   **Lining up at the start:** Ibid.

54   **Although Lewis was a freed Black man:** Hollingsworth, *The Kentucky Thoroughbred*, 24.

54   **The grand prize that day:** "Lexington (KY) Races," *Spirit*, 186.

54   **The winnings totaled:** Mackay-Smith, *The Race Horses of America*, 55 (Viley paid Lewis $500 per annum, continuing even after Lewis was too old to work).

55   **A few weeks before, Smith had assembled:** "Great State Post Stake," *Spirit of the Times*, April 2, 1853, 78; "Sweepstakes—Metairie Course New Orleans," *Spirit of the Times*, May 7, 1853, 141.

55   **The *Spirit of the Times* was calling the Great State:** "On Dits in Sporting Circles," *Spirit of the Times*, May 7, 1853, 138.

55   **Smith told Warfield to name his price:** Hervey, *Racing in America*, 2:283.

56   **Not long after Smith's departure:** Ibid.

56   **Smith and Ten Broeck weren't the only ones:** Ibid. (recounts only the attempts made by Smith and Ten Broeck); Hollingsworth, *The Kentucky Thoroughbred*, 25 ("Several people had approached Dr. Warfield and offered to buy his colt").

56   **The Citizens' Stakes for three-year-old horses:** "Lexington (KY) Races," *Spirit*, 186.

56   **The problem was that Warfield:** Hervey, *Racing in America*, 2:284.

57   **Captain Willa Viley, the man who gave:** Mackay-Smith, *The Race Horses of America*, 53.

57   **And like Warfield, Captain Viley:** "Genealogies of Kentucky Families," *The Register of the Kentucky Historical Society,* 2:571, courtesy International Museum of the Horse.

57   **"I'll go half with you on the horse":** Hervey, *Racing in America,* 2:284.

57   **Ward was also a member:** "Junius Ward and the Thoroughbred Horse," Ward Hall, accessed November 7, 2022, wardhall.net/history/article1.html.

58   **There, they met with General Abe Buford:** "Memories of Distinguished Kentucky Turfmen, Col. Wm. Buford," *Kentucky Live Stock Record,* April 9, 1875, 153; Hollingsworth, *The Kentucky Thoroughbred,* 25.

58   **Old Harry looked point-blank:** Hotaling, *The Great Black Jockeys,* 145.

59   **He lost the first heat:** "Lexington (KY) Races," *Spirit,* 186.

59   **"Take him":** Bruce, "Memoir of Lexington," 9.

59   **Assuming that as Darley's new owners:** Hervey, *Racing in America,* 2:284.

59   **But Lewis stood his ground:** Ibid.

60   **A month before, he had raced his mare Sallie Waters:** "Metairie Jockey Club Races," *Spirit of the Times,* April 23, 1853, 116.

60   **He wrote, "I have purchased Dr. Warfield's Boston colt:** "Racing at the South-West," *Spirit of the Times,* June 11, 1853, 198.

CHAPTER 5: GETTING THERE

61   **Twenty-two years earlier:** "Lexington & Ohio Railroad," LexHistory.org, accessed May 10, 2020; Jessie Munday, "The Railroads of Kentucky 1861–1865" (master's thesis, University of Louisville, 1925), 4–7.

61   **A gang of dockhands:** "Embarkment of Cavalry, a Scene," *Spirit of the Times,* May 27, 1854, 173 (description of slinging horses on board ship and its difficulties, applied to Lexington scene).

62   **In a six-month period in 1851:** Author's compilation, made from review of *The New York Times* Archives digital database.

62   **Cypress trees growing along the river's banks:** Nichols, "Down the Mississippi," *Harper's New Monthly Magazine,* 840.

63   **Sometimes decks on ships:** "Shipping Horses," *New England Farmer, and Horticultural Register,* January 10, 1844, 217.

63   **At times they were shoved:** M. Horace Hayes, *Horses On Board Ship: A Guide to Their Management* (London: Hurst & Blackett, Limited, 1902), 218.

63   **In a heavy gale:** Fred Smith, *Veterinary Hygiene* (London: Baillière, Tindall, and Cox, 1887), 296 (eighty horses killed after being bashed against the sides of the ship when stall fittings unhinged during a gale); Arthur Shirley, *Remarks on the Transport of Cavalry and Artillery with Hints for the Management of Horses, Before, During, and After a Long Sea Voyage* (London: Parker, Furnivall & Parker, n.d.), 18 (forty-six horses snapped their stall fittings "like pieces of timber" during a violent storm).

63   **Negotiating rough waters:** Shirley, *Remarks on the Transport of Cavalry,* 25.

63   **Horses could slip and fall:** Hayes, *Horses On Board Ship,* 95.

63   **The bulk of a horse's natural balance:** Sharon Cregier, "Alleviating Surface Transit Stress on Horses" (PhD diss., Walden University, 1981), 105.

63   **Slings added pressure:** Smith, *Veterinary Hygiene,* 298 (Dr. Smith considered slings a "positive evil" and "quite unnecessary").

64   **Horse care was often relegated:** Hayes, *Horses On Board Ship,* 186, 188. (A few transports were lucky to have a skilled team specifically assigned to the horses. The

division was one man to every fifteen horses. The job was seventeen hours a day. The men followed a schedule, usually rising at 5:30 in the morning to water and feed, and repeating the routine every two hours until 10:00 in the evening. In addition to taking an hour for afternoon tea if it was a British crew, the men also performed daily rubdowns of idle legs, followed by brisk grooming to increase circulation.)

64 **When Lexington's sire, Boston:** "Old Boston's Early Life," *Spirit,* 486.

64 **Following a two- or three-week voyage:** Smith, *Veterinary Hygiene,* 305.

CHAPTER 6: LOST LIGHT

66 **Hailing from Virginia:** "The Pryor Family," *The Virginia Magazine of History and Biography* (January 1900), 325–26.

66 **Pryor had worked for a Mississippi:** Hervey, *Racing in America,* 2:194.

67 **But Pryor and Frances Ann's:** 1871 England Census; 1880 United States Census.

67 *Sans peur et sans reproche:* "Testimonial to the Trainer of Lexington," *Spirit of the Times,* May 12, 1855, 147.

67 **And it would take a fearless man:** "The Horse: Horse Portraiture," *Turf, Field and Farm,* 258.

67 **Clothing was so paramount:** "Thoughts on Blood Horses," *American Turf Register,* December 1831, 158; "Thoughts on Blood Horses," *American Turf Register,* January 1832, 217.

68 **Even though horses frequently gnashed:** "Thoughts on Blood Horses," *American Turf Register,* December 1831, 159.

68 **Fully swathed, Lexington was ridden:** The account of how Lexington was slowly trained, with gaits added incrementally over weeks of time, was taken from the following sources on nineteenth-century American racehorse training and preparation for heat racing: "Thoughts on Blood Horses," *American Turf Register,* December 1831, 160–63; "Thoughts on Blood Horses," *American Turf Register,* March 1832, 325–30; "Thoughts on Blood Horses," *American Turf Register,* April 1832, 383–87.

69 **Now, free to roam:** Bruce, "Memoir of Lexington," *Kentucky Live Stock Record,* December 11, 1880, 104 (J. B. Pryor's account of Lexington's corn bingeing).

70 **Feeding racehorses was a task:** "Instructions for Training Race Horses," *American Turf Register,* June 1830, 475–77; "Thoughts on Blood Horses," *American Turf Register,* January 1832, 211.

70 **Minor had heard the rumors:** Bruce, "Memoir of Lexington," 104.

71 **Lexington ran sluggishly:** Ibid.

71 **Pryor bled the horse:** Ibid.

71 **But the corn bingeing had done:** Ibid.

71 **The overeating and subsequent workout:** Claire Latimer, DVM, MS, DACVO, Rood & Riddle Equine Hospital, Lexington, Kentucky, telephone calls with author on possible causes of and factors leading to Lexington's blindness, August 6, 2020, and July 9, 2022.

72 **"I have no doubt that working the horse full brought it about":** Bruce, "Memoir of Lexington," 104.

72 **Horses see differently than humans:** Equine vision contrasted to human vision taken from the following sources: Michael A. Ball, *Understanding the Equine Eye*

(Lexington, Ky: The Blood-Horse, Inc., 1999); Jack Murphy, Carol Hall, and Sean Arkins, "What Horses and Humans See: A Comparative Review," *International Journal of Zoology,* 2009; Les Sellnow, "The Equine Eye," *The Horse,* October 15, 2001, thehorse.com/14895/the–equine–eye; Laura Hillenbrand, "Leading the Blind," *Equus* 229, 71–79; "Monocular Vision," Wikipedia, accessed March 8, 2019, en.wikipedia.org/wiki/Monocular_vision; "Binocular Vision," Wikipedia, accessed March 8, 2019, en.wikipedia.org/wiki/Binocular_vision.

73 **When a prey animal:** Steve Smith, owner, Rolling Dog Farm, email exchange with author, March 15, 2019 (caring for blind horses at Rolling Dog Farm); Jessica Pye, gold medal eventer, FEI North American Junior & Young Rider Championships, conversation with author, June 2018 (on competing her Thoroughbred Zephyr before and after he became partially blind); Hillenbrand, "Leading the Blind"; Jennifer Forsberg Meyer, "Horse Blindness Solutions," *Horse & Rider,* horseandrider.com/horse-health-care/horse-blindness-solutions; Heather Smith Thomas, "Caring for the Blind Horse," *The Horse,* November 1, 2012, thehorse .com/118812/caring-for-the-blind-horse; "Caring for a Blind Horse," accessed March 14, 2019, blindhorses.org/caring-for-a-blind-horse; "Fan Favorite Patch Prepping for 4-Year-Old Debut This Weekend," Paulick Report, paulickreport .com; Bill Finley, "Horse Racing; One-Eyed Colt Shows Derby Promise," *New York Times,* March 6, 2004.

75 **And only in November:** Hervey, *Racing in America,* 2:285.

75 **The track was heavy slop:** "The Great Match Race at New Orleans," *Spirit of the Times,* December 17, 1853, 523.

76 **Grooms flung off her linen blankets:** Ibid.

76 **The sight of his four white socks:** Ibid.

77 **"A racehorse, *sure*":** "Match Race—Sallie Waters vs. Lexington," *Spirit of the Times,* December 17, 1853, 522.

77 **But the horse's eyes were glassy:** "The Great Match," *Spirit,* 523.

77 **He approached Smith and offered:** Bruce, "Memoir of Lexington," 10.

77 **Lexington dug into the mud:** "The Great Match," *Spirit,* 523; "Match Race—Sallie Waters," *Spirit,* 522.

78 **When bettors saw her at the post:** "The Great Match," *Spirit,* 523; "Match Race—Sallie Waters," *Spirit,* 522.

78 **However, the *Spirit* reported:** "On Dits in Sporting Circles," *Spirit of the Times,* January 7, 1854, 558.

78 **After the race, Porter wrote for the *Picayune:*** "The Great Match," *Spirit,* 523.

78 **There were easily one hundred horses:** "The Most Brilliant Sporting Event," *Picayune.*

80 **As he had always done:** Hervey, *Racing in America,* 2:288–89.

80 **Running for Mississippi:** "New Orleans Races, Post State Stake, Etc.," *Spirit of the Times,* February 11, 1854, 618.

CHAPTER 7: KENTUCKY'S HORSE

82 **"The most brilliant sporting event of the age":** "The Most Brilliant Sporting Event," *Picayune.*

82 **Indeed, as one Alabama man:** "Mobile," *Picayune,* March 31, 1854.

83   **In 1854, there were over two thousand:** Robert C. Reinders, *End of an Era: New Orleans, 1850–1860* (New Orleans: Pelican Publishing Co., 1964), 168–69.

83   **People bet on endless oddities:** "Human Versus Horse Flesh," *Spirit of the Times*, February 4, 1837, 408; "One Hundred and Three Miles Between Sunrise and Sunset!," *Spirit of the Times*, June 6, 1840, 159; "Pedestrianism in New Orleans," *Spirit of the Times*, January 18, 1845, 558; "Challenge Extraordinary," *Spirit of the Times*, August 19, 1848, 301.

83   **One Catholic priest decried:** Eliza Ripley, *Social Life in Old New Orleans* (New York and London: D. Appleton and Company, 1912), 27.

83   **James Buckingham, a visiting Englishman:** James Silk Buckingham, *The Slave States of America* (London: Fisher, Son & Co., 1842), 1:331.

84   **Frederick Law Olmsted:** Frederick Law Olmsted, *A Journey in the Seaboard Slave States* (New York: G. P. Putnam's Sons, 1904), 2:229.

84   **To spare its patrons:** Martha Ann Peters, "The St. Charles Hotel: New Orleans Social Center 1837–1860," *Louisiana History: The Journal of the Louisiana Historical Association* 1, no. 3 (Summer 1960): 195.

84   **People clustered:** Fossier, *New Orleans: The Glamour Period*, 391; Reinders, *End of an Era*, 169.

84   **The French Quarter showcased:** Reinders, *End of an Era*, 151.

84   **The overflow trickled back up:** Ibid., 158–59.

85   **"The race for everybody, and everybody for the race!":** "The Great State Post Stake," *Spirit of the Times*, April 15, 1854, 103; "The Great State Post Stake," *Picayune*, April 2, 1854.

85   **another group from Fayette County:** "Recollections of a Famous Race," *Thoroughbred Record*, November 19, 1910, 242.

85   **In Louisiana, several sugar planters:** Ibid.

85   **Since then, the North had been climbing:** "On Dits in Sporting Circles," *Spirit of the Times*, April 29, 1854, 126. New Yorkers had bet an estimated $100,000 on the Great State. See "The State Stake Result in New York," *Picayune*, April 15, 1854.

85   **The *Spirit of the Times* noted:** "The Great State Stake," *Spirit of the Times*, March 4, 1854, 30.

86   **Arriving six days ahead of time:** "Millard Fillmore in New Orleans," *Picayune*, March 25, 1854.

86   **Memoirist Eliza Ripley:** Ripley, *Social Life in Old New Orleans*, 60.

86   **"The men," wrote Grace King:** Grace King, *New Orleans: The Place and the People* (New York: The Macmillan Co., 1917), 169.

87   **The Metairie Jockey Club had committed:** "The Most Brilliant Sporting Event," *Picayune*.

87   **On March 30, 1854, L. H. Filie:** "Metairie Course, Surveyor's Department, City Hall," *Picayune*, March 31, 1854.

87   **Of the Kentucky women:** Ripley, *Social Life in Old New Orleans*, 247.

87   **The mayor of New Orleans:** "Recollections of a Famous Race," *Thoroughbred Record*.

87   **That morning, all the avenues leading:** William Henry Herbert, *Frank Forester's Horse and Horsemanship of the United States and British Provinces of North America* (New York: Stringer & Townsend, 1857), 1:331; Ripley, *Social Life in Old New Orleans*, 247; "The Great State Post Stake," *Picayune* (all sources consulted for the scene on Shell Road en route to the Metairie's Great State Post Stake).

88   **The same rain-and-wind storm:** "The Great State Post Stake," *Picayune*.

88   **Mud, eight inches in depth:** Kentuck, "The Great State Post Stake!," *The Kentucky Statesman,* April 11, 1854.

88   **In the *Spirit,* one man predicted:** Larkin, "Sporting Epistle from a Western Sportsman," *Spirit of the Times,* February 11, 1854, 618.

89   **In the odds, Lexington trailed:** Kentuck, "The Great State."

89   **By two o'clock, the Metairie's grandstand:** New Orleans's laws and ordinances for 1857 seem to corroborate Dale Somers and John Dizikes in their statements that the city's horse races were inclusive, at least regarding freed Blacks, who were treated differently than enslaved people. The ordinances forbade enslaved persons from assembling in any "street, road, public square, meat markets or in any house, cabaret, grocery or coffee house, or on the levee, or any other place whatsoever in the city." On Sundays, enslaved persons could congregate at funerals, or at church "during the hours consecrated to divine service," and—Sundays only—on any public commons for the purpose of dancing or playing ball or cricket, with the mayor's permission. See City of New Orleans Ordinance § 753. The ordinances further stated that freed Blacks were allowed to congregate anywhere, and with anyone, except with the enslaved. Ordinances provided that if freed persons of color were invited to attend a public ball—making clear that ethnic races did comingle—the same ball must not include the enslaved. See City of New Orleans Ordinance § 755. In his visit of New Orleans in 1855, Frederick Law Olmsted wrote of seeing the marketplace crowded with "Spanish, French, English, Celtic, and African persons." Olmsted, *A Journey in the Seaboard,* 230–31.

89   **President Fillmore labored up:** "The Great State Post Stake," *Picayune.*

90   **Nearby, J. B. Pryor wiped Lexington's nostrils:** "Thoughts on Blood Horses," *American Turf Register,* May 1832, 444.

90   **He knew every dip in the Metairie's track:** Kentuck, "The Great State."

90   **The horse was underweight:** Ibid.

91   **At three o'clock, the drum tapped:** Ibid. "The Great State Post Stake," *Picayune.*

92   **During the forty-five-minute cooling period:** "Thoughts on Blood Horses," *American Turf Register,* May 1832, 444–46.

92   **At the drum's tap, Lexington:** Kentuck, "The Great State"; "The Great State Post Stake," *Picayune.*

94   **"The uproar became quite deafening":** Ripley, *Social Life in Old New Orleans,* 248.

94   **The exertion of corralling the stallion's extreme drive:** Boston, "Lecomte's 7:26–7:38 ¾," *Spirit of the Times,* June 17, 1854, 210.

95   **The *Picayune* labeled his silence "gracious":** "The Great State Post Stake," *Picayune.*

95   **The text was simple: KENTUCKY VICTORIOUS!:** "The Great State Post Stake, Kentucky Victorious!," *Spirit of the Times,* April 15, 1854, 103.

CHAPTER 8: LECOMTE

96   **It was either that or the more elaborate:** "The Great State Post Stake Race," *Boston Herald,* April 5, 1854.

96   **The *New-York Daily Times:*** "Great Race at New Orleans," *New York Times,* April 4, 1854.

96   **The *Louisville Daily Courier:*** "Kentucky Triumphant," *Louisville Daily Courier,* April 5, 1854.

97   **The inscription read:** Bowl on display at the Keeneland Library, Lexington, Kentucky.

97   **The *Nashville Union:*** "Great Race—Kentucky Victorious," *Nashville Union and American,* April 9, 1854, 2.

98   **Turf historian John Hervey:** Hervey, *Racing in America,* 2:198.

98   **Wells trained his colt at Wellswood:** "Lecomte Bred Near Alexandria," *Picayune,* February 18, 1958, 18.

98   **Lecomte started racing in April 1853:** Race records of Lecomte, October 30, 1852, through April 1854, contained in *The Spirit of the Times.* See also H. Crickmore, ed., *Famous Horses of America* (Philadelphia: Porter and Coates, 1877), 13.

99   **He even set a mile record:** "Metairie Jockey Club," *Spirit of the Times,* April 23, 1853, 115; "Sporting Epistle from 'Observer,'" *Spirit of the Times,* December 31, 1853, 548.

99   **Hark told Wells frankly:** "Lecomte," *Spirit of the Times,* January 27, 1855, 594; Annie Johnson, "A Legacy of Triumph: More Stories of Duncan F. Kenner and Abe Hawkins at Ashland Plantation," *Deep South Magazine,* March 3, 2014.

99   **Before that race, he had moved from Mississippi:** Hotaling, *The Great Black Jockeys,* 143–45; Johnson, "A Legacy of Triumph: More Stories," *Deep South Magazine;* Annie Johnson, "A Legacy of Triumph: The Red Fox of the South & Old Abe of Ashland Plantation," *Deep South Magazine,* March 3, 2014; "When Americans were Betting Abe on Abe," *Chronicles of the Black Jockeys,* vol. 2 archive.

99   **Abe Hawkins's skills made him:** Bob Roesler, "Lecomte vs. Lexington," *The Town Talk,* (Alexandria, La.), December 1, 1998, 9.

100 **General Wells arranged:** Hotaling, *The Great Black Jockeys,* 147.

100 **Perhaps the voodoo priestess:** Author's visit to the Cabildo, New Orleans, October 2015.

100 **Time had been a silent contender:** "English Racing—English Racehorses—Importation of English Stallions," *American Turf Register,* January 1834, 236. (Flying Childers ran Newmarket's Beacon Course—four miles, one furlong, 138 yards—in 7:30. Matchem ran four miles at Newmarket in 7:20.)

101 **With all the buzz:** Hervey, *Racing in America,* 2:289. According to Hervey, Ten Broeck chose to race Lexington again because he saw the chance to draw another big crowd at the Metairie. This scenario seems likely, given Ten Broeck's proprietorship of the Metairie. By his admission, he placed his bet on Lexington. See "Lexington to Lecomte—Another Challenge," *Spirit of the Times,* July 8, 1854, 246–47. Throughout his racing career, which spanned decades and two continents, Ten Broeck was known to back only his horses, good or bad; see "A Noted Turfman Dead," *Kentucky Live Stock Record,* August 6, 1892, 89; "English View of Mr. Ten Broeck," *The Thoroughbred Record,* September 28, 1895, 154 ("He always backed his horses heavily, and when they won, owned to the soft impeachment; if they were beaten he adopted an air of wisdom, and allowed it to be supposed that he did not fool his money away.").

101 **Lecomte was already entered:** Hervey, *Racing in America,* 2:289.

101 **"Sometimes inflammation comes on rapidly":** "Thoughts on Blood Horses," *American Turf Register,* June 1832, 495.

101 **Post-race observation and management:** Ibid., 493–505.

102 **Instead, Viley ordered the stallion's shoes:** Hervey, *Racing in America,* 2:289.

102 **In the end, Viley packed his bags:** Ibid.

102 **At the Metairie, odds fell heavily on Lexington:** "Fastest Time on Record," *Spirit of the Times*, April 22, 1854, 115.

103 **As patrons tossed money:** Ibid.

103 **The trainer said as much, strongly objecting:** "Lexington to Lecomte," *Spirit*, 247.

103 **"Keeping a horse in condition is hard":** "Thoughts on Blood Horses," *American Turf Register*, December 1831, 158.

104 **Pryor drove him forward:** "A Friend of Lexington to the Friends of Lecomte," *Spirit of the Times*, July 15, 1854, 259.

104 **When the drum tapped:** "Fastest Time on Record," *Spirit*, 115; "Lexington to Lecomte," *Spirit*, 247; Bruce, "Memoir of Lexington," 16–18.

105 **At the cooling circle:** Hervey, *Racing in America*, 2:290 (Lexington distressed); John Stewart, "Stable Economy," *American Turf Register*, May and June 1839, 334 (signs of distress).

106 **In 1898, American historian Lyman Horace Weeks:** Lyman Horace Weeks, *The American Turf: An Historical Account of Racing in the United States* (New York: The Historical Company, 1898), 387.

106 **The *American Turf Register* advised:** "Thoughts on Blood Horses," *American Turf Register*, August 1832, 605.

106 **The journal's very specific advice:** Ibid., 605–6.

107 **The exhausted jockey jerked:** "A Friend of Lexington to the Friends of Lecomte," *Spirit*, 259.

107 **But just as Lexington's rider:** Ibid., 246–47.

108 **From the crowd, Meichon heard "Pull up!":** Ibid., 247, 259 (John Hunter, the owner of Reube, the third competing horse, allegedly yelled at Meichon, "Pull up! The race is over!"); "Lecomte's 7:26," *Spirit*, 210.

108 **Hawkins looked back:** "On Dits in Sporting Circles," *Spirit of the Times*, May 27, 1854, 174.

108 **John G. Cocks, president of the Metairie:** "Lecomte's 7:26," *Spirit*, 210.

108 **As Wells's horse crossed the finish leading Lexington:** "Observer's Reply to a Turfman," *Spirit of the Times*, June 10, 1854, 199.

108 **A correspondent later wrote:** "Lecomte's 7:26," *Spirit*, 210.

108 **Meichon couldn't even keep:** Ibid.

109 **On April 9, the *Picayune* wrote:** "Great Four Mile Day—Fastest Time on Record," *Picayune*, April 9, 1854.

109 **That same day, Ten Broeck:** "Letter from Equus: Lecomte's Time," *Spirit of the Times*, June 10, 1854, 200.

110 **In late April 1854, the governing minds in Albany:** "Revival of Racing in New York!," *Spirit of the Times*, April 29, 1854, 126.

110 **In 1853, Frenchmen had pulled off:** *The Spirit of the Times* vol. 22, 366.

110 **Spurred by American pride:** "America's Cup Held Here Since 1851," *New York Times*, February 22, 1920.

111 **Tayloe wrote to the *Spirit*:** "English and American Horses," *Spirit of the Times*, October 25, 1851, 423.

111 **The answer was Richard Ten Broeck:** "Challenge from Lexington," *Spirit of the Times*, June 3, 1854, 186.

CHAPTER 9: TIME IS A MIGHTY GOOD HORSE

112 **Under the care of William A. Stuart:** "Revival of Racing in New York!," *Spirit*, 126; Hervey, *Racing in America*, 2:293.

112 **The *Picayune* called his recent victory:** "Great Four Mile Day," *Picayune*.

112 **Even Ten Broeck conceded:** "Lexington to Lecomte," *Spirit*, 247.

112 **The general's horse was so inspiring:** "Lecomte's Heat of 7:26," *Spirit of the Times*, June 10, 1854, 198 (poem); "Lecomte," *Spirit of the Times*, January 27, 1855, 594; "The Lecomte Medals," *Spirit of the Times*, February 17, 1855, 555.

112 **T. S. Moise, the celebrated equine artist:** "Portrait of Lecomte," *Picayune*, June 20, 1854.

113 **He was not the type to blame:** "Lexington to Lecomte," *Spirit*, 259.

114 **On April 30, 1854, he wrote a letter:** "Challenge from Lexington," *Spirit*, 186.

115 **"It is improbable that the best time":** "The Great Match Against Time," *Spirit of the Times*, April 14, 1855, 102.

115 **Other pundits claimed:** "Observations of the American Turf," *Spirit of the Times*, February 3, 1855, 606.

115 **Ten Broeck's straight-faced proposal:** "Lexington's Challenge Against Time Accepted," *Spirit of the Times*, June 17, 1854, 210.

115 **The *Spirit of the Times*, whose offices:** Ibid.

116 **For several days Lexington:** "The New National Course," *Spirit of the Times*, June 17, 1854, 210 (Lexington arrives to the National Course); "Lexington to Lecomte," *Spirit*, 247 (Lexington suffering from inflamed eyes).

116 **Ten Broeck withdrew Lexington:** "The Challenge from Lexington," *Spirit*, 247.

117 **I learn from a paper of New York:** "Lexington to Lecomte," *Spirit*, 247.

117 **Cholera had first appeared:** Charles Rosenberg, "The Cause of Cholera: Aspects of Etiological Thought in Nineteenth Century America," *Bulletin of the History of Medicine* 34, no. 4 (1960): 331–54.

117 **A month after Lexington arrived:** Hervey, *Racing in America*, 2:293.

117 **He found one in New Jersey:** "On Dits in Sporting Circles," *Spirit of the Times*, August 26, 1854, 330; Hervey, *Racing in America*, 2:293.

118 **While Lexington was rebuilding muscle:** "Sporting Intelligence," *Picayune*, July 9, 1854.

118 **Ten Broeck had at long last:** "Lexington to Lecomte," *Spirit*, 247.

118 **"For an owner to defend":** Ibid., 246.

118 **"I feel sure":** Ibid., 259.

118 **Jockeys had to spur Lecomte:** "Union Jockey Club Races," *Picayune*, March 28, 1855.

119 **According to one man who saw:** "Letter from Equus: Lecomte's Time," *Spirit*, 200.

119 **Even Wells conceded:** Ibid.

119 **On August 19, 1854, the *Spirit*:** "Challenge to the World!," *Spirit of the Times*, August 19, 1854, 318.

119 **The proposal sparked:** "Lexington to Lecomte," *Spirit*, 247.

119 **But one morning, while wrestling to have his head:** "Accident to Lexington," *Spirit of the Times*, September 16, 1854, 366.

120 **There, he would prepare to face Time:** "On Dits in Sporting Circles," *Spirit of the Times*, December 30, 1854, 546.

121 **One expert declared, "Lexington's condition":** "Lexington's Great Time Match," *Spirit of the Times*, March 24, 1855, 67.

122 **The previous day's morning paper:** "The Great Match Against Time," *Spirit*, 102.

122 **In preparation for the race:** "The New Orleans Spring Meeting," *Spirit of the Times*, May 12, 1855, 145.

122 **Uncharacteristically for New Orleans, rain had been scarce:** Meteorological Records for New Orleans, January 1855 through April 1855, Southern Regional Climate Center / Louisiana Office of State Climatology.

122 **With no rainwater to moisten the sand:** "Lexington and Lecomte, the Great Turf Events of the Past Season," *Spirit of the Times*, September 8, 1855, 355.

122 **The New Orleans *Crescent:*** "The Great Match Against Time," *Spirit*, 102.

123 **Almost all the bets placed:** "The Great Race—Lexington Against Time," *Spirit of the Times*, April 14, 1855, 103. (The *Spirit,* quoting from the New Orleans *True Delta:* "Bets were made freely, but by far the majority of them against Lexington, success in the effort being deemed out of the question. It is estimated that not less than half a million dollars were staked.")

123 **The debate reached the stage of:** Hervey, *Racing in America*, 2:295.

123 **After Lexington's loss to Lecomte:** "The Great Race," *Picayune*, April 3, 1855.

124 **But on race day, Gilpatrick, saddle in hand:** Ibid.

124 **By early Monday morning of race day:** "The Great Race—Lexington Against Time," *Spirit*, 103.

124 **At three o'clock, as if by some malevolent force:** Meteorological Records for New Orleans (Louisiana State University weather records indicate the wind blew south—Metairie is laid out on an east-to-west plane); "The Spring Meeting," *Picayune*, April 29, 1855 ("A strong wind prevailed during the effort," referring to Lexington's match against Time).

125 **Just a "consciousness of superiority":** "The Great Race," *Picayune*.

125 **The horse appeared in such splendid:** Ibid.

125 **Gilpatrick trotted Lexington:** Lexington race against Time scene taken from "The Great Race," *Picayune*.

127 **The boy ran the paper over to the telegraph room:** "Nine Cheers for Lexington! 7:26 Beaten!," *Spirit of the Times*, April 7, 1855, 90.

127 **Lexington had just broken the world speed record:** "English Racing—English Racehorses," *American Turf Register*, 236.

127 **When the result was announced:** "The Great Race," *Picayune*.

128 **Half of the right side of one of his shoes:** Ibid.

128 **In that era blacksmiths used iron:** "On the Manufacture of Horse-Shoes," *Spirit of the Times*, October 1, 1853, 391.

128 **One news article from the time:** Ibid.

128 **Some in the crowd clicking their own chronometers:** "The Great Race," *Picayune*.

128 **Late that afternoon, Lexington's figure of 7:19 ¾:** Trevathan, *American Thoroughbred*, 291.

129 **But it was New Orleans, they said:** Ibid.

130 **Three days after the race against Time:** Meteorological Records for New Orleans. See also "The Best Race of Three Mile Heats Ever Run," *Picayune*, April 11, 1855.

130 **Back in December 1854:** "Lecomte at New Orleans—Challenge," *Spirit of the Times,* January 6, 1855, 558.

130 **In early March 1855, a couple of weeks:** "Great Racing Events at New Orleans: Lexington's Match vs. Time," *Spirit of the Times,* March 10, 1855, 42.

130 **On March 31, 1855, two days before Lexington:** "The Great Four Mile Race at New Orleans," *Spirit of the Times,* March 31, 1855, 78.

CHAPTER 10: THE WAVING FLAG OF LEXINGTON

131 **Seven days after Lexington:** "Lecomte's Time Beaten," advertisement, *Picayune,* April 11, 1855.

132 **The *Picayune* wrote, "For several days":** "The Great Four Mile Race: Lexington the Winner!," *Picayune,* April 15, 1855.

132 **They filed into New Orleans's grand hotels:** "The City," *Picayune,* April 1, 1855. ("Our city continues to be full of visitors. The observance of Lent so very generally in New Orleans has a visible effect upon gaiety, which it holds in check from the Carnival till the Easter holidays, that are now rapidly approaching. Yet still there is so little of it visible here and there. The opera, the concert room, and the theatre, are well attended; the streets are not without the attractiveness imparted to them by numerous promenades and shoppers, and the hotels keep up the numbers on their registers without material diminution. The approach of the racing season, which commences tomorrow with the great match of Lexington against 7:26, in four miles, is producing some excitement, and we look to see a fresh infusion of visitors from day-to-day.")

132 **Every moment added to what:** "Metairie Jockey Club Races," *Picayune,* April 8, 1855.

132 **Every day, people continued to swoop in:** "Yellow Fever Deaths in New Orleans, 1817–1905," Louisiana Division, New Orleans Public Library, nutrias.org /facts/feverdeaths.htm.

132 **Six days before the rematch:** The 1850 United States Census reported a New Orleans population of 116,375.

132 **They waited for daily bulletins from the two stables:** "The Great Four Mile Race," *Picayune.*

132 **There is not anyone to be met:** Ibid.

133 **More Lexington-brand tobacco was shipped:** "Lexington," *Picayune,* April 14, 1855.

133 **Every merchant tried to take advantage:** "Advertisements—Coleman's Undulatory Mill," *Picayune,* April 13, 1855.

133 **Puns abounded:** "The Spirit of the Times," *Picayune,* February 24, 1855.

133 **Meanwhile, the *Picayune* was keeping a close eye:** "Lexington and Lecomte Again," *Spirit of the Times,* November 17, 1855, 474.

133 **"They reasoned," he reported:** Herbert, *Frank Forester's Horse and Horsemanship,* 332.

134 **"It is to me a matter of imperfect indifference":** "Lexington to Lecomte," *Spirit,* 247.

134 **"All over the sunny South went the word 'Lexington'":** Trevathan, "The Last Race of Lexington," *American Thoroughbred,* 305.

134 **In the early morning hours of Monday, April 9:** "Lexington and Lecomte Again," *Spirit,* 474; letter from William Minor to the editor of the *Spirit of the Times,*

William J. Minor Horse Racing Papers, box 2, folder 40, Beinecke Rare Books Library and Archives, Yale University.

135 **Lecomte ran a quarter mile:** Letter from William Minor to editor, Yale University.

135 **However, for the rest of the day:** "Lexington and Lecomte Again," *Spirit,* 474.

135 **Lecomte was drowsy, with cool skin:** Letter from William Minor to editor, Yale University; "Lexington and Lecomte Again," *Spirit,* 474.

135 **The *Picayune* reported that the "celebrated Lecomte":** "The Great Race," *Picayune,* April 13, 1855. See also "The Celebrated Lecomte," *Spirit of the Times,* April 21, 1855, 114.

135 **By Thursday, April 12, two days before the rematch:** "Lexington and Lecomte Again," *Spirit,* 474.

135 **By April 13, the day before the Jockey Club Purse:** "The Great Four Mile Race," *Picayune.*

135 **Even more people decided to cast bets:** "Capt. Dollis," *Picayune,* April 14, 1855.

136 **The general and his friends strolled:** "The Great Four Mile Race," *Picayune.*

136 **At nine o'clock on the eve of the race:** Herbert, *Frank Forester's Horse and Horsemanship,* 330.

136 **Out on the clogged streets, carriages battled:** "The Great Four Mile Race," *Picayune.* See also Herbert, *Frank Forester's Horse and Horsemanship,* 331 ("All the roads leading to the track streamed with pedestrians and vehicles, and the line condensed toward the gateway into a choked column that could move onward and in, only by the most tedious series of instalments").

136 **At the Metairie, ticketless racegoers:** "The Great Four Mile Race," *Picayune;* "Metairie Jockey Club Races," *Picayune* ("Those who are desirous of enjoying the week's sport, should profit by the knowledge, and obtain badges before leaving the city").

137 **Ticket-holders packed the two public stands:** Herbert, *Frank Forester's Horse and Horsemanship,* 331.

137 **Other patrons crowded inside the roped area:** Hotaling, *The Great Black Jockeys,* 149; Herbert, *Frank Forester's Horse and Horsemanship,* 331.

137 **Herbert wrote, "Even the gamblers":** Herbert, *Frank Forester's Horse and Horsemanship,* 331.

137 **From her reserved seat up high:** Amelia M. Murray, "A High Mettled Racer," *Letters from the United States, Cuba and Canada* (New York: Negro Universities Press, 1969), 284.

138 **According to Herbert, who saw Lexington standing:** Herbert, *Frank Forester's Horse and Horsemanship,* 333.

138 **He stated so to several men hovering:** "The Great Four Mile Race," *Picayune.*

138 **The track, having been restored by the heavy rainfall:** Ibid.

138 **Anchored by two grooms, Lecomte tossed:** Ibid.

138 **Lexington ran inside and in to the lead:** Race scene constructed from "The Great Four Mile Race," *Picayune;* Herbert, *Frank Forester's Horse and Horsemanship,* 334–35.

139 **Lecomte tried to answer his jockey's call, but "when his tail fell":** Herbert, *Frank Forester's Horse and Horsemanship,* 335.

139 **Down the backstretch for the last time:** Ibid.

139 **Refusing to relinquish his bit:** Ibid.

140 **After a few minutes of deliberation:** "The Great Four Mile Race," *Picayune.*

140 **"No one who saw Lexington walk quietly":** Herbert, *Frank Forester's Horse and Horsemanship*, 336.

140 **Lexington ran the race carrying 3 ¾ pounds more:** Ibid.

140 **Three days after the rematch, Ten Broeck contacted:** "The Celebrated Race-Horse Lexington," *Picayune*, April 18, 1855.

141 **T. S. Moise, the artist:** Ibid.

141 **So did Nathaniel Ives:** "Lexington," *Picayune*, June 23, 1855.

141 **Seven days after the race, His Excellency, Governor Hébert:** "Testimonial to the Trainer of Lexington," *Picayune*, April 21, 1855.

141 **Ten Broeck had been tapped:** "R. Ten Broeck, Esq.," *Spirit of the Times*, April 12, 1851, 90.

142 **Ever the promotional wizard:** Dizikes, *Sportsmen & Gamesmen*, 148.

142 **At that time, "the name of Lexington":** Trevathan, "The Last Race of Lexington," *American Thoroughbred*, 305.

142 **Lexington's purse earnings:** Hervey, *Racing in America*, 2:299.

CHAPTER 11: THE FALL

145 **He could rattle off:** William J. Minor Papers, Yale University.

145 **Wells's grumblings distilled to a belief:** William J. Minor to T. J. Wells, May 12, 1855, William J. Minor Papers, Louisiana State University.

145 **Wells argued in the pages of the newspaper:** T. J. Wells, "Letter to the Editors," *Picayune*, May 13, 1855.

145 **In addition to his proffer:** Ibid.

146 **The *Picayune* responded incredulously:** "The Spring Meeting," *Picayune*, April 29, 1855.

146 **William Minor eventually responded:** Minor to Wells, May 12, 1855.

146 **If anything, Minor said, Duncan Kenner:** Ibid.

146 **Since Lecomte's loss to Lexington, chatter circulated:** Ibid. ("Kenner then told me that Graves had told him some time previously that Hark was giving Lecomte too much work, and that if he continued it, Lecomte would not be able to beat anything"); "The Spring Meeting," *Picayune*, April 29, 1855.

146 **I shall endeavor to draw that Lecomte:** Minor to Wells, May 12, 1855.

147 **Minor added that he happened:** Ibid.

147 **Ten Broeck retorted, "That's a lie!":** Ibid.

147 **A correspondent identified as "Kentuck":** "Notes on Kentucky Horses and 'Pizen,'" *Spirit of the Times*, June 30, 1855, 235.

147 **In a letter to the *Spirit*:** "Lexington and Lecomte," *Spirit of the Times*, September 8, 1855, 355.

148 **Replying to Minor's letter, the *Spirit*:** "Lexington and Lecomte," *Spirit of the Times*, September 29, 1855, 391.

148 **The *Picayune* was even less forgiving:** "Lexington and Lecomte Again," *Picayune*, September 15, 1855 ("The revival of the old 'pizen' story will perhaps prove the signal for an earnest, if not angry, renewal of a discussion that we deemed to have been forever terminated").

148 **Wells wrote to Minor, who wrote back in vain:** Minor to Wells, September 12, 1855.

148 **Minor cautioned, "What I am now going to state":** Ibid.

148 Graves told Minor that Hawkins had no money: Ibid.
148 But Minor had defended Lecomte's training schedule: Minor to editor, Yale University.
148 Graves continued on with Minor, arguing that if the horse: Minor to Wells, September 12, 1855.
149 They corroborated the jockey's innocence: Ibid.
149 Nevertheless, seven months after the match race: "Lexington and Lecomte Again," Spirit, 474–75.
150 Minor wrote to the Spirit: Ibid., 475.
150 Eight months after Lecomte's loss to Lexington: "New Orleans Races, Metairie Course," Spirit of the Times, December 22, 1855, 535.
150 Wells, through Minor, wrote: "Lecomte and Arrow," Spirit of the Times, January 19, 1856, 582.
150 James Valentine, secretary of the Metairie: "Arrow and Lecomte," Spirit of the Times, February 16, 1856, 6.
151 Wells, in a surprising move: "Sale of Blood Stock," Spirit of the Times, May 24, 1856, 174.
151 Wells had named her Poison: Ibid.

CHAPTER 12: THE KING'S HORSES

155 As a diplomatic gesture: Sources for infusion of Eastern blood into the king's royal stables include Sidney, The Book of the Horse, 6–35; Prior, The Royal Studs; Weatherby's General Stud Book (London: J. Weatherby, 1793).
156 Captain Byerley had imported to England in 1690: Prior, The Royal Studs, 83.
156 Then, twelve years later, in 1702, Thomas Darley: Ibid., 126, 129.
156 Although the British royals initiated: "Breeding, Training," American Turf Register, January 1838, 8.
156 The incentive behind the plates: C. M. Prior, The History of the Racing Calendar and Stud-Book (London: Sporting Life, 1926), 97.
157 The Jockey Club, founded in 1750: Prior, History of the Racing Calendar, 114.
157 Along with establishing rules to govern racing: "Dissertation on the Blooded Stock of the United States," American Turf Register, August 1833, 613.
157 Weatherby's General Stud Book reads: General Stud Book, 1793.
158 Regulus, a chestnut son of the Godolphin Arabian: Fairfax Harrison, The Equine F.F.Vs.: A Study of the Evidence for the English Horses Imported into Virginia Before the Revolution (Richmond, Va.: The Old Dominion Press, 1928), 98.
158 Races were cut down: American Turf Register, June 1841, 305.
158 "The most important quality in a horse is speed": "English Racing—English Racehorses," American Turf Register, 234.
158 In 1873, the respected English turfman Admiral Henry Rous: Sidney, The Book of the Horse, 62.
159 Whether the losing horses were short on bottom or speed: Ibid.
159 To satisfy everyone, in 1851: Prior, History of the Racing Calendar, 221.
159 As one correspondent explained it: "English Racing—English Racehorses," American Turf Register, 231.
160 As one horseman wrote in the American Turf Register: "Breeding, Training," American Turf Register, April 1838, 155.

160 **Admiral Rous agreed, saying the system:** "Foreign Sporting Intelligence: Laws and Practice of Horse Racing by the Honorable Capt. Rous," *Spirit of the Times,* April 16, 1850, 81.

160 **Now, wealthy Virginia farmers who coveted:** Harrison, *Equine F.F.Vs.,* 43.

160 **The fantasy of owning a Matchem or a Regulus:** Ibid., 44.

160 **Bulle Rock was followed by Jolly Roger:** Ibid., 45.

160 **Owning a Thoroughbred was a coming-of-age:** Ibid., 44.

161 **The first was purchased by John Baylor:** Fairfax Harrison, "The Equine F.F.Vs.," *The Virginia Magazine of History and Biography* 35 (1927), 355–56.

161 **In 1764, Baylor sent a letter to John Backhouse:** Harrison, *Equine F.F.Vs.,* 99.

162 **A striking deep bay, Fearnought:** Fairfax Harrison, *Early American Turf Stock, 1730–1830.* 2 vols. (Richmond, Va.: The Old Dominion Press, 1934), 2:116 (Fearnought pedigree and characteristics); J. H. Wallace, *Wallace's American Stud-Book* (New York: W. A. Townsend and Adams, 1867), 1:156 (Baylor's stud entry for Fearnought); Hervey, *Racing in America,* 1:76 (Fearnought's king's plates winnings).

162 **Fairfax Harrison praised Fearnought's:** Harrison, *Equine F.F.Vs.,* 102.

163 **A few miles from Fredericksburg:** Hervey, *Racing in America,* 1:113; Randall Shrock, "Alexander Spotswood (1676–1740)," *Encyclopedia Virginia,* January 29, 2013, encyclopediavirginia.org/Spotswood_Alexander_1676-1740; accessed approx. 2014.

163 **On February 8, 1710:** Shrock, "Alexander Spotswood"; Harrison, *Equine F.F.Vs.,* 83.

163 **In 1757, he began importing:** "Lexington's Taproots," *The Thoroughbred Record,* November 22, 1924, 145; *General Stud Book,* 1793; Harrison, *Early American Turf Stock,* 1:165.

163 **While Spotswood was busy importing:** Hervey, *Racing in America,* 1:112–14.

163 **Washington once wrote to Fitzhugh:** Ibid., 1:113.

163 **Washington, likely through Fitzhugh:** Ibid., 1:113–14; "Lexington's Taproots," *The Thoroughbred Record,* 145.

163 **Fitzhugh purchased Diana I from John Spotswood:** Harrison, *Early American Turf Stock,* 1:167. Lexington's maternal pedigree has been questioned over the years. Dr. Warfield's stud book entry for Alice Carneal states that she traced to the Cullen Arabian mare, otherwise known as Diana I. According to the stud entry, Diana I was bred to a horse named Jack of Diamonds, a stallion that has not been authenticated in American pedigrees (or British, for that matter), to produce a mare in Lexington's lineage. Alice Carneal's maternal line, as relayed in her stud book entry, also contains an unnamed mare referred to simply as the Fearnought mare. This author has conducted extensive research into Lexington's pedigree. The most likely scenario is that Diana I was not bred to the mythical Jack of Diamonds but was instead bred to Baylor's Fearnought to produce Diana II, and Diana II is most likely the Fearnought mare mentioned by Dr. Warfield in the stud entry for Alice Carneal. See "Carolinian, Ratler," *American Turf Register,* September 1837, 496 (certificate of Lynaugh II Fitzhugh stating that Diana II was owned by his father, William Fitzhugh of Chatham; based on Chatham's stud book entries, which also refer to Diana II as "the Fearnought Mare").

164 **There was no reliable way to know:** Harrison, *Early American Turf Stock,* 1:7. (Many pre-Revolutionary importations and their descendants are mythological; a review of advertisements in eighteenth- and early-nineteenth-century American

newspapers, as well as attestations of the horsemen, "showed them to be of unequal value as historical evidence.")

164 **J. H. Wallace, who compiled his own stud book:** Wallace, *Wallace's American Stud-Book,* 13.

164 **Edgar was a friend of many American breeders:** Hervey, *Racing in America,* 2:98; Wallace, *Wallace's American Stud-Book,* 14.

165 **In defense of their respective countries' breeding efforts:** "Letter from an American Gentleman on Affairs of the Turf, Character, and Value of English Horses," *American Turf Register,* May 1834, 453; "Opinions Entertained in England of Horses Exported to America," *American Turf Register,* September 1831, 5.

CHAPTER 13: ROBERT ALEXANDER'S PURCHASE

167 **From the first time he walked along the cobblestone streets:** "Richard Ten Broeck," *Baily's Monthly Magazine of Sports and Pastimes,* May 1866, 55–59.

167 **The Duke and Duchess of Badminton:** Ten Broeck, "Some Personal Reminiscences," *Spirit,* 872.

167 **There was scarcely a social soirée:** Author's review of *Bell's Life in London,* a periodical pertaining to the time frame surrounding Ten Broeck's arrival to England, British Newspaper Archives digital database, accessed June 2016, britishnews paperarchive.co.uk.

168 **They crossed paths at the Goodwood Racecourse:** Jonelle Fisher, *For All Times: The Story of Lucas Brodhead* (St. Crispian Press, 2002), 16–17.

168 **His name had been published once or twice:** "Imported Cattle for Kentucky," *Spirit of the Times,* September 2, 1854, 348.

168 **He asked Ten Broeck if Lexington was for sale:** Fisher, *For All Times,* 17.

168 **Ten Broeck told Alexander that he had never considered selling:** Ibid.

169 **Alexander could become Lexington's new owner:** Hervey, *Racing in America,* 2:302.

169 **No one had ever paid that much:** "Race Horses Sold," *The Richmond Whig,* September 9, 1856, 2.

169 **Robert Aitcheson Alexander—R.A. to just about everyone:** Author relied on a reproduction of Jean Édouard Lacretelle's painting of Alexander that hangs in Woodburn Farm's private collection. Lacretelle's painting is currently the only known image of the breeder. Author also relied on descriptions contained in a clipping from the New York *Sun,* Alexander Family Papers, Kentucky Historical Society.

170 **He was the namesake son:** Dan M. Bowmar III, *Giants of the Turf* (Lexington, Ky.: The Blood-Horse, Inc., 1960), 3.

170 **Robert—R.A.'s father—had graduated from Cambridge:** Hervey, *Racing in America,* 2:321.

170 **Franklin chose Robert:** Bowmar, *Giants of the Turf,* 3.

170 **When Franklin left France to return to America:** Ibid.

170 **Because the land bordered Elkhorn Creek:** Ibid.

170 **Robert then set out to distinguish himself:** "Robert Aitcheson Alexander," *Turf, Field and Farm,* December 14, 1867, 369.

170 **It was there that he met:** "Descendants of William Alexander," unknown source or author, list of descendants, Alexander Family File, Woodford County Historical Society.

170 **On October 25, 1819, Robert Aitcheson Alexander:** Ibid.

171 **He was headed to Scotland:** Bowmar, *Giants of the Turf,* 4.

171 **In New York, R.A. shuttled from the train:** Author's review of Alexander Family Papers, including a photograph of Airdrie House in Scotland, Kentucky Historical Society.

171 **It would be the first of many that went unanswered:** Author's review of Alexander Family Papers, which contain letters to Robert Alexander from his brother, William Alexander, as well as from his son, R.A., Kentucky Historical Society.

171 **Sir William even admonished his brother:** Sir William Alexander to Robert Alexander, n.d., Alexander Family Papers, Kentucky Historical Society.

171 **Worried that R.A. wouldn't be able to pursue:** Ibid.

172 **As if R.A.'s poor health wasn't enough:** Ibid.

172 **There, R.A.'s ancestors had constructed:** Christine Alexander, *Airdrie, Scotland* (Philadelphia: published by the author, 1875), 5; James Knox, *Airdrie: A Historical Sketch* (Airdrie, Scotland: Baird & Hamilton, Ltd., 1921), 64.

172 **He was never expected to return to Kentucky:** Hervey, *Racing in America,* 2:323.

172 **Still, despite his father's absence, R.A. persisted:** Alexander Family Papers, Kentucky Historical Society.

173 **In February 1841, Robert was thrown from a carriage:** William Preston Mangum II, *A Kingdom for the Horse* (Louisville: Harmony House Publishers, 1999), 9.

173 **A man of wealth, he'd naturally had the foresight:** Last Will & Testament of Robert Alexander, Woodford County Historical Society.

173 **One year later, Sir William followed:** Mangum, *A Kingdom for the Horse,* 9.

173 **In 1849, he chose a farmer's life:** "Robert Aitcheson Alexander," *Turf, Field and Farm,* 369.

173 **He petitioned the Kentucky Legislature:** Henry Deedes, *Sketches of the South and West; or: Ten Months' Residence in the United States* (Edinburgh and London: William Blackwood and Sons, 1869); Allison Brownell Tirres, "Ownership Without Citizenship: The Creation of Noncitizen Property Rights," *Michigan Journal of Race & Law* 19, no. 1 (Fall 2013): 14.

173 **In 1851—about the time Ten Broeck bought the Metairie:** "Imported Cattle for Kentucky," *Spirit,* 348.

173 **In his youth, Alexander had sat at his Trinity College desk:** Hervey, *Racing in America,* 2:325.

174 **The course of self-education took him two years:** Dennis Domer, "Inventing the Horse Farm," *Kentucky Humanities,* October 2005, 5.

174 **By 1856, he was ready to purchase a stallion:** "Robert Aitcheson Alexander," *Turf, Field and Farm,* 369.

174 **He told his friend that it wouldn't do:** Arnold Kirkpatrick, "Most Famous Thoroughbred of the 1850s, Lexington, Was Foaled, Raced, off Loudon," *The Bluegrass Historian,* n.d., 5.

175 **So Alexander hunted down Ten Broeck:** Deed of sale of Lexington from Richard Ten Broeck to R. A. Alexander for $15,000, Alexander Family Papers, Kentucky Historical Society.

175 **The *Cleveland Plain Dealer* skeptically:** *Cleveland Plain Dealer,* January 15, 1857.

175 **"Have you seen him?":** Letter from Ten Broeck, writing from Florence, Italy, to R. A. Alexander, October 26, 1856, Alexander Family Papers, Kentucky Historical Society.

CHAPTER 14: WOODBURN FARM

177 **Alexander built the limestone wall:** "The Stone Fences of Fayette County," Lexington-Fayette Urban County Government, Division of Planning, November 1990.

177 **The wall was a trademark in many respects:** "Mr. Alexander and Woodburn Farm," *Turf, Field and Farm,* December 1, 1866, 344.

177 **Inside Woodburn, post-and-rail oak fencing:** Clipping from New York *Sun* describing layout of Woodburn Farm, and photographs of old fencing at Woodburn Farm, Alexander Family Papers, Kentucky Historical Society.

178 **Each section contained a series of European-style barns:** "Visit to R.A. Alexander's," *Spirit of the Times,* July 7, 1860, 255; Domer, "Inventing the Horse Farm," 7–9.

178 **Many of them were Irish and Scottish:** 1860 United States Census for Woodford County, Kentucky.

178 **When it came to his racehorses in training:** Mackay-Smith, *The Race Horses of America,* 224 (Mackay-Smith writes that Ansel Williamson gained his freedom under Alexander, although he provides no date for that occurrence); Hervey, *Racing in America,* 2:330 (Alexander utilizing training services of Ansel Williamson, whom Hervey identifies as an ex-slave).

178 **The Alexander family papers do contain:** 1857 contract to lease services of "Bill," a farmhand, agreeing therein to pay the man's owner as well as Bill, Alexander Family Papers, Kentucky Historical Society.

178 **Woodburn's enslaved were freed:** Author's review of Woodburn Farm's estate ledgers showing payments made to, among others, Ansel Williamson, Alexander's racehorse trainer; and Jarrett, Lexington's groom; Alexander Family Papers, Kentucky Historical Society.

179 **In all, Woodburn employed:** Domer, "Inventing the Horse Farm," 5.

179 **In addition to the stone-cut barns and homes:** Ibid., 8–9; "Visit to R.A. Alexander's," *Spirit,* 255.

179 **On an adjacent hill lay the racehorse training:** "Woodburn and Other Gossip," *Turf, Field and Farm,* October 16, 1874, 287; Domer, "Inventing the Horse Farm," 10.

179 **Alexander sought mares that were proven racehorses:** "The Lessons of Twenty Years at Woodburn Farm, Kentucky," *Wallace's Monthly,* May 1879, 242.

180 **"I have now," Alexander wrote:** Fisher, *For All Times,* 17.

180 **His ability to withstand various types of racing:** "Poetical Comparison," *Lowell* (Ma.) *Daily Citizen and News,* June 17, 1859, 2.

180 **"His foot set on like a hook":** Hervey, *Racing in America,* 2:313.

180 **Francis T. Porter, editor of the *Picayune*'s:** Ibid., 2:311.

180 **He was fast, and temperamentally even-keeled:** Ibid., 2:315.

180 **Sanders D. Bruce, who later compiled the *American Stud Book:*** Sanders Dewees Bruce, introduction to *The Horse-Breeder's Guide and Hand Book* (New York: Turf, Field and Farm, 1883).

181 **Nick breeding involves putting a selection of mares:** Matthew Binns and

Tony Morris, *Thoroughbred Breeding: Pedigree Theories and the Science of Genetics* (UK: J. A. Allen, 2010), 160.

181 **A mere day after winning the cup:** Hervey, *Racing in America*, 2:141.

181 **He retired as a champion:** Ibid., 2:141–42.

181 **He started buying up Glencoe mares:** Ibid., 2:326.

181 **He opened Lexington's breeding rights:** 1857 Woodburn Farm catalog, "Terms of Breeding," requiring that owners submit their mares' pedigrees so that they may be recorded, collection of the Keeneland Library. Lexington, Kentucky.

182 **To entice other horsemen to bring their mares:** 1857 Woodburn Farm catalog.

183 **The horse would later run for Ten Broeck in Great Britain:** "Mr. Richard Ten Broeck's Stables in England, 1857 to 1867," *Spirit of the Times,* January 12, 1878, 636. See also Ten Broeck, "Some Personal Reminiscences," *Spirit,* 874–75.

183 **One turf historian called these foals:** "The Law of Breeding—Facts and Theories," *Turf, Field and Farm,* March 1, 1878, 129.

184 **Each year, the sale's grand finale was the exhibition of Lexington:** "Visit to R.A. Alexander's," *Spirit,* 255.

184 **"Report speaks well of them":** "Arrow," *Porter's Spirit of the Times,* October 30, 1858, 136.

184 **On Saturday, October 8, 1859, twenty thousand people:** "Movements of Distinguished Horses," *Porter's Spirit of the Times,* October 8, 1859, 88.

184 **Competing for the title alongside Woodburn's horse:** Mackay-Smith, *The Race Horses of America,* 161.

185 **When Revenue wasn't traveling around the country winning blue ribbons:** "Movements of Distinguished Horses," *Porter's Spirit,* 88.

185 **a horse whose get were already proven:** Crickmore, *Famous Horses of America,* 21.

185 **The cacophony of the fair made Lexington:** "The Horse: Horse Portraiture," *Turf, Field and Farm,* February 10, 1866, 81–82.

185 **They chanted his name:** Ibid., 82.

186 **Author Joseph Cairn Simpson was on hand:** Ibid., 81.

186 **The horse walked alone:** "Lexington at the St. Louis Fair," *Wilkes' Spirit of the Times,* October 15, 1859, 87.

186 **He startled only for a moment:** "Horse Portraiture," *Turf, Field and Farm,* 82 (garlanded with a wreath of flowers, "he strode out of the ring with elastic step, his unrivalled pasterns enabling him to walk as gracefully as though he could see the way").

186 **Over the following weeks, his loss sparked a fury:** "Challenge from Kentucky to Virginia," *Spirit of the Times,* November 12, 1859, 474; "Lexington to Revenue," *Wilke's Spirit of the Times,* November 26, 1859, 184; "Another Challenge—Lexington vs. Revenue," *Spirit of the Times,* December 3, 1859, 510.

186 **Another man, identified only as "GERF":** "Lexington at the St. Louis Fair," *Wilke's Spirit,* 87.

CHAPTER 15: WAR

189 **General Ulysses S. Grant later called the war:** Ulysses S. Grant, *Personal Memoirs of U.S. Grant* (New York: Charles L. Webster & Company, 1885), 1:219 ("Now the right of revolution is an inherent one. When people are oppressed by their

government, it is a natural right they enjoy to relieve themselves of the oppression, if they are strong enough, either by withdrawal from it, or by overthrowing it and substituting a government more acceptable. But any people or part of a people who resort to this remedy, stake their lives, their property, and every claim for protection given by citizenship—on the issue").

189 **But Kentucky—fiercely independent:** Basil W. Duke, *History of Morgan's Cavalry* (Cincinnati: Miami Printing and Publishing Co., 1867), 38–41.

189 **On September 4, 1861:** Ibid., 47.

190 **On September 11, amid incoming pleas:** Ibid., 51.

190 **At dusk on September 20, 1861:** Ibid., 88–89.

191 **By late 1861, Lexington had been at stud:** Hervey, *Racing in America,* 2:303.

191 **Three years earlier, Alexander had answered:** "An Interview with Napoleon Belland," *The Thoroughbred Record,* August 6, 1921, 62.

192 **"Riding him was a thorough pleasure":** Hervey, *Racing in America,* 2:313.

192 **"At such times, with his head carried level":** Ibid., 2:313.

193 **There, he painted the Arab horses:** Mackay-Smith, *The Race Horses of America,* 174–85.

193 **Troye sketched and painted the horse:** Ibid. (author's tabulation of Troye's Lexington sketches and paintings identified by Mackay-Smith).

193 **About the time Belland was riding Lexington over the hills:** Clipping from New York *Sun,* Alexander Family Papers, Kentucky Historical Society.

193 **There they remained until the next fastest boat:** Frederick Way, Jr., *She Takes the Horns: Steamboat Racing on the Western Waters* (Cincinnati: Young and Klein, Inc., 1953).

193 **By 1862, the Lexington Rifles had grown to over:** Duke, *History of Morgan's Cavalry,* 281.

194 **Even though they could now officially be called soldiers:** Stephen Towne and Jay G. Heiser, "Everything Is Fair in War: The Civil War Memoir of George A. 'Lightning' Ellsworth, Telegraph Operator for John Hunt Morgan," *The Register of the Kentucky Historical Society* 108, no. ½ (Winter/Spring 2010): 31.

194 **As Basil Duke, Morgan's right-hand commandant:** Duke, *History of Morgan's Cavalry,* 108–9.

194 **Discipline, according to Duke, would render:** Ibid., 83–84.

194 **Near the northern Kentucky town of Cynthiana:** *The War of the Rebellion: A Compilation of the Official Records of the Union and Confederate Armies.* Washington, D.C.: Government Printing Office, 1897, 29, no. 1, 59. Hereafter cited as ORWR.

195 **They even pointed guns at a Mrs. Hamilton:** *ORWR* 39, no. 1, 77–80.

195 **Then they headed toward Morgan's hometown:** Towne and Heiser, "Everything Is Fair in War," 32, 53. Hereafter cited as ORWR.

195 **Morgan gave the order, "Light up the town!":** *ORWR* 39, no. 1, 67–70.

195 **Morgan's men kicked the doors open:** "The Civil War in Kentucky" mentions the name of the Lexington, Kentucky, bank, nps.gov/nr/travel/lexington/civilwar.htm.

195 **Captain George H. Laird, the Union quartermaster:** *ORWR* 39, no. 1, 71–72.

196 **With the pillaging of Kentucky's deposit banks:** *ORWR* 39, no. 1, 74–75 (Report of H. L. Glinter, Commanding Col. of the First Cavalry Brigade reporting on Morgan's theft of $80,000 from the Mount Sterling bank).

196 **There was no guessing what a Union or Confederate:** Joan E. Cashin, "Tro-

phies of War: Material Culture in the Civil War Era," *Journal of the Civil War Era* 1, no. 3 (2011): 339–67.

196 **Tiffany's, earlier known as Tiffany, Young & Ellis:** "Notice," *Spirit of the Times,* December 22, 1849, 528.

196 **The pure-silver Woodlawn Vase, as the cup came to be known:** "Woodlawn Association—Challenge Vase," *Spirit of the Times,* May 18, 1861, 232.

197 **Alexander then took the Woodlawn Vase and other family silver:** "Westchester's Final Strids," *Turf, Field and Farm,* October 25, 1902, 1026.

198 **Southern cotton was by far the most exported:** Worthy P. Sterns, "The Foreign Trade of the United States from 1820 to 1840," *Journal of Political Economy* 8, no. 1 (December 1899): 34–57.

199 **Lightning Ellsworth's Thoroughbred, Maud:** Towne and Heiser, "Everything Is Fair in War," 70–71.

199 **Ellsworth always suspected the reason to be that Fleetfoot:** Ibid., 78.

199 **A good horse was more valuable to a soldier:** Ibid., 71.

199 **A horse with stamina, speed, and courage could carry:** John Davis Billings and Charles W. Reed, *Hardtack and Coffee; or: The Unwritten Story of Army Life* (Boston: George M. Smith & Co., 1887), 328 (Private Billings wrote that on average, a horse could take hits from five bullets before dying. On the sounds of impact, he wrote, "A peculiar dull thud indicated that the bullet had penetrated some fleshy part of the horse sounding much as a pebble does when thrown into the mud. . . . When a bullet struck the bone of a horse's leg in the lower part, it made a hollow snapping sound."); Ibid., 326–27; Towne and Heiser, "Everything Is Fair in War," 85 (Ellsworth wrote, "My horse had traveled 150 miles in less than three days' time, and was in no condition for racing, although it was no trouble for him to lead that scrub stock up the mountains. He was a Thoroughbred").

199 **Colonel James B. McPherson's horse was shot:** Grant, *Personal Memoirs,* 1:353. ("On examination it was found a ball had struck [the horse] forward of the flank just back of the saddle, and had gone entirely through. In a few minutes the poor beast dropped dead; he had given no sign of injury until we came to a stop.")

199 **"Running low and swift, as in a race":** "Farnsworth's Charge and Death," *Battles and Leaders of the Civil War* (New York: Thomas Yoseloff, 1956), 3:396.

199 **Of his own horse Parsons wrote:** Ibid.

199 **In his memoir, *Hardtack and Coffee:*** Billings and Reed, *Hardtack,* 180.

200 **On June 15, 1864, the Fourth Iowa Cavalry:** ORWR 39, no. 1, 138.

200 **On July 8, 1864, the Thirty-seventh Kentucky Infantry:** Ibid., 138–43.

200 **The devastation only worsened:** Ibid., 311.

200 **During a march by the First Ohio Heavy Artillery:** Ibid., 369. See also John B. Jones, *A Rebel War Clerk's Diary at the Confederate States Capital* (Philadelphia: J. B. Lippincott & Co., 1866), 1:21. (Heavy artillery "monster guns" weighed 22 tons, carriages were 60 tons, the cannonballs weighed 700 pounds, and the shells whopped in at 480 pounds. It took 40 pounds of powder to fire one of these cannons—all of it was carried or pulled by fatigued and underfed horses and mules.)

200 **On average, a thousand–pound war horse:** "Animal Management," *Horsemanship and Horsemastership* (Ft. Riley, Kans.: Cavalry School, 1946), vol. 2, part 3, 222–24.

200 **To preserve muscle and flesh:** Ibid., 206.

201 **Most of the time, the impressing by both sides:** Billings and Reed, *Hardtack,* 231, 234, 237, 240–41. (Sherman's Special Field Order 120, dated November 9,

1864: Foraging parties may take mules or horses as well as wagons belonging to inhabitants "freely and without limit." "In all foraging of whatever kind, the parties engaged will refrain from abusive or threatening language, and may, where the officer in command thinks proper, give written certificates of the facts, but no receipts.")

201 **Morgan often issued one-week furloughs:** Towne and Heiser, "Everything Is Fair in War," 57, 77.

201 **Woodburn had already amassed:** Ibid., 33.

201 **But when it came to horse recruitment:** Ibid.

201 **"And the men," Ellsworth later wrote:** Ibid.

202 **Attached to a pole anchored to the roof:** Ibid., 30.

202 **"We need fast hosses":** "Humphries" to A. J. Alexander, Alexander Family Papers, Kentucky Historical Society; "The Racers of Kentucky—Morgan's Men," *Wilkes' Spirit of the Times,* July 2, 1864, 281.

202 **Alexander's farm superintendent, Daniel Swigert:** "Humphries" to Alexander, Kentucky Historical Society; "The Racers of Kentucky—Morgan's Men," *Wilkes' Spirit,* 281.

202 **Already the raid had impacted:** R. A. Alexander to A. J. Alexander, advising that his auction had failed due to fear from the Morgan raid, Alexander Family Papers, Kentucky Historical Society.

203 **In September 1864, John Hunt Morgan was killed:** *ORWR* 39, no. 1, 488, 492.

203 **His regiments, scattered, were left to fend for themselves:** *ORWR* 39, no. 1, 488.

203 **But it was there where he was called out:** *United States v. Jerome Clarke,* affidavit of M. Jerome Clarke appended to trial transcription, U.S. National Archives.

203 **He vowed he would never leave his Kentucky home:** *United States v. Samuel Berry,* trial transcript, testimony of Berry, U.S. National Archives.

CHAPTER 16: THE SHE-DEVIL

204 **Marcellus Jerome Clarke galloped his horse out of Springfield:** Robbery of Springfield scene taken from *United States v. Henry Magruder,* trial transcript, testimony of Grandison Robertson, U.S. National Archives, 243–50; *United States v. Jim Davis,* trial transcript, testimony of Grandison Robertson, U.S. National Archives, 72–84.

204 **Clarke wore a black velvet hat:** *United States v. Magruder,* trial transcript, 22, 82; Marcellus Clarke daguerreotype with inscription on the back ("The photograph was given by Mundy to my father. A silver moon is noted on Mundy's hat. It was said he was never without it—he considered it brought him good luck"), Filson Historical Society.

204 **Strapped to Clarke's belt were as many as four Navy Colt:** *United States v. Magruder,* trial transcript, 19. (Clarke and his men had double-barreled shotguns, carbines, and other arms used by soldiers. They each carried five or six pistols at a time.)

205 **One brave fellow, Grandison Robertson, a livery stable keeper:** *United States v. Davis,* 73.

205 **One of Clarke's twelve men was Jim Davis, alias Harvey Welles:** John M. Palmer, *Personal Recollections of John M. Palmer: The Story of an Earnest Life* (Cincinnati: R. Clarke Co., 1901), 275.

206 **Then Davis, who frequently decorated himself in war paint:** *United States v. Davis,* trial transcript, 16 ("I have seen [Davis] painted as an Indian").

206 **At dusk on Friday, October 7, a stagecoach negotiated the uneven:** "Guerrilla Desperadoes in Mercer County: A Female Guerrilla," *Louisville Daily Journal,* October 11, 1864.

207 **Although a Whig and a friend of President Lincoln:** L. L. Valentine, "Sue Mundy of Kentucky," part 1, *The Register of the Kentucky Historical Society* 62, no. 3 (July 1964): 185.

207 **Long before Lincoln's proclamation of martial law:** Louis De Falaise, "General Stephen Gano Burbridge's Command in Kentucky," *The Register of the Kentucky Historical Society* 69, no. 2 (April 1971): 110.

207 **And, significantly to Prentice, Burbridge forbade any newspaper:** De Falaise, "General Burbridge," 109–10.

207 **Burbridge issued General Order No. 59, which stated:** Ibid., 112.

208 **Rather than slowing down guerrilla warfare:** Ibid., 114–18.

208 **Underneath the paper's logo they read:** Valentine, "Sue Mundy of Kentucky, part 1," 191–92 (footnote 67 identifies Susanna Munday as a woman whose arrest record Prentice likely used to depict his woman guerrilla).

208 **Young E. Allison, a former editor:** Young E. Allison, "Sue Mundy: An Account of the Terrible Kentucky Guerrilla of Civil War Times," *The Register of the Kentucky Historical Society* 57, no. 4 (October 1959): 300.

208 **In crafting Lieutenant Flowers, Prentice put his creative pen into overdrive:** "Guerrilla Desperadoes," *Louisville Daily Journal,* October 11, 1864.

209 **Gifted with dark features that jumped out:** Daguerreotypes of Clarke, Filson Historical Society. See also "Sue Mundy Was Not a Woman," *The Hartford Herald,* August 31, 1898.

209 **His narrow waist and long hair:** "The Execution of Sue Mundy," *The Louisville Daily Journal,* March 16, 1865.

209 **He frequently sat unshakably still in a swaggered pose:** Daguerreotypes of Clarke, Filson Historical Society.

209 **It was no secret that during his days with Morgan's brigade, Clarke masqueraded:** The inscription on the back of one of Clarke's daguerreotypes tells a story of him assuming the dress and role of a woman to cross enemy lines and secure information. On one occasion he, dressed as a woman, seduced a Union soldier, and took the man's uniform. Filson Historical Society. See also "Time Removes Bitter Feeling: Half Century Ago, Soldier Furnished Theme," newspaper clipping dated July 4, 1940, Simpson County Historical Society Archives.

209 **To complicate matters, Clarke hired a local tailor to outfit him:** *United States v. Magruder,* trial transcript, 19 (black velvet, silk, and red flannel jackets); ibid., 22 (the guerrillas had a "fancy dress," described as velvet trimmed with gold lace, roundabouts, large pants, high-topped black boots); ibid., 62 ("The man they called Sue Mundy was dressed in red I believe. He was dressed in red"); ibid., 82 ("They had tinsel on their sleeves. Some had red velvet coats"); ibid., 86 ("Mundy had a red coat with yellow tinsel"); *United States v. Davis,* 65 (dressed in red flannel suit and carried pistols).

209 **spurs in the shape of daisies:** "Sue Mundy's War Spur," *The Bourbon News,* March 10, 1882.

209 **sometimes he wore a brown leather jacket:** "Charles S. Robison," *The Courier-*

Journal, September 19, 1964, 33 (Marcellus Clarke, the Confederate guerrilla called Sue Mundy, dressed as a woman).

210 **That same blue dress:** "Time Removes Bitter Feeling."

210 **On raids, as Clarke stripped gold rings, watches:** *United States v. Magruder,* trial transcript, 24, 43 ("Did he answer to it when he was called Sue Mundy?" Witness answer: "Yes, sir"); ibid., 63 ("This one they called Sue Mundy and the other Magruder"); ibid., 250 ("Clarke or Sue Mundy, they call him"); ibid., 262 ("and a man named Clarke, called 'Sue Mundy'"); *United States v. Davis,* trial transcript, 76 ("He introduced Sue Mundy, as they called him, to us, by the name of Clarke").

210 **The theater in Louisville sold out several performances:** Allison, "Sue Mundy," 305.

211 **Every train derailment, all robberies of pedestrians:** The depiction of Sue Mundy and "her" deeds was reported by Prentice. This author incorporates accounts of acts alleged to have been committed by Sue Mundy taken from eyewitness testimony contained in the court-martial proceedings from six of Clarke's gang members. The testimony is replete with details of Sue Mundy's atrocities. For instance, *United States v. Magruder,* trial transcript, 51: "Sue Mundy came into my hotel, kicked the barroom door open, and kicked the back door open and came in with a pistol in each hand and demanded to know where the [telegraph] operator was. He afterward demanded my money." Ibid. 77. See also 87: "They came in like savages and took everything. Then they took his mare and shot him five times. One over the left eye and other shots as he fell, three in the breast and one in the neck. He was on furlough for his father's funeral and his dead brother. They circled him on their horses and shot him down. Sue Mundy got on the stolen mare."

211 **She burned down the Masonic Hall in Bloomfield:** Henry C. Magruder, *Three Years in the Saddle: The Life and Confession of Henry C. Magruder, the Original Sue Munday* (Louisville, Ky.: published by his captor, Maj. Cyrus J. Wilson, 1865), 83, 86.

211 **Sue Mundy was a born leader:** "General News: That She-Guerrilla Sue Mundy," *New York Times,* December 14, 1864; "The Rebellion," *New York Times,* January 12, 1865.

212 **Napoleon Belland was pulled from the stallion's riding:** "An Interview with Napoleon Belland," *The Thoroughbred Record,* 62.

212 **If his groom Jarrett was late with a feeding:** According to this author's research, the first time Jarrett is mentioned in history by name is on November 11, 1865, in an account in the *Turf, Field and Farm,* describing a painting of Lexington by Thomas J. Scott: "Jarrett, the black groom of Lexington, walks in front while Lexington follows. . . ." To date, this painting has never surfaced; Genevieve Baird Lacer, Edward Troye and equine art historian and author) email message to author, October 21, 2022.

212 **The horse still romped across his paddock:** "Lexington," *Wilkes' Spirit of the Times,* January 2, 1864, 281.

212 **The *Cleveland Plain Dealer* published:** "The Old Racer Lexington," *Cleveland Plain Dealer,* December 11, 1874, 3.

213 **But not all of Lexington's war foals fell into such disuse:** Frazier Hunt and Robert Hunt, *Horses and Heroes* (New York: Charles Scribner's Sons, 1949), 127–32.

213 **The general agreed and, according to historian Frazier Hunt:** Ibid., 128.

213 **His 1857 filly Idlewild beat some of the nation's:** Crickmore, *Famous Horses of America*, 25, quoting from the *Spirit of the Times*.

214 **Bent over and physically frail, he had taken to wrapping:** Domer, *Inventing the Horse Farm*, 12 (quoting from the *Spirit of the Times:* "Every day at the early dawn, the frail man, with his chest-wrappings about him, was on the course, his timing dial in his hands").

214 **It was on one of those mornings that the chronometer:** R. A. Alexander to A. J. Alexander, Alexander Family Papers, Kentucky Historical Society.

215 ***Wilkes' Spirit of the Times* wrote, "This king among horses":** "Lexington," *Wilkes' Spirit*, 281.

215 **"How very strange that [Sue Mundy] isn't caught":** "Sue Mundy," *Louisville Daily Journal*, January 27, 1865.

CHAPTER 17: THE UNDEFEATED ASTEROID

216 **On October 27, 1864, the sun was at high noon:** The facts of the theft of the Woodburn horses were taken from the eyewitness testimonies of Henry Granison and R. A. Alexander in the court-martial proceedings of Jim Davis: *United States v. Davis*, U.S. National Archives. The initial scene of the arrival of the guerrillas was never explored in depth in the trial testimony of Granison. This author has pieced together the likely scenario of their arrival based on what was known about the guerrilla band, including the number of pistols they carried and how they approached most horse thefts. Noteworthy is that Sue Mundy had first been named by George Prentice only sixteen days prior to this incident. The atrocities of Clarke's guerrilla band grew more violent over time. Clarke's fancy clothing, whether his velvet and lace roundabouts or his blue dress, became his norm as Sue Mundy escalated in popularity and as his confidence grew in his ability to evade the Union.

217 **A mile away, Alexander had just sat down for lunch:** *United States v. Davis*, trial transcript, testimony of R. A. Alexander, 85. (According to the court-martial records, Alexander had been ill at the time of Davis's trial. Alexander's testimony had been postponed to accommodate his illness. When he did appear to testify, his health was still weakened. *United States v. Davis*, 94.)

217 **The equine painter Edward Troye:** Mackay-Smith, *The Race Horses of America*, 223.

217 **Suddenly, in the middle of this reverie:** *United States v. Davis*, trial transcript, testimony of R. A. Alexander, 85.

217 **For a moment, Alexander smiled slightly:** Ibid.

217 **Only a few days earlier, Alexander had written:** R. A. Alexander to A. J. Alexander, October 13, 1864, Alexander Family Papers, Kentucky Historical Society.

218 **Again, the kitchen door slammed open:** *United States v. Davis*, trial transcript, testimony of R. A. Alexander, 86.

218 **A field hand then came hurtling over the hill:** Ibid.

218 **Alexander turned to his friends:** Ibid.

218 **The men, with Granison as their hostage:** *United States v. Davis*, trial transcript, testimony of Henry Granison, 96. (Sadly, and troublingly, defense counsel objected to Granison's testimony being considered as evidence on the basis he was Black. Thankfully, the court-martial overruled the objection and allowed the testimony to be admitted into evidence. However, Granison's status as a Black man in that era may be the reason his testimony was never fully developed by trial counsel.)

219 Alexander, his friends—possibly Troye too: *United States v. Davis,* trial transcript, testimony of R. A. Alexander, 86.

219 Clarke stopped near a blacksmith's shop: *United States v. Davis,* trial transcript, testimony of Granison, 97.

219 For over three hours the groom had held: Ibid.

219 During their escape through Woodford County: Ibid., 96.

220 Then he noticed the sprigs of pokeberries tucked snugly: Ibid., 98.

220 When they reached a farm known as the Nichols's place: *United States v. Davis,* trial transcript, testimony of R. A. Alexander, 87.

220 He felt his body weakening: Ibid., 93.

220 As Alexander's group neared the fork in the road: Ibid., 88.

221 Just as the marauders noticed them: Ibid.

221 The racehorses jumped, reared, frantically sidestepped: Ibid., 89.

221 Granison, now the least of their concerns: *United States v. Davis,* trial transcript, testimony of Granison, 97.

221 Alexander saw one of his racehorses: *United States v. Davis,* trial transcript, testimony of R. A. Alexander, 90.

221 On rounding the turn, Alexander saw three more: Ibid., 91.

221 By the time Alexander and his group reached the river: Ibid.

222 The men debated whether to return home: Ibid., 91–92.

222 Before the men could leave: Ibid., 92.

222 Nugent aimed his rifle: Ibid.

222 The day had taxed what little reserves: Ibid., 93.

222 "They did not appear to mind my shots": Ibid.

222 He fired, hitting the guerrilla's foot: Ibid.

222 Alexander and his men climbed on their horses: Ibid.

223 The *Chicago Tribune* wrote: "From Louisville," *Chicago Tribune,* October 31, 1864, 1.

223 *Wilkes' Spirit of the Times* in New York: "Asteroid Stolen by Guerrillas," *Wilkes' Spirit of the Times,* November 5, 1864, 156.

223 By the time those articles were being read: "WBB" to A. J. Alexander, October 28, 1864, Alexander Family Papers, Kentucky Historical Society; "Stories of Maj. Warren Viley," *Woodford Sun,* (Versailles, Ky.), January 30, 1902, 1.

224 Their journey eventually led them: Ibid.

224 To gain their trust, Viley told them: Ibid.

224 Viley and Henry rode a few miles: Ibid.

224 He told them he was here for the bay horse: Ibid.

224 As a final thought, the man told Viley: Ibid.

225 Foolishly, Viley agreed: "Rebel Outrages by Guerrillas in Kentucky: Murder of John Harper," *Wilkes' Spirit of the Times,* November 19, 1864, 185.

225 For their bravery, nearly one hundred people: "Stories of Maj. Warren Viley," *Woodford Sun,* 1.

226 Troye painted Asteroid: Mackay-Smith, *The Race Horses of America,* 223.

226 But a few days later, that very man: "Stories of Maj. Warren Viley," *Woodford Sun,* 1.

226 Viley later said that the man: Ibid.

226 Within a matter of days: "Rebel Outrages by Guerillas in Kentucky—Murder of John Harper—Asteroid Recovered," *Wilkes' Spirit of the Times,* November 12, 1864, 164.

226 **In the wake of the October 1864 guerrilla raid:** William A. Penn, *The Civil War in Midway, Kentucky* (Midway, Ky.: Historic Midway Museum Store, 2012), 9.

227 **Quantrill had read about:** "Quantrell's Death," *The Courier-Journal,* November 1, 1890, 9; William Elsey Connelley, *Quantrill and the Border Wars* (Cedar Rapids, Iowa: The Torch Press, 1910), 461.

227 **They rode out of Missouri:** O. S. Barton, *Three Years with Quantrill: A True Story Told by His Scout John McCorkle* (Armstrong, Mo: Armstrong Herald Print, 1914), no page numbers.

CHAPTER 18: SMOKE SCREENS

228 **As a boy in Canal Dover, Ohio:** Connelley, *Border Wars,* 42; Thomas Shelby "Bob" Watson, *The Silent Riders—WAKY News Documentary* (Louisville: Beechmont Press, 1971), 8. (*The Silent Riders* first appeared as a radio broadcast on the WAKY Radio Documentary Series in 1971. WAKY news director Bob Watson researched and wrote the program about William Quantrill and his scourge of Kentucky.)

228 **He once shot a pig:** "Quantrell's Mother," *Courier-Journal,* March 20, 1898.

228 **On one occasion, he locked a girl up high in the belfry:** Connelley, *Border Wars,* 43.

229 **En route, the escort discovered him in the middle of the night:** Ibid., 63–64.

229 **It could've been over a whipping:** Ibid., 44.

229 **He had once written to his mother:** Ibid., 101.

229 **Disguised in Union blue, they eased through:** Barton, *Three Years with Quantrill;* John Newman Edwards, *Noted Guerrillas, or, The Warfare of the Border* (St. Louis: Bryan, Brand & Co., 1877), 390.

229 **rode their horses over the blood, dust, and gore:** Lawrence massacre eyewitness Hugh Fisher, letter 1, Kansas Memory Collection, Kansas Historical Society.

230 **How gallantly Old Charlie had led the Raiders:** William H. Gregg, "A Little Dab of History Without Embellishment," part 1 (unpublished manuscript, The State Historical Society of Missouri, Columbia, n.d.), 63; Lawrence massacre eyewitness Mary Savage, letter, Kansas Memory Collection, Kansas Historical Society.

230 **When he returned to the blacksmith:** Barton, *Three Years with Quantrill.*

230 **Quantrill said, "It is fate. So be it":** Edwards, *Noted Guerrillas,* 390.

230 **Stopping at Greenville's Federal livery stable:** Ibid.

230 **Quantrill paid the tab:** Barton, *Three Years with Quantrill.*

230 **Amused, Quantrill told them:** "Quantrell, the Guerrilla: The History and Exploits of the Most Noted Bandit of Modern Times," *The Courier-Journal,* April 29, 1874, 3.

231 **As the main column marched on, the Raider team farthest:** Ibid.

231 **Minus their escort, Quantrill and his men continued:** *ORWR* 49, no. 1, 657.

231 **They'd then proceeded to burn down:** *United States v. Magruder,* 31–66.

232 **Throughout this latest rampage:** Ibid., 38, 62.

232 **At the Union headquarters, Quantrill informed Colonel Shanks:** *ORWR* 49, no. 1, 657.

232 **Along the way, Quantrill and his Raiders beat and shot:** Ibid.

233 **On January 28, Marcellus Clarke stopped at a house:** Thomas Shelby Watson and Perry A. Brantley, *Confederate Guerrilla Sue Mundy* (Jefferson, N.C.: McFarland & Company, Inc., 2008), 132.

233 **His authority, though self-appointed, received nods from Governor:** *ORWR* 49, no. 1, 667.

233 **He shot guerrillas on the front porches:** Watson and Brantley, *Confederate Guerrilla*, 115.

233 **Only the day before, editor George Prentice:** "Sue Mundy," *The Louisville Daily Journal*, January 27, 1865.

233 **And, as if that weren't enough:** "Sue Mundy," *The Louisville Daily Journal*, January 10, 1865.

234 **Rather than wait to be caught, Clarke:** Lewis Collins and Richard H. Collins, *History of Kentucky* (Berea, Ky.: Kentucke Imprints, 1976), 1:153.

234 **Clarke didn't stick around long enough:** Watson, *Silent Riders*, 28–29.

234 **The next day, Quantrill and his men, still disguised:** *ORWR* 49, no. 1, 18, 612.

234 **But one message got through:** Ibid.

234 **Riding southward down the same road:** History doesn't record the exact meeting between Marcellus Clarke and William Quantrill. According to one source, the meeting didn't happen until sometime in January 1865. Another source claims Quantrill and Sue Mundy operated together at Danville on January 29, 1865, and were together possibly as early as January 23, 1865, near Chaplaintown, Kentucky. *ORWR* supports this contention. George Prentice also connected Marcellus Jerome Clarke with the January 29 Danville raid. On his deathbed, Henry Magruder confessed that he and Marcellus Clarke had joined Quantrill in Kentucky, although Magruder never specified a date. It does appear that either before the January 29 Danville raid or shortly after, Quantrill met Marcellus Clarke and Henry Magruder. They operated together until about the end of February 1865.

235 **On February 2, 1865, in the early evening, Midway:** "Another Daring Guerrilla Outrage," *Lexington Observer & Reporter*, February 4, 1865. See also *ORWR* 49, no. 1, 635; "Guerrilla Operations," *Louisville Daily Journal*, February 4, 1865 ("Quantrell and Sue Mundy were reported in command of the gang. They left in the direction of Versailles").

235 **Along the way, they stopped at Stonewall Farm:** Willa Viley's obituary claims that the guerrilla group stopped at midnight at the farm of a friend of his by the name of Thomas Payne. According to the write-up, Willa Viley was then staying at Payne's home. The guerrillas stole Payne's horse, prompting Viley, an elderly man, to heroically leave Payne's house dressed only in his nightshirt, chasing down the guerrillas on horseback and reclaiming Payne's horse. The obituary states that when Viley caught up to them, they aimed their revolvers and took him hostage. The more likely scenario is that Marcellus Clarke remembered the broken promise in the woods over Asteroid and rode to Warren Viley's Stonewall Farm to right what he considered to be Viley's failed part of the bargain. When Warren wasn't home, Clarke took the man's father as hostage to use as leverage at his next stop, only a few miles down the road from Stonewall.

CHAPTER 19: THE HEIST OF WOODBURN

236 **Assuming the worst, Alexander ordered his staff:** Deedes, *Sketches of the South*, 20–30. The scenes described in this chapter, including the conversations between Alexander and the guerrillas, were constructed from Alexander's letter to Henry Deedes, dated February 6, 1865. As far as we know, Deedes printed the let-

ter verbatim in his book. A typed copy also exists in the Alexander Family Papers, Kentucky Historical Society.

237 **He'd been warned that he'd be raided again:** R. A. Alexander to A. J. Alexander, January 27, 1865, Alexander Family Papers, Kentucky Historical Society.

237 **"What will you have, gentlemen?":** Deedes, *Sketches of the South*, 21.

237 **"Well, I suppose if you are bound to have horses":** Ibid., 22.

237 **"Then you shall have two horses":** Ibid.

238 **"Captain, I have these arms for my own protection":** Ibid., 23.

238 **"If a gun shall be fired, it will be your fault":** Ibid.

238 **"Where are those horses? I'm in a hurry":** Ibid.

239 **Alexander offered the captain $10,000:** Ibid., 80.

239 **Alexander hurried to the stable barracks and found F.V.R. Hull:** Ibid., 25.

239 **"We must have a few horses. Good ones":** "The Story of Woodburn," *The Morning Herald*, January 27, 1898, 3.

239 **When Alexander arrived at his house, two Raiders:** Deedes, *Sketches of the South*, 25–26.

240 **Alexander tightened his grip on the Raider's arms:** Ibid., 26–27.

240 **Alexander yelled back, "I won't let him go":** Ibid., 28.

241 **"Do you promise me on the word and honor":** Ibid.

241 **He told Mary not to open the door:** Ibid.

241 **His first thought was for Lexington:** Ibid., 29.

241 **He ordered one of the grooms there:** Ibid.

242 **Williamson watched them go:** "Mr. Alexander's Horses," *Wilkes' Spirit of the Times*, March 18, 1865, 41.

242 **That night, the guerrillas left Woodburn:** Deedes, *Sketches of the South*, 29–30.

242 **At Cane Spring, a neighboring farm, Willa Viley:** "Guerrilla Raid," *Louisville Daily Journal*, February 5, 1865.

243 **Hobson ordered troops to move in various directions:** *ORWR* 49, no. 1 (series of confused dispatches), 634 ("Rebels under Clarke or Sue Munday burned down depot at Midway to-night. They are going in the direction of Versailles"); 633 (about fifty miles northwest of Midway, "Sue Munday's command, about thirty men, well mounted, passed through Smithfield this morning at 2 o'clock, in direction of New Castle"); 634 ("The gang is not the same we were after. I have fifty men here. Maj. Hamilton, 12th Kentucky Cavalry, is here with sixty-five men. What must we do?"); 635 (about forty-seven miles north of Midway, "We have chased Sue Munday's gang into Henry [County]. Our horses are worn out, can't do anything without fresh horses. Please send some, if only fifty. Quantrill is with the gang"); 641 (by February 3, the Union army was in a tailspin. Hobson dispatched his command in Frankfort: "No necessity for [your captain] to be in Owen or Henry Counties. Troops now there. If he can hear of Sue Munday's gang, it will be well for him to look after her").

243 **Circling in, the Home Guards:** "The Late Guerrilla Raid," *The Louisville Daily Journal*, February 10, 1865.

243 **Some of them slashed sabers:** Ibid.

243 **But Bay Chief outran them:** Ibid.

243 **As Home Guards overcame them, the captain jumped:** Ibid.

244 **Unshod and unconditioned for work:** "The Story of Woodburn," *The Morning Herald*, 3.

244 Abdallah was found where the Raiders: Ibid.

244 Other Woodburn horses were found abandoned: Ibid.

245 "Matters have at length become so unsatisfactory": Deedes, *Sketches of the South*, 20.

245 On the platform, Lexington stood, neck stretched high: Susan Rhodemyre, "Woodburn Stud," *The Thoroughbred Record*, January 7, 1981, 36.

245 There, several barges were waiting, bobbing: "Lexington," *Florida Horse*, September/October 1975, 86.

245 Lexington and his progeny rode the Ohio River: "The Story of Woodburn," *The Morning Herald*, 3.

246 A few days after Lexington left Woodburn: Ibid.

CHAPTER 20: LOUISVILLE

247 President Lincoln sat in his office chair, a towel wrapped: Palmer, *Personal Recollections*, 224–45.

247 John Palmer, a staunch abolitionist: Ibid., 94–95.

248 He told Palmer, "Go to Kentucky": Ibid., 225.

248 As Lincoln met with General Palmer, two hundred: *ORWR* 49, no. 1, 698–99.

248 Some of them were even ordering dinners: Ibid., 715.

248 All he could manage was to order: Ibid.

248 After meeting with Governor Bramlette: Ibid., 741.

248 Editor George Prentice wrote: "Major General Palmer," *The Louisville Daily Journal*, February 10, 1865.

248 Palmer's presidential orders mandated: *ORWR* 49, no. 1, 671.

249 He hired Edwin Terrell, who had survived: Watson, *Silent Riders*, 44.

249 On March 3, 1865, Clarke, Magruder, and fellow gang: Valentine, "Sue Mundy," part 1, 204–5.

249 The Confederacy was now ordering: *ORWR* 49, no. 1, 764.

249 They agreed and secreted their companion inside a tobacco barn: Valentine, "Sue Mundy," part 1, 204–5; L. L. Valentine, "Sue Mundy of Kentucky," part 2, *The Register of the Kentucky Historical Society* 62, no. 4 (October 1964): 279.

249 Turning again to his off-the-books approach, Palmer: Valentine, "Sue Mundy," part 2, 281.

250 As the dawn broke on the morning of March 12: *United States v. Jerome Clarke, alias Sue Mundy*, U.S. National Archives, trial transcript, testimonies of Cyrus J. Wilson, 6–11, and Capt. Lewis Marshall, 11–15.

250 After a few minutes of silence, Clarke called for Major Wilson: *United States v. Clarke*, trial transcript, testimony of Cyrus J. Wilson, 8.

250 Clarke stood a few feet from the entrance: Ibid.

250 Wilson told him fifty infantrymen: Ibid.

250 They rolled and smoked: Ibid.

251 "Major, if I surrender to you": Ibid., 8–11 (dialogue between the men).

251 From his bed on the barn floor, Magruder: Ibid., 9.

251 Clarke had escaped from the Union prison: L. F. Johnson, *Famous Kentucky Tragedies and Trials* (Louisville: The Baldwin Law Book Co., 1916), 188.

252 On another occasion, he reportedly jumped: "Time Removes Bitter Feeling."

252 **Finally, Clarke said, "I have only one object":** *United States v. Henry Metcalf,* U.S. National Archives, 16.

252 **"Are you Sue Mundy":** *United States v. Clarke,* testimony of Lewis Marshall, 13.

252 **Marshall took Clarke, Metcalf, and Magruder:** Ibid.

252 **Prentice later wrote, "Sue Mundy is a rosy-cheeked boy":** "Capture of Three Notorious Outlaws," *The Louisville Daily Journal,* March 14, 1865.

252 **The *Daily Democrat,* which had previously:** Valentine, "Sue Mundy," part 2, 285.

253 **The one-day trial consisted of testimony:** *United States v. Clarke,* court-martial proceedings.

253 **On March 13, the day before Clarke's trial, General Palmer:** Ibid., "Order of Execution." Clarke was indeed summarily tried and convicted. General Palmer undoubtedly wanted to make an example of Clarke / Sue Mundy. Still, testimony in the subsequent court-martial proceedings of Clarke's fellow gang members reveals that Palmer had overwhelming evidence with which to properly convict Clarke, should he have afforded the man a fair trial.

253 **The Union army stationed in Louisville had hung guerrillas:** Valentine, "Sue Mundy," part 2, 303.

253 **They roped up oak beams and constructed a crude platform:** Allison, "Sue Mundy," 311.

253 **By three o'clock that afternoon, four thousand:** "Execution of Marcellus Jerome Clark, Alias Sue Mundy," *The Louisville Daily Democrat,* March 16, 1865.

253 **At noon that day, Father Jeremiah J. Talbot:** "From Kentucky," *New York Times,* April 26, 1865.

254 **Clarke had not, and said, "I suppose I shall be shot":** "The Execution of Sue Mundy," *The Louisville Daily Journal.*

254 **"*Oh!*" Clarke remarked:** Ibid.

254 **At twenty-five minutes past three o'clock, four Union soldiers:** Ibid.

254 **Clarke slid into the seat, slumped down:** Ibid.

254 **Four companies of Union soldiers in uniform raised:** Ibid.

254 **The Thirtieth Wisconsin band played the "Dead March":** Valentine, "Sue Mundy," part 2, 303–4; Watson, *Silent Riders,* 43.

254 **A wagon carrying a pine coffin traveled past:** Allison, "Sue Mundy," 313.

254 **Clarke put his baptismal handkerchief over his eyes:** "The Execution of Sue Mundy," *Louisville Daily Journal.*

254 **The carriage stopped at the steps to the left:** "Execution of Marcellus Jerome Clark," *The Louisville Daily Democrat;* "From Kentucky," *New York Times.*

254 **Instead, he muttered over and over:** "The Execution of Sue Mundy," *Louisville Daily Journal.*

255 **Captain George Swope counted out loud:** "Execution of Marcellus Jerome Clark," *Louisville Daily Democrat.*

255 **After three long minutes, Clarke's convulsions:** Clarke's body was exhumed in 1914 and examined. Several of his neck bones had broken due to his struggles at the rope. Long, dark hair still clung to his skull. L. L. House Mortuary Records, entry dated July 25, 1914, recounting exhumation of the body of Marcellus Jerome Clarke, inspection of remains, and reburial, Clarke Family File, Simpson County Archives.

255 **After twenty minutes, the Company D soldiers cut the rope:** "The Execution of Sue Mundy," *Louisville Daily Journal.*

255 **As Clarke lay dead, three men brawled:** Allison, "Sue Mundy," 314.

255 **"Green & Green," the finest milliners:** Ibid.

255 **On most occasions, hundreds of stacked guns:** Emmanuel Dabney, "City Point During the Civil War," *Encyclopedia Virginia*, October 2015, www.Encyclopedia Virginia.org/City_Point_During_the_Civil_War. Accessed on February 9, 2018 (photograph of City Point wharf during the Civil War).

255 **When the boat was moored, Lincoln descended the stairs:** Gen. Horace Porter, *Campaigning with Grant* (New York: The Century Co., 1897), 217.

256 **Grant himself hoisted the president up on the general's favored horse:** Ibid., 216–17.

256 **By the time they reached the troops, the president appeared:** Ibid., 218–19.

257 **On March 26, 1865, in preparation for another troop inspection:** Ibid., 412.

257 **Bypassing his two other war mounts, he ordered Cincinnati:** Hunt, *Horses and Heroes*, 129.

257 **On April 15, 1865, the day President Lincoln died:** "A Graphic Story," *The Morning Herald*, March 27, 1898.

257 **Ed Terrell had been on General Palmer's payroll:** Watson, *Silent Riders*, 55.

258 **Near Smileytown, as the skies darkened above Quantrill:** Edwards, *Noted Guerrillas*, 428.

258 **He replied, "Boss, there was a gang just went":** Ben R. Kirkpatrick, affidavit about "The Career of William Clark Quantrill in Kentucky and His Ending," Kansas Historical Society.

258 **At the end of the field, Terrell spotted the Raiders:** Watson, *Silent Riders*, 56.

258 **He yelled, "Here they are!":** Ibid., 55–56; Edwards, *Noted Guerrillas*, 428.

258 **According to one account:** Watson, *Silent Riders*, 51.

259 **Other accounts vary slightly:** Kirkpatrick affidavit; Connelley, *Border Wars*, 474.

259 **"If you give me a parole":** Dialogue constructed from "A Graphic Story," *The Morning Herald*; Watson, *Silent Riders*, 60; Kirkpatrick affidavit.

259 **As Quantrill lay paralyzed on the ground:** Kirkpatrick affidavit.

259 **By the following morning, Ed Terrell:** Watson, *Silent Riders*, 63; Kirkpatrick affidavit; Connelley, *Border Wars*, 480.

260 **Riding up to the wagon master, Terrell told him:** Kirkpatrick affidavit.

260 **Palmer ordered Quantrill to be taken:** Connelley, *Border Wars*, 480.

260 **Instead, Quantrill may have handled death:** Ibid., 35, 60, 482n6.

260 **Instead, he instructed the Sisters of Charity:** Ibid., 480.

260 **On July 26, 1865 Quantrill's remaining Raiders:** Ibid., 479.

CHAPTER 21: THE BEQUEST

262 **By the end of the war, the number of New York racecourses:** Hervey, *Racing in America*, 2:378.

262 **By the time of his thirtieth birthday, in 1863:** W. S. Vosburgh, *Racing in America, 1866–1921* (New York: The Jockey Club), 9.

263 **In 1863, during the heartache of the war:** Ibid., 21.

263 **Among them was Senator Henry Clay's son John M. Clay:** Ibid., 71.

263 **The following year, Hunter sent Kentucky:** Ibid.

263 **The most anyone was willing to risk:** "The Saratoga Race Meeting," *New York Times*, August 4, 1864.

264 **A curly-haired Californian named Theodore Winters:** Vosburgh, *Racing in America,* 72–73.

264 **After the Jersey Derby, he bought Norfolk on the spot, paying:** R. A. Alexander to A. J. Alexander, advising of sale of Norfolk for $15,001, Alexander Family Papers, Kentucky Historical Society.

264 **"He so completely outclassed his contemporaries":** Vosburgh, *Racing in America,* 69.

264 **Intensifying their apprehension and angst:** "The Jockey Club Meeting," *New York Times,* September 26, 1866.

265 **By the time he returned to Woodburn at war's end:** R. A. Alexander to A. J. Alexander, April 9, 1864, Alexander Family Papers, Kentucky Historical Society.

265 **He required a regime of round-the-clock care:** R. A. Alexander to A. J. Alexander, postmarked July 9, 1964, Alexander Family Papers, Kentucky Historical Society.

265 **In November 1865, only eight months after:** R. A. Alexander to Henry Deedes, November 27, 1865, Alexander Family Papers, Kentucky Historical Society.

265 **He'd put Asteroid up for sale—along with his entire:** "Large Number of Thoroughbred and Trotting Horses for Sale," *Turf, Field and Farm,* August 5, 1865, 15.

265 **Most astonishing, Lexington too was up:** Ibid.

266 **"My pockets," wrote Alexander to A.J.:** R. A. Alexander to A. J. Alexander, April 25, 1866, Alexander Family Papers, Kentucky Historical Society.

266 **About Woodburn Alexander expressed unrelenting concerns:** Ibid.

266 **John Hunter sent out a bugle call:** "A Bugle Call to Asteroid!," *Wilkes' Spirit of the Times,* July 8, 1865, 297.

266 **Match races, he said, required "more gambling":** "Response of Mr. Alexander," *Wilkes' Spirit of the Times,* August 5, 1865, 361.

267 **But even though the vase once again decorated Alexander's fireplace:** "An Accident to Asteroid," *Turf, Field and Farm,* May 19, 1866, 312.

267 **Alexander shipped Asteroid back to Woodburn:** "Visit to Kentucky," *Turf, Field and Farm,* August 25, 1866, 118.

267 **Racegoers sat in the parlor of Saratoga's Grand Union Hotel:** "Saratoga, Week After the Races," *Turf, Field and Farm,* August 25, 1866, 115.

267 **According to the *Turf, Field and Farm,* people speculated:** Ibid.

267 **Having returned from Canada, where he had taken a string:** "An Interview with Napoleon Belland," *The Thoroughbred Record,* 62.

268 **"It is the only picture we have seen":** Mackay-Smith, *The Race Horses of America,* 215.

268 **The prizefighter John Morrissey:** "Saratoga, Week After the Races," *Turf, Field and Farm,* 115.

268 **"He's praying for Asteroid to be here":** Ibid.

269 **Still, his veterinarian, Dr. Herr:** "Visit to Kentucky," *Turf, Field and Farm,* 118.

269 **Despite the warning, on September 8, 1866:** "Asteroid, Eastward Bound," *Turf, Field and Farm,* September 15, 1866, 168.

269 **Jerome Park was built in 1866 in Fordham, New York:** Vosburgh, *Racing in America,* 3–5. See also Brian Kachejian, "History of Jerome Park Racetrack in the Bronx," Classic New York History, accessed September 6, 2021, classicnewyork history.com/history-of-the-jerome-park-racetrack.

269 **With news that the long-awaited match race:** "The Jockey Club Meeting," *New York Times.*

269 **"Once more," wrote Vosburgh:** Vosburgh, *Racing in America,* 70.

270 **On September 22, during a deluge of rain:** "Asteroid," *Turf, Field and Farm,* September 29, 1866, 201.

270 **He walked off the track with a limp:** Ibid.

270 **The rain hadn't stopped in the last twenty-four hours:** "Sporting Matters," *New York Times,* September 25, 1866, 8.

271 **But he soon pulled Asteroid up:** Ibid.

271 **Idlewild, foaled in 1859 out of one of Alexander's:** Crickmore, *Famous Horses of America,* 25.

271 **Although the mare was more talented:** "The Jockey Club Meeting," *New York Times.*

271 **Before Asteroid broke down at Jerome Park:** "Mr. Alexander and Woodburn Farm," *Turf, Field and Farm,* December 1, 1866, 344.

271 **Despite *The New York Times*'s prior warnings that the rain:** "Sporting Matters," *New York Times,* 8.

272 **Some funneled past Kentucky's stall in hopes:** "The Jockey Club Meeting," *New York Times.*

272 **The first race scheduled that day:** Ibid.

272 **Crouched over the saddle:** From a 1901 article in the London *Times,* courtesy International Museum of the Horse: "One great rider of the day who in my opinion never had a superior in inducing a horse to make the greatest effort he was capable of, rode in the manner which the best of our jockeys made familiar to race-goers. This was Old Abe Hawkins. I saw Gil Patrick and John Ford and Abe ride in a race in 1864 in St. Louis, with Hawkins crouching over the mare's neck, knees pressed firmly against her shoulder, a clear space between him and the saddle, specks of froth from between closely set teeth flecking the intensely black visage, eyes flashing, he seemed the very incarnation of frantic energy inspiring the animal to win."

272 **General Ulysses S. Grant arrived slightly late:** "The Jockey Club Meeting," *New York Times.*

272 **With Hawkins in the saddle, Idlewild took the lead:** Ibid.

273 **He led wire to wire:** Ibid.

273 **On the heels of that success, Leonard Jerome:** "Kentucky and Asteroid," *Turf, Field and Farm,* October 13, 1866, 233.

273 **Instead, he set his eyes on breaking:** Vosburgh, *Racing in America,* 71.

273 **The match against Time took place a year later:** Trevathan, *American Thoroughbred,* 326; Vosburgh, *Racing in America,* 71–72.

273 **A year after he faced Lexington's Time, he was brought:** Vosburgh, *Racing in America,* 72.

274 **Decades later historian Charles E. Trevathan:** Trevathan, *American Thoroughbred,* 327.

275 **Earlier in the day, Alexander had driven a carriage:** R. A. Alexander to A. J. Alexander, November 26, 1866, Alexander Family Papers, Kentucky Historical Society.

275 **As he wrote, Alexander heard his cook Betsy in the kitchen:** Ibid.

276 **A few days later, the *Turf, Field and Farm* published:** "Mr. Alexander's Retirement from the Turf," *Turf, Field and Farm,* December 29, 1866, 409.

276 **By 1865, Alexander was offering the horse's stud services to outside:** Hervey, *Racing in America*, 2:303.

277 **In May 1867, Alexander sold six colts and fillies:** "A New Addition to the Preakness Stable," *Turf, Field and Farm*, May 11, 1867, 296.

277 **He sold sixty-six colts, the majority:** "R. A. Alexander's Sale," *Turf, Field and Farm*, June 22, 1867, 388.

277 **The average selling price per colt was $4,000:** William E. Railey, "Woodford County," *The Register of the Kentucky State Historical Society* 18, no. 53 (May 1920): 68.

277 **In early November 1867, a reporter from New York:** "Robert Aitcheson Alexander," *Turf, Field and Farm*, November 16, 1867, 312.

277 **He had organized a tour of Woodburn's expansive:** Ibid.

278 **Later, he introduced the entourage to Betsy:** Ibid.

278 **The New York reporter later wrote of Alexander:** Ibid.

278 **On the morning of December 1, 1867, he whispered words:** "Robert Aitcheson Alexander," *Turf, Field and Farm*, December 14, 1867, 369.

278 **Soon after Alexander's death, the *Turf, Field and Farm* wrote:** "Death of Robert Aitcheson Alexander," *Turf, Field and Farm*, December 7, 1867, 360.

278 **In a later publication, B. G. Bruce wrote:** "Robert Aitcheson Alexander," *Turf, Field and Farm*, 369.

279 **Swigert took over the breeding operations:** Hervey, *Racing in America*, 2:333.

279 **He responded courteously and honestly:** Ibid., 2:334.

CHAPTER 22: THE FOUR-MILE HORSE

283 **J. M. Womack was treasurer of the Louisville Jockey Club:** "Race History Told by Downs' Officer," *Louisville Courier-Journal*, September 11, 1910.

284 **"I've been a very active man":** Ibid.

284 **He'd imported the stallion Phaeton from England:** Hervey, *Racing in America*, 2:252–53; "An Eminent Turfman," *The Daily Graphic*, August 13, 1874; "Richard Ten Broeck," *Territorial Enterprise*, August 22, 1874; "Hurstbourne," *Louisville Courier-Journal*, September 8, 1884.

285 **Harper named him Ten Broeck:** Crickmore, *Famous Horses of America*, 51.

285 **There, he faced Aristides again:** "1875: Aristides," www.kentuckyderby.com /history/year/1875; Vosburgh, *Racing in America*, 100.

285 **Then, in the last three months of 1875:** Crickmore, *Famous Horses of America*, 51.

286 **On August 20, 1874, a year before Ten Broeck:** Vosburgh, *Racing in America*, 98; *American Racing Calendar of 1876* (New York: Turf, Field and Farm, 1876), 179–85.

286 **Harper then enlisted the one man who knew:** "Sketch of Ten Broeck," *New York Times*, September 28, 1876.

286 **On September 27, 1876, at Churchill Downs:** *American Racing Calendar of 1876*.

287 **When Lexington's Time was bested, the ribbon:** "Kentucky's Largest Farm," clipping from New York *Sun*, Woodburn Farm Papers, Kentucky Historical Society.

287 **The next day, the New York *Sun* reporter:** Ibid.

287 **Brodhead explained the old custom:** Ibid.

287 **For the two decades that those antlers had hung:** Fisher, *For All Times*, 47.

CHAPTER 23: CATALOG NO. 16020

288 **By 1872, he had been listed:** "Annual Leading Sire—Money Won," *The American Racing Manual, 2013,* (New York: Daily Racing Form Press, 2013), 870–71.

288 **Over the years he had learned the placement of each tree:** "Lexington," *Wilkes' Spirit of the Times,* January 2, 1864, 281.

288 **"His deeds," noted the** *Turf, Field and Farm:* "Lexington," *Turf, Field and Farm,* October 11, 1872, 232.

288 **A few years before General George Armstrong Custer:** "Nomad in the Blue Grass Country—The Famous Breeding Studs," *Turf, Field and Farm,* December 1, 1871, 337–38.

289 **He stood still in his straw-bedded stall:** Ibid., 337.

289 **Custer wrote:** Ibid.

289 **The groom led Lexington out into the barn's aisle:** Ibid.

289 **Custer marveled at his appearance:** Ibid.

289 **Custer later bought a horse:** Kim Mariette, "The Mystery of General Custer's War Horse, Victory," *American Racehorse,* Spring 2018, 47–49.

289 **The** *Turf, Field and Farm* **wrote:** "Lexington," *Turf, Field and Farm* 232.

290 **On the morning of July 1, 1875, a stable hand told:** "Lexington," *Kentucky Live Stock Record,* July 9, 1875, 18.

290 **He held his head erect and shifted his hindquarter:** Ibid.

290 **A few months before, Doctors Herr and Harthill:** Ibid., 17.

290 **The mass that had formed underneath:** Print of a photograph taken of Lexington in 1872 by George Francis Schreiber, Alexander Family Papers, Kentucky Historical Society.

290 **About the same time the vets visited, Lexington's digestive tract:** "Woodburn and Other Gossip," *Turf, Field and Farm,* October 16, 1874, 287.

291 **Sensing the worst, Brodhead led Lexington:** Fisher, *For All Times,* 77.

291 **Word of his condition spread among Woodburn's grooms:** "Old Lexington: The Great Racer Is Dead," newspaper clipping dated July 4, 1875, Lexington, Kentucky (contained in accession file #121040), Smithsonian Institution Archives. ("Among the grooms and stable boys Lexington was known familiarly as Jack, and when, on Friday morning, it was whispered around that 'Jack' was dead, the laborers on the great farm put on an air of mourning as though some respected member of Mr. Alexander's family had departed this life.")

292 **Nearing twelve o'clock that night, Lexington finally lowered:** "Lexington," *Kentucky Live Stock Record,* 18.

292 **The** *Turf, Field and Farm* **wrote, "The hero":** "The Death of Lexington," *Turf, Field and Farm,* July 9, 1875, 31.

292 **Lexington's former trainer, J. B. Pryor, had written:** "Lexington," *Kentucky Live Stock Record,* 18.

293 **The** *Kentucky Live Stock Record* **wrote:** Ibid., 17.

293 **While men prepared his grave, Brodhead stationed:** Fisher, *For All Times,* 77.

293 **When the grave was prepared, a harness was attached:** Ibid.

293 **The** *Kentucky Live Stock Record* **only briefly described:** "Lexington," *Kentucky Live Stock Record,* 18.

293 **After he was buried, the elk's antlers:** "Old Lexington: The Great Racer Is Dead."

294 **In November, four months after Lexington's death, Professor Spencer Baird:** Baird to A. J. Alexander, November 2, 1875 (accession file #121040), Smithsonian Institution Archives.

295 **The food had seeped inside Lexington's cranial cavity:** "The Bones of Lexington," *Turf, Field and Farm,* November 12, 1875, 376.

295 **Lexington was reported to have had a jaw:** Ibid.

295 **On November 20, 1875, the *Spirit of the Times* reported:** "Lexington," *Spirit of the Times,* November 20, 1875, 353.

295 **Of the two methods, maceration was the better process:** William T. Hornaday, *Taxidermy and Zoological Collecting: A Complete Handbook for the Amateur Taxidermist, Collector, Osteologist, Museum-Builder, Sportsman, and Traveller* (New York: Charles Scribner's Sons, 1891), 282.

296 **According to Hornaday, "a greasy bone":** Ibid.

296 **Based on Hornaday's book, we can surmise:** The maceration and articulation processes are much more involved than what is relayed here. This author consulted Hornaday's text as well as an 1894 text edited by Dr. Albert Buck to describe the abbreviated process. See Albert H. Buck, ed., *Handbook of the Medical Sciences Embracing the Entire Range of Scientific and Practical Medicine and Allied Science,* vol. 6, *Preparation of Skeletons* (New York: William Wood & Co., 1894).

296 **"Maceration of a skeleton," wrote Hornaday, "is a question of time":** Hornaday, *Taxidermy and Zoological Collecting,* 283.

296 **It would take Ward two years:** "History," Ward's Natural Science, February 5, 2005, web.archive.org/web/20050206022312/http://wardsci.com/article.asp?ai=3.

296 **"But," warned Hornaday, "if you're going to study bones":** Hornaday, *Taxidermy and Zoological Collecting,* 283.

297 **The Centennial International Exhibition of 1876 encompassed:** "International Exhibition, 1876 Official Catalogue" (Philadelphia: John R. Nagle and Company, 1876). (Noteworthy is the fact that Lexington is not listed by name therein. However, the Smithsonian's exhibits were displayed at the Main Exhibition Building. Based on the written conversations between the Smithsonian and A. J. Alexander, Lexington's bones were donated in part so that they could be displayed at the Centennial. The assumption is that this loan specification was indeed complied with by the Smithsonian.)

299 **"Lexington holds a record":** *The American Racing Manual: Edition of 1936* (Chicago: Regal Press, 1936), 595.

299 **Lexington stood on display until the middle of the twentieth century:** "Super Runner, Super Sire, Out to Pasture in MNH," *The Torch* [monthly newspaper of the Smithsonian Institution], May 1969, 2.

CHAPTER 24: STANDING ON ALL FOURS: NINETY-FIVE YEARS LATER

301 **He finally stopped in front of an articulated skeleton:** Gerald R. Strine, "Hideout in the Attic," *The Blood-Horse,* September 5, 1970, 2861.

301 **The chain of calls ended with Frank Greenwell, taxidermist:** Strine, "Hideout," 2859; Ingrid Rochon, museum technician, Smithsonian Institution, email exchange with author regarding Frank Greenwell and his team on the construction of the Fénykövi Elephant, July 24, 2020.

301 **"I don't know why he's up here":** Strine, "Hideout," 2859.

301 **A maze of gangplanks stretched across steel beams:** Photograph of Frank Greenwell with Lexington in the Smithsonian's attic, Smithsonian Institution Archives.

302 **Three floors below—and one wrong step—was the *Life in the Sea:*** Peter Chew, "Great Stallion's Skeleton Is Stabled in Museum Attic," *Smithsonian,* May 1974, 74.

302 **As Strine negotiated the gangplank, he passed a horde of antlers:** Photograph of Greenwell with Lexington in the Smithsonian's attic; see also Strine, "Hideout," 2859.

302 **"This horse was a very healthy specimen":** Strine, "Hideout," 2861.

302 **"But don't worry," Greenwell assured:** Ibid., 2859.

303 **"The policy here," said Helena Weiss:** Ibid., 2860.

304 **Then Cowan offered a glimmer of hope:** Ibid.

304 **In response to mounting pleas from racing fans:** Frank T. Phelps, "Skeleton of Lexington May Return to Bluegrass," *Lexington Herald-Leader,* August 18, 1974.

304 **Chew wrote an article emphasizing Lexington's triumphs:** Chew, "Great Stallion's Skeleton."

304 **According to one of those, "Since Lexington's present disposition":** Internal memorandum dated March 1, 1974, Smithsonian Institution Archives, box 8 of 32, Record Unit 363.

305 **After a few more memoranda between:** Ibid.

305 **Finally, on July 29, 1974, the Thoroughbred Racing Association:** Thoroughbred Racing Association press release, "Lexington File," Keeneland Library.

305 **Ever since the Smithsonian acquired Lexington's bones:** Amy Wilson, "Lexington Back in Lexington at Last," *Lexington Herald-Leader,* September 1, 2010.

305 **Smithsonian officials had even discussed disassembling the bones:** Internal memorandum dated March 1, 1974, Smithsonian Institution Archives.

306 **Then, in 1999, Timex came knocking:** "One Hundred Sixty Years After His Birth, a Racehorse's Bones Return to Lexington," Smithsonian Insider, November 17, 2010, insider.si.edu/2010/11/after-160-years-racehorse-lexingtons-bones -returned-to-the-town-of-his-birth/.

306 **The four-thousand-square-foot exhibit:** Ken Ringle, "At the Tone the Time Will Be . . . ," *Washington Post,* November 25, 1999.

306 **There, the King of Time stood as an example:** "One Hundred Sixty Years," Smithsonian Insider.

307 **He was a step in the evolution of a breed:** Phelps, "Skeleton of Lexington."

307 **Cooke believed Lexington was "the horse who definitively":** Wilson, "Lexington Back."

307 **In August 1988, the City of Lexington's Urban Council:** "Council Seeks Return of Horse's Remains," *Lexington Herald-Leader,* August 26, 1988.

307 **In a renewed effort, Bill Cooke picked up his pen:** Tom Eblen, "Lexington Namesake Might Come Home," *Lexington Herald-Leader,* March 15, 2009.

308 **Back at the Bone Hall, Lexington's display spot had been filled:** "One Hundred Sixty Years," Smithsonian Insider.

308 **In the back of the storage room:** "Condition Report and Treatment Proposal & Treatment Report Mounted Skeleton of the Lexington," April 2010, Smithsonian Institution Archives.

308 **After Lexington's condition was documented, he was vacuumed:** Ibid.

308 **"It's a lost art":** "One Hundred Sixty Years," Smithsonian Insider.

309 **"He arrived in very good condition":** Bill Cooke, telephone call with author, October 25, 2013.

309 **Lexington's homecoming was banner news:** "Thoroughbred Daily News Industry Info Press Release: Lexington's Remains Coming to Kentucky Horse Park," August 31, 2010, "Lexington File," Keeneland Library.

310 **To celebrate Lexington's return, the city of Lexington:** Eblen, "Lexington Namesake."

310 **The city named him "Big Lex" and used Troye's painted:** Beverly Fortune, "Horse Logo of a Different Color," *Lexington Herald-Leader,* May 30, 2009.

310 **Although some citizens found the color:** "Logo, Blue Horse Doesn't Please All," *Lexington Herald-Leader,* May 30, 2009; "Blue Horse Logo: Questionable Logo and Decision-Making," *Lexington Herald-Leader,* June 7, 2009.

EPILOGUE

312 **But he exists in a staggeringly high number of them:** Unpublished report on a pedigree search of every graded stakes winner from 1994 to 2014 that contains a cross of Lexington, prepared for the author by the Jockey Club on the author's commission.

312 **The daughter side of Lexington, therefore, carried:** Hervey, *Racing in America,* 2:307.

312 **Thoroughbred bloodstock consultant Alan Porter:** Edward L. Bowen, "Thoroughbred Boulevard," *Keeneland Magazine,* Spring 2022, 106.

313 **Without Lexington, Porter told me:** Alan Porter, telephone call with author, July 15, 2022.

313 **As of this writing:** Author's compilation, made from review of the pedigrees of Triple Crown and various stakes winners as contained in the following online sources: Thoroughbred Horse Pedigree Query, pedigreequery.com; "Kentucky Derby Winners," kentuckyderby.com/history/kentucky-derby-winners; "Preakness Stakes Winners," usracing.com/preakness-stakes/winners; "Belmont Stakes Winners," belmontstakes.com/history/past-winners/; "Travers Stakes Winners," tbheritage.com/TurfHallmarks/racecharts/USA/TraversStakes.html; "Saratoga Cup Winners," tbheritage.com/TurfHallmarks/racecharts/USA/SaratogaCup .html; "Jerome Handicap," en.wikipedia.org/wiki/Jerome_Stakes.

314 **In honor of his racing accomplishments, Lexington was inducted:** "Hall of Fame," search function on the website for the National Museum of Racing and Hall of Fame, racingmuseum.org/.

316 **one painted not by Edward Troye:** Trevathan, *American Thoroughbred,* 312.

BIBLIOGRAPHY

ARCHIVES, DOCUMENTS, AND DIGITAL COLLECTIONS

Alexander Family Collection File. Woodford County Historical Society, Versailles, Kentucky.

Alexander Family Papers, 1509–1969. Kentucky Historical Society, Frankfort, Kentucky.

Black Horsemen of the Kentucky Turf. Exhibit Collection. International Museum of the Horse, Lexington, Kentucky.

Clarke Family Papers. Simpson County Historical Society Archives, Franklin, Kentucky.

Court-Martial Case Files, 1809–1917. United States National Archives, Washington, D.C.

Edward Troye Collection. National Sporting Museum and Library, Middleburg, Virginia.

Elisha Warfield Collection File. Keeneland Library, Lexington, Kentucky.

Elisha Warfield Collection File. Kentucky Historical Society, Frankfort, Kentucky.

Henry Augustus Ward Papers. Rare Books, Special Collections, and Preservation. River Campus Libraries, Rochester, New York.

John Winston Coleman, Jr., Collection on Slavery in Kentucky, 1780–1940. University of Kentucky Special Collections, Lexington, Kentucky.

Kansas Memory Archives. Kansas Historical Society, Topeka, Kansas.

Lexington 2010 Condition Report; various internal memorandums regarding placement of the skeletal remains of Lexington; various newspaper clippings pertaining to Lexington's racing career, his death, and his exhibit placements; photographic images of Lexington in the Smithsonian Natural History Museum's attic. Smithsonian Institution Archives, Washington, D.C.

Lexington Accession File 121040. Smithsonian Institution Archives, Washington, D.C.

Lexington Collection File. International Museum of the Horse, Lexington, Kentucky.

Lexington Collection File. Keeneland Library, Lexington, Kentucky.

Marcellus Jerome Clarke "Sue Mundy" Archives. Filson Historical Society, Louisville, Kentucky.

Metairie Cemetery. National Register of Historic Places. United States Department of the Interior National Park Service.

Pre–World War I United States Army Service Records. United States National Archives, Washington, D.C.

Prints & Photographs Online Catalog. Library of Congress, Washington, D.C.

Richard Ten Broeck, West Point Correspondence Papers and Resignation Documents. Records of the Adjutant General's Office (Record Group 94, Entry 212). United States National Archives, Washington, D.C.

Robert N. Dennis Collection of Stereoscopic Views. Digital Collections. New York Public Library.

Southern Regional Climate Center / Louisiana Office of State Climatology. Meteorological Register, April through May 1855. Louisiana State University Archives.

West Point Archives. United States Military Academy, West Point, New York.

William J. Minor Horse Racing Papers. Beinecke Rare Books Library and Archives, Yale University, New Haven, Connecticut.

William J. Minor Papers, 1845–1862. Louisiana State University Special Collections, Baton Rouge, Louisiana.

Woodburn Farm Collection File. Keeneland Library, Lexington, Kentucky.

Woodburn Farm Collection File. Woodford County Historical Society, Versailles, Kentucky.

BOOKS

Abbott, John S. C. *The History of the Civil War in America*. 2 vols. Springfield, Mass: Gurdon Bill & Co., 1863.

Armistead, Gene C. *Horses and Mules in the Civil War*. Jefferson, N.C.: McFarland & Company, Inc., 1947.

Ball, Michael A., DVM. *Understanding the Equine Eye*. Lexington, Ky.: The Blood-Horse, Inc., 1999.

Barton, O. S. *Three Years with Quantrill: A True Story Told by His Scout John McCorkle*. Armstrong, Mo.: Armstrong Herald Press, 1914.

Beatty, John. *The Citizen-Soldier; or: Memoirs of a Volunteer*. Cincinnati: Wilstach, Baldwin & Co., 1879.

Billings, John Davis, and Charles W. Reed. *Hardtack and Coffee; or: The Unwritten Story of Army Life*. Boston: George M. Smith & Co., 1887.

Binns, Matthew, and Tony Morris. *Thoroughbred Breeding: Pedigree Theories and the Science of Genetics*. London: J. A. Allen, 2010.

Bird, T. H. *Admiral Rous and the English Turf*. London: Putnam, 1939.

Bowmar, Dan M., III. *Giants of the Turf: The Alexanders, the Belmonts, James R. Keene, the Whitneys*. Lexington, Ky.: The Blood-Horse, Inc., 1960.

Brereton, J. M. *The Horse in War*. New York: Arco Publishing, 1976.

Bruce, B. G. *Memoir of Lexington*. No publishing information.

Bruce, Sanders Dewees. *The Horse-Breeder's Guide and Hand Book (1883)*. New York: Turf, Field and Farm, 1883.

Buckingham, James Silk. *The Slave States of America*. Vol. 1. London: Fisher, Son & Co., 1842.

Busbey, Hamilton. *Recollections of Men and Horses*. New York: Dodd, Mead & Co., 1907.

Campanella, Catherine. *Images of America, Metairie*. Charleston, S.C.: Arcadia Publishing, 2008.

Carter, Samuel, III, *The Last Cavaliers: Confederate and Union Cavalry in the Civil War*. New York: St. Martin's Press, 1979.

Collins, Lewis, and Richard H. Collins. *History of Kentucky.* 2 vols. Berea, Ky.: Kentucke Imprints, 1976.

Connelley, William Elsey. *Quantrill and the Border Wars.* Cedar Rapids, Iowa: The Torch Press, 1910.

Crickmore, H., ed. *Famous Horses of America.* Philadelphia: Porter and Coates, 1877.

Crutchfield, James A. *It Happened on the Mississippi River.* Kearney, Neb: Morris Book Publishing, LLC, 2009.

Dana, Charles A. *The Life of Ulysses S. Grant.* Springfield, Mass.: Gurdon Bill & Co., 1868.

Day, William. *Turf Celebrities I Have Known.* London: F. V. White & Co., 1891.

Day, William, and Alfred J. Day. *The Racehorse in Training.* London: Cassell & Company, Ltd., 1880.

Deedes, Henry. *Sketches of the South and West; Or, Ten Months' Residence in the United States.* Edinburgh and London: William Blackwood and Sons, 1869.

Devereux, Frederick L., Jr. *The Cavalry Manual of Horse Management.* Cranbury, N.J.: A. S. Barnes & Co., 1979.

Devol, George H. *Forty Years a Gambler on the Mississippi.* Cincinnati: Devol & Haines, 1887.

Dizikes, John. *Sportsmen & Gamesmen.* Columbia: University of Missouri Press, 2002.

Druid, The. *The Post & the Paddock.* London: Frederick Wayne and Co., n.d.

Duke, Basil W. *History of Morgan's Cavalry.* Cincinnati: Miami Printing and Publishing Co., 1867.

Edwards, John Newman. *Noted Guerrillas, or, The Warfare of the Border.* St. Louis: Bryan, Brand & Co., 1877.

Emerson, Edwin, Jr. *A History of the Nineteenth Century Year by Year.* 3 vols. New York: P. F. Collier and Son, 1901.

Evans, Oliver. *New Orleans.* New York: The Macmillan Co., 1959.

Fisher, Jonelle. *For All Times: The Story of Lucas Brodhead.* St. Crispian Press, 2002.

Fossier, Albert E. *New Orleans: The Glamour Period, 1800–1840.* Gretna, La.: Pelican Publishing Co., 1998.

Gandolfo, Henri A. *Metairie Cemetery, an Historical Memoir: Tales of Its Statesmen, Soldiers and Great Families.* New Orleans: Stewart Enterprises, 1981.

Gandy, Joan W., and Thomas H. Gandy. *The Mississippi Steamboat Era in Historic Photographs: Natchez to New Orleans, 1870–1920.* New York: Dover Publications, 1987.

Giberti, Bruno. *Designing the Centennial: A History of the 1876 International Exhibition in Philadelphia.* Lexington: The University Press of Kentucky, 2002.

Gleason, Oscar Rudolph. *How to Handle and Educate Vicious Horses.* Ithaca, N.Y.: Cornell University, n.d.

Goodman, Thomas M. *A Thrilling Record Founded on Facts and Observations Obtained During Ten Days' Experience with Colonel William T. Anderson (the Notorious Guerrilla Chieftain).* Edited by Capt. Harry A. Houston. Des Moines, Iowa: Mills & Co., 1868.

Goss, Warren Lee. *Recollections of a Private: A Story of the Army of the Potomac.* New York: Thomas Y. Crowell & Co., 1890.

Grant, Jesse R. *In the Days of My Father General Grant.* New York: Harper & Brothers, 1925.

Grant, Ulysses S. *Personal Memoirs.* 2 vols. New York: Charles L. Webster & Company, 1885.

Gregg, William H. "A Little Dab of History Without Embellishment," Part 1. Unpublished manuscript. The State Historical Society of Missouri, Columbia, Missouri.

Grimsgaard, M. C. *Original Handbook for Riders*. New York: The Winthrop Press, 1911.

Harrison, Fairfax. *Early American Turf Stock, 1730–1830*. 2 vols. Richmond, Va.: The Old Dominion Press, 1934.

———. *The Equine F.F.Vs.: A Study of the Evidence for the English Horses Imported into Virginia Before the Revolution*. Richmond, Va.: The Old Dominion Press, 1928.

Hayes, M. Horace. *Horses On Board Ship: A Guide to Their Management*. London: Hurst & Blackett, Limited, 1902.

Hennessey, Louis J. *The Fair Grounds Race Course: A Time-Honored American Institution,* 1947.

Herbert, Henry William. *Frank Forester's Horse and Horsemanship of the United States and British Provinces of North America*. New York: Stringer & Townsend, 1857.

Hervey, John L. *Racing in America, 1665–186*. 2 vols. New York: The Jockey Club, 1944.

Hervey, John L., and Worcester Smith. *Life of Lexington*. N.p.: published by the author, n.d. In circulation, Lexington Public Library.

Hewitt, Abram S. *The Great Breeders and Their Methods*. Lexington, Ky.: Thoroughbred Publishers, Inc., 1982.

Hildreth, Samuel C., and James R. Crowell. *The Spell of the Turf: The Story of American Racing*. London and Philadelphia: J. B. Lippincott Company, 1926.

Hinds, John. *Grooms' Oracle and Pocket Stable-Directory*. 2nd ed. London: Hurst, Chance, and Co., 1830.

Hollingsworth, Kent. *The Great Ones*. Lexington, Ky.: The Blood-Horse, Inc. 1970.

———. *The Kentucky Thoroughbred*. Lexington: The University Press of Kentucky, 1976.

Hore, J. P. *The History of Newmarket, and the Annals of the Turf*. 3 vols. London: A. H. Baily and Co., 1886.

Hornaday, William T. *Taxidermy and Zoological Collecting: A Complete Handbook for the Amateur Taxidermist, Collector, Osteologist, Museum-Builder, Sportsman, and Traveller*. New York: Charles Scribner's Sons, 1891.

Horsemanship and Horsemastership. Vol. 2, part 3. Fort Riley, Kans.: The Cavalry School, 1946.

Horse-Racing: Its History and Early Records of the Principal and Other Race Meetings. London: Saunders, Otley, and Co., 1863.

Hotaling, Edward. *The Great Black Jockeys: The Lives and Times of the Men Who Dominated America's First National Sport*. Rocklin, Calif.: Prima Publishing, 1999.

Howland, S. A. *Steamboat Disasters and Railroad Accidents in the United States: To Which Is Appended Accounts of Recent Shipwrecks, Fires at Sea, Thrilling Incidents, etc.* 2nd ed. Worcester, Mass.: Dorr, Howland & Co., 1840.

Hunt, Frazier, and Robert Hunt. *Horses and Heroes: The Story of the Horse in America for 450 Years*. New York: Charles Scribner's Sons, 1949.

Jackson, Joy J. *New Orleans in the Gilded Age: Politics and Urban Progress, 1880–1896*. 2nd ed. Baton Rouge: Louisiana State University Press, 1997.

Johnson, L. F. *Famous Kentucky Tragedies and Trials*. Louisville, Ky.: The Baldwin Law Book Co., 1916.

Jones, J. B. *A Rebel War Clark's Diary at the Confederate States Capital*. 2 vols. Philadelphia: J. B. Lippincott & Co., 1866.

Kidd, J. H. *Personal Recollections of a Cavalryman with Custer's Michigan Cavalry Brigade in the Civil War*. Ionia, Mich.: Sentinel Printing Co., 1908.

King, Grace. *Creole Families of New Orleans*. New York: The Macmillan Co., 1921.

————. *New Orleans: The Place and the People.* New York: The Macmillan Co., 1917.

Knox, James. *Airdrie: A Historical Sketch.* Airdrie, Scotland: Baird & Hamilton, Ltd., 1921.

Lacer, Genevieve Baird. *Edward Troye: Painter of Thoroughbred Stories.* Prospect, Ky.: Harmony House, 2006.

Leet, Karen M., and Joshua A. Leet. *Civil War—Lexington, Kentucky: Bluegrass Breeding Ground of Power.* Charleston, S.C.: The History Press, 2011.

Lehndorff, G. *Horse-Breeding Recollections.* Philadelphia: Porter and Coates, 1887.

Leovy, Henry J. *The Laws and Revised Ordinances of the City of New Orleans.* New Orleans: E. C. Wharton, 1857.

Leslie, Edward E. *The Devil Knows How to Ride: The True Story of William Clarke Quantrill and His Confederate Raiders.* New York: Random House, 1996.

Mackay-Smith, Alexander. *Speed and the Thoroughbred: The Complete History.* New York: The Derrydale Press, 2000.

————. *The Race Horses of America, 1832–1872: Portraits and Other Paintings by Edward Troye.* Saratoga Springs: The National Museum of Racing, 1981.

Magruder, Henry C. *Three Years in the Saddle: The Life and Confession of Henry C. Magruder, the Original Sue Munday.* Louisville, Ky.: published by his captor, Maj. Cyrus J. Wilson, 1865.

Mangum, William Preston, II. *A Kingdom for the Horse.* Louisville, Ky.: Harmony House Publishers, 1999.

Mason, Richard. *The Gentleman's New Pocket Farrier: Comprising a General Description of the Noble and Useful Animal, the Horse.* Philadelphia: Grigg & Elliot, 1841.

Mooney, Katherine C. *Race Horse Men: How Slavery and Freedom Were Made at the Racetrack.* Cambridge, Mass.: Harvard University Press, 2014.

Murray, Amelia M. *Letters from the United States, Cuba and Canada.* New York: Negro Universities Press, 1969.

Nolan, Lewis Edward. *The Training of Cavalry Remount Horses.* London: Parker, Son & Bourn, 1859.

O'Connor, John L. *Notes on the Thoroughbred from Kentucky Newspapers.* Lexington, Ky.: Transylvania Printing Co., n.d.

Olmsted, Frederick Law. *A Journey in the Seaboard Slave States.* 2 vols. New York: G. P. Putnam's Sons, 1904.

Palmer, John M. *Personal Recollections of John M. Palmer: The Story of an Earnest Life.* Cincinnati: R. Clarke Co., 1901.

Penn, William A. *The Civil War in Midway, Kentucky.* Midway, Ky.: Historic Midway Museum Store, 2012.

Peter, Robert. *History of Fayette County, Kentucky.* Chicago: O. L. Baskin & Co., 1882.

Porter, Horace. *Campaigning with Grant.* New York: The Century Co., 1897.

Pratt, O. S. *The Horse's Friend: The Only Practical Method of Educating the Horse and Eradicating Vicious Habits.* Buffalo, N.Y.: private publication, 1876.

Prior, C. M. *The History of The Racing Calendar and Stud-Book.* London: The Sporting Life, 1926.

————. *The Royal Studs of the Sixteenth and Seventeenth Centuries.* London: Horse & Hound Publications, Ltd., 1935.

Raff, Lyne. *My Heart Is Too Full to Say More: The Horse in the Civil War.* United States: Art Horse Press, 2010.

Ralph, Julian. *Dixie, or Southern Scenes and Sketches.* New York: Harper & Bros., 1896.

Ranck, George W. *History of Lexington, Kentucky: Its Early Annals and Recent Progress.* Cincinnati: Robert Clarke & Co., 1872.

Reinders, Robert C. *End of an Era: New Orleans, 1850–1860.* New Orleans: Pelican Publishing Co., 1964.

Richardson, Charles. *The English Turf: A Record of Horses and Courses.* New York: Dodd, Mead & Co., 1901.

Ripley, Eliza. *Social Life in Old New Orleans: Being Recollections of My Girlhood.* New York and London: D. Appleton and Company, 1912.

Robertson, William H. P. *The History of Thoroughbred Racing in America.* New York: Bonanza Books, 1964.

Roesler, Bob. *The Fair Grounds: Big Shots & Long Shots.* New Orleans: Arthur Hardy Enterprises, Inc., 1998.

Rules and Regulations for the Government of Racing, Trotting, and Betting, as Adopted by the Principal Turf Associations Throughout the United States. New York: M. B. Brown & Co., 1866.

Runk, Emma Ten Broeck. *The Ten Broeck Genealogy: Being the Record; and Annals of Dirck Wesselse Ten Broeck of Albany and His Descendants.* New York: The De Vinne Press, 1897.

Shapiro, Dean M. *Historic Photos of Steamboats on the Mississippi.* Nashville: Turner Publishing Co., 2009.

Shirley, Arthur. *Remarks on the Transport of Cavalry and Artillery with Hints for the Management of Horses, Before, During, and After a Long Sea Voyage.* London: Parker, Furnivall & Parker, 1854.

Sickles, John. *The Legends of Sue Mundy and One-Armed Berry: Confederate Guerrillas.* Merrillville, Ind.: Heritage Press, 1999.

Sidney, S. *The Book of the Horse.* 3rd ed. London: Cassell & Company, Ltd., 1884–86.

Skinner, John S., ed. *American Farmer.* Vols. 1–15. Baltimore: John D. Toy, 1824 *et al.*

———. *American Turf Register and Sporting Magazine.* Vols. 1–15. Baltimore: John D. Toy, 1830 *et al.*

Smith, Fred. *Veterinary Hygiene.* London: Baillière, Tindall, and Cox, 1887.

Smith, Thomas Ruys. *Blacklegs, Card Sharps, and Confidence Men: Nineteenth-Century Mississippi River Gambling Stories.* Baton Rouge: Louisiana State University Press, 2010.

Somers, Dale A. *The Rise of Sports in New Orleans, 1850–1900.* Baton Rouge: Louisiana State University Press, 1972.

Stall, Gasper J. *Louisiana COD (Cities of the Dead).* Metairie, La.: published by the author, 2000.

Stroyer, Jacob. *My Life in the South.* Salem, Mass.: Newcomb & Gauss, 1898.

Taunton, Thomas Henry. *Portraits of Celebrated Racehorses of the Past and Present Centuries.* Vol. 1. London: Sampson Low, Marston, Searle & Rivington, 1887.

Trevathan, Charles E. *The American Thoroughbred.* New York: The Macmillan Co., 1905.

Troye, Edward. *The Race Horses of America.* 1st ed. 1887.

Vosburgh, W. S. *Racing in America, 1866–1921.* New York: The Jockey Club, 1922.

Warburton, R. E. *The Race Horse: How to Buy, Train, and Run Him.* London: Sampson Low, Marston & Co., 1892.

Ward, Henry A. *Catalogue of Human Skeletons and Anatomical Preparations.* Rochester, N.Y.: Ward's Natural Science Establishment, n.d.

Watson, Thomas Shelby. *The Silent Riders—WAKY News Documentary.* Louisville, Ky.: Beechmont Press, 1971.

Watson, Thomas Shelby, and Perry A. Brantley. *Confederate Guerrilla Sue Mundy: A Biog-*

raphy of Kentucky Soldier Jerome Clarke. Jefferson, N.C.: McFarland & Company, Inc., 2007.

Watson, William. *Life in the Confederate Army*. New York: Scribner & Welford, 1888.

Way, Frederick, Jr. *She Takes the Horns: Steamboat Racing on the Western Waters*. Cincinnati: Young and Klein, Inc., 1953.

Weeks, Lyman Horace. *The American Turf: An Historical Account of Racing in the United States, with Biographical Sketches of Turf Celebrities*. New York: The Historical Company, 1898.

Wentworth, Lady. *Thoroughbred Racing Stock and Its Ancestors*. New York: Charles Scribner's Sons, 1938.

Whipple, Henry Benjamin. *Bishop Whipple's Southern Diary, 1843–1844*. Minneapolis: The University of Minnesota Press, 1937.

Wiecek, William M. *The Sources of Anti-Slavery Constitutionalism in America, 1760–1848*. Ithaca, N.Y.: Cornell University Press, 1977.

MAGAZINES AND NEWSPAPERS

Albany Argus (NY)
American Racehorse
Baily's Magazine of Sports and Pastimes (UK)
Bell's Life in London (UK)
Boston Herald
Boston Journal
Boston Traveler
Charleston Courier (SC)
Chicago Tribune
Cincinnati Daily Gazette
Cleveland Plain Dealer
Cynthiana News (KY)
Daily Free Democrat (Milwaukee, WI)
Daily Racing Form
Deep South Magazine
Delaware State Reporter
Equus
Evening Bulletin (San Francisco, CA)
Florida Horse
Georgetown Herald (KY)
Harper's New Monthly Magazine
Hearth and Home
Hopkinsville Kentuckian
Intelligencer Journal (Lancaster, PA)
Interior Journal (Stanford, KY)
Keeneland Magazine
Kentucky Ancestors
Kentucky Humanities
Kentucky Leader (Lexington)
Kentucky Live Stock Record
Lexington Herald-Leader (KY)
Lexington Observer & Reporter (KY)

Los Angeles Herald
Louisville Daily Courier
Lowell Daily Citizen and News (MA)
Miami Herald
Morning Olympian (Olympia, WA)
Nashville Union and American
National Aegis (Worcester, MA)
National Republican (Washington, DC)
New England Farmer, and Horticultural Register
New Hampshire Patriot
New York Herald
New York Sportsman
Norwich Courier (CT)
Ottawa Daily Citizen (Ontario, Canada)
Porter's Spirit of the Times
Practical Horseman
Prairie Farmer
Public Ledger (Maysville, KY)
Riverside Daily Press (CA)
Rock River Democrat (Rockford, IL)
Sacramento Daily Union
San Francisco Chronicle
Smithsonian
Southern Sentinel (Plaquemine, LA)
Spirit of the Times
State Gazette (Trenton, NJ)
Tampa Tribune
Territorial Enterprise (Virginia City, NV)
The Adair County News (KY)
The Alexandria Gazette (VA)
The Backstretch
The Baltimore Sun

The Belfast News Letter (Northern Ireland)
The Blood-Horse
The Bluegrass Historian
The Buffalo Daily Reporter (NY)
The Canton Repository (OH)
The Centinel of Freedom (Newark, NJ)
The Charlotte Observer (NC)
The Cincinnati Enquirer
The Commonwealth (Frankfort, KY)
The Daily Advocate (Baton Rouge, LA)
The Daily American (Nashville, TN)
The Daily Delta (New Orleans, LA)
The Daily Globe (Washington, DC)
The Daily Graphic
The Daily Inter Ocean (Chicago, IL)
The Daily Picayune
The Dallas Weekly Herald
The Denver Post
The Evening Post
The Galveston News (TX)
The Hartford Herald (KY)
The Hartford Republican (KY)
The Indiana Progress (Indiana, PA)
The Indianapolis Sentinel
The Kansas City Star (MO)
The Kansas City Times (MO)
The Kentucky Statesman (Lexington)
The Kentucky Tribune (Danville)
The Kingsport Times (TN)
The Louisiana Democrat (Alexandria)
The Louisville Daily Democrat
The Louisville Daily Journal
The Magazine Antiques

The Mississippi Free Trader (Natchez, MS)
The Morning Herald (Lexington, KY)
The National Police Gazette
The News Democrat (Franklin, KY)
The New York Times
The Patriot (Harrisburg, PA)
The Pittsburg Press
The Pittsfield Sun (MA)
The Richmond Whig
The St. Matthews Voice (KY)
The Salt Lake Tribune
The San Francisco Call
The Sporting Life (UK)
The Sporting Magazine (UK)
The Sun (New York)
The Tacoma Daily News
The Thoroughbred of California
The Thoroughbred Record
The Torch (monthly newspaper of the Smithsonian Institution)
The Town Talk (Alexandria, LA)
The Washington Post
The Weekly Shelby News (Shelbyville, KY)
The Woodford Sun (Versailles, KY)
Tri-Weekly Kentucky Yeoman (Frankfort, KY)
Turf and Sport Digest
Turf, Field and Farm
United States Economist, Dry Goods Reporter, and Bank, Railroad, and Commercial Chronicle
Wallace's Monthly
Washington Sentinel (Washington, DC)
Wilkes' Spirit of the Times

JOURNALS

Allison, Young E. "Sue Mundy: An Account of the Terrible Kentucky Guerrilla of Civil War Times." *The Register of the Kentucky Historical Society* 57, no. 4 (October 1959): 295–316.

Cashin, Joan E. "Trophies of War: Material Culture in the Civil War Era." *Journal of the Civil War Era* 1, no. 3 (September 2011): 339–67.

Cohen, Kenneth. "The Entreaties and Perswasions of our Acquaintance: Gambling and Networks in Early America." *Journal of the Early Republic* 31, no. 4 (Winter 2011): 599–638.

De Falaise, Louis. "General Stephen Gano Burbridge's Command in Kentucky." *The Register of the Kentucky Historical Society* 69, no. 2 (April 1971): 101–27.

Dunn, Jacob P. "Indiana's Part in the Making of the Story of 'Uncle Tom's Cabin.'" *The Indiana Quarterly Magazine of History* 7, no. 3 (September 1911): 112–18.

Harrison, Fairfax "The Equine F.F.Vs." *The Virginia Magazine of History and Biography* 35, (1927): 345–46.

Jeter, Katherine Brash. "A Racing Heritage." *Louisiana History: The Journal of the Louisiana Historical Association* 30, no. 1 (Winter 1989): 5–22.

Johnson, Paul. "Northern Horse: American Eclipse as a Representative New Yorker." *Journal of the Early Republic* 33, no. 4 (Winter 2013): 701–26.

Mangum, William Preston, II. "Disaster at Woodburn Farm: R. A. Alexander and the Confederate Guerrilla Raids of 1864–1865." *The Filson Club History Quarterly* 70, no. 2 (April 1996): 143–85.

Martin, James B. "Black Flag over the Bluegrass: Guerrilla Warfare in Kentucky, 1863–1865." *The Register of the Kentucky Historical Society* 86, no. 4 (Autumn 1988): 352–75.

Murphy, Jack, Carol Hall, and Sean Arkins. "What Horses and Humans See: A Comparative Review." *International Journal of Zoology* (2009).

Peters, Martha Ann. "The St. Charles Hotel: New Orleans Social Center, 1837–1860." *Louisiana History: The Journal of the Louisiana Historical Association* 1, no. 3 (Summer 1960): 191–211.

Rosenberg, Charles. "The Cause of Cholera: Aspects of Etiological Thought in Nineteenth Century America." *Bulletin of the History of Medicine* 34, no. 4 (1960): 331–54.

Shoup, Francis A. "Uncle Tom's Cabin Forty Years After." *The Sewanee Review* 2, no. 1 (November 1893): 88–104.

Sterns, Worthy P. "The Foreign Trade of the United States from 1820 to 1840." *Journal of Political Economy* 8, no. 1 (December 1899): 34–57.

Struna, Nancy L. "The North-South Races: American Thoroughbred Racing in Transition, 1823–1850." *Journal of Sport History* 8, no. 2 (Summer 1981): 28–57.

"The Pryor Family. (Continued.)" *The Virginia Magazine of History and Biography* 7, no. 3 (January 1900): 325–26.

Tirres, Allison Brownell. "Ownership Without Citizenship: The Creation of Noncitizen Property Rights." *Michigan Journal of Race & Law* 19, no. 1 (Fall 2013): 1–52.

Tolson, John, and Wray Vamplew. "Derailed: Railways and Horse-Racing Revisited." *The Sports Historian* 18, no. 2 (November 1998): 34–49.

Towne, Stephen E., and Jay G. Heiser. "Everything Is Fair in War: The Civil War Memoir of George A. 'Lightning' Ellsworth, Telegraph Operator for John Hunt Morgan." *The Register of the Kentucky Historical Society* 108, no. ½ (Winter/Spring 2010): 3–110.

Valentine, L. L. "Sue Mundy of Kentucky." Part 1. *The Register of the Kentucky Historical Society* 62, no. 3 (July 1964): 175–205.

———. "Sue Mundy of Kentucky." Part 2. *The Register of the Kentucky Historical Society* 62, no. 4 (October 1964): 278–306.

Wilson, Henry. "History of the Rise and Fall of the Slave Power in America." *The North American Review* 120, no. 246 (January 1875): 47–83.

Winston, James E. "Notes on the Economic History of New Orleans, 1803–1836." *The Mississippi Valley Historical Review* 11, no. 2 (September 1924): 220–26.

SERIES AND REFERENCE SOURCES

Battles and Leaders of the Civil War. 4 vols. New York: Thomas Yoseloff, Inc., 1956.

Biographical Cyclopedia of the Commonwealth of Kentucky. Chicago: John M. Gresham Co., 1896.

Buck, Albert H., ed. *Handbook of the Medical Sciences Embracing the Entire Range of Scientific and Practical Medicine and Allied Science.* Vol. 6, *Preparation of Skeletons.* Ithaca, New York: William Wood & Co., 1894.

"Steward to Trowbridge." *Dictionary of American Biography.* Vol. 18. New York: Charles Scribner's Sons, 1936.

ONLINE RESOURCES

1850 and 1880 United States Census Records. Ancestry.com.

"A History of Steamboats." United States Army. n.d. www.sam.usace.army.mil.

"Airdrie Stud History." Airdrie Stud. n.d. www.airdriestud.com/history.html.

"America (yacht)." Wikipedia. Accessed July 6, 2016. en/wikipedia.org.wiki/America_%28yacht%29.

"America's Cup Held Here Since 1851." *The New York Times.* February 22, 1920. timesmachine.nytimes.com/timesmachine/1920/02/22/118263432.html?page Number=18.

"Applying for Affiliation." Smithsonian Affiliations. n.d. affiliations.si.edu/applying-for-affiliation/.

"Approach to Civil War: America in the 1840s & 1850s." Sage American History. n.d. sageamericanhistory.net/civil war/topics/background_1850s.html.

"Binocular Vision." Wikipedia. en.wikipedia.org/wiki/Binocular_vision.

"Blind Horse Insights." BlindHorses.org.

"Born Blind and Deaf, Tough Sunday Finds the Winner's Circle at Del Mar." Paulick Report. November 2017. www.paulickreport.com.

British Newspaper Archives digital database. www.britishnewspaperarchive.co.uk.

"By Ship." National Army Museum. Accessed July 2016. URL not recorded.

"Caring for a Blind Horse." BlindHorses.org. blindhorses.org/caring-for-a-blind-horse/.

"Chronicles of the Black Jockeys, vol. 2: When Americans Were Betting 'Abe' on 'Abe.'" www.ealymaysartworks.com/news/art-narratives-in-focus/282-chronicles-of-the-black-jockeys-when-americans-were-betting-abe-on-abe#sthash.uerCINFb.dpuf.

Dabney, Emmanuel. "City Point During the Civil War." October 2015. *Encyclopedia Virginia.* Accessed February 9, 2018. www.encyclopediavirginia.org/city-point-during-the-civil-war.

Eblen, Tom. "Lexington's Bones May Return to Kentucky." March 2009. tomeblen.bloginky.com/2009/03/14/lexingtons-bones-may-return-to-kentucky/.

"Equine Recurrent Uveitis." U.C. Davis. March 2020. ceh.vetmed.ucdavis.edu/health-topics/equine-recurrent-uveitis.

"Fan Favorite Patch Prepping for 4-Year-Old Debut This Weekend." Paulick Report. May 2018. paulickreport.com/news/thoroughbred-racing/fan-favorite-patch-prepping-for-4-year-old-debut-this-weekend/.

Finley, Bill. "Horse Racing: One-Eyed Colt Shows Derby Promise." *The New York Times.* March 2004. www.nytimes.com/2004/03/06/sports/horse-racing-one-eyed-colt-shows-derby-promise.html.

"Frank Greenwell: Stories from the Museum: Explore Our History: Celebrating 100 Years." National Museum of Natural History.

"Gambling on the Race Course." State Library of Louisiana. louisianadigitallibrary.org/islandora/object/state-lwp%3A8097.

Hedrick, Benjamin. "A Nation Divided: The Political Climate of 1850s America." Civil War Era NC. n.d. cwnc.omeka.chass.ncsu.edu./exhibits/show/benjamin-hedrick/polticalclimate.

Hillenbrand, Laura. "Leading the Blind." *Equus* 229. PDF downloaded from BlindHorses
.org.

"Historical Background on Traveling in the Early 19th Century." TeachUSHistory.org.
Accessed April 28, 2013. www.teachushistory.org/detocqueville-visit-united-states
/articles/historical-background-traveling-early-19th-century.

"History." Ward's Natural Science. February 2005. Accessed March 23, 2018. Archived at web.archive.org/web/20050206022312/http://wardsci.com/article.asp?ai
=3. web/20050206022312/http://wardsci.com/article.asp?ai=3.

"How Fast Does a Racehorse Run?" Horse Racing Nation. www.horseracingnation
.com/content/how_fast_racehorse_run.

"International Museum of the Horse Becomes Smithsonian Affiliate." *Equus*. July 2006.
equusmagazine.com/horse-world/imhsmithsonian_072806.

JSTOR.org digital database.

"Keeping a Blind Horse." Kentucky Equine Research. October 2011. ker.com/equinews
/keeping-blind-horse/.

"Kentucky River." Wikipedia. en.wikipedia.org/wiki/Kentucky_River.

Koch, Robert G. "Henry A. Ward." 3 parts. *The Crooked Lake Review*. Accessed
March 23, 2018. crookedlakereview.com /articles /34 _66 /57dec1992 /57kock
.html.

"Lexington's Skeleton to Return to Kentucky." Horsetalk .co .nz. August 2010. www
.horsetalk.co.nz/news/2010/08/210.shtml.

Livingston, Barbara. "Man o' War's Funeral: Remarkable Final Tribute for Majestic
Champion." *Daily Racing Form*. February 2011. www.drf.com/blogs/man-o-wars
-funeral-remarkable-final-tribute-majestic-champion.

Meyer, Jennifer Forsberg. "Horse Blindness Solutions." *Horse & Rider*. May 2018.
horseandrider.com/horse-health-care/horse-blindness-solutions.

"Monocular Vision." Wikipedia. en.wikipedia.org/wiki/Monocular_vision.

Newspapers.com digital database.

"Old Frankfort Pike National Scenic Byway." oldfrankfortpike.org/old-frankfort-pike
-national-scenic-byway/.

"One Hundred Sixty Years After His Birth, a Racehorse's Bones Return to Lexington."
Smithsonian Insider. November 17, 2010. Accessed November 23, 2012. smithsonian
science.org/2010/11/aafter-160-years-racehorse-lexingtons-bones-return-to
-lexington.

"On Time: Mechanizing Time 1820–1880: The Race Is On." Smithsonian National
Museum of American History. https://americanhistory.si.edu/ontime/mechanizing
/index.html.

"Saratoga Cup Winners." Thoroughbred Heritage. www.tbheritage.com/TurfHallmarks
/racecharts/USA/SaratogaCup.html.

Sellnow, Les. "The Equine Eye." *The Horse*. October 2001. thehorse.com /14895 /the
-equine-eye/.

"Skeletal System of the Horse." Wikipedia. en.wikipedia.org/wiki/Skeletal_system_of
_the_horse.

Spitzner, K. "History of the Steam Engine." Steamboats.com. n.d. steamboats.com
/museum/engineroom.html#tour.

"The Finest Piece of Architecture in the New World: The Old St. Charles Hotel." Old
New Orleans. old-new-orleans.com/NO_StCharlesHotel.html.

"The History of Churchill Downs." Churchill Downs. www.churchilldowns.com/visit
/about/churchill-downs/history/.

The New York Times Archives digital database.

Thomas, Heather Smith. "Caring for the Blind Horse." *The Horse.* November 2012. thehorse.com/118812/caring-for-the-blind-horse/.

Thomson, Candus. "Story of Woodlawn Vase Has Many Twists—and Some Are Even True." *The Baltimore Sun.* May 2011. Accessed November 23, 2012. www.baltimore sun.com/sports/horse-racing/bs-sp-preakness-trophy-20110505-story.html.

Thoroughbred Horse Pedigree Query. www.pedigreequery.com.

"Top 5 Myths & Tips." BlindHorses.org. blindhorses.org/top-5-myths-tips.

"Transporting Horses by Road and Air: Recommendations for Reducing the Stress." CEH Horse Report. July 2013. PDF downloaded from https://ceh.vetmed.ucdavis .edu/sites/g/files/dgvnsk4536/files/local_resources/pdfs/pubs-July2013HR-sec.pdf.

Waldridge, Bryan. "Gastrointestinal Tract Basics: The Horse's Hindgut." Kentucky Equine Research. May 2014. ker.com/equinews/gastrointestinal-tract-basics-horses -hindgut/.

"Yellow Fever Deaths in New Orleans, 1817–1905." New Orleans Public Library. January 2003. nutrias.org/facts/feverdeaths.htm.

DISSERTATIONS

Cregier, Sharon. "Alleviating Surface Transit Stress on Horses." PhD diss., Walden University, 1981.

Morrison, James L. "The United States Military Academy, 1833–1866: Years of Progress and Turmoil." PhD diss., Columbia University, 1970 (West Point Library).

Munday, Jessie. "The Railroads of Kentucky 1861–1865." Master's thesis, University of Louisville, 1925 (Electronic Theses and Dissertations, Paper 1026).

LAWS AND REGULATIONS

"Laws of the State of New York." Fiftieth Session, Albany, January 1827.

"The Stone Fences of Fayette County." Lexington-Fayette Urban County Government Division of Planning, Lexington, November 8, 1990.

COMPILATIONS

American Racing Calendar of 1876. Part I. New York: Turf, Field and Farm, 1876.

The American Racing Manual: Edition of 1936. Chicago: Regal Press, 1936.

The American Racing Manual: 1992 Edition. New York: Daily Racing Form Press, 1992.

The American Racing Manual, 2013. New York: Daily Racing Form Press, 2013.

The New York Clipper Annual for 1893. New York: The Frank Queen Publishing Company (Ltd.), 1893.

The War of the Rebellion: Official Records of the Union and Confederate Armies. Washington, D.C.: Government Printing Office, 1897.

MISC. RESOURCES

1860 United States Census for Woodford County, Kentucky. Kentucky Historical Society, Frankfort, Kentucky.

"International Exhibition, 1876 Official Catalogue." Philadelphia: John R. Nagle and Company, 1876.

Mackay-Smith, Alexander. "Portraits of Lexington." *National Sporting Library Newsletter,* December 1978.
Map of the Old French Quarter. Courtesy Ritz-Carlton, New Orleans, October 2015.
Metairie Cemetery Map showing old racecourse layout incorporated into cemetery. Courtesy Metairie Cemetery, October 2015.
The Jockey Club. Database search of Thoroughbreds containing traces of Lexington in their pedigrees; search restricted to graded stakes winners on the American turf from 1994 through 2014. Search commissioned by author, 2014.

BONES, OBJECTS, PLACES, AND SCULPTURES UTILIZED TO FORM NARRATIVE

Brown, Joseph. *Richard Ten Broeck.* Engraving, circa 1870s. National Portrait Gallery, London.
Nau Civil War Collection. Private collection of John L. Nau III, Houston, Texas.
Pullen, Tessa. *Bridled Veterans.* Memorial sculpture, 1997. Middleburg, Virginia.
Shrady, Henry. Ulysses S. Grant Memorial, 1924. Washington, D.C.

PERSONAL COMMUNICATIONS

Brehe, Kyle, Louisiana State University Southern Regional Climate Center. Email message to author, April 7, 2016.
Cooke, Bill, director emeritus, International Museum of the Horse. Telephone call with author, October 25, 2013.
Latimer, Claire, DVM, MS, DACVO, Rood & Riddle Equine Hospital. Telephone calls with author, August 6, 2020, and July 9, 2022.
Peterson, Michael, PhD, Professor, Biosystems and Agricultural Engineering, Race Track Surfaces, University of Kentucky. Telephone call with author, May 12, 2021.
Pye, Jessica, gold medal eventer, FEI North American Junior & Young Rider Championships. Conversation with author, June 2018.
Rochon, Ingrid, museum technician, Smithsonian Institution. Email exchange with author, July 24, 2020.
Smith, Steve, owner, Rolling Dog Farm. Email messages to author, March 10, 15, 16, and 19, 2019.
Vera, Angell, Maryland Jockey Club. Email message to author, November 1, 2013.
Williams, Joey, assistant director, Museum of Osteology. Email message to author, June 25, 2015.

PHOTO CREDITS

INDEX

Page numbers in *italics* indicate illustrations.

KIM WICKENS grew up in Dallas, Texas, and practiced as a criminal defense lawyer in New Mexico for twenty years. She subsequently turned her attention to writing, which she studied at Kenyon College, and has devoted the last several years to researching this book. She lives with her husband and son in Lexington, Kentucky, where she trains in dressage with her three horses.

kimwickensauthor.com
Twitter: @WickensKim
Instagram: @kwick700
Find Kim Wickens on Facebook

ABOUT THE TYPE

This book was set in Bembo, a typeface based on an old-style Roman face that was used for Cardinal Pietro Bembo's tract *De Aetna* in 1495. Bembo was cut by Francesco Griffo (1450–1518) in the early sixteenth century for Italian Renaissance printer and publisher Aldus Manutius (1449–1515). The Lanston Monotype Company of Philadelphia brought the well-proportioned letterforms of Bembo to the United States in the 1930s.